PENGUIN HANDBOOKS

The CTC Route Guide

The authors, who compiled the routes when working
in the CTC's touring department, researched the
material with the help of CTC members whose first-
hand experience ensures that the information is
reliable. Nicholas Crane and Christa Gausden have
themselves tested many of the routes and are well
aware of the needs of cyclists.

The C T C Route Guide

TO CYCLING IN BRITAIN AND IRELAND

Christa Gausden and Nicholas Crane

PENGUIN BOOKS

in association with Oxford Illustrated Press

Penguin Books Ltd, Harmondsworth, Middlesex, England
Penguin Books, 625 Madison Avenue, New York, New York 10022, U.S.A.
Penguin Books Australia Ltd, Ringwood, Victoria, Australia
Penguin Books Canada Ltd, 2801 John Street, Markham, Ontario, Canada L3R 1B4
Penguin Books (N.Z.) Ltd, 182-190 Wairau Road, Auckland 10, New Zealand

First published by Oxford Illustrated Press 1980
Published in Penguin Books 1981

Made and printed in Great Britain by
Richard Clay (The Chaucer Press) Ltd,
Bungay, Suffolk
Set in Monotype Plantin

CONTENTS

ACKNOWLEDGEMENTS

Of all the people involved in the production of this book we would like to thank in particular Elaine Russell-Wilks, who designed many of the Irish routes. Less directly, many hundreds of CTC members gave assistance, for during our time working in the CTC's Touring Department we were lucky enough to talk to cyclists from all over the world, and build up an idea of the type of routes that are required for touring Britain and Ireland. Thanks are also due to the many members who tested individual routes for us and whose invaluable comments have lent extra interest.

CHRISTA GAUSDEN and NICHOLAS CRANE, 1979

Maps by Oxford Illustrators Ltd

Line drawings by Frank Patterson of:
The Old Oast House, Pounsley   14
Bossington, Exmoor   85
Malham, North Yorkshire   143
The Long Mynd   226
Glen More   271
Near Coleraine, Co. Londonderry   336

The route maps used in this book derive from Ordnance Survey maps, with the sanction of the Controller of HM Stationery Office. Crown copyright reserved.

INTRODUCTION

The British Isles lend themselves to exploration by bicycle. The landscape, enriched by centuries of habitation, is of unrivalled variety and there is always something to delight the eye. The cyclist with a week or fortnight to spend can see one or two areas in detail or opt to pass through several, getting just an idea of each. A more fortunate person with plenty of time can cycle for several months and constantly find new scenery and places of interest.

The intimate scale of the British countryside is ideally suited to the cyclist's pace which allows time to notice and enjoy lesser-known places that are often missed by the faster traveller. In particular the network of lanes which covers so much of the countryside makes cycling in Britain unique. The lanes could have been designed for the cyclist though in fact they are the result of many different uses over a very long time: prehistoric ways or drovers' roads over distances, or local farm tracks and cottage paths linking villages. Many of these old routes are now surfaced with tarmac and give good access to the depths of the countryside. The cyclist rarely needs to use the busier classified A and B roads.

Cycling in Britain has some practical advantages over cycling in less populated countries as well as more crowded ones. For example, there are villages in all but the most remote areas which means that accommodation and provisions are nearly always to hand, and the cyclist can travel light. The climate, too, is kind. The summer days will allow you to keep going without roasting you, and the long daylight hours mean that you can make the most of your time. At the other extreme, during the winter months snow and ice do not often linger long enough for you to put away your bicycle altogether.

By recommending specific cycling routes this Guide reduces to manageable numbers the enormous choice of good routes. Drawing upon our own experience and that of many CTC members, we have devised the best possible combination of routes, taking into account certain conditions for cyclists. We selected quiet roads, preferably lanes, that pass through good scenery and which give easy access to places of interest. In addition, each route had to fit into the whole network; some were influenced by available ferries, major cities or Ministry of Defence land. For the most part, the routes do not avoid hilly terrain where this would otherwise mean omitting a place of interest or using a busier road. Inevitably, some fine cycling roads and some famous places do not feature in the routes—to include everything in a land of such variety would have meant a cycling route on every lane and a mention of every listed building!

The 365 routes are interconnected to form an intricate pattern over the British Isles. The peculiarities of the landscape mean that the pattern is far from regular; there are for example large spaces around the cities of the Midlands, while fine touring areas such as the Lake District attract a lot of routes. A very few routes were chosen not so much for their scenic merit but more for their usefulness in linking two touring areas across less interesting or built-up places. To ensure you do not use them for the wrong reasons there is a note at the head of these routes to that effect.

Planning the Tour

If you are new to cycle-touring in Britain it would be advisable to read at this stage the Appendices on pages 415–431 as these may well affect your choice of touring area. The variations and possibilities offered by the routes are many and to get the most out of this Guide some advice on how to use it is offered below.

When you have decided how many days, weeks or even months you have available for your tour, roughly estimate the miles (kilometres) you wish to cycle each day. Then calculate the approximate total distance of the whole tour, remembering that this figure can be flexible as the route network allows you to make adaptations during a tour. The length of each route has no significance in relation to distance: they are not equivalent to one day's cycling and in fact vary from ten to one hundred miles.

Next, decide which area or areas interest you, referring to the Touring Areas map and key (pages 11–13). To simplify matters we have divided the British Isles into six regions, each having its own section of the Guide. If your knowledge of the British Isles is a little hazy then you may find it useful to read the introduction to each region, which describes in more detail the scenery, interesting features and cycling terrain. Each regional introduction has two supporting maps: one a route key and the other a touring areas map showing the various features mentioned in the text.

Having picked the region or regions, look at the route map for each region and compare this with the adjacent touring areas map. List all the routes which go through areas you would like to visit, remembering that your tour can of course cross regional boundaries. Turn to each of the routes that you have picked and see which ones attract you particularly, eliminating those that don't hold so much interest for you. For example, one route may visit a fine castle while an alternative explores the mountains; another may offer rough-stuff and its alternative coastal scenery.

In selecting the routes, experiment with the various ways of linking them together to form a tour. You can make a circular tour, starting and finishing at the same place, or a linear tour where you finish in a different place, perhaps taking a train to reach one of the ends. Linear tours generally mean that you cycle through a greater variety of areas, while circular tours are good for exploring one area in detail.

Before deciding finally on your routes, just add up the total distances shown at the head of each one and make sure that the grand total is not too great a distance to cycle in the time that you have available. In hilly country remember that you will manage a lower daily distance from that possible in flat areas. You do not of course have to follow each route exactly and you will probably find opportunities to adapt them here and there. Chances to cut corners occur particularly near route nodes (the places where routes join) where you can cut across from one route to its neighbour without cycling all the way to the points where the routes meet. You may like to do this where the node has nothing of special interest (some nodes were chosen only because they are at the junction of good cycling roads) though many, such as Cambridge, have plenty to offer.

To give you an idea of some of the possibilities of this Guide we have suggested several tours of differing lengths and characters which appear on pages 412–414.

All that you now need to do is read the following notes on using the routes, make sure that your bike is roadworthy, pack your bags—and go!

How to use the Routes

The great number of roads in the British Isles is a blessing to cyclists but it can make navigation tricky. It is important therefore that you are equipped with commercial maps of a suitable scale (see Appendix 3). The routes have been designed for use with commercial maps which will in any case give you the freedom to adapt the routes or visit off-route features according to your interests. The relevant maps are given at the head of each route. Those marked 'just' are maps which cover either a very short distance of the route, or a direct stretch of road where no navigation is needed.

The route map shows precisely where the route goes. It is a good idea to follow it through on a commercial map before setting out to see whether there are any hills you want to avoid or short cuts you wish to make. Turn the book so that north is 'up' if this helps. All the A and B road turn-offs are shown on the route map but not the lane turn-offs. No routes are shown through the shaded areas of cities and towns, partly because of ever-changing one-way systems which mean you will have to get used to

Key to Route Maps

Map symbol	Key	Map symbol	Key
———	*A and B roads*	+++++	*railway*
———	*unclassified roads or lanes*	●	*on-route place*
— — —	*alternative route*	○	*off-route place*
....	*track or path—see Appendix 1*	▲	*on-route youth hostel*
▰▰	*built-up areas*	△	*off-route youth hostel*
╱	*sea or inland waters*		
a, b, c,	*refers to text comments in italics regarding the cycling*		
CHESTER	*capitals: node (place where two or more routes meet)*		
Wing	*bold type: indicates that the place features in the route text*		
Cheviots	*italic type: indicates a natural feature e.g. a hill or lake*		

detective work involved in 'city-escape', and also because you may in any case want to wander about in them.

Some of the places marked on the route maps are not shown on one or other of the Bartholomew's or Ordnance Survey (OS) 1:250 000 series (the OS 1:50 000 is the last word in completeness). Also there are occasional discrepancies in, for example, the shape of a lane and so one or other series has to disagree with the route map. Neither of these points should cause problems: we have made sure that the route maps can be easily deciphered. A number of the places which feature in the routes will not be marked on the OS 1:250 000 and Bartholomew's maps simply because they are small features. You may have to ask locally to find them, especially where they lie away from roads: prehistoric man, for one, did not place his monuments with accessibility to 20th-century roads in mind!

Key to Route Text

Text symbol	Feature
DoE	*in the care of the Department of the Environment*
NM	*a registered National Monument in Ireland*
NT	*in the care of the National Trust*
NTS	*in the care of the National Trust for Scotland*
open	*open to the public at certain times. A house, castle, ruin or garden mentioned without the 'open' comment can be viewed from the outside only. Churches, cathedrals, museums and prehistoric monuments can be assumed to be open unless otherwise stated*
italicized text	*comments relevant to the practical aspects of travelling the route*

The route texts give the lengths of the main rather than the alternative routes, details of the places of interest on or near the route, and information regarding the cycling itself. Before riding the route be sure to read any comments which appear directly below the map listing, and it is a good idea to consider which of the points of interest you wish to visit. You must decide how you can best detour to off-route features given your overall plans, and you are advised to check the opening times of stately houses, etc. either in the public library or in relevant publications (see Appendix 7) before you set out, or by asking locally.

British Isles Touring Areas

a **North and South Downs and Weald** Smooth grassy South Downs; North Downs with more woods and villages; Low Weald with thick woods and pastures; steep hills of High Weald; medieval buildings; coastal resorts.

b **Chilterns** Steeply folded hills; long valleys; beech woods; grassy fields; old churches, brick and flint houses; commuter towns; steep roads.

c **East Anglia** Gently undulating; easy touring; rich farmland; rural atmosphere; flat low coastline; not many towns; flint cottages, half-timbered buildings.

d **Lincolnshire Wolds** Rolling grassy downland hills; level ridge-top roads; well farmed; small villages in valleys.

e **New Forest** Flattish; ancient oaks and beeches; forestry plantations; unfenced heaths with ponies and cattle; few buildings.

f **The Wessex Downs** Rounded low hills; winding valleys, clear streams; brick and flint houses; some rough sheep pasture; prehistoric monuments; chalk-cut motifs of beasts and men.

g **The Cotswolds** Ridges and valleys, steep in the west, shallow in the east; fertile fields; stone walls, hedges; beautiful villages of honey-coloured stone; rich medieval 'wool' churches.

h **The Dorset Hills** Expansive ridges and valleys; fertile, warm-coloured stone villages; some rugged coast; strenuous.

i **The West Country Hills** Large rolling hills; granite walls, high hedges; stone houses, some thatch; rugged cliffs, sandy bays, wooded creeks; open moorland of Exmoor, Dartmoor and Bodmin; strenuous.

j **The Peak District** Deep, winding valleys; limestone outcrops, caves and drystone walls; green pastures, sombre moorlands; grey stone inland cliffs; strenuous.

k **The Yorkshire Dales** Broad valleys; swift rivers; green fields; white inland cliffs and gorges; long straight white walls; stone villages and field barns; some heather and peat moorland.

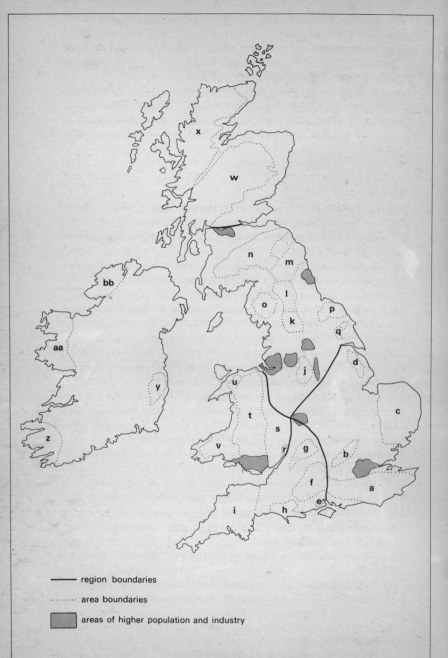

region boundaries
area boundaries
areas of higher population and industry

l   **The North Pennines** Wild moorland; farmed valleys; few habitations; long or steep slopes.

m   **Northumberland** Low sandy coast; undulating low farmland, hedges and a few trees; smooth, high Cheviot Hills; pine forests; low heathery wastes and bogs; Hadrian's Wall.

n   **The Southern Uplands** High, barren, rounded hills, more rugged in the west; bracken, heather and sheep; few roads and villages.

o   **The Lake District** Rugged mountains; flat green valleys; mountain tarns, valley lakes; lowland woods; whitewash and slate cottages; strenuous.

p   **The North York Moors** Bleak heathery plateau; wide valleys, green fields rising high; grey stone walls; small villages; long ridge and valley roads.

q   **The Yorkshire Wolds** Farmed hills; steep-sided winding valleys, some wooded, some rough grass; lost villages; stone buildings.

r   **Wye Valley and Forest of Dean** Deep and wooded Wye Valley; beauty spots; thick deciduous woods of Forest of Dean; steep roads.

s   **Welsh Borders** Grassy hills and broad vales; woods; cattle and sheep farms; stone buildings, castles and interesting towns.

t   **Cambrian Mountains** Wild mountains and hills with rough grass; deep valleys; huge forests; lakes; hill farms and sheep; few villages and towns; long and steep hill climbs; strenuous.

u   **Snowdonia** Rugged mountains; sheer-sided valleys; lakes; busy roads; few buildings.

v   **Pembrokeshire Coast** Rocky coast; high cliffs; bays; castles; well-farmed inland; stone buildings; partly hilly, partly flat.

w   **Grampians** High desolate mountains; moor, rough grass and heather slopes, rocky ridges; lochs; sheep farming; few roads and buildings.

x   **North West Scotland** Fjord-like coast; rugged steep sided mountains with long rocky ridges; many lochs; sheep on lower grassy slopes; crofts; fishing ports; many islands.

y   **The Wicklow Mountains** Rounded, high mountain block; peat and heather summits; deep valleys with pastures and woods.

z   **Kerry** Peninsulas with rocky coasts; low coastal farmlands; spines of high mountains with some bare red rock; occasional luxuriant woods; whitewash and thatch cottages.

aa   **Connemara and Mayo** Open, low expanses; bog; bared pale rock; heather, gorse, few trees; many small loughs (lakes); isolated mountains and mountain groups; whitewash and thatch cottages.

bb   **Donegal** Rugged mountains; coastal lowlands dotted with farms; whitewash and thatch cottages; rocky coast; few trees.

SOUTH-EAST ENGLAND

For a great many people the south-east is the most accessible of the six regions. The comparatively mild terrain is comfortable for a first tour and covers areas that have long been enjoyed by cyclists from the cities of southern England, while foreign visitors will find the region well supplied with seaports and international airports. Escape from the towns can quickly be made by train to all the prime cycling areas.

Broadly speaking the region is one of undulating lowland with several well-defined, long and narrow ranges of hills. Few parts are level, the largest being the man-made Fens, and the steepest gradients are to be found in the North and South Downs, High Weald, the Chilterns, parts of Northamptonshire, Oxfordshire and Leicestershire and the Lincolnshire Wolds. Other parts of the region such as East Anglia and lowland Lincolnshire can be toured comfortably with a three-speed gear or even a single speed. Although there are no barren moors or mountain areas (as there are in the five other regions), it is still easy to get away from it all and once out of town or village you will find quiet lanes. Civilization is never far away and shops and accommodation are fairly easy to find. Some of the villages are a delight with a traditional group of old cottages round the village green and a small shop and pub to add colour to any day's cycling.

The southern half of England does of course include large built-up areas: try to avoid altogether the Midlands, London and their environs. A small number of routes have been selected as useful links rather than on scenic merit, notably 17 and 32 and to a lesser extent 27, 31, 58 and 65. While they do contain much of interest, these routes pass close to towns and tend to involve cycling on busier roads. Main roads are continually being modified in the south-east and up-to-date maps are particularly advisable.

From the hills of Hampshire, the chalk ridge of the North Downs curves eastwards before plunging into the English Channel at the White Cliffs of Dover. For more than half their length the Downs butt on to the southern suburbs of London, providing an immediate sanctuary for the city dweller. Here the hills form a dividing line between the urban sprawl to the north and the Weald to the south. They vary in width and at their western end are so narrow that the steep-sided hill called the Hog's Back carries only one road; over in the east by Canterbury the Downs are lower, less steep and about 10 miles (16 km) wide. Many of the slopes are heavily wooded, while flatter hilltops and valleys have been turned to pasture for sheep and cattle.

In the hills lanes wind between high banks and hedges and under arcades of trees. They sometimes slice through deep cuttings hacked out years ago in an attempt to reduce the severity of the gradients. There are frequent junctions with other roads. From the top of the steep south-facing slope of the Downs there are fine views over the valleys of the Weald. Below, at the foot of the scarp slope, is the Pilgrim's Way, an ancient track which leads to Canterbury Cathedral.

Several main roads cross the Downs and large dormitory towns such as Guildford, Dorking, Reigate and Sevenoaks occupy strategic gaps in them. In the western part of this range careful map reading is needed. A mile in the wrong direction may result in an unnecessary hill climb or a ride along a busy main road. Further east, where lanes are more abundant and main roads fewer, it is much easier to wander as you please.

The chalk rim of the North and South Downs encloses a roughly oval area known as the Weald which can be separated into the High and the Low Weald. Villages are liberally scattered and timbered houses, willow-fringed ponds, old bridges, castles and churches contribute to the very 'English' scenery. A variation in Kent is the conical oast house, used in the hop drying process.

The steep sides of the High Weald rise to around 600 feet (160 metres), culminating in the bracken covered slopes of Ashdown Forest. At one time the great primeval forest of Andreas Wald covered the whole Weald, but

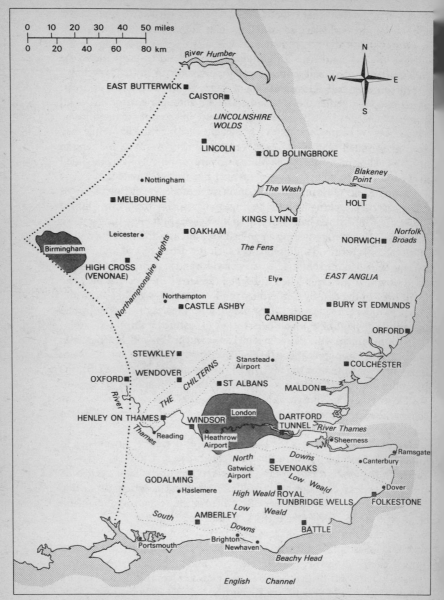

over the centuries it has been decimated by ship builders, iron workers and others needing timber. A large-scale map reveals old 'hammer' ponds, once used by the iron smelters, and there are many crooked medieval buildings among these hills. Several parts of the High Weald are still wooded. The

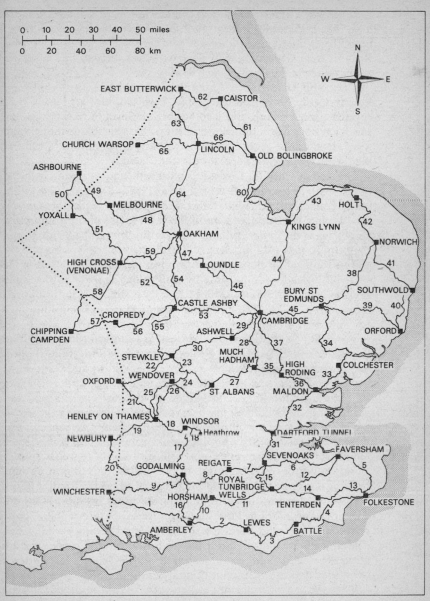

Scale:
0   10   20   30   40   50 miles
0   20   40   60   80 km

EAST BUTTERWICK
62   CAISTOR
63   61
CHURCH WARSOP   66
65   LINCOLN
OLD BOLINGBROKE
ASHBOURNE   64   60
50   49   43   HOLT
MELBOURNE   42
YOXALL   48   KINGS LYNN
51   NORWICH
OAKHAM   44   41
59   47   38
HIGH CROSS   54   OUNDLE   BURY ST   SOUTHWOLD
(VENONAE)   46   EDMUNDS
52   39   40
58   CASTLE ASHBY   45   ORFORD
CROPREDY   53   CAMBRIDGE
57   55   ASHWELL   29
CHIPPING   56   28   37   34
CAMPDEN   30   MUCH
STEWKLEY   23   HADHAM   35   HIGH   COLCHESTER
22   27   RODING   33
WENDOVER   24   36
OXFORD   25   26   ST ALBANS   MALDON
21   32
HENLEY ON THAMES   18   WINDSOR
19   Heathrow
NEWBURY   18   DARTFORD TUNNEL
17   31
20   GODALMING   REIGATE   SEVENOAKS   FAVERSHAM
8   7   6   5
ROYAL   15   12
9   TUNBRIDGE   14   13
WINCHESTER   HORSHAM   WELLS   11   TENTERDEN   FOLKESTONE
16   10   4
AMBERLEY   2   LEWES   BATTLE
3

lanes here tend to have steep gradients.

Surrounding the High Weald is a great horseshoe of gently undulating countryside known as the Low Weald. Here you can pedal for many miles without finding a serious hill in your path, and roads are fewer.

At the western end of the Weald, around Haslemere, is another group of hills. The highest, Blackdown, rises to 919 feet (280 metres). Narrow, twisty lanes offer glimpses between trees of the South Downs beyond. Route 9 from Godalming to Winchester passes through the impressive amphitheatre of the Devil's Punch Bowl.

The South Downs stretch from the Hampshire hills to the cliffs of Beachy Head. The rounded tops and downland folds are largely grass covered though more arable land has been claimed in recent years. An excursion along one of the many bridleways that scramble up the northern scarp slope will be rewarded with views back to the wooded Weald and then south down gentle slopes towards the Channel.

The eastern end of the Downs is popular with motorists, being bounded on the south by resorts such as Brighton and crossed by several busy main roads. Lanes here are few but further west the Downs become broader and good cycling lanes explore some of the valleys. One of the main upland attractions is the designated long distance bridleway, the South Downs Way. Its 80-mile (128 km) length is signposted to help you keep to the correct route. On a clear summer day there are few better places in the south of England, with the hard, dry chalk rolling beneath the wheels and skylarks singing overhead. At times the track is strenuous and some parts are too steep to cycle. The surface can be bumpy and in wet weather turns to a mire defying even the most determined cyclist.

The tightly folded Chiltern Hills extend in a long and narrow belt from the reaches of the Thames near Henley to beyond the town of Luton where they merge with gentler slopes to continue towards Cambridge. Their highest point is reached along the north-west facing scarp which rises abruptly from the Vale of Oxford to around 800 feet (250 metres). Remnants of the huge forest that once covered the Chilterns can be seen in the beech woods on the hillsides of the western part of the range. It was these trees that supplied the furniture-making industry of West Wycombe though, in spite of the centuries of felling, many large woods such as Burnham Beeches remain. At their eastern end the Chilterns can be quite bare and windswept where woodland has given way to farmland.

Chiltern towns tend to stretch along the valley bottoms. Many are commuter towns for London. The villages are less discriminating in choice of site, and are found on ridge tops and hillsides. There are old Norman churches and traditional brick and flint houses. Several scenic areas are owned by the National Trust, and most of the Chilterns falls within a designated Area of Outstanding Natural Beauty.

The main ways through the Chilterns are used by A roads, railways and motorways which run south-east to converge on London. However, there are many peaceful if hilly lanes. If you are cycling along the range you will be going 'against the grain' of the valleys which means many a swooping descent usually followed by a hard ascent. Make sure that you have low gears or good walking shoes. Many of the valleys have lanes along their floors which provide gentler access to the hilltops, while the ridge roads offer fine views.

East Anglia roughly comprises Norfolk, Suffolk and north Essex. Little in this sympathetic terrain demands effort and it is one of the most extensive 'easy' touring areas in the British Isles. The countryside is mainly low and undulating with gentle slopes and slow rivers meandering along shallow valleys to the coastline. Gradients are seldom steep, and when they are it is for but a short distance. The area is a prime one for arable land and views will often be over fields of barley and wheat against small patches of woodland and beneath open skies—a landscape painted by the 19th-century artist John Constable.

Relatively unaffected by industrial and urban development, East Anglia has a distinct character. The few large towns that do exist (such as Norwich, Bury St Edmunds and Ipswich) are widely spaced and have strong regional atmospheres. Once out in the countryside you will find compact villages, isolated farmsteads and the occasional small market town. The latter became important when the wool trade flourished in the Middle Ages but are now mainly quiet backwaters. With relatively few main roads and a good network of lanes, in East Anglia you should easily avoid traffic.

Within East Anglia there is some variety of landscape. On the north Norfolk coast deposition by the sea has led to the formation of salt marshes; the long shingle spit of Blakeney Point and Scolt Head island are a haven for birds. With its expanse of sand dunes, small fishing villages of flint-built cottages and low horizons studded with church towers, it has a desolate quality rarely found in southern England. North-east of Norwich are the rivers and shallow reed-fringed lakes of the Norfolk Broads, a favourite area for water-borne holiday makers.

Suffolk is noticeably hillier than Norfolk, with narrower river valleys and rounded slopes tucked around the villages. However you will find three gears quite adequate for exploring this unspoilt landscape. Many of the towns and villages have old timbered buildings and you will come across abbeys, mansions, old mills and grand churches. Backed by sandy heathland, the Suffolk coast is flat and empty; its estuaries, shingle banks and marshes are most frequented by yachtsmen and birds.

In the north-west corner of East Anglia are the Fens, one of the largest truly flat areas in the British Isles. But before turning your handlebars Fen-wards, just pause to check which way the wind is blowing. You may find yourself pumping the pedals furiously into a strong headwind to reach all of five miles per hour when crossing these levels. Conversely, a following wind over the long, flat, straight roads is really exhilarating. It was not until the 18th century that this once great waste of marsh was drained to produce the rich arable land of today. Both Cambridge and Ely, the latter built on one of the original islands that stood above the marsh, are fascinating places to visit after a relatively featureless ride across the Fens.

Between the Fens and the industrial Midlands are the counties of Bedfordshire, Northamptonshire and Leicestershire. A web of busy main roads has developed between the many large towns in these counties, although there are quiet lanes which keep the cyclist well away from them. Low hills near the Fens give way further west to the rolling slopes of the Northamptonshire Heights.

From the Humber the rounded hills of the Lincolnshire Wolds stretch southwards to merge with the Fens. Fields of barley, wheat and grass spread across their smooth contours while hillsides dip to deep valleys. You will seldom find a hill climb unrewarded by good views, particularly from the long and fairly level ridge-top roads. There are not many villages but small county towns are found on the edges of the hills. You will probably notice signposts mentioning places with names ending in 'by' and 'thorpe'; these were settlements founded by the Danes around the 9th century. If you wish to cycle the east coast of England, the Lincolnshire Wolds provide an enjoyable alternative to the relatively flat and less scenic landscapes to either side.

Route 1
WINCHESTER — AMBERLEY

50 miles   80 km

OS 1:250 000 no. 9
Bartholomew's 1:100 000 nos 5, 6
OS 1:50 000 nos 185, 197

Between Buriton and Houghton, and running parallel and south of the main route is an alternative route along the South Downs Way. It forms part of a designated long distance bridleway, and in good weather has a reasonable surface, but during and after rain this deteriorates to sticky mud. Cycles have to be pushed on the steeper parts. In several places roads link the main route to the South Downs Way providing chances to cycle shorter sections of downland rough-stuff. Navigation of these tracks requires the use of 1:50 000 maps.

Winchester Important in Roman times, it was the capital in the times of King Alfred and William the Conqueror. The Norman cathedral, said to be Europe's longest, is the burial place of many famous people, and contains the Cathedral Treasury and Library with a fine, illustrated bible. The 13th-century Castle Hall contains King Arthur's round table (in fact it dates from the 16th century); it is the assizes where Walter Raleigh was condemned to death, and where Judge Jeffreys presided. Famous Winchester College; many fine buildings and museums; the superb Norman Chapel of St Cross and almshouses dating from the 12th century. The YH is in the City Mill (NT, open). Links with Routes 9, 95, 97, 100.

Cheesefoot Head A great natural amphitheatre possibly used by the Romans, and where in 1944 Eisenhower addressed Allied troops before the D-Day landings. It can be reached by public bridleway from Morestead.

West Meon Thomas Lord, first owner of the famous Lord's cricket ground in London, is buried here and the pub is named after him. Guy Burgess, the political defector is also buried here. The church walls are of knapped flint, and there are some charming cottages.

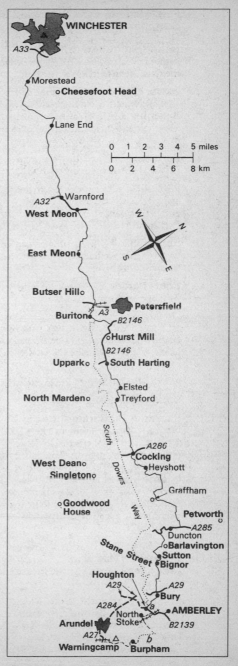

East Meon A beautiful village with a fine church containing a marble font. Opposite the church is a 15-century court house. Izaak Walton, 17th-century author of *The Compleat Angler*, fished in the river Meon here.

Butser Hill Fine views from the 888 foot (270 m) summit. Close by, near the A3, is Butser Iron Age farm, an experimental site where ancient farming techniques are practised.

Buriton The 18th-century historian Edward Gibbon spent his boyhood here.

Petersfield Attractive Georgian houses and market square, and once an important coaching stop on the London to Portsmouth road.

Hurst Mill Delightfully situated garden, with waterfall, mill stream, bog garden, trees and shrubs (open).

South Harting The novelist Anthony Trollope lived here.

Uppark A romantic 17th-century house set high on the Downs (open), with 18th-century furnishings, a Queen Anne doll's house, Victorian kitchen and landscaped garden.

North Marden Tiny Norman church.

Cocking Pebbledash church.

Singleton The Weald and Downland Open Air Museum occupies a lovely 35-acre site used for re-erecting historic buildings from south-east England: 15th-century Wealden hall, a 14th-century farmhouse, an Elizabethan treadwheel, a blacksmith's forge, and the Titchfield market hall are a few. The museum is also a country park, and has a woodland nature trail.

West Dean West Dean Gardens (open) have rare and unusual trees, a pergola, gazebo, bamboo garden, wild garden and ornamental birds.

Goodwood House A Jacobean house with fine Sussex flintwork (open) and a collection of Louis XV furniture and famous paintings by artists such as Canaletto, Van Dyck and Stubbs. There are specimen trees in the Park and High Wood, and to the north the Goodwood Race Course and 676 foot (206 m) high Trundle Hill.

Petworth Magnificent 17th-century Petworth House (NT, open) has a fine deer park landscaped by Capability Brown, the Carved Room decorated by Grinling Gibbons, paintings by Turner (who visited here often) and others. Delightful medieval town with narrow winding streets, an 18th-century town hall, the Somerset almshouses, and Tudor and Georgian buildings.

Barlavington Perfect early English church.

Sutton The very unusual rectory is made of mud bricks.

Bignor The site of one of the largest Roman villas discovered in Britain (open).

Stane Street A Roman road built in AD 70 to link London and Chichester. It can be reached by a steep lane climbing up the Downs from Bignor to Bignor Hill. From there a public bridleway follows its course for 2½ miles (4 km) in a south-westerly direction before meeting another lane.

Bury The remains of a jetty mark where a ferry once crossed to Amberley. John Galsworthy, author of *The Forsyte Saga* lived in Bury House.

Houghton Charles II called at the 16th-century George and Dragon inn in 1651 after the Battle of Worcester.

a The alternative route detours south to the interesting town of Arundel, passing the YH and Burpham, and involving the use of a track over the South Downs.

Arundel The massive keep, walls and towers of restored Arundel Castle (open) guard the valley through the Downs; tremendous views from the top of the 12th-century keep, and in the huge park is 18th-century Hiorn's Tower. There are many fine old houses, and the Norfolk Arms coaching inn in the town. Potter's Museum of Curiosity displays the work of the Victorian naturalist and taxidermist Walter Potter.

Warningcamp Arundel YH.

Burpham The author Mervyn Peake lived here for a while and his grave can be seen in the churchyard.

b The southern end of the track starts from a sharp corner in the lane north of Burpham leading to Peppering High Barn, while the northern end of the track starts at the end of the lane leading eastwards up the hill from North Stoke.

Amberley See Route 2. Also links with Routes 10, 16.

Route 2   28 miles   45 km
AMBERLEY — LEWES

OS 1:250 000 no. 9
Bartholomew's 1:100 000 no. 6
OS 1:50 000 nos 197, 198

Running parallel and south of the main route is the South Downs Way, offering an exciting alternative route. If you wish to sample just a part of the South Downs Way you are recommended to follow the section between Amberley and Bramber and use the
main route for the remainder. 1:50 000 maps will be needed. (See also Route 1 comments.)

Amberley A delightful old village with a medieval atmosphere, ruins of a great 14th-century castle and a Norman church. In summer it is bright with flowers. Links with Routes 1, 10, 16.

a For an interesting detour over the South Downs to Arundel, see Route 1.

Parham House An Elizabethan house (open) with an important collection of Elizabethan, Jacobean and Georgian portraits, fine furniture and needle work.

Chanctonbury Ring Beech trees planted in 1760 by Charles Goring stand within the mounds of an Iron Age earthwork which was also the site of a Roman temple. It stands at 783 feet (238 m); good views to the sea.

Cissbury Ring A 60-acre Iron Age camp with strong ramparts enclosing the sites of early flint mines. There are fine views.

Steyning Fine 12th-century church.

Bramber This was once the provincial capital of William the Conqueror, and the fragment of a Norman castle can be seen on a huge mound. St Mary's is an out-

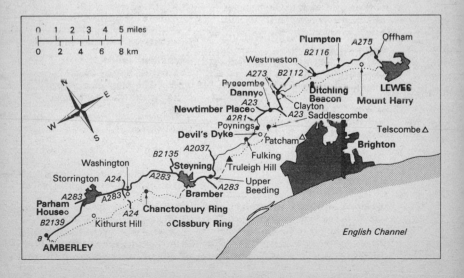

standing example of late 15th-century timber framing (open) and has panelling, costumes, a collection of handicrafts, a music room and garden.

Devil's Dyke According to legend, the Devil cut this valley into the Downs with the intention of flooding the Weald with the sea.

Newtimber Place A moated house with Etruscan style wall paintings (open).

Danny An Elizabethan house (open) dating from 1593.

Brighton The best known building in this famous resort is the exotic Royal pavilion (open), built for King George IV, and lavishly decorated inside in a Chinese style. The town has many graceful Georgian and late Victorian houses, and endless entertainments. Preston Manor (open) is a Georgian house containing fine pictures, furniture, silver and china. Also of interest are the Brighton Museum and Art Gallery, the Booth Museum of Natural History, and Grange Art Gallery and Museum.

Ditchling Beacon The highest point on the South Downs, with superb views.

Plumpton The V-shaped plantation of trees on the Downs to the south was planted to commemorate the Golden Jubilee of Queen Victoria in 1887.

Mount Harry On the eastern slopes of this hill a battle took place in 1264, when Henry III was beaten by Simon de Montfort and his barons.

Lewes The town grew around the castle, built soon after the Norman Conquest to subdue the English. There are remains of a Cluniac Priory. View the town from the castle keep. Once a river port, Lewes has many Georgian houses, particularly in the high street. The 15th-century Anne of Cleves House has collections including old household equipment and firebacks (open); Barbican museum of the archaeology and history of Sussex. Southover Grange was the home of John Evelyn, the diarist. Links with Route 3.

Route 3   38 miles   62 km
BATTLE — LEWES

OS 1:250 000 no. 9
Bartholomew's 1:100 000 no. 6
OS 1:50 000 nos 198, 199

Battle The Abbey was built by William the Conqueror in thanks for his victory over King Harold at the Battle of Hastings, fought on a nearby hill. The remains are being actively dug (DoE, open). Deanery church with brasses. Langton House has a museum including a collection about the Sussex iron industry. Links with Route 4.

Ashburnham Place The house is set in a large park laid out by Capability Brown. A public footpath crosses the park from Steven's Crouch.

a A bridleway passes through the grounds of Herstmonceux Castle parallel and just south of a drive. The alternative route follows roads to the north.

Herstmonceux Castle A 15th-century moated castle built of brick. The Royal Greenwich Observatory moved here when the London air became too smoky for astronomical observations. Isaac Newton Telescope building.

Pevensey Pevensey Castle (DoE, open); 14th-century Old Minthouse, with panels, frescoes and a hiding-hole (open).

Michelham Priory Priory with one of England's largest moats, a Tudor barn, wheelwright's forge and watermill grinding wholemeal flour (open).

b The main route detours to the South Downs and the alternative follows the A27.

The Long Man Visible from Wilmington is the Long Man, one of England's three impressive, ancient figures cut out of the turf on the chalk hillside.

Litlington Charleston Manor Gardens are set around a house combining Norman, Tudor and Georgian architecture, having a fine Romanesque window (grounds open).

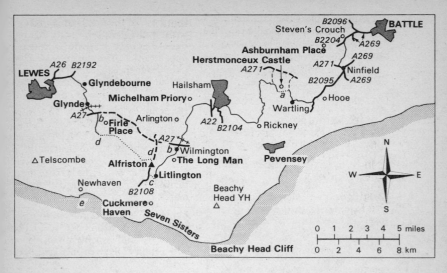

Cuckmere Haven Country park in the Cuckmere valley.

Seven Sisters Seven chalk cliffs formed where the South Downs meet the sea. This is considered to be south-east England's finest coastal scenery, and it can be enjoyed by walks on the open grass downland above the cliffs, accessible from Cuckmere Haven.

Beachy Head Cliff A single chalk cliff whose name derives from the French 'Beau Chef', as it used to be a vital landmark to sailors in the Channel.

c This short bridleway is well-surfaced and runs from just south of Alfriston YH to a bend just south of Litlington.

Alfriston Pretty village; 14th-century thatched Clergy House was the first building acquired by the NT (open). The 15th-century Star Inn has fine carved woodwork.

d Here the main route follows the South Downs Way; further information in Route 1 comments. It is reached from Alfriston by side-roads going west, starting from opposite the church.

Firle Place The house contains important collections of paintings, china, and objects with American interest (open).

e Ferries from Newhaven to Dieppe.

Glynde The 16th-century flint and brick Glynde Place is open.

Glyndebourne Famed for festivals of opera and music.

Lewes See Route 2.

Route 4   46 miles   74 km
FOLKESTONE — BATTLE

OS 1:250 000 no. 9
Bartholomew's 1:100 000 no. 10
OS 1:50 000 nos 189, 199

Folkestone A popular holiday, yachting and cruising centre since the railway era. Victorian resort architecture. Museum and art gallery. Walks in the Warren. Links with Routes 5, 13.

a Ferries from Folkestone to continental ports including Ostend, Calais and Boulogne.

Hythe St Leonard's church is built on a slope. Norman Saltwood Castle, said to have been the subject of a quarrel between Thomas à Becket and Henry II, and the place from which Becket's assassins rode out, contains an armoury collection (open). Local history museum; terminus for the light gauge railway.

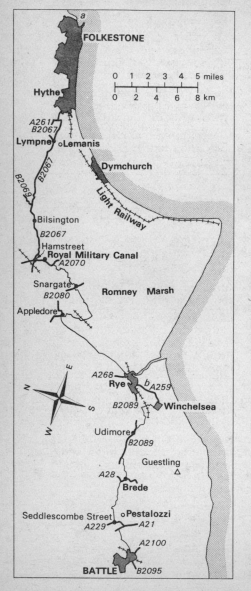

Romney, Hythe and Dymchurch Light Railway This 15-inch gauge railway claims to be the world's smallest public railway. The miniature steam trains reach speeds of 20 mph. During th Second World War it was used by the army.

Dymchurch Two Martello Towers, par of the Napoleonic defences, are in the care of the DoE (open). New Hall (16th century) was the meeting hall for the Lords of the Level who used to govern Romney Marsh. It is the home of the fictional Dr Syn, smuggler and clergyman.

Lympne The 14th-century restored castle has terraced grounds (open). Port Lympne wildlife sanctuary is set around a 20th-century Dutch colonial style house (open).

Lemanis Also called 'Stutfall', Lemanis is the remains of a Roman fortification.

Royal Military Canal Here the route crosses over a canal which was built as a barrier to Napoleonic forces.

Romney Marsh The vast, flat expanse of Romney Marsh is land which has been formed by the piling together of shingle by two meeting sea currents within geologically recent time. The landward parts of it, where the rich silt has lost much of its sea-salt, are said to be one of the world's best sheep areas.

Rye An ancient town with steep, cobbled streets, many of which have very old houses. Georgian Lamb House was Henry James' home (NT). The 13th-century Ypres Tower houses a museum of local interest. St Mary's church has a 16th-century clock. There is a medieval hospital and a 17th-century grammar school.

b The road between Rye and Winchelsea is heavily used by tourist traffic, but is the only reasonable way of linking these two marvellous towns.

Winchelsea In 1287 the sea flooded Old Winchelsea and the present hill-top town was laid out to a grid plan (c.1290) though the building was never completed. It is today a charming Georgian town. Winchelsea was a cinque port before the sea receded. The church is most unusual, being just the chancel of a huge 14th-century church, and containing fine modern glass and coats of arms. Museum of local interest and the history of the cinque ports.

Brede Early English church with brasses.

Pestalozzi Children's village for refugees.

Battle See Route 3.

Route 5   36 miles   57 km
FAVERSHAM — FOLKESTONE

OS 1:250 000 no. 9
Bartholomew's 1:100 000 no. 10
OS 1:50 000 no. 179, 178 (just)

Faversham There have been pre-historic, Roman and Anglo-Saxon settlements near the site of present-day Faversham. Abbey Street and Market Place have a richness of Tudor, Stuart and Georgian architecture. St Mary's church has fine misericords and brasses. The 13th-century Maison Dieu houses finds from the Roman cemetery (DoE, open). Davington priory church. Links with Routes 6, 12.

Canterbury Belgic and Roman settlements existed here, but Canterbury gained the importance it has today as head of the Anglican Communion when St Augustine was appointed Archbishop in 597, and built his first cathedral. It has a Norman crypt; the Black Prince's tomb; ancient and modern stained glass; some 800 coats of arms in the cloisters. There are many ancient churches; medieval city walls; the Roman pavement; the Weavers, half-timbered houses with old looms, a reminder of the industry introduced by Walloon and Huguenot refugees. Remains of St Augustine's Abbey (DoE, open). Several old buildings and museums. Ducking stool and tuck shop. The Chequers Inn immortalized in the Canterbury Tales.

a This bridleway is a good farm road. At the Canterbury end it crosses a railway bridge to lead into Pilgrims Road, a turning off St Augustine's Road which turns off the A2.

Patrixbourne Fine Norman carving and early glass is seen in the church.

Barfreston Church with outstanding Romanesque carving; statue carving of Thomas à Becket.

Lower Eythorne The church contains a lead font, and is associated with Joan Burchen who was martyred by burning.

Dover There are two YHs. Old cinque port, with a castle on an imposing site,

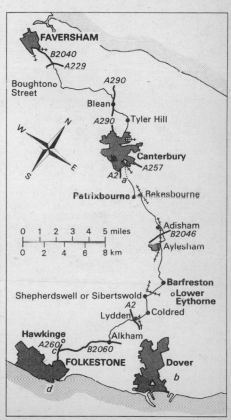

with remains of Roman lighthouse, a Knights Templars chapel and underground passages (DoE, open).

b Ferries from Dover go to many Contin- ental *ports including Zeebrugge, Ostend, Dunkirk, Calais and Boulogne.*

Hawkinge Tiny medieval church.

c If you next intend to follow Route 13 to Tenterden, you can turn to it here.

d Ferries from Folkestone to Continental ports including Ostend, Calais and Boulogne.

Folkestone See Route 4. Also links with Route 13.

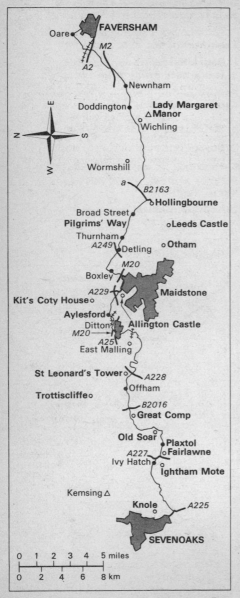

Route 6   44 miles   71 km
FAVERSHAM — SEVENOAKS

OS 1:250 000 no. 9
Bartholomew's 1:100 000 no. 10
OS 1:50 000 nos 178, 188

Between Ditton and Boxley this route has to pass through the busy Maidstone area as there are no other practical crossings over the river Medway. Patience and care with navigation is particularly vital there.

Faversham See Route 5. Also links with Route 12.

Lady Margaret Manor Doddington YH.

a For ferries to Holland, go generally north on the B2163 to Sittingbourne and then the B2005 and A249 to Sheerness.

Hollingbourne Fifteenth-century Eyhorne Manor is a timbered house with a laundry museum (open).

Pilgrims' Way This stretch of lanes between Hollingbourne and Boxley below the North Downs follows the route of the ancient pilgrims' way to Canterbury.

Leeds Castle Henry VIII made this medieval castle a royal palace; sited on two lake islands; landscaped parkland and gardens (open).

Otham Stoneacre (NT, open) is a yeoman's half-timbered hall house.

Maidstone A pleasant group of 14th-century buildings comprising the Archbishop's Palace, a church, the College and 'tithe barn', which was probably a stable. There is a museum of carriages.

Allington Castle A 13th-century, turretted castle with collections of icons and Renaissance art (open).

Kit's Coty House The stones remaining form an impressive cromlech (DoE).

Aylesford The Friars is a 13th-century Carmelite friary (open); there is a 14th-century bridge.

St Leonard's Tower The tower of an ancient chapel (DoE).

Trottiscliffe A large prehistoric group of stones, thought to have been a royal tomb.

Great Comp Seven acres of botanical gardens (open).

Old Soar Manor containing the solar block of a knight's house (DoE, NT, open).

Plaxtol The church was opened during the Civil War, and therefore has no dedication.

Ightham Mote An ancient, moated manor house (open).

Knole A magnificent 15th-century private house, containing large collections, and set in huge grounds where deer roam. The house has strong associations with the Sackville family (NT, open).

Sevenoaks See Route 7. Also links with Routes 15, 31.

Route 7   24 miles   39 km
SEVENOAKS — REIGATE

OS 1:250 000 no. 9
Bartholomew's 1:100 000 no. 9
OS 1:50 000 nos 187, 188

This route is of necessity fairly tortuous, as it seeks to avoid the many main roads and built-up areas on London's southern fringes.

Sevenoaks Famous boys' school founded by Sir Sevenoaks, a 15th-century foundling of the town who took its name. The Long Barn is a 14th-century house, said to have been the birthplace of

William Caxton (open). Links with Routes 6, 15, 31.

a The alternative route between Sevenoaks and Crockham Hill is longer but less hilly, as it explores the level lanes running by the foot of the North Downs, rather than the convoluted hills to the south.

Knole See Route 6.

b If you next intend to follow Route 15 to Tunbridge Wells, turn to it here.

Emmetts Garden of rare trees renowned for seasonal colours (NT, open).

Chartwell The house which was Winston Churchill's home for many years (NT, open).

Bat and Ball This place is so named as it prospered at one time on the manufacture of cricket bats.

Otford A picturesque grouping of buildings by the village pond.

c If you next intend to follow Route 31 to the Dartford Tunnel, turn to it here.

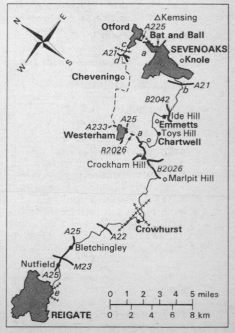

d The track used in this route is actually an old lane which was blocked off to cars when the new A21 was built. The lane passes a quarry entrance, and is connected to the A21 by a short sloping footpath at right angles to the lane. The A21 must be walked across.

Chevening The 16th-century church stands opposite some attractive 18th- and 19th-century estate cottages. Chevening House (17th-century) is thought to be one of the earliest departures from the Jacobean style. It belongs to Prince Charles. There are footpaths through the grounds.

Westerham Quebec House was General Wolfe's home (NT, open). Squerryes Court, also with Wolfe connections, has collections including Dutch paintings (open). The church has a Burne-Jones window commemorating Wolfe.

Crowhurst There is a very large and old yew tree, with a Civil War cannonball inside it.

e The lane between Reigate and Nutfield passes just south of the gas holders and just north of the cemetery in the Reigate outskirts.

Reigate See Route 8.

Route 8   25 miles   41 km
REIGATE — GODALMING

OS 1:250 000 no. 9
Bartholomew's 1:100 000 no. 9
OS 1:50 000 nos 186, 187

Reigate A castle mound is all that remains of an 11th-century castle. The Barons' Cave, traditionally said to be where the Barons met prior to meeting King John at Runnymede, is an underground court with a complex of long tunnels (sometimes open). The Redhill Royal Earlswood Hospital Museum of medical history is here. Links with Route 7.

a This right of way has a decayed tarmac surface. If you are following this route from east to west, turn off the old main road at South Holmwood onto Moorhurst Lane. If you are following this route from west to east,

turn off the lane onto the bridleway next to the drive to Spring Copse.

Leith Hill On the hill summit is the 18th century Leith Hill Tower, the construction of which brought the effective height of Surrey's highest point to over 1000 feet. There are panoramic views to the Channel.

Cranleigh England's first cottage hospital was founded here in 1859. During the First World War, Canadian soldiers planted the Canadian maples on the main road.

b This bridleway is very clear, having an almost entirely rideable surface, and it offers fine views. Follow the track as it turns through a right angle near Nore Farm.

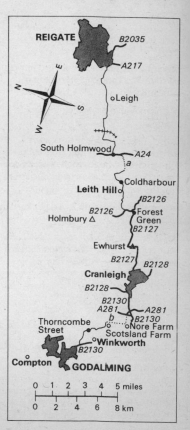

Winkworth NT arboretum, where the variety of trees is well displayed on a steep hillside.

Compton Norman church with a unique two storey chancel. A memorial chapel to the painter George Watts was built by his widow and the village people in art noveau style. There is also a Watts gallery.

Godalming See Route 9. Links with Routes 16, 17, 20.

Route 9	46 miles	74 km

GODALMING — WINCHESTER

OS 1:250 000 no. 9
Bartholomew's 1:100 000 nos 8, 9
OS 1:50 000 nos 185, 186

Godalming The town was the halfway stop on the old London to Portsmouth coach route; prisoners to be deported were exercised in the King's Arms yard. Local history museum in The Pepperpot; heavily restored ancient church. Charter-house school has mock Gothic and modern buildings. Cyclists' Touring Club has its headquarters here. Links with Routes 8, 16, 17, 20.

Compton See Route 8.

Enton Mill A picturesque pond-side hamlet.

Witley Common NT heathland; there is a centre explaining its ecology.

a If you are following this route from east to west, cross from the lane over the A3 on to a track, then keep right at subsequent track junctions. If you are following this route from west to east, follow the lane south out of Thursley as it becomes a beech-lined track. Bear left at the first opportunity, and keep left to cross the A3 on to a lane.

Devil's Punchbowl Hindhead YH.

Thursley A long-established church with an Anglo-Saxon window. There is a graphic gravestone depicting a traveller being murdered by three men.

Liphook The Hollycombe steam railway and agricultural machinery collection.

Selborne The Wakes museum of Gilbert White, author of *The Natural History of Selborne*. Scott Polar expedition display.

Chawton House Jane Austen's home.

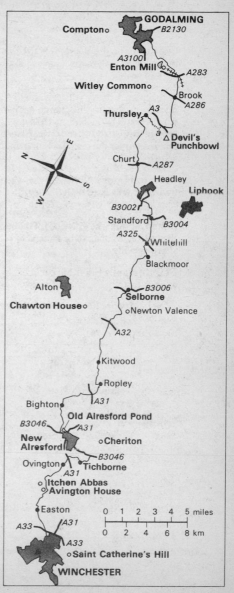

Old Alresford Pond The remains of a 12th-century reservoir built to make the River Itchen navigable as far as Bishops Sutton.

New Alresford A 'new town' laid out by the Bishop of Winchester in the 12th century.

Cheriton The site of a Civil War battle involving 20,000 troops. Grave mounds are still visible.

Tichborne A pretty village with old houses and thatch. The church has old woodwork. The Tichborne Dole is a charity supported by lands which were marked out for the purpose by a dying woman.

Avington House A house in the Wren tradition, associated with Shelley, and Charles II and Nell Gwynn (open).

Itchen Abbas The grave of J. Hughes, the last Englishman to be hanged for sheep-stealing.

St Catherine's Hill A hill encircled by ancient earthworks with a mizmaze.

Winchester See Route 1. Also links with Routes 95, 97, 100.

Route 10   17 miles   27 km
HORSHAM — AMBERLEY

OS 1:250 000 no. 9
Bartholomew's 1:100 000 no. 6
OS 1:50 000 nos 197, 198, 187 (just)

Horsham A market town and home for London commuters. The Horsham Museum is in 16th-century gabled Causeway House and has collections of local history, domestic, rural and industrial exhibits from Sussex life including a blacksmith's forge, and early bicycles. Links with Route 11.

Christ's Hospital The famous bluecoat school, which moved to Horsham in 1902, the buildings designed by Sir Aston Webb.

West Chiltington The church has a shingled spire, and wall paintings.

a If you next intend to follow Route 16 to Godalming, you can turn to it here.

Parham House See Route 2.

b For an interesting detour over the South Downs to Arundel, see Route 1.

Amberley See Route 2. Also links with Routes 1, 16.

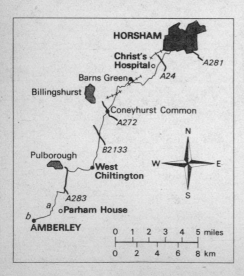

Route 11   37 miles   60 km
ROYAL TUNBRIDGE WELLS — HORSHAM

OS 1:250 000 no. 9
Bartholomew's 1:100 000 no. 6
OS 1:50 000 nos 188, 187

Royal Tunbridge Wells An elegant spa town best known for the Pantiles, a delightful shaded walk lined with a colonnade of 18th- and 19th-century houses and shops with Italianate columns. The Church of King Charles the Martyr has an impressive wooden cupola and marble font. There is a museum and art gallery. Links with Routes 12, 14, 15.

Groombridge An attractive village with 18th-century tiled cottages and a triangular green.

Ashdown Forest A large area of heath and wood with plenty of opportunity for good walks. It is a remnant of the huge Wealden Forest of Anderida, which stretched for 120 miles (192 km) across south-east England in Roman times.

Forest Row The Spring Hill Wildfowl Park has an extensive private collection of over one thousand birds from one hundred different species (open).

Kidbrooke Park An 18th-century sandstone house and stables (open).

Weir Wood Reservoir Delightfully set among woodlands.

Standen The house was built in 1894 (NT, open) and has William Morris wallpapers and textiles.

Tanyard A medieval tannery (open) with great oak beams, open fireplaces and a walled garden.

The Bluebell Railway To the northwest of Horsted Keynes is the northern end of this delightfully restored section of railway line. Steam locomotives and original rolling stock carry passengers along the line, which is run largely by volunteers from the Bluebell Railway Preservation Society.

West Hoathly Once a centre of the iron industry and haunt of smugglers. The 15th-century Priest House has a museum of old furniture, bygones, dolls and embroideries.

Wakehurst Place The Garden has a collection of exotic trees and shrubs, and several lakes (NT, open).

Borde Hill A large garden of great botanical interest, with rare trees, shrubs, view and walks (open).

Cuckfield Pleasant old buildings, and Cuckfield Park, an Elizabethan manor house and gatehouse.

Heaselands Over 20 acres of gardens (open) with water gardens, trees, shrubs and an aviary.

Nymans A garden with 30 acres of rare and beautiful plants, shrubs and trees from all over the world (NT, open).

Lower Beeding North of the village there is a hammer pond. Leonardslee (open) to the south, has gardens, and a chain of hammer ponds. Old Woldringfold (open) has a woodland garden and

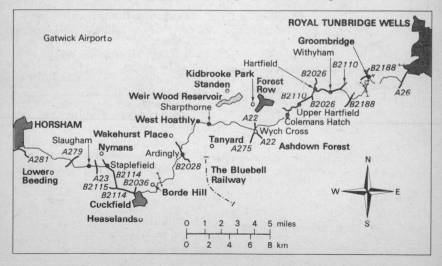

fine trees, and South Lodge (open) has flowering trees, a rock garden and rhododendrons.

Horsham See Route 10.

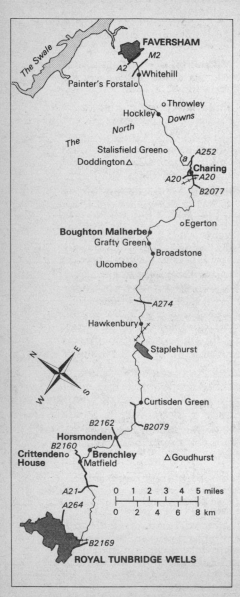

Route 12   41 miles   65 km
FAVERSHAM —
ROYAL TUNBRIDGE WELLS

OS 1:250 000 no. 9
Bartholomew's 1:100 000 no. 10
OS 1:50 000 nos 188, 189, 178

The network of lanes in the county of Kent is dense and can be confusing, so pay extra attention to map reading.

Faversham See Route 5. Also links with Route 6.

a A short section of lane is not shown on the Bartholomew's map of 1975.

Charing A palace of the Archbishops of Canterbury once stood here. The church has a timbered roof and medieval pulpit.

Boughton Malherbe There is a fine view over the Weald from the church.

Horsmonden A 17th-century gun-maker, John Browne, designed guns for both Charles I and Cromwell in the bar of the old Gun Inn.

Brenchley The village has several Tudor cottages, and is set in orchard country. An avenue of three hundred and fifty year old yew trees leads up to the 13th-century church.

Crittenden House An interesting garden (open) planned on labour-saving lines.

Royal Tunbridge Wells See Route 11. Also links with Routes 14, 15.

Route 13   29 miles   47 km
TENTERDEN — FOLKESTONE

OS 1:250 000 no. 9
Bartholomew's 1:100 000 no. 10
OS 1:50 000 nos 189, 179

Tenterden An important wool trading centre in medieval times with a 15th-century church. There are many attractive Elizabethan and Georgian houses, and old inns. Links with Route 14.

Smallhythe Place The 15th-century

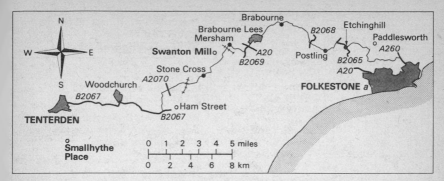

home of the actress Ellen Terry, who died in 1928. The delightful house (open) now contains a museum of her personal and theatrical mementos.

Swanton Mill A watermill in working order (open).

a Ferries from Folkestone to continental ports including Ostend, Calais and Boulogne.

Folkestone See Route 4. Also links with Route 5.

Route 14   26 miles   42 km
ROYAL TUNBRIDGE WELLS —
TENTERDEN

OS 1:250 000 no. 9
Bartholomew's 1:100 000 no. 10
OS 1:50 000 nos 188, 189

Royal Tunbridge Wells See Route 11. Also links with Routes 12, 15.

Bayham Abbey Built of local sandstone, these are among the most complete monastic ruins in lowland England (DoE, open).

Owl House A 16th-century half-timbered, tile-hung, wool smuggler's cottage (open), with gardens, roses and woodland walks.

Lamberhurst Once a centre of iron production.

Scotney Castle A romantic landscape garden (NT, open) surrounds the ruins of a 14th-century moated castle.

Finchcocks An early 18th-century house (open) containing a historic collection of keyboard instruments.

Twyssenden Manor Goudhurst YH.

Goudhurst A pretty village which prospered from the weaving industry of the Middle Ages. The church has marks on it said to have been caused by archers sharpening their arrows before going to fight in the Battle of Agincourt. The Star and Eagle Inn was once the headquarters of the Hawkhurst Gang, 18th-century smugglers, whose leader was caught in 1796 and hanged by the villagers.

Pattenden Manor A magnificent 15th-century timbered house, once the home of the standard bearer of Henry VIII and Elizabeth I (open).

Bedgebury Pinetum A Forestry Commission park (open) with an extensive collection of landscaped conifer trees and rhododendrons.

Ladham House Bog garden, heather garden, flowering shrubs and roses (open).

Angley Park A large variety of trees, with shrubs and rhododendrons, woods and a lake (open).

Cranbrook The town prospered from the weaving industry and has a fine medieval church dubbed 'Cathedral of the Weald'. The three-storied windmill, Union Mill, was built in 1814, and is kept in full working order.

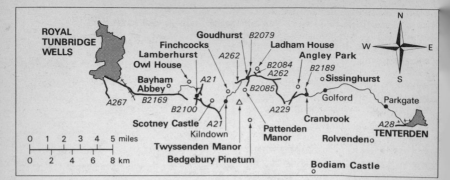

Sissinghurst Sir Harold Nicholson and Vita Sackville West created Sissinghurst Castle Garden (open) which incorporates a number of small gardens of different character, e.g. the white garden, and the remains of an Elizabethan house. Sissinghurst Court, towards Cranbrook, has a garden with attractions varying from ornamental cherries to lily pools (open).

Bodiam Castle One of the best-preserved examples of medieval military architecture built in the 14th century as a protection from French raids. It has a beautiful moat, and most of the walls and towers remain (NT, open).

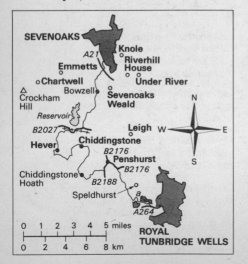

Rolvenden Great Maytham Hall (open) was built in 1910 by Sir Edwin Lutyens.

Tenterden See Route 13.

Route 15   22 miles   35 km
**SEVENOAKS —
ROYAL TUNBRIDGE WELLS**

OS 1:250 000 no. 9
Bartholomew's 1:100 000 no. 10
OS 1:50 000 no. 188

Sevenoaks See Route 7. Also links with Routes 6, 31.

Knole See Route 6.

Riverhill House A fine collection of trees and a terraced garden with shrubs and roses (open).

Under River Built in the 14th century, Black Charles (open) was the home of John de Blakecherl and his descendants for over four hundred years.

Sevenoaks Weald Long Barn is a restored 14th-century house (open) with fine beams, fireplaces and a galleried hall. William Caxton, the first English printer, is said to have been born here.

Emmetts and **Chartwell** See Route 7.

Leigh Hall Place Gardens (open) have many interesting trees and shrubs, and an 11-acre lake.

Hever The delightful 14th-century moated castle was the home of Henry VIII's second wife, Anne Boleyn, mother of Queen Elizabeth I (open).

Chiddingstone A virtually original Elizabethan village (NT) with a 19th-century castle (open) containing pictures, furnishings, swords, and Stuart and ancient Egyptian collections. There is a 13th-century church, oasthouses, and the 'Chiding Stone' where, according to legend, villagers would chide any women whose nagging annoyed them.

Penshurst Splendid Penshurst Place (open) is built in the English Gothic style, and has a great hall dating from 1340, an armoury, state rooms, picture gallery and a toy museum. There is a nature trail and an agricultural display in the park.

a A short section of this lane is not marked on the Bartholomew's map of 1975.

Royal Tunbridge Wells See Route 11. Also links with Routes 12, 14.

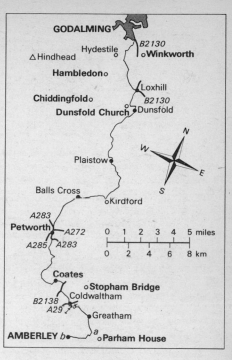

Route 16 28 miles 45 km
GODALMING — AMBERLEY

OS 1:250 000 no. 9
Bartholomew's 1:100 000 no. 6
OS 1:50 000 nos 186, 197

Godalming See Route 9. Also links with Routes 8, 17, 20.

Winkworth See Route 8.

Hambledon Feathercombe Gardens (open), with good views.

Dunsfold Church The pews were made by local farm workers.

Chiddingfold Situated on the edge of a large green with a pond is the 14th-century timbered Crown Inn, once visited by Edward VI, and with the oldest licence in Surrey. The church contains locally made medieval glass.

Petworth See Route 1.

Coates Manor gardens (open).

Stopham Bridge An attractive medieval bridge spans the river Arun.

a If you next intend to follow Route 10 to Horsham, you can turn to it here.

Parham House See Route 2.

b For an interesting detour over the South Downs to Arundel, see Route 1.

Amberley See Route 2. Also links with Routes 1, 10.

Route 17 29 miles 46 km
WINDSOR — GODALMING

OS 1:250 000 no. 9
Bartholomew's 1:100 000 no. 9
OS 1:50 000 nos 186, 176

This route is intended as a link between the pleasant cycling country of southern England, and Windsor, close to west London and Heathrow Airport. It involves cycling in built up areas and on some busy roads. Navigation in the northern section is quite complicated.

Windsor William the Conqueror founded the castle in this strategic position, then conveniently near to hunting forests. The present structure is medieval, Stuart and Regency, and is the

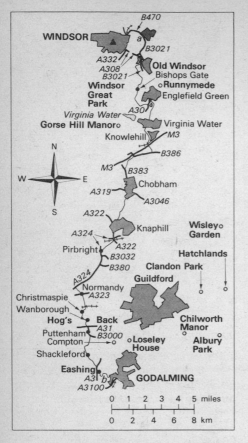

WINDSOR

B470

a

B3021

A332
A308
B3021

Windsor
Great
Park

Old Windsor
Bishops Gate
o**Runnymede**
oEnglefield Green

Virginia Water
A30
Gorse Hill Manoro

Virginia Water

Knowlehill
M3

N

B386

W   E

M3   *B383*

S

A319

Chobham

A3046

A322

Knaphill

Wisleyo
Garden

A324

Pirbright

A322
B3032
B380

Hatchlands

Clandon Park

A324

Guildford

Normandy
A323

o   o

Christmaspie
Wanborough

Hog's   **Back**
A31
Chilworth
Manor

Puttenham
Compton
B3000

o**Loseley**
House

o**Albury**
Park

Shackleford

Eashing
A3
A3100

GODALMING

0   1   2   3   4   5 miles
0   2   4   6   8 km

world's largest inhabited castle. It has a
wealth of interesting features including
the state apartments, St George's Chapel
and Queen Mary's Dolls' House. Castle
and some of the grounds are open.
Windsor town has attractive Georgian
and Victorian buildings. St John's
Church has work by Grinling Gibbons.
Links with Route 18.

*a For the link route between Windsor and
Heathrow Airport, see Route 18.*

Windsor Great Park A huge park open
to the public by courtesy of the Crown.
There are three-mile rides, including one
leading dramatically to a statue of George
III. Savill Garden contains plants of
botanical and horticultural interest.

Man-made Virginia Water is nearby, with
curios including imported Roman ruins
and a totem pole. Polo is played in the
park.

Old Windsor The palace of Edward the
Confessor was here.

Runnymede In 1215 King John sealed
the preliminary draft of the Magna Carta
here, and the domed temple at the foot of
Cooper's Hill is a memorial to the event.
Halfway up the hill is the John F.
Kennedy Memorial to United States Air
Force men killed in the Second World
War. Fine views.

Gorse Hill Manor A 3-acre garden
(open) with over 450 varieties of trees and
shrubs.

Wisley Garden A 300-acre garden of
magnificent variety maintained by the
Royal Horticultural Society (open).

Hatchlands An 18th-century house built
for Admiral Boscawen (NT, open) and
decorated by Robert Adam.

Clandon Park A Palladian house (NT,
open) built in about 1733 with one of the
finest 18th-century interiors in Britain. It
houses important collections of furniture
and porcelain.

Guildford The county town of Surrey,
with an attractive high street, featuring
17th-century almshouses, the Angel
Hotel, and a great gilded clock. There are
fine views from the top of the Norman
keep. St Mary's Church dates from
Anglo-Saxon times, and the modern
Gothic cathedral stands on a hillside
above the town. Guildford Museum has
items of archaeological and historical
interest.

Albury Park A country mansion
designed by Pugin (open).

Chilworth Manor A garden laid out in
the 17th-century (open) with 11th-
century stewponds (for keeping fish).

Loseley House An Elizabethan country
house (open) built of stone taken from
Waverley Abbey.

Hog's Back Excellent views.

Eashing Medieval bridge (NT).

b If you next intend to follow Route 20 to Newbury, you can turn to it here.

Godalming See Route 9. Also links with Routes 8, 16, 20.

Route 18   20 miles   32 km
**HENLEY-ON-THAMES —
WINDSOR**

OS 1:250 000 no. 9
Bartholomew's 1:100 000 no. 9
OS 1:50 000 no. 175 (176 for Heathrow Airport)

Henley-on-Thames A pretty town with many old inns and an active brewery. Henley Royal Regatta, held in July, began as a university boatrace in 1829. There is an 18th-century bridge. Links with Routes 19, 21, 25, 26.

a If you next intend to follow Route 26 to St Albans, you can turn to it here.

White Waltham Two great barns, stocks and a whipping post. Prince Arthur, elder brother of Henry VIII, lived for a time in a farmhouse by the church.

Shottesbrooke Beside the 18th-century mansion stands the collegiate church in the decorated style. There are brasses within.

Windsor Safari Park Open to the public.

Windsor Great Park See Route 17.

Eton An ancient town. The famous public school was founded by Royal Charter in 1440, and has architecture from that era and many thereafter. Superb Perpendicular style chapel with fan-vaulting. There is a 15th-century cockpit near the parish stock, and a whipping post; also a museum of British natural history.

b It is impossible to reach or leave Heathrow Airport without some use of very busy roads, in particular the A4. The distance from Windsor to Heathrow is 9 miles (15 km) by the route given here.

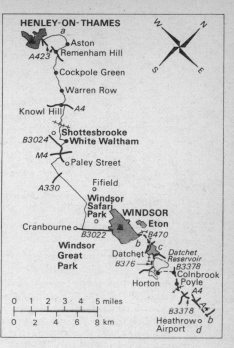

c If you next intend to follow Route 17 to Godalming, turn to it here.

d The road entrance to Heathrow Airport is prohibited to cycles. Cyclists should wheel their machines through the pedestrian tunnel.

Windsor See Route 17

Route 19   26 miles   42 km
**HENLEY-ON-THAMES —
NEWBURY**

OS 1:250 000 no. 9
Bartholomew's 1:100 000 no. 8
OS 1:50 000 nos 174, 175

Henley-on-Thames See Route 18. Also links with Routes 21, 25, 26.

Rotherfield Greys The church has a fine Elizabethan monument.

Greys Court A Jacobean manor house and garden (open), set amid the remains of a 14th-century fortified house, with an early Tudor donkey wheel well house.

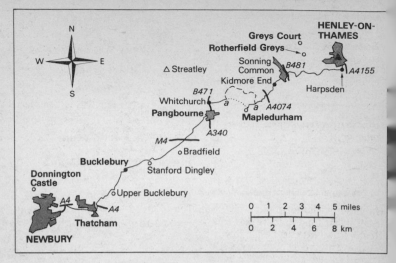

Mapledurham Pretty cottages, an old water-mill and some 17th-century alms-houses, on the banks of the Thames. The great 16th-century Mapledurham House (open) has moulded ceilings, a great oak staircase and a collection of paintings. The 14th-century church has some fine monuments, and a Roman Catholic chapel built for the Blount family, who lived in the house.

a   The main route follows a public bridleway along a well-defined track running between Mapledurham, and a sharp corner in the lane one mile east of Whitchurch. The alternative route detours north on lanes.

Pangbourne Kenneth Grahame, author of *Wind in the Willows*, lived and died here, and Jerome K. Jerome's heroes in *Three Men in a Boat* paused at the Swan Inn.

Bucklebury On the chancel window of the church a 17th-century artist has painted a curiously realistic fly.

Thatcham Traces of a mesolithic settlement, 6000–4000 BC.

Donnington Castle The impressive 14th-century gatehouse (DoE, open) is all that remains from the huge castle that once stood here. It was successfully defended three times by the Royalists during the Civil War. A footpath leads to the castle from Newbury.

Newbury See Route 20. Also links with Routes 94, 95.

Route 20   52 miles   83 km
NEWBURY — GODALMING

OS 1:250 000 no. 9
Bartholomew's 1:100 000 nos 8, 9
OS 1:50 000 nos 174, 185, 186

Newbury The town was situated on the main route to the west of England. In the 16th century Jack of Newbury, the famous clothier, brought prosperity to the town through the cloth trade. At one time he had over two hundred looms and a thousand employees, and entertained Henry VIII. He paid for the rebuilding of St Nicholas's church, which was later used as a guard room and hospital during the Civil War, which brought two battles to the town. Jacobean Cloth Hall Museum; Newbury Museum. Links with Routes 19, 94, 95.

Burghclere The Sandham Memorial Chapel (NT) has wall paintings depicting war scenes by Stanley Spencer.

Ladle Hill There are traces of an Iron Age fort on the top.

Beacon Hill On the 858-foot (262 m) summit of this hill is the grave of the 5th Earl of Caernarvon, who led the excavation of Tutankhamen's tomb in 1922. There is also an impressive Iron Age fort and wonderful views.

Seven Barrows Bronze Age burial mounds.

Watership Down Made famous in the book of the same name by Richard Adams.

a The main route uses a well-defined track which forms part of an ancient routeway called the Harroway, between a point just south of a T-junction at the western end, and a point where a track crosses the B3051 at the eastern end. The alternative route follows the B3400 in the valley, and a lane.

b The main route follows a well-defined track which runs between a T-junction by Sutton Common at its western end, and a point on a lane just south of Well at its eastern end. The alternative route follows lanes via Long Sutton.

Jenkyn Place A well-planned garden of variety and interest (open) with a collection of rare shrubs.

Farnham The 12th-century castle (DoE, open) entertained Royalty from Edward I to Queen Victoria, and was besieged by Cromwell. There are Georgian houses in Castle Street and West Street, some Tudor houses and 17th-century almshouses. William Cobbett, the writer and politician best remembered for his *Rural Rides*, was born in the house which is now the Jolly Farmer Inn. Willmer House was built in 1718 and has a front of cut and moulded brick, fine carving and panelling inside, and a walled garden. It houses the Farnham Museum.

Waverley Abbey The ruins of the first English Cistercian Abbey.

Tilford Old Kiln agricultural museum.

Elstead Medieval five-arched bridge, a 14th-century church and watermill.

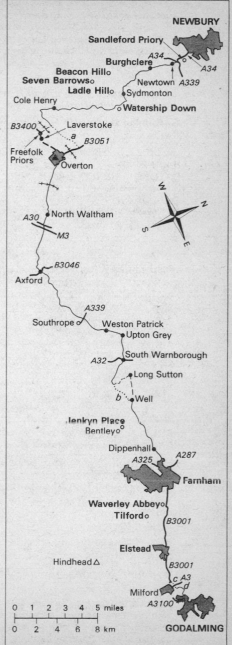

c The main route follows a track between a sharp bend in the B3001 and a point on the lane running north from Milford. It crosses the A3 involving a right then left turn before continuing on the track. An alternative route is to cycle to the junction of the B3001 and A3 in Milford.

d If you next intend to follow Route 17 to Windsor, you can turn to it here.

Godalming See Route 9. Also links with Routes 8, 16, 17.

Route 21   26 miles   43 km
OXFORD — HENLEY-ON-THAMES

OS 1:250 000 no. 9
Bartholomew's 1:100 000 nos 8, 14
OS 1:50 000 nos 164, 175

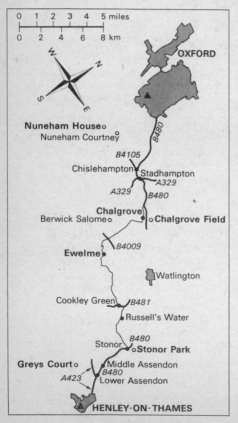

Oxford The earliest mention of Oxford is in the *Anglo-Saxon Chronicle* for 912, and the D'Oilly tower and remaining city walls testify to its importance before the University was founded in the 13th century. Christ Church, the cathedral of Oxford, has much 12th-century work; Tom Tower contains the famous bell of that name. Merton College library is among the most ancient extant medieval libraries. Wren built the Sheldonian Theatre, Vanbrugh the Clarendon Building, home of Oxford University Press. In the Civil War Oxford was a Royalist stronghold and Charles I had his base there. Walks in Christ Church Meadows rowing and punting on the Thames (Isis) and Cherwell rivers. Britain's oldest botanic gardens (1621); museums include the Ashmolean, the History of Science Museum and the Pitt Rivers. Oxford has now expanded to take in many villages: Iffley has one of England's finest Norman churches. A Mr Morris started a cycle-making concern in Cowley which developed into the making of Morris cars. The Oxford ring road has a cycle track. Links with Routes 22, 67, 87, 91.

Nuneham House A Palladian house by the Thames, set in grounds by Mason and Capability Brown (open).

Chalgrove A pretty village with thatch buildings and two roadside streams. The 12th-century church has some 14th-century frescoes, covered during the Civil War, and uncovered about a hundred years ago.

Chalgrove Field The site of a Civil War battle in which Prince Rupert was victorious. Nearby is a monument to John Hampden, whose objection to Charles I's Ship Tax was the cause of the Civil War.

Ewelme Fine church with the tomb of humorous writer Jerome K. Jerome. The 15th-century village school is one of the oldest in England.

Stonor Park A beautiful Tudor mansion (open). It claimed to have belonged to one family for longer than any other house in England. There is a public footpath

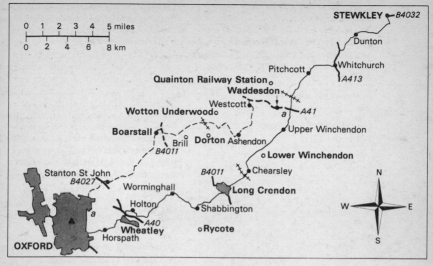

through the park, leaving the B480 north of Stonor.

Greys Court A Jacobean mansion with a donkey-wheel well-house (NT, open).

Henley-on-Thames See Route 18. Also links with Routes 19, 25, 26.

Route 22   30 miles   49 km
STEWKLEY — OXFORD

OS 1:250 000 no. 9
Bartholomew's 1:100 000 no. 14.
OS 1:50 000 nos 164, 165

Stewkley Norman church. Links with Routes 23, 30, 55.

a The main route follows a low ridge beside the Thames valley for quite some distance. The alternative route climbs over the saddle between two hills, and brings you to different points of interest.

Quainton Railway Station Standard gauge working railway museum.

Waddesdon Manor built in French Renaissance style; large grounds with aviary (NT, open).

Wotton Underwood An 18th-century house built to the same plan as Buckingham Palace, and set in grounds by Capability Brown (open).

Dorton The House is a Jacobean mansion with fine ceilings (open).

Lower Winchendon Nether Winchendon House (open) was the home of an 18th-century governor of New Jersey and Massachusetts.

Long Crendon Some 16th- and 17th-century cottages and two manor houses in an attractive village that was once a lace-making centre. The 14th-century Court House, originally a wool-store, and later belonging to Catherine of Aragon, was used for manorial courts (NT).

Boarstall A ancient working duck decoy, sometimes open. Gatehouse (NT, open).

Rycote Rycote Chapel (DoE, open).

Wheatley Parish pit and lock-up.

Oxford See Route 21. Also links with Routes 67, 87, 91.

Route 23   27 miles   44 km
STEWKLEY — ST ALBANS

OS 1:250 000 no. 9
Bartholomew's 1:100 000 no. 15
OS 1:50 000 nos 165, 166

Stewkley Norman church. Links with Routes 22, 30, 55.

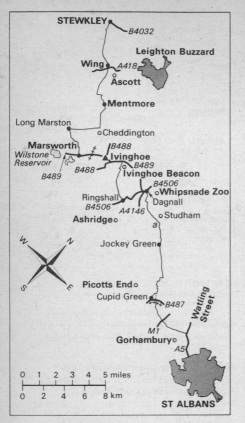

Marsworth At the south end of the village is the Grand Union Canal with a series of locks. Waterfowl on the canal and nearby reservoirs.

Ivinghoe Walter Scott's *Ivanhoe* is derived from Ivinghoe. Lovely church with a fine roof and medieval carved pews. The King's Head is an ancient pub. Nearby is Pitstone windmill, one of Britain's oldest postmills (NT, open).

Ivinghoe Beacon This hill at the end of the Chilterns was once used for signalling by fire. A footpath leads to the summit which commands panoramic views.

Ashridge Ashridge House is Gothic Revival, though it has a 13th-century crypt and Tudor barn. The gardens are by Repton (NT, open).

Whipsnade Zoo One of the first zoos to keep animals in large, 'natural' enclosures, Whipsnade has a good breeding record.

a If you next intend to follow Route 24 to Wendover, you can turn to it here.

Piccotts End A 14th-century house (open) with some remarkable wall paintings dating from the 15th century, a priest's hide and medieval well.

Gorhambury An 18th-century, modified classical style manor house, with 16th-century enamelled glass (open).

Watling Street The A5 follows the course of the Roman Watling Street, which, in the 18th-century, was an early turnpiked road as it was the London to Holyhead coach route.

St Albans See Route 26. Also links with Routes 24, 27.

Route 24   31 miles   50 km
WENDOVER — ST ALBANS

OS 1:250 000 no. 9
Bartholomew's 1:100 000 no. 15
OS 1:50 000 nos 166, 165

Wendover See Route 25.

Tring The Zoological Museum is

Leighton Buzzard An old market town with some brick and timber thatched cottages. The market place has some buildings of architectural interest and a fine 14th-century market cross.

Wing Some 17th- and 18th-century cottages. All Saints church has a Saxon crypt, brasses from the era of the Wars of the Roses and a 16th-century screen.

Ascott House containing Anthony de Rothschild's collections of pictures, furniture and Oriental porcelain. The gardens have rare plants and a topiary sundial (NT, open).

Mentmore The village lies within the park of Mentmore House, whose sumptuous collections were auctioned in 1977.

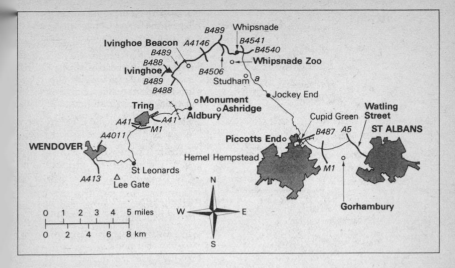

particularly comprehensive, and has stuffed animals from all over the world.

Aldbury A pretty village with old stocks and a whipping post on the green. There are a timbered manor house, some tiny almshouses and a fine church which has monuments, brasses and a medieval stone screen.

Ashridge See Route 23.

Monument High on the hill stands the Bridgewater monument, erected to commemorate the 3rd Duke of Bridgewater, who pioneered Britain's canal system. There are steps leading to the top, which commands a fine view.

Ivinghoe, Ivinghoe Beacon, Whipsnade Zoo, Piccotts End, Gorhambury and **Watling Street** See Route 23.

a If you next intend to follow Route 23 to Stewkley, you can turn to it here.

St Albans See Route 26. Also links with Routes 23, 27.

___

Route 25   26 miles   41 km
**WENDOVER —
HENLEY-ON-THAMES**

___

OS 1:250 000 no. 9
Bartholomew's 1:100 000 no. 15
OS 1:50 000 nos 175, 165

Wendover There are many timbered buildings and several old inns. Links with Route 24.

Wellwick Farm This once belonged to Judge Jeffreys, the 17th-century English judge notorious for his cruelty and corruption.

Coombe Hill Footpaths from the B4010 lead to the summit of the hill, where there is a monument to the men of Buckinghamshire who died in the South African War. There are excellent views.

Chequers The country home of prime ministers, given to the nation as a thank-offering for the end of the First World War.

Whiteleaf On the side of the hill above this hamlet is the 80-foot (24-metre) Whiteleaf Cross.

Princes Risborough An expanding residential town, but with many 16th-century cottages, attractive houses and a brick market house with a wooden cupola. The red-bricked manor house (NT, open) is 17th-century.

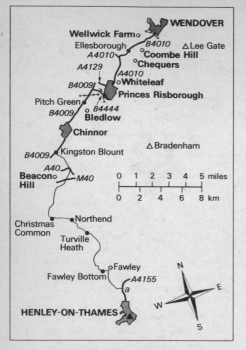

St Albans A Belgic settlement existed here prior to the important Roman tow. The shrine of St Alban, the first British martyr, is the 11th-century Abbey, whic has decorated ceilings, brasses, mediev: paintings. Links with Routes 23, 24, 27

Flaunden The Victorian church was designed by Sir George Gilbert Scott.

Sarratt A pretty village with a green, some 17th-century farmhouses and a church with an unusual saddleback roo

Chenies Attractive village with the Manor House (open) and garden dating from Tudor times.

Lee Gate Ancient church with Oliver Cromwell window.

Chequers See Route 25.

Great Hampden Hampden House was the home of John Hampden who died fighting in the Civil War, which began after his objection to the Ship Tax imposed by Charles I without the authority of Parliament. Hampden was buried in the churchyard here. Public footpaths and bridleways lead through the park.

Green Hailey The lane running north-west from Hampden Row through Greer Hailey offers superb views.

Bradenham Benjamin Disraeli lived here.

Hughenden Manor Once the home of Benjamin Disraeli (NT, open).

West Wycombe Park A magnificent palladian house built for Sir Francis Dashwood in the 18th century, with a park and lake (NT, open). On a hilltop is the church with a huge gilded ball on its tower which with the caves (open) below, was used as a meeting place by the notorious Hell Fire Club.

a The alternative route climbs up to Bledlow Ridge, whereas the main route is gentler and more direct.

Bedlow Ridge The road to the north-west of the village offers fine views.

Bledlow This village has herringbone-brick cottages, a 13th-century church and 17th-century inn.

Chinnor The church has two excellent 14th-century stained glass windows, and fine early brasses. Cut in the hillside to the east is a large Greek cross.

Beacon Hill Nature Reserve.

a If you next intend to follow Route 26 to St Albans, you can turn to it here.

Henley-on-Thames See Route 18. Also links with Routes 19, 21, 26.

Route 26   50 miles   80 km
**ST ALBANS —
HENLEY-ON-THAMES**

OS 1:250 000 no. 9
Bartholomew's 1:100 000 no. 15
OS 1:50 000 nos 175, 165, 166

The section between Bedmond and Kings

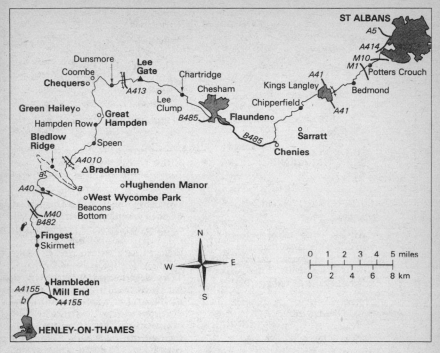

Fingest One of the finest old churches in the country, with a rare Norman tower topped by twin gables. The Chequers Inn is three hundred years old.

Hambleden An attractive village with a large church containing a panel believed to have been the bedhead of Cardinal Wolsey.

Mill End White-timbered Hambleden Mill on the Thames dates from 1338. A footpath crosses the river on the lock.

b If you next intend to follow Route 25 to Wendover, turn to it here.

Henley-on-Thames See Route 18. Also links with Routes 19, 21, 25.

Route 27　　　　25 miles　40 km
MUCH HADHAM — ST ALBANS

OS 1:250 000 no. 9
Bartholomew's 1:100 000 no. 15
OS 1:50 000 nos 167, 166

The roads are likely to be busy with traffic around the towns of Hertford, Welwyn and St Albans.

Much Hadham An attractive village which was for centuries the country seat of the Bishops of London. Their palace (birthplace of Edmund Tudor, father of Henry VII) stands near the church which has brasses. Links with Routes 28, 35.

Wadesmill The route east and west of Wadesmill offers pleasant views.

Hertford County town, with a few remains of the Norman castle built to protect London from the Danes. The town centre has a Victorian Corn Exchange, 18th-century Shire Hall, many fine buildings and decorated plasterwork. The Hertford Museum contains items of local history and geology.

Welwyn Garden City The town was begun in 1919, and planned by Ebenezer Howard, who envisaged a 'garden city' of spacious housing. It was a significant

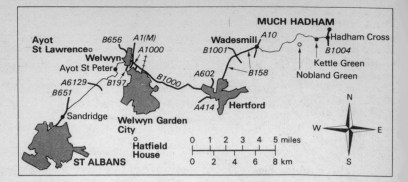

development in 20th century town planning.

Hatfield House One of the finest Jacobean houses in Britain, and the childhood home of Queen Elizabeth I (open). It contains mementos of the Queen; delightful gardens and a park.

Welwyn A five-roomed Roman villa, built in the 1st century AD, has been excavated here and its ground plan marked in turf and brick.

Ayot St Lawrence Shaw's Corner (NT, open) was the home of George Bernard Shaw from 1906 until his death in 1950. In the garden is the revolving summerhouse where he used to retreat to work. The lovely little Church of St Lawrence has a Grecian style front. Georgian Ayot House contains the Lullingstone Silk Farm where raw silk is produced (open).

St Albans See Route 26. Also links with Routes 23, 24.

Route 28   30 miles 48 km
CAMBRIDGE — MUCH HADHAM

OS 1:250 000 no. 9
Bartholomew's 1:100 000 nos 15, 20
OS 1:50 000 nos 154, 167

Cambridge The city is historically and culturally one of Britain's most important. A Roman town was established on the site by AD 70, and since that time Cambridge has evolved into one of the world's foremost centres of learning. It is also a busy commercial centre. There is much to see and visit, and several days can enjoyably be spent exploring. One of the most famous buildings is King's College Chapel, which contains Ruben's painting 'The Adoration of the Magi'. The college courtyards, chapels, dining halls and certain gardens can be visited at most times (see especially the Old Court of Corpus Christi, the President's Lodge of Queens' and Trinity's Wren Library); there are many delightful walks by the river along 'The Backs'. Punts can be hired. There are museums of geology, folk, aerial photography, archaeology and ethnology, mineralogy and petrology, zoology, and history of science. The Fitzwilliam Museum has a magnificent collection of fine and decorative arts, and the Scott Polar Research Institute has a museum of polar expedition. Also notable are the Botanic Gardens (second only to Kew), the Holy Sepulchre Church, Great St Mary's Church (the town can be viewed from the tower). Links with Routes 29, 37, 44, 45, 46, 53.

Grantchester A favourite haven for generations of students and tutors from the University, and immortalized in a famous poem by Rupert Brooke, who lived in the vicarage before the First World War. There are several thatched and timber cottages, an old church and pleasant riverside walks. Just to the south is Byron's Pool, frequented in the past by Chaucer, Spenser, Milton and Dryden, but less attractive now.

Trumpington In the church is a memorial brass to Sir Roger de Trumpington dated 1289, making it the second oldest brass in the country. The Green Man inn is 16th century. The first milestone to be set up in Britain since Roman times was erected here in 1727.

Turnpike Road Milestones along the B1368 indicate that this road was improved and maintained by a Turnpike Trust, and financed by tolls from users.

Barley Pretty cottages and a three hundred year old inn, the Fox and Hounds. Town House dates from Tudor times, and there is a brass in the church. Two vicars from Barley have become Archbishop of Canterbury; one of them crowned Henry VIII.

Anstey The church has a Norman font and misericords.

Furneux Pelham The 13th-century church has an inscription round the clock on the tower 'Time flies—mind your business', and inside, a fine monument with brass figures.

Little Hadham Old timber framed cottages, a windmill and two 15th-century brasses in the church.

Much Hadham See Route 27. Also links with Route 35.

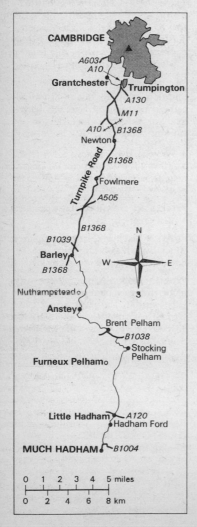

Route 29	19 miles	31 km

CAMBRIDGE — ASHWELL

OS 1:250 000 no. 9
Bartholomew's 1:100 000 nos 15, 20
OS 1:50 000 nos 165, 153, 154

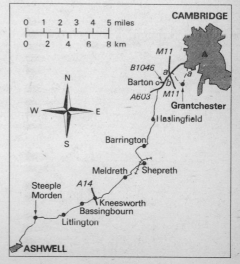

Cambridge See Route 28. Also links with Routes 37, 44, 45, 46, 53.

a The alternative route detours on lanes to Grantchester, while the main route follows the A603.

Grantchester See Route 28.

b If you next intend to follow Route 53 to Castle Ashby, turn to it here.

Ashwell See Route 30.

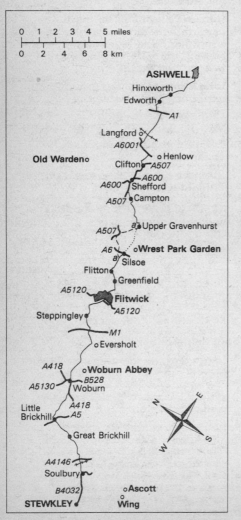

Route 30   33 miles   52 km
ASHWELL — STEWKLEY

OS 1:250 000 no. 9
Bartholomew's 1:100 000 nos 15, 20
OS 1:50 000 nos 153, 165

Ashwell St John's Guildhall in the high street was built in the 17th century, and the adjoining cottages have fine decorative plasterwork, or pargeting. There is a 14th-century church with graffiti on the tower referring to the Black Death. The Ashwell Village Museum illustrates the life of the village. Arbury Banks, to the south-west, is an Iron Age hill-fort. Links with Route 29.

Old Warden At the aerodrome is the Shuttleworth Collection of historical aeroplanes, cars, carriages and bicycles, many of which are unique and in working order.

a The main route follows a public bridle-way across Wrest Park while the alternative route detours on lanes and the A507 to the north.

Wrest Park Garden A fine example of a formal canal garden (DoE, open).

Flitwick Just north-west of the church, which has a 12th-century font, are the remains of a small motte and bailey castle.

Woburn Abbey A huge 18th-century home with a famous collection of paintings, furniture and silver (open). There are fourteen state apartments and in the 3000-acre park, the well known Wild Animal Kingdom.

Ascott and **Wing** See Route 23.

Stewkley See Route 22. Also links with Routes 23, 55.

Route 31   16 miles   26 km
DARTFORD TUNNEL — SEVENOAKS

OS 1:250 000 no. 9
Bartholomew's 1:100 000 no. 10
OS 1:50 000 nos 188, 177

The northern part of this route, between the

Dartford Tunnel and Darenth, involves cycling on busy roads.

Dartford Tunnel Links with Route 32.

a Cycles must be carried through the Dartford Tunnel on a trailer which passes through at regular intervals.

b A ferry which carries cycles crosses the Thames between Tilbury and Gravesend.

Dartford Dartford District Museum has local historical and geological displays.

St John's Jerusalem Pleasant garden and small sections of the church of a commandery of the Knights Hospitallers (NT, open).

Farningham Many 18th century houses, a fine old inn, and a weather-boarded mill by the river. Captain Bligh of the 'Bounty' once lived in the old manor house. South of here the route follows Sparepenny Lane, so called because carters used it to avoid paying tolls on the main road.

Eynsford Medieval houses, a 15th-century bridge and an interesting church. It was Thomas Becket's excommunication of William de Eynsford that precipitated his murder in Canterbury Cathedral by knights of Henry II. Eynsford was once, in 1936, selected as the site for London Airport! Outside the village stand the ditch and ruined walls of a Norman castle (DoE, open).

Roman Villa Occupied between the 1st and 5th century AD (DoE, open) with good wall paintings, mosaics, and an early Christian chapel; small museum of objects found.

Lullingstone Castle Built in the 18th century incorporating a gateway dating from the reign of Henry VII, the castle contains family portraits, armour, a church and lovely grounds (open).

Shoreham The church has a good screen, a Burne-Jones window, and porch of huge timbers. The white cross cut in the hillside is a war memorial. The artist Samuel Palmer lived at Water House for five years, much of

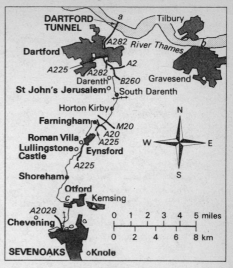

his best work being accomplished during this stay.

c If you next intend to follow Route 7 to Reigate, you can turn to it here.

Otford and **Chevening** See Route 7.

Knole See Route 6.

Sevenoaks See Route 7. Also links with Routes 6, 15.

Route 32 33 miles 54 km
MALDON — DARTFORD TUNNEL

OS 1:250 000 no. 9
Bartholomew's 1:100 000 no. 16
OS 1:50 000 nos 177, 167, 168

The purpose of this route is to provide a means of cycling between East Anglia and south-east England, without having to enter London. The southern half of this route is not scenically attractive.

Maldon The church has a unique triangular tower, and rich decoration inside. There is a fishing harbour, and some pleasant buildings, among them the Moot Hall, Blue Boar Hotel, Swan Hotel and vicarage. Beeleigh Abbey houses the library of W. Foyle (open). Links with Routes 33, 36.

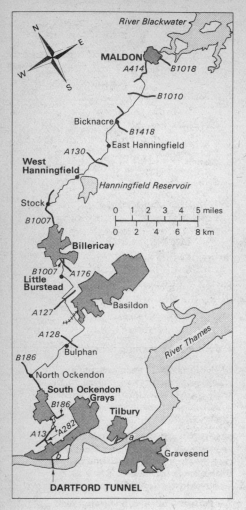

West Hanningfield The church has old brasses and a wooden belfry.

Billericay In 1620 the Pilgrim Fathers met in Mayflower Hall before their famous journey to America. The town was the scene of the peasants' revolt in 1379, when the followers of Jack Straw were captured.

Little Burstead The Hall clock has figures made of blackened bones.

South Ockendon The 12th-century church has a round tower.

Grays Museum of local history.

Tilbury The Thurrock Riverside Museum describes the history of the Thames; Tilbury Fort (DoE, open).

a A ferry on which cycles may be carried crosses the River Thames from Tilbury to Gravesend.

b Cycles must be carried through the Dartford Tunnel on a trailer which passes through at regular intervals.

Dartford Tunnel Links with Route 31.

Route 33   21 miles   34 km
COLCHESTER — MALDON

OS 1:250 000 no. 9
Bartholomew's 1:100 000 no. 16
OS 1:50 000 no. 168

Much of the north bank of the River Blackwater is bounded by dykes overlooking fairly empty countryside. The various dead-end lanes leading from the B1026 to the dyke footpaths can be found most easily with the 1:50 000 map.

Colchester Traces of Bronze Age settlements give Colchester a claim to being Britain's oldest town. It was the first Roman city in Britain, although it fell temporarily to Queen Boadicea. The Norman keep, built over a Roman temple, is the largest in Europe and now houses a museum of Roman Colchester and the archaeology of Essex. The Balkerne Gateway was the city wall gate on the London road. The 18th-century Holly Trees house contains a museum of social history. Minories art gallery is in a Georgian house. Essex natural history museum; country craft museum. Remains of St Botolph's Priory; St John's Abbey gatehouse; Lexden prehistoric earthworks enclose a huge area (all DoE, open). Bourne Mill, built in the 16th century as a fishing lodge, has working machinery (NT, open). Links with Route 34.

Elmstead Market The landscaped, 3-

acre garden of White Barn House has unusual plants (open).

Wivenhoe Attractive boat-building quayside. Rich brass in the church. Superb example of pargeting on the plaster wall of a house in East Street.

Rowhedge Old fishing port.

Fingringhoe The 17th-century hall was rebuilt in the Georgian style. The tide mill was one of the few in the country. The quay to the east gives a good view of Wivenhoe.

Peldon A zeppelin crashed here in the First World War.

Layer Marney Towers A 16th-century Tudor brick mansion with an enormous gate tower (open).

Tolleshunt D'Arcy A 15th-century moated hall. Georgian-fronted D'Arcy House. A good collection of brasses in the church.

Beckingham Hall A 16th-century hall with an interesting gatehouse.

Maldon See Route 32. Also links with Route 36.

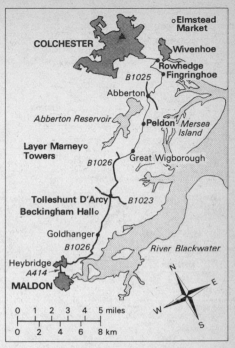

Route 34   52 miles   84 km
**BURY ST EDMUNDS —
COLCHESTER**

OS 1.250 000 no. 9
Bartholomew's 1:100 000 nos 16, 21
OS 1:50 000 nos 155, 168

Bury St Edmunds The city has a Georgian appearance, but has many buildings dating from much earlier times. The Abbey, of which there are a few remains, was once one of the greatest in the country, and the cathedral is 16th century. Worth seeing are the Unitarian Chapel with its double decker pulpit, the Town Hall, Guildhall, Provost's House, Cupola House, Abbot's Bridge, Theatre Royal (NT, open), Athenaeum, Hengrave Hall, and the Angel Hotel which has associations with Dickens, and the Nutshell which is one of the smallest inns in the country. Hardwick Hall has some of the finest cedar trees in Britain and

Angel Corner (NT, open) contains a collection of clocks. Moyse's Hall Museum is a 12th-century dwelling house with displays of local history. Links with Routes 38, 39, 45.

Ickworth Park This 700-foot (215 m) long building (NT, open) was built in the early 19th century by the eccentric Bishop Frederick Hervey. The Park was designed by Capability Brown.

Lavenham This beautiful town, which flourished on the cloth trade, has many timbered and pargeted buildings. The church has a fan-vaulted porch and misericords. Its bell of 1625 has been thought the finest-toned in the world. The 16th-century Guildhall (NT), is now a local museum. Little Hall, a 15th-century hall house (open). Old Wool Hall; De Vere House and Tudor shops.

Kentwell Hall Moated Elizabethan mansion in brick, standing in grounds with a fine lime avenue (open).

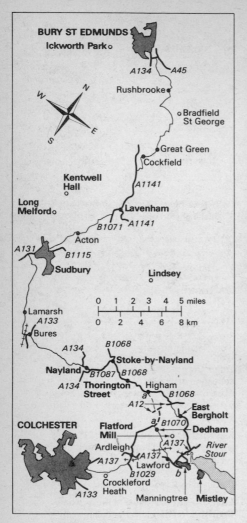

BURY ST EDMUNDS
Ickworth Park o

A134   A45

Rushbrooke •

o Bradfield
St George

• Great Green
Cockfield

**Kentwell
Hall**
o

A1141

**Long
Melford** o

Lavenham

B1071   A1141

A131

Acton
B1115

Sudbury

Lindsey
o

0   1   2   3   4   5 miles
0   2   4   6   8 km

• Lamarsh
A133
† Bures
A134   B1068

Stoke-by-Nayland

Nayland B1087   B1068

A134   **Thorington   Higham
Street**
a   B1068
A12

**East
Bergholt**

COLCHESTER   **Flatford
Mill**   a   B1070
Dedham
Ardleigh   A137
A137   A137   *River
Stour*
Lawford
A133   B1029   b
Crockleford
Heath   Manningtree   **Mistley**

with its portraits can be visited. Old houses in Stour Street. Early Victorian Corn Exchange. The head of a murdered 14th-century Archbishop is preserved in St Gregory's Church vestry.

Nayland The church has an altarpiece by John Constable. Alston Court (15th-century) has superbly carved timbering.

Stoke-by-Nayland A pretty village with half-timbered cottages, a Tudor brick mansion and a 16th-century Guildhall and Maltings. The church has many good brasses, and its tower was one of Constable's favourite subjects.

Thorington Street The 16th-century, gabled Thorington Hall (NT).

a The loop of the main route makes unavoidable use of some main roads in order to explore places associated with John Constable.

East Bergholt John Constable was born here. The churchyard contains an unusual 16th-century bell house.

Flatford Mill The mill and Willy Lott's cottage (NT), which are immortalized in Constable's paintings.

Mistley An unsuccessful attempt was made in the 18th century to make this a spa. The Mistley Towers (DoE, open) were built by Robert Adam as part of a hall.

b From Manningtree the B1352 and A604 lead east to Harwich for ferries to the Continent and Scandinavia.

Dedham The village has many associations with Constable, who went to the 18th-century grammar school. Castle House, the home of Sir Alfred Munnings, contains an art collection with his own works (open).

Colchester See Route 33.

Route 35   17 miles   27 km
MUCH HADHAM — HIGH RODING

OS 1:250 000 no. 9
Bartholomew's 1:100 000 no. 16
OS 1:50 000 no. 167

Long Melford Described as 'Britain's stateliest small town', Long Melford has a long high street with many fine houses, an attractive green, and a church said to be Suffolk's loveliest. The 16th-century brick-built Melford Hall has a Regency interior (NT, open).

Lindsey St James's Chapel (DoE).

Sudbury The painter Thomas Gainsborough was born here, and his house

Much Hadham See Route 27. Also links with Route 28.

Bishop's Stortford Some old buildings testify to the medieval origin of the town, which also has some good Victorian architecture. There is a 17th-century malthouse and a granary.

Hatfield Forest This NT land is a remnant of the ancient royal forests of Essex. It has fine walks among some splendid trees, especially hornbeams.

a If you next intend to follow Route 37 to Cambridge, you can turn to it here.

High Roding See Route 36. Also links with Route 37.

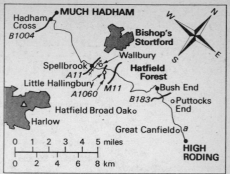

Route 36   21 miles   34 km
HIGH RODING — MALDON

OS 1:250 000 no. 9
Bartholomew's 1:100 000 no. 16
OS 1:50 000 nos 167, 168

High Roding Church with 13th-century ironwork. Links with Routes 35, 37.

Pleshey The village is encircled by a Norman castle ditch.

Boreham Boreham House (18th century), with its impressive façade overlooking a straight lake, lies west of the village. To the south lies New Hall, originally built by Henry VIII and also with a fine façade.

Maldon See Route 32. Also links with Route 33.

Route 37   37 miles   60 km
CAMBRIDGE — HIGH RODING

OS 1:250 000 no. 9
Bartholomew's 1:100 000 nos 16, 20
OS 1:50 000 nos 154, 167

Cambridge See Route 28. Also links with Routes 29, 44, 45, 46, 53.

Whittlesford Station Nearby is Duxford Chapel (DoE, open).

Duxford To the west lies a Battle of Britain airfield, now an aviation museum.

Audley End The Jacobean mansion, built after the dissolution of an abbey on the site, has state rooms, a great hall and a fine collection of pictures, and is set in grounds by Capability Brown with a temple and ice house lodge (DoE, open). To the west is Ring Hill, topped by remains of an Iron Age hill-fort.

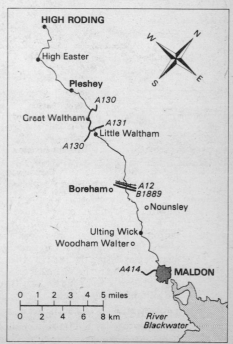

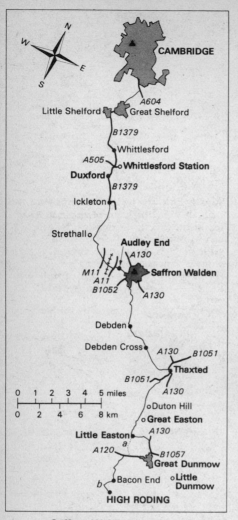

Saffron Walden Past prosperity based on the cloth trade and the growing of saffron for medicine and dyeing paid for several fine buildings with pargeted plaster, particularly the Sun Inn. The Church of St Mary the Virgin has excellent carvings, roofs and brasses. There is a town maze and local museum.

Thaxted Pretty cottages with pargeted plaster; great church; 15th century guildhall; tower windmill.

Great Easton Remains of a motte and bailey by the church.

Little Easton The church has 12th-century paintings, fine monuments and brasses.

a A bridleway links Little Easton church and the A120, keeping just east of a stream in the north section and a wood in the south section.

Great Dunmow The 16th-century Clock House was the home of Sir George Beaumont, art patron.

Little Dunmow Here the famous Dunmow Flitch of bacon is awarded to couples who can prove that they have lived for a year and a day without quarrelling. The flitch winners' chair is in the church.

b If you next intend to follow Route 35 to Much Hadham you can turn to it here.

High Roding See Route 36. Also links with Route 35.

Route 38   45 miles   72 km
NORWICH — BURY ST EDMUNDS

OS 1:250 000 nos 9, 6
Bartholomew's 1:100 000 nos 21, 26
OS 1:50 000 nos 155, 144, 134

Norwich In medieval times Norwich was second only to London in importance. Today it is a thriving commercial centre, and has a small port. The great keep of the Norman castle now houses a collection of art (including works by the Norwich School) and a museum. The fine Norman cathedral has the second highest spire and the largest cloisters in Britain. Inside there is fine carving and a bishop's throne thought to be a thousand years old. Nurse Edith Cavell is buried in the precinct. The many old buildings of Norwich include the Guildhall, Pulls Ferry, the Assembly House (gallery and tea rooms) and Cow Tower (DoE). The Maddermarket is a replica Elizabethan theatre. There are 32 medieval churches within the area of the old city walls; close by the market place is St Peter Mancroft.

St Peter Hungate houses a collection of ecclesiastical art and is situated in picturesque Elm Hill. Strangers Hall is now a museum of urban domestic life, and the Bridewell Museum has exhibits relating to local industry. At the University of East Anglia, the Sainsbury Centre houses modern art collections. Links with Routes 41, 42.

Swardeston Nurse Edith Cavell, who was executed in Belgium in 1915 for helping British prisoners to escape from the Germans, was born in this village, and there is a memorial to her in the church.

Mulbarton One of the largest village greens in Norfolk.

a The main route follows a quiet and fairly intricate series of lanes through a succession of small villages. The shorter alternative route uses mostly B roads, which in this case do not usually carry much traffic.

Forncett St Peter The church has a Saxon tower; there is a pleasant inn.

Diss This attractive market town has several fine buildings including the Kings Head, the former Dolphin Inn, the Greyhound Inn, the Corn Exchange, Lacon's Maltings and the Shambles (Victorian shops). The poet John Skelton, tutor to Henry VIII, was rector here.

Redgrave Cardinal Wolsey was once rector of the church.

Banham International motor museum.

Ixworth Just outside the village are the remains of a Roman building and camp. Ixworth Abbey has 12th-century monastic buildings (open).

Stowlangtoft The 14th-century church has good carvings and there are some moated farms around the village.

Pakenham The old mill still grinds corn and there is an interesting Norman church. A Stone Age camp and Roman village were sited here.

Bury St Edmunds See Route 34. Also links with Routes 39, 45.

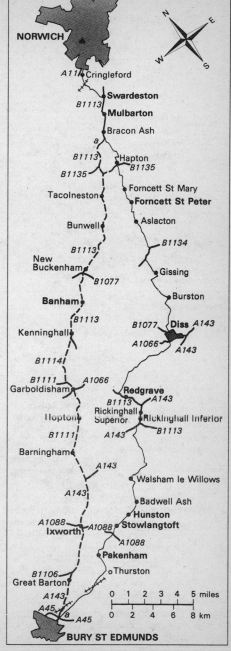

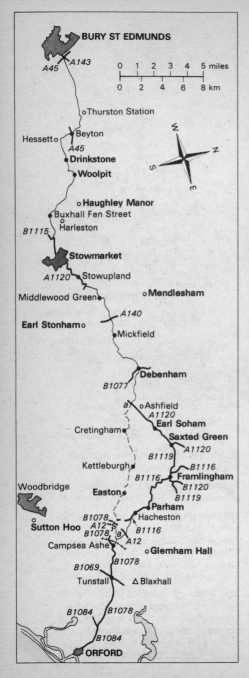

BURY ST EDMUNDS

A45   A143

0   1   2   3   4   5 miles
0   2   4   6   8 km

o Thurston Station

Hessett o   Beyton
A45
● **Drinkstone**
● **Woolpit**

o **Haughley Manor**
● Buxhall Fen Street
B1115   o Harleston

◼ **Stowmarket**
A1120   Stowupland
Middlewood Green ●   o **Mendlesham**
A140
Earl Stonham o
● Mickfield

● **Debenham**
B1077

a o Ashfield
A1120
Earl Soham
Cretingham ●   **Saxted Green**
A1120
B1119
Kettleburgh ●   B1116
B1116   ● **Framlingham**
Woodbridge   B1120
Easton o   B1119
Parham ●
B1078   Hacheston
A12
Sutton Hoo   B1078   a   B1116
Campsea Ashe   A12
o **Glemham Hall**
B1078
B1069
Tunstall   △ Blaxhall
B1084   B1078
B1084
◼ **ORFORD**

Route 39   46 miles   74 km
BURY ST EDMUNDS — ORFORD

OS 1:250 000 no. 9
Bartholomew's 1:100 000 no. 21
OS 1:50 000 nos 155, 156

Bury St Edmunds See Route 34. Also links with Routes 38, 45.

Drinkstone Windmill and craft centre.

Woolpit Attractive Tudor and Georgian houses. The church has a magnificent double hammerbeam roof, and a brass eagle lectern said to have been a gift of Queen Elizabeth I.

Haughley Manor Jacobean house set in parkland (open).

Stowmarket Georgian and early 19th-century houses flank the market place. The Church of SS Peter and Paul has an old wig-stand. In Abbots Hall and surrounding land is the museum of East Anglian rural life.

Mendlesham Collection of 15th- to 17th-century armour in the church.

Earl Stonham Church with a hammerbeam roof and a pulpit provided with four hour-glasses.

Debenham Church with a fine west porch and a hammerbeam roof.

a The main route follows B roads to visit several points of interest, whereas the alternative uses rural lanes in the river Deben valley.

Earl Soham Inscriptions on the church buttresses commemorate its builders.

Saxted Green Fine traditional Suffolk postmill (DoE, open).

Framlingham Impressive remains of a castle dating from the 12th century (DoE, open). Church with good tombs and an unusual roof. Old shops and two sets of almshouses in Market Hill.

Parham Parham Hall is a lovely 16th-century house, moated and timber-framed. Village buildings with picture carvings.

Easton Picturesque village. Crafts are demonstrated at Easton Park Farm.

Glemham Hall A brick-built Elizabethan house with panelling, Queen Anne furniture and a walled garden (open).

Sutton Hoo Here is the site of England's most significant archaeological discovery of the Dark Ages. Excavation of a mound uncovered an 89-foot (27-m) long rowing boat, burial ship of a great East Anglian king. Silverware and other finds from the site are now in the British Museum.

Orford The keep of England's earliest documented castle (DoE, open). The town is known for smoked fish, particularly a type of smoked herring called the 'Orford Butley'. Links with Route 40.

Route 40   24 miles   39 km
SOUTHWOLD — ORFORD

OS 1:250 000 no. 9
Bartholomew's 1:100 000 no. 21
OS 1:50 000 no. 156

Southwold A fishing port since Norman times, now a seaside resort with cliffs and beaches. After a great fire in 1659, the town was rebuilt interspersed with wide green spaces to halt spread of fire. The Church of St Edmund has beautiful carved and painted woodwork, including a fine screen of c. 1500. Museum of local interest. Links with Route 41.

Blythburgh The splendid church with its interesting woodwork was built when Blythburgh was a busy port, in the 15th century. Later, vessels were too large for the shallow channels and the town declined.

a The alternative route involves the use of a heathland track.

Dunwich The encroaching sea destroyed most of the town chartered by King John and once large enough to need seven churches. The present village was frequented by writers such as Henry James and J. K. Jerome.

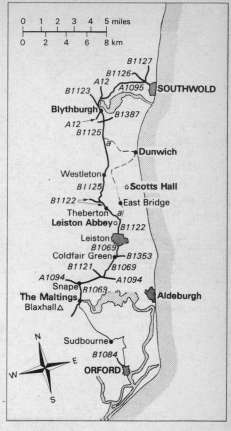

Scotts Hall Bird reserve in an area of heathland, marshes and cliffs.

Leiston Abbey Some 14th-century abbey remains (DoE, open).

Aldeburgh A declined 16th-century port, with a 16th-century timber-framed Moot Hall; Elizabethan brasses in the Church of SS Peter and Paul. Elizabeth Garrett Anderson, a native, was England's first woman mayor.

The Maltings A varied group of early industrial buildings, one of which has been converted into a concert hall, a centre for the Aldeburgh Festival inspired by Benjamin Britten.

Orford See Route 39.

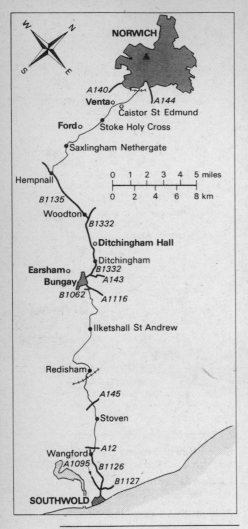

NORWICH

A140
Venta
A144
Caistor St Edmund
Ford
Stoke Holy Cross
Saxlingham Nethergate

0	1	2	3	4	5 miles
0	2	4	6	8 km	

Hempnall
B1135
Woodton
B1332
Ditchingham Hall
Ditchingham
B1332
Earsham
Bungay   A143
B1062   A1116

Ilketshall St Andrew

Redisham
A145
Stoven

Wangford   A12
A1095   B1126
B1127
SOUTHWOLD

The Iceni people probably settled here after their defeat in Queen Boadicea's revolt against the Romans.

Ford Pretty ford beside the parkland of Shotesham estate.

Ditchingham Hall An 18th-century hall in grounds landscaped by Capability Brown.

Earsham An Otter Trust is situated here.

Bungay Remains of a 12th-century castle, which could be made to collapse on an enemy by removing its supports from tunnels under the foundations. St Mary's Church belonged to a 12th-century nunnery. Georgian houses by the market place. A 17th-century butter cross.

Southwold See Route 40.

Route 42   33 miles   53 km
HOLT — NORWICH

OS 1:250 000 no. 6
Bartholomew's 1:100 000 no. 26
OS 1:50 000 no. 133

Holt An old market town. Gresham's school (Old School House at top of High Street) was founded by Sir Thomas Gresham, 1555. Links with Route 43.

Baconsthorpe Hall Gatehouse and other remains of a moated hall (DoE, open).

Mannington Hall Lovely gardens set around the ruin of a Saxon church and a 15th-century moated house (gardens open).

Blickling Jacobean Blickling Hall has a great gallery and collections of paintings and tapestries. The grounds contain a good 19th-century orangery (NT, open).

Duel Stone A roadside stone near the Woodrow Inn marks the site of a duel fought in 1698.

Cawston Church with a carved

Route 41   37 miles   60 km
NORWICH — SOUTHWOLD

OS 1:250 000 nos 6, 9
Bartholomew's 1:100 000 nos 21, 26
OS 1:50 000 nos 134, 156

Norwich See Route 38. Also links with Route 42.

Venta The earthworks and some remnants of wall of Roman Venta Icenorum.

hammerbeam roof and a painted screen.

Sall A 15th-century church with a high tower, fine woodcarvings, brasses and monuments.

Reepham The early 18th-century Dial House stands by the attractive market place. The churchyard is shared by two churches and the scant remains of a third.

Norwich See Route 38. Also links with Route 41.

Route 43   46 miles   74 km
HOLT — KINGS LYNN

OS 1:250 000 no. 6
Bartholomew's 1:100 000 no. 26
OS 1:50 000 nos 132, 133

Holt See Route 42.

Letheringsett An iron bridge spans the River Glaven here.

Glandford The river is crossed by a wide, pretty ford (there is a footbridge). Unique shell museum.

Cley-next-the-Sea Windmill and fine, huge church; the village was once a busy port.

Blakeney Point A good walk along the shingle spit ends at the dunes and beaches of this desolate sanctuary of many rare birds (NT).

Blakeney Once a port of some importance, now favoured by yachtsmen; ferries at high water to the Point. The smaller of the church's two towers was a beacon for guiding mariners. The Guildhall (DoE, open) dates from the 15th century.

Binham Impressive remains of a Benedictine priory (DoE, open).

Warham An interesting church; outside the village is the site of an Iron Age hill-fort.

Little Walsingham A charming village where successive shrines have attracted

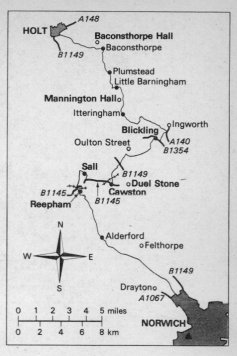

pilgrims for centuries. The ruins of the 15th-century priory and 13th-century friary are open. The Shirehall Museum has a near-perfect courtroom and displays of local history.

Houghton St Giles Slipper Chapel where pilgrims halted to remove their shoes so that they walked barefoot the final mile to the shrine at Walsingham.

Wells-next-the-Sea A resort and small port; Georgian houses around the attractive green known as the Buttlands. A good bathing beach one mile to the north.

Holkham Hall A grand Palladian mansion (open) containing fine paintings and furnishings; grounds laid out by Capability Brown.

Burnham Market The church's battlemented parapet has unusual carvings.

Burnham Thorpe The birthplace of Horatio Nelson.

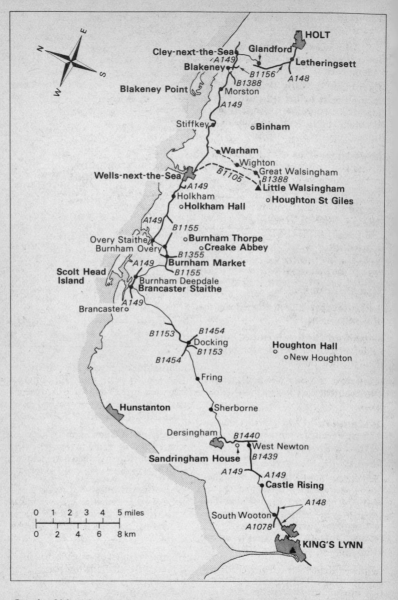

Creake Abbey In 1206 the August-inians founded an abbey, the impressive, though small, remains of which can be seen (DoE, open). The church has a good hammer-beam roof.

Scolt Head Island This shingle ridge, with its dunes and marram grass is popular among naturalists (NT). It is well known for its wide variety of birds, some of which are rare.

Brancaster Staithe A popular boating centre from where you can take a small ferry to Scolt Head Island.

Hunstanton The town grew as a Victorian resort. To the north are the famous striped cliffs.

Houghton Hall One of the finest examples of Palladian architecture in England, built for Robert Walpole, first British Prime Minister (open).

Sandringham House The gardens of this country retreat of the Royal Family are open when they are not resident. The Royal Parish Church of St Mary Magdalene has much rich decoration.

Castle Rising The great keep of the 12th-century castle is one of the largest in England and is surrounded by spectacular earthworks. The village was once a port. There are nine 17th-century brick-and-tile almshouses, with a court, chapel and treasury (open). The Church of St Lawrence is famous for its Norman west front.

King's Lynn See Route 44. Also links with Route 60.

Route 44   50 miles   80 km
KING'S LYNN — CAMBRIDGE

OS 1:250 000 no. 9, 6
Bartholomew's 1:100 000 nos 20, 25
OS 1:50 000 nos 154, 143, 132

This route crosses the broad expanse of the Fens. Once covered by sea, now rich agricultural land, the flat landscape is broken by long, straight ditches, rivers and occasional roads. The Fens have an empty beauty, characterized by huge skies and steady breezes. The latter, which can be persistent, will often decide the progress of the cyclist.

King's Lynn A seaport, market town and agricultural centre for the surrounding rich farmlands. The town was once a walled city of some importance, and contains many interesting buildings. These include Trinity Guildhall, (1423), now the town hall; Custom House (1683); Hanseatic warehouses, Greenland

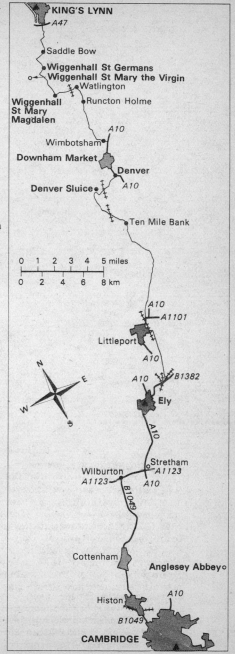

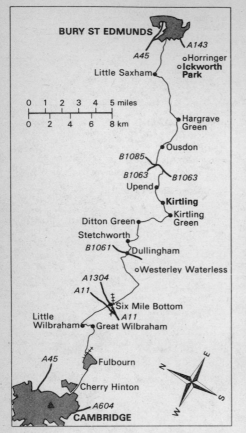

BURY ST EDMUNDS

A143
A45
Horringer
Ickworth Park
Little Saxham

0 1 2 3 4 5 miles
0 2 4 6 8 km

Hargrave Green

Ousdon
B1085

B1063   B1063
Upend

Kirtling
Kirtling Green
Ditton Green
Stetchworth
B1061   Dullingham

Westerley Waterless

A1304
A11
Six Mile Bottom
A11
Little Wilbraham
Great Wilbraham

A45
Fulbourn

Cherry Hinton

A604
CAMBRIDGE

in these villages contain fine wood carvings.

Downham Market In earlier centuries the town was an important centre. Interesting buildings include Howdale Home (an Elizabethan style workhouse), Mount Tabor chapel and the clock tower.

Denver On the edge of the village is a fine windmill once used for grinding corn.

Denver Sluice Vermuyden, a Dutch engineer, built the first sluice here in 1652 in order to drain this part of the Fens, so bringing agricultural prosperity to the area. The original sluice used wind mills as water pumps. Water control of the Fens continues to this day.

Ely Until the Fens were drained, the town stood on an island. The great cathedral has a magnificent west tower and unique octagonal lantern. The King's School, the Ely Porta (the three storey gatehouse to the original abbey), and the Bishop's Palace are open; Isleham Priory (DoE, open). A pleasant walk from the cathedral to Cherry Hill Park follows the bank of the river Ouse.

Anglesey Abbey The house was built in about 1600 and contains collections of furniture and paintings (NT, open). There is an outstanding hundred-acre garden.

Cambridge See Route 28. Also links with Routes 29, 37, 45, 46, 53.

Route 45   35 miles   56 km
**BURY ST EDMUNDS —
CAMBRIDGE**

OS 1:250 000 no. 9
Bartholomew's 1:100 000 nos 20, 21
OS 1:50 000 nos 154, 155

Bury St Edmunds See Route 34. Also links with Routes 38, 39.

Ickworth Park See Route 34.

Kirtling Kirtling Tower (NT) is a fine

Fishery House; Clifton House and Thoresby College. St George's Guildhall (1407) is the largest surviving medieval example of its kind in England and has an adjoining medieval warehouse and Tudor house (NT), and is now an annual festival centre, theatre and art gallery. In the 'Saturday Market Place' stands St Margaret's parish church (1100) containing magnificent brasses. Lynn Museum of local history; museum of social history. Links with Routes 43, 60.

Wiggenhall St Germans, Wiggenhall St Mary the Virgin and **Wiggenhall St Mary Magdalen** All three churches

tower gatehouse, built in 1530. The village church is Norman.

Cambridge See Route 28. Also links with Routes 29, 37, 44, 46, 53.

Route 46   41 miles   66 km
OUNDLE — CAMBRIDGE

OS 1:250 000 no. 9
Bartholomew's 1:100 000 no. 20
OS 1:50 000 nos 154, 153, 142, 141 (just)

Oundle A pretty country town on the river Nene, with buildings of stone and Colly-weston tiles. There are many ancient inns, a famous public school, and some almshouses. Links with Route 47.

Lyveden New Bield The shell of a four-winged house built by Sir Thomas Tresham, which was unfinished following his involvement in the Gunpowder Plot (NT, open).

Great Gidding The Baptist chapel, built in 1790, has original furnishings.

Sawtry The old lock-up can be seen standing on the village green. William Sawtry, burnt in chains in 1401, and the first Christian martyr to be burnt in England after the conquest, was born here.

Huntingdon The Black Death of 1348 cost this country town its prosperity. The 12th-century hospital became a grammar school, attended by both Oliver Cromwell and Pepys. The Falcon Inn may have been Cromwell's headquarters during the Civil War. A fine medieval bridge separates the town from Godmanchester. There is a museum devoted to the Cromwellian period.

Hinching Brooke House A 13th-century nunnery which later became the home of the Cromwells (open).

Godmanchester An ancient Roman town with thatched brick and timber cottages. The parish church of St Mary has misericords, a rare mass dial and a fine brass. The delightful Chinese bridge leads to islands in the Ouse.

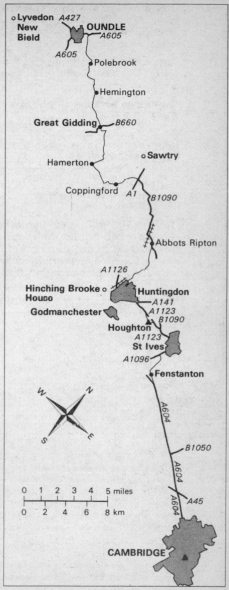

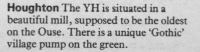

Houghton The YH is situated in a beautiful mill, supposed to be the oldest on the Ouse. There is a unique 'Gothic' village pump on the green.

St Ives A chapel stands on the medieval bridge. Oliver Cromwell had a farm near here, and his statue can be seen in the market place.

Fenstanton The home village and burial place of Capability Brown, the famous landscape architect.

Cambridge See Route 28. Also links with Routes 29, 37, 44, 45, 53.

Route 47   31 miles   50 km
OAKHAM — OUNDLE

OS 1:250 000 nos 6, 9
Bartholomew's 1:100, 000 nos 20, 25
OS 1:50 000 nos 141, 142 (just)

Oakham This small country town has a late 12th-century Norman castle notable for its magnificent hall, the interior of which is decorated with an extraordinary collection of horseshoes given by various peers of the realm (open). A set of stocks and an old butter cross can be seen in the

market square, and there is a fine church Rutland County Museum has interesting local history and archaeology collections and the town was the birthplace of Titus Oates, the renegade Anglican priest who fabricated the 'Popish Plot' of 1678. Links with Routes 48, 54, 59, 64.

Upper Hambleton The tower and spire of the church are typical of the style found in what used to be the county of Rutland.

Wing The church has some good Norman carving, and there is a rare turf maze at the east end of the village.

North Luffenham This old-established village has a 16th-century hall and barn. The hall has a hole in one wall through which food used to be passed to the poor. During the Civil War the hall was besieged, hence the dry ditch.

Uppingham A quiet old market town with the fine buildings of the public school founded in the 16th century.

Lyddington An attractive village with several delightful old cottages. The church has an unusual altar rail, and jars built into the wall to improve the acoustics. Bede house, well known for its great hall, was the palace of the bishops of Lincoln until it was dissolved by Henry VIII (DoE, open).

Gretton This hill-top village with its magnificent views over the Welland valley has old stocks on the green, and a whipping post last used in the mid 19th century.

Rockingham Standing high above this delightful village with fine views is the much restored castle (open). It was built by William the Conqueror and later used as a hunting lodge by King John. More recently, Charles Dickens was a frequent visitor.

Kirby Hall Although largely in ruins, the hall and gardens are still a splendid sight (DoE, open).

Deene The grand house of Deene Park is of great historic and architectural interest; the extensive grounds have rare trees and shrubs (open).

a The alternative route follows the valley of Willow Brook, through pretty villages built of local stone, although it misses Southwick.

Southwick A manor house dating from 1300. Rebuilt in Tudor times, and with 18th century additions, the hall now houses an exhibition of Victorian dresses.

Fotheringhay The mound of historic Fotheringhay Castle can be seen on the edge of the village. It was here that Mary Queen of Scots was executed in 1587, and the Scotch thistles found in the grounds are said to have been planted by Mary during her imprisonment. It was here also that the future King Richard III was born. There are many old cottages. The church has a fine lantern tower, and an attractive pulpit which was given by Edward IV.

Cotterstock The hall is a 17th-century stone manor house with a large garden (open). Dryden wrote his 'Fables' here.

Oundle See Route 46.

Route 48   46 miles   74 km
MELBOURNE — OAKHAM

OS 1:250 000 no. 6
Bartholomew's 1:100 000 no. 24
OS 1:50 000 nos 128 (just), 129, 141

This is essentially a link route through an area which has pleasant rural scenes but also significant amounts of industry, and it is to avoid the latter that the route is indirect.

Melbourne Melbourne Hall is famous for its large formal gardens and attractive house which has an important collection of works of art. The town has an impressive Norman church, and a medieval tithe barn. Lord Melbourne was born in the Hall, and gave his name to the Australian city. Links with Route 49.

Staunton Harold By a lovely Georgian country house stands a unique church built in Cromwellian times (NT).

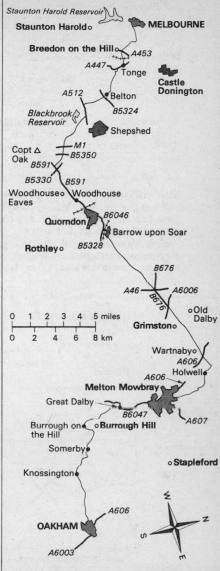

Breedon on the Hill On the hill summit the earthworks of an Iron Age encampment enclose a church incorporating parts of an 8th-century Anglo-Saxon monastery which stood on the site and was destroyed by the Danes.

Castle Donington Museum relating to transport history including bicycles.

Quorndon This part of Leicestershire has long been hunting country, the Quorn being one of the most famous. The station serves a main line steam trust railway.

Rothley The statue of a Knight Templar stands by an ancient preceptory of the Knights Templars. A worn Anglo-Saxon cross is in the churchyard.

Grimston Stocks on the village green.

Melton Mowbray Here is 'Leicester's stateliest church', and a Maison Dieu of 1640. The town is renowned for its pork pies and Stilton cheese. In the 19th century it was the haunt of the 'Tip Top Meltonians', the dashing extravagent men who came to ride with the very best hunts.

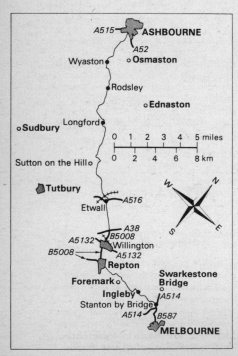

Stapleford The park, set about a house dating from 1500, has a miniature railway, ships on the lake and a lion reserve (open). The house contains a collection of Victorian Staffordshire figures (NT).

Burrough Hill Some earthworks remain of a 12-acre Iron Age hill-fort.

Oakham See Route 47. Also links with Routes 54, 59, 64.

Route 49   24 miles   39 km
ASHBOURNE — MELBOURNE

OS 1:250 000 no. 6
Bartholomew's 1:100 000 no. 24
OS 1:50 000 no. 128

Ashbourne The church of St Oswald is known as the 'Pride of the Peak'. The church wall still bears marks caused by Parliamentary artillery in 1644. Charles I prayed here following his defeat at the Battle of Naseby one year later. Ashbourne gingerbread is famous, the recipe having been handed down from French prisoners billetted here during the Napoleonic Wars. Church Street has many fine buildings. Links with Routes 50, 113, 149, 151.

Osmaston Pretty village.

Ednaston Ednaston Manor has 9 acres of beautiful gardens and woodlands (open).

Sudbury A model 17th-century village. The church has a window given by Queen Victoria. The 17th-century brick built Sudbury Hall has fine plasterwork, murals and carvings (open); the Hall also has a museum of childhool exhibits.

Tutbury This attractive town has a fine Norman church, and castle ruins on a dramatic site that has been the location for forts since the Iron Age. The town had an ancient ceremony of bull running—if the townsfolk could catch the bull before he crossed the river, he would be theirs; if not, he would go to the bishop.

Repton This was once the capital of Mercia, and is the home of one of England's oldest public schools. The school incorporates parts of the ruined priory, and has a museum of school and town history.

Foremark The church has a Renaissance interior and a three-tiered pulpit. There is a walk to the Anchor Church, a hermit's cave near the river.

Ingleby There are many ancient Danish burial mounds around the village.

Swarkestone Bridge Medieval bridge with seventeen arches; the causeways stretch for ¾ mile.

Melbourne See Route 48.

Route 50   23 miles   37 km
ASHBOURNE — YOXALL

OS 1:250 000 nos 6 or 7
Bartholomew's 1:100 000 no. 24
OS 1:50 000 no. 128

Ashbourne See Route 49. Also links with Routes 113, 149, 151.

Mayfield Thomas Moore lived here. Bonnie Prince Charlie reached this far south in his campaign. Scottish rebels were said to have been hanged on the Hanging Bridge, following the rebellion of 1745; the church door is bullet-scarred from the skirmish.

Wootton Lodge The lodge was the setting for George Eliot's *Adam Bede*, and it can be viewed from the road.

Norbury A 14th-century church with a sedilia, and the tomb and brasses of its founder.

Sudbury See Route 49.

Uttoxeter A stone-carved conduit in the market place depicts Dr Johnson's penitence for his refusal to serve at his father's bookstall as a boy.

Abbots Bromley This charming village, with half-timbered buildings and a butter cross, is where the ancient horn dance is performed (September).

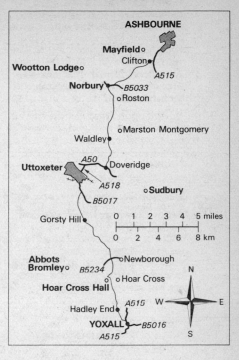

Hoar Cross Hall The Elizabethan-style hall, set in landscaped and terraced grounds, contain collections of arms and armour (open). Nearby is an unusually lovely 19th-century church which a young widow had built after her bereavement.

Yoxall Links with Route 51.

Route 51   41 miles   66 km
YOXALL — HIGH CROSS

OS 1:250 000 nos 6, 9
Bartholomew's 1:100 000 nos 19, 24
OS 1:50 000 nos 128, 140

The southern end of this route passes through a fairly industrialized area, and involves some main roads and many junctions; patient navigation is necessary.

Yoxall Links with Route 50.

Lichfield Early English cathedral in red sandstone, famed for its three spires and

carvings on its imposing west front.
Dr Johnson's birthplace and museum of
mementoes. Letocetum Roman bath
house, at a Watling Street posting station,
and museum of finds (NT, DoE, open).
Art gallery and local history museum.
Memorial to the last Englishman burnt
for heresy in 1612.

Burton upon Trent Famous brewing
town. The town hall, two churches and

other buildings were built by Michael
Bass in the 19th century. Bass Museum of
brewing; local history musem; art gallery.

Clifton Campville Church with a
beautiful spire and fine carvings.

Appleby Magna Good glass in the
church. By Moat House is a grouping of a
well, gatehouse and dovecot.

Tamworth Castle The Norman castle,
with medieval keep and tower and
Jacobean state apartments, houses a local
history museum (open).

Barton in the Beans The name derives
from the staple food crop of the area in
Roman times.

Market Bosworth A market town,
important in medieval times, now with
some pretty thatched buildings. Fine
English Renaissance hall in brick and
stone. Tudor grammar school, where
Samuel Johnson was a master.

Sutton Cheney There is a 17th-century
almshouse. The Lancastrian (King's)
army were encamped here before the
battle of Bosworth Field.

Bosworth Field Accessible by a right of
way on foot from Sutton Cheney, this was
the site of the conclusive battle which
ended the Wars of the Roses, thus bringing the House of Tudor to the throne.

Stoke Golding Church with some
delightful details and a lovely five-light
window.

High Cross See Route 52. Also links with
Routes 58, 59.

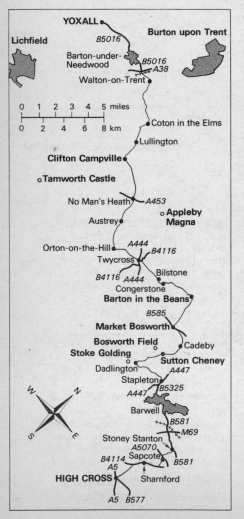

Route 52   39 miles   62 km
HIGH CROSS — CASTLE ASHBY

OS 1:250 000 no. 9
Bartholomew's 1:100 000 no. 19
OS 1:50 000 nos 140, 141, 152

High Cross At this site was the Roman
settlement of Venonae, at the junction of
Watling Street which linked London to
Wales, and the Foss Way which linked
Bath, Cirencester, Leicester and Lincoln.
Links with Routes 51, 58, 59.

a If you next intend to follow Route 59 to Oakham, you can turn to it here.

Lutterworth Medieval doom-painting in the Church of St Mary. Pretty 18th-century bridge. Some thatched, timber-framed cottages.

Stanford Hall The William and Mary house has antique kitchen equipment, a motor museum and a walled rose-garden (open); it also possesses a model of the flying machine of 1898, the original of which belonged to pioneer aviator Percy Pilcher.

Naseby Field Here Charles I was defeated by Oliver Cromwell in the battle which determined the outcome of the Civil War. The site is marked by two memorials.

Guilsborough A bird and pet park are in the grounds of a country house (open).

Coton A collection of tropical birds including flamingoes in a particularly fine English garden (open).

Brixworth The Church of All Saints was first built in the 7th century by the monks of Peterborough, using in part Roman tiles still seen in the fabric.

Lamport Lamport Hall, built in the 17th and 18th centuries, has a music hall and good 18th-century plasterwork (open).

Boughton House The 15th-century monastery, now converted into a stately home with seven courtyards, has fine furnishings and grounds (open).

Overstone Church with 16th-century glass and 18th-century monuments.

b If you next intend to follow Route 54 to Oakham, you can turn to it here.

Mears Ashby A 17th-century hall; church with a Norman font and a Viking wheel cross.

Earls Barton The Saxon tower of the church is said to be one of England's finest.

Whiston Church with fine carvings.

Castle Ashby See Route 53. Also links with Routes 54, 55, 56.

Route 53   46 miles   74 km
CASTLE ASHBY — CAMBRIDGE

OS 1:250 000 no. 9
Bartholomew's 1:100 000 no. 20
OS 1:50 000 nos 152, 153, 154

Castle Ashby An Elizabethan mansion with an Inigo Jones facade, containing

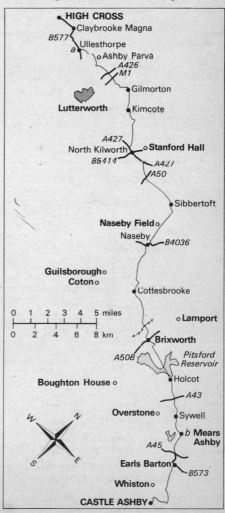

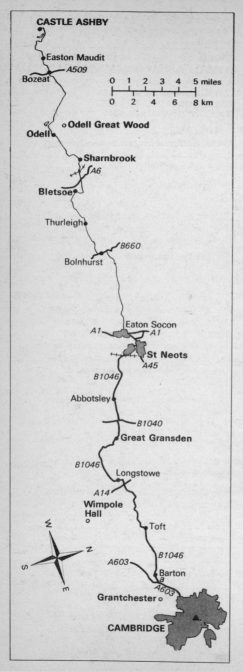

good ceilings and panelling, and set in grounds by Capability Brown (open). Links with Routes 52, 54, 55, 56.

Odell A pretty village with thatched cottages, by the mound of a Norman castle. The 15th-century church has its original rood screen and some old glass.

Sharnbrook Built near the site of an Iron Age settlement, Sharnbrook is attractive, with old cottages, a Victorian post office, a 17th-century manor with 20th-century additions, and Georgian Colworth House.

Bletsoe The remains of a castle where Elizabeth I was a guest are incorporated in a present farmhouse. Edward Fitzgerald, the translator of *The Rubaiyat of Omar Khayyam*, often stayed at the Falcon Inn.

St Neots This market town grew around a 10th-century Benedictine priory, now destroyed but for its foundations. There is a spacious market place, and some 17th-century inns. St Mary's church is beautiful.

Great Gransden A picturesque village with cottages of plaster and thatch. The 17th-century almshouses are still in use. Elizabethan Rippington Hall and 17th-century moated Great Gransden Hall. East of the village is a wooden postmill.

Wimpole Hall Elegant house set in fine landscaped park (NT, open).

a If you next intend to follow Route 29 to Ashwell, you can turn to it here.

Grantchester See Route 28.

Cambridge See Route 28. Also links with Routes 29, 37, 44, 45, 46.

Route 54   39 miles   63 km
OAKHAM — CASTLE ASHBY

OS 1:250 000 nos 6, 9
Bartholomew's 1:100 000 nos 20, 25
OS 1:50 000 nos 141, 152

Oakham See Route 47. Also links with Routes 48, 59, 64.

Brooke Church of Elizabethan work. Brooke Priory gatehouse was converted into a dovecot in the 18th century.

Wing and **Uppingham** See Route 47.

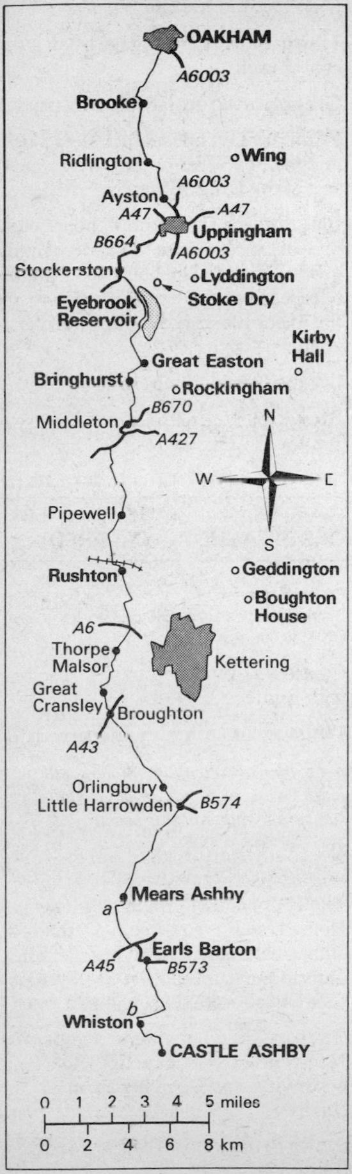

Eyebrook Reservoir Frequented by many wildfowl, including rare birds of passage.

Stoke Dry Church with wall paintings. This was the home village of Sir Digby who was hanged for financing the Gunpowder Plot.

Lyddington, Rockingham and **Kirby Hall** See Route 47.

Great Easton Like many villages in the area, this one has many houses built in the local, attractive ironstone.

Bringhurst Views over the Welland Valley.

Rushton The grounds of 16th-century Rushton Hall, which was the home of Tresham, betrayer of Guy Fawkes, can be visited. The Triangular Lodge was built with as many features as possible in threes, as a symbol of the Trinity (DoE, open).

Geddington Lovely village with several thatched buildings; church with fine screens; medieval bridge. A beautiful Eleanor Cross, one of several erected by Edward I to mark the resting places of his Queen's coffin on the way to Westminster.

Boughton House, Mears Ashby, Earls Barton and **Whiston** See Route 52.

a If you next intend to follow Route 52 to High Cross, you can turn to it here.

b If you next intend to follow Route 56 to Cropredy you can turn to it here.

Castle Ashby See Route 53. Also links with Routes 52, 55, 56.

Route 55   36 miles   59 km
CASTLE ASHBY — STEWKLEY

OS 1:250 000 no. 9
Bartholomew's 1:100 000 nos 14, 19
OS 1:50 000 nos 152, 165

This route swings to the west for reasons of interest rather than in order to avoid any large towns, and more direct but still pleasant routes between Castle Ashby and

Stewkley can easily be picked out by those wishing to make good time.

Castle Ashby See Route 53. Also links with Routes 52, 54, 56.

Stoke Bruern Waterways museum by the Grand Union Canal. The towpath walk north-west leads to the entrance of a two-mile canal tunnel.

Stoke Park Two 17th-century pavilions and a colonnade, all by Inigo Jones, can be visited in the park.

Shutlanger Priests' house.

Towcester This town used to be an important coaching stop on the London to Holyhead run, when it had over twenty inns. The Saracen's Head, still a pleasant pub, is featured in Dickens' *Pickwick Papers*.

a If you next intend to follow Route 56 to Cropredy, you can turn to it here.

Thornton A pretty village by an ivy-clad church.

Great Horwood Jacobean cottages.

Winslow Old houses including a hall said to be by Wren (open). It was once the seat of the King of Mercia.

Claydon An 18th-century house with unusual rococo state rooms containing good carvings. The house has a museum of relics from the Crimean war and about the life of Florence Nightingale (NT, open).

Swanbourne Picturesque village.

Stewkley Norman church. Links with Routes 22, 23, 30.

Route 56   36 miles 58 km
CASTLE ASHBY — CROPREDY

OS 1:250 000 no. 9
Bartholomew's 1:100 000 no. 19
OS 1:50 000 nos 151, 152

Castle Ashby See Route 53. Also links with Routes 52, 54, 55.

Whiston Church with fine carvings.

a If you next intend to follow Route 52 to High Cross, or Route 54 to Oakham, you can turn to either at this point.

Northampton Delapre Abbey, 16th century, is now used as offices (open). The 15th-century Abington Manor House contains a museum of ethnography, folk and natural history. The Central Museum and Art Gallery includes shoe and shoemaking exhibits.

Gayton Church with misericords, a 14th-century wooden effigy and a tomb portraying a wife and her eighteen children.

Stoke Bruern and **Towcester** See Route 55.

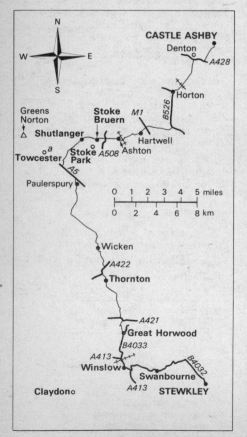

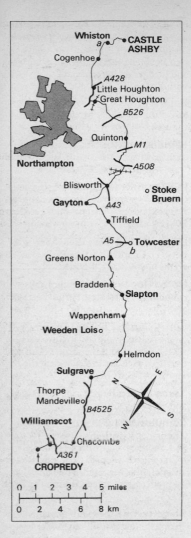

equipped old kitchen, and the family arms of stars and stripes carved over the door.

Williamscot Charles I stayed at the small house of Williamscot after the fierce Civil War battle at nearby Cropredy Bridge, as there was smallpox at the larger manor house.

Cropedy See Route 57.

Route 57   24 miles   39 km
**CROPREDY —
CHIPPING CAMPDEN**

OS 1:250 000 no. 9
Bartholomew's 1:100 000 no. 14
OS 1:50 000 no. 151

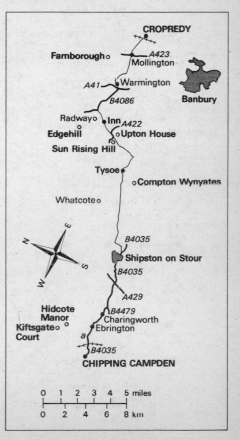

b If you next intend to follow Route 55 to Stewkley, you can turn to it here.

Slapton Primitive church.

Weeden Lois A monument by Henry Moore surmounts the grave of Dame Edith Sitwell, the poetess.

Sulgrave The homely Elizabethan manor was George Washington's ancestral home (open). It has a completely

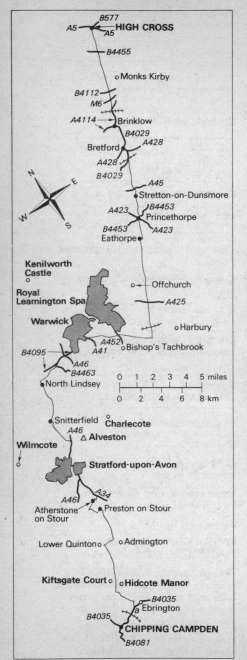

Cropredy In the church are cannon balls and an eagle lectern, hidden in the river during a fierce Civil War battle and only rediscovered years later. Interesting locks and bridges on the canal and river. Links with Route 56.

Banbury Museum of local interest, with an exhibition of the changing landscape of the area.

Farnborough An 18th-century house with excellent plasterwork, and a terrace walk with temples (NT, open).

Inn The tower which marked the site of Charles I's standard before the Battle of Edgehill has now become the Castle Inn Hotel.

Edgehill The site of a Civil War battle between Charles I and the Parliamentarians involving 28,000 men.

Upton House A 17th-century house containing Brussels tapestries, porcelain and 18th-century furniture (NT, open).

Sun Rising Hill The Red Horse carved on the hillside is the last of a succession of such horses, and is the subject of ancient practices such as the Scouring of the Horse on Palm Sunday.

Tysoe Middle Tysoe has pretty cottages and an 11th-century church.

Compton Wynyates A picturesque Tudor house with many secret rooms and passages, and with a famous topiary garden (open). The rare Restoration church was built with stones of its predecessor, ruined during the Civil War.

Shipston on Stour Old inns and Georgian houses testify to the past prosperity of this one-time sheep-market town.

a If you next intend to follow Route 58 to High Cross, you can turn to it here.

Hidcote Manor The garden here is considered to be one of the loveliest in England (NT, open).

Kiftsgate Court A garden with many rare plants, including a large collection of old rose species (open).

Chipping Campden See Route 86. Also links with Routes 58, 87, 88, 89.

Route 58   48 miles   77 km
HIGH CROSS —
CHIPPING CAMPDEN

OS 1:250 000 no. 9
Bartholomew's 1:100 000 nos 14 (just), 19
OS 1:50 000 nos 140, 151

Between Warwick and High Cross, the route picks its way through a fairly industrialized area, and traffic can sometimes be busy. The straight part of the route follows the Foss Way, part of which is classified and so has some traffic. If travelling in a busy season, you may prefer to use quieter lanes roughly parallel to the Foss Way.

High Cross See Route 52. Also links with Routes 51, 59.

Kenilworth Castle Massive, 12th-century keep, and gatehouse (DoE, open).

Royal Leamington Spa This late 18th-and early 19th-century spa was dubbed 'Royal' because of Queen Victoria's patronage. Pump Room; fine Georgian, Regency and Victorian terraces; riverside gardens; museum.

Warwick Of early importance, because of its strategic riverside site, Warwick was largely rebuilt after a great fire in 1694. The superb castle dating back to the 14th century in parts, contains classical paintings and is set in grounds by Capability Brown (open). The Lord Leycester Hospital, a group of 14th-century buildings, is still an active almshouse (open). There are pre-fire buildings in Castle Street; Warwick-shire museum; St John's House museum of bygones and period dress; a doll museum.

Stratford-upon-Avon A market town since the 12th century, Stratford has some good Tudor and Georgian buildings. It is famed as Shakespeare's town and the home of the Shakespeare festival. Shakespeare's birthplace (open).

Thatched cottage of Anne Hathaway, Shakespeare's wife (open). Tudor Hall's Croft with walled garden was Shakespeare's daughter's home (open). At New Place traces of Shakespeare's last home are preserved in an Elizabethan garden (open). Royal Shakespeare Theatre; 16th-century Harvard House, ancestral home of the founder of America's Harvard University (open).

Wilmcote Mary Arden's House, a Tudor farm with a dovecot and farm museum, was the home of Shakespeare's mother.

Alveston Stratford-upon-Avon YH.

Charlecote A 16th-century house with brewhouse, kitchens and a collection of carriages, set in a deer park where Shakespeare was charged with poaching (open).

Kiftsgate Court and **Hidcote Manor** See Route 57.

a If you next intend to follow Route 57 to Cropredy, you can turn to it here.

Chipping Campden See Route 86. Also links with Routes 57, 87, 88, 89.

Route 59   41 miles   66 km
OAKHAM — HIGH CROSS

OS 1:250 000 nos 6, 9
Bartholomew's 1:100 000 nos 19, 24
OS 1:50 000 nos 140, 141

Oakham See Route 47. Also links with Routes 48, 54, 64.

Braunston Many of the houses were built of local dark-brown ironstone.

Brooke See Route 54.

Withcote Rich modern glass in the church adjoining Withcote Hall.

Church Langton Langton Hall is a small, medieval country house containing collections of dolls and contemporary art works, and set in gardens in the French style (open).

Foxton Walks beside the Grand Union Canal. There are ten locks nearby.

Market Harborough This was created a market town by Henry II, and still has an attractive square. The Church of St Dionysius has one of England's best steeples. The Royalist army had their headquarters here before their defeat at the Battle of Naseby. The half-timbered grammar school is 17th-century. Wrought iron sign of the Three Swans; local history museum.

Arnesby Restored windmill.

a If you next intend to follow Route 52 to Castle Ashby, you can turn to it here.

High Cross See Route 52. Also links with Routes 51, 58.

Route 60	60 miles 96 km

OLD BOLINGBROKE — KING'S LYNN

OS 1:250 000 no. 6
Bartholomew's 1:100 000 nos 25, 30
OS 1:50 000 nos 122, 131, 132

This route crosses the flat expanses of the Fens. In the few instances where it has not been practical to avoid using main roads, extra care should be taken as cross winds and some heavy traffic can make cycling difficult.

Old Bolingbroke One of the finest villages in the Lincolnshire Wolds, site of John of Gaunt's castle and the birthplace of his son, Henry IV. The castle was destroyed by the Parliamentarians following their victory at the Battle of Winceby. There are 18th-century houses and shops, and by the church doorway are two worn stone heads thought to be those of John of Gaunt's parents, Edward III and Queen Philippa. Links with Routes 61, 66.

East Keal Good views over the Fens to the Boston Stump.

Boston The town used to be an important seaport in the 13th century, but declined with the growth of ports on the west coast and the silting up of the Wash. The 272-foot (83-metre) high tower of 14th-century St Botolphs Church, known as the 'Stump', was a landmark for shipping and has a superb view; the interior has a magnificent roof and carvings. Fydell House (open) contains the Pilgrim College with a room reserved for visitors from Boston, Massachusetts; Shodfriars Hall; the Peacock and Royal Hotel; Customs House and ruin of Blackfriars Hall. Emigrants from Boston named the American town after their own, and each year on 4 July the Stars and Stripes is flown.

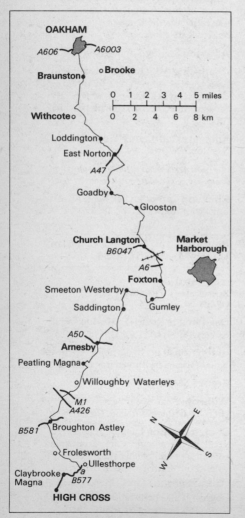

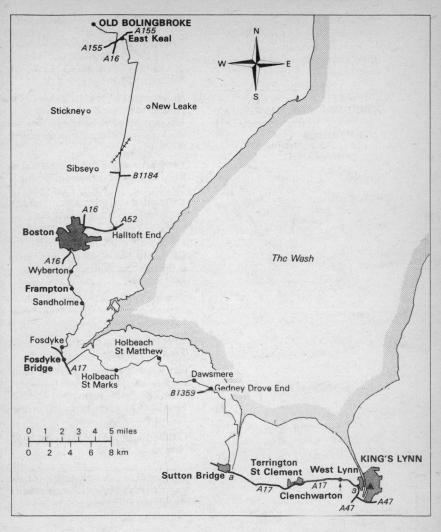

Frampton The village has several old cottages, 18th-century houses and Georgian Frampton House.

Fosdyke Bridge The iron bridge was built in the years 1910 and 1911.

Sutton Bridge The river Nene here was the site of an unsuccessful port scheme. It was here in 1216 that King John tried to cross the Wash and lost his 'treasure'.

a The A17 road between Sutton Bridge and King's Lynn often carries heavy traffic. It can be avoided by using the lanes to the north, between the main road and the sea.

Terrington St Clement Victorian shops and an interesting church.

Clenchwarton There is a monument in the church referring to the floods of 1735; 17th and 18th-century houses.

West Lynn From the waterfront there is a good view of King's Lynn across the river.

King's Lynn See Route 44. Also links with Route 43.

Route 61   29 miles   46 km
CAISTOR — OLD BOLINGBROKE

OS 1:250 000 no. 6
Bartholomew's 1:100 000 no. 30
OS 1:50 000 nos 113, 122

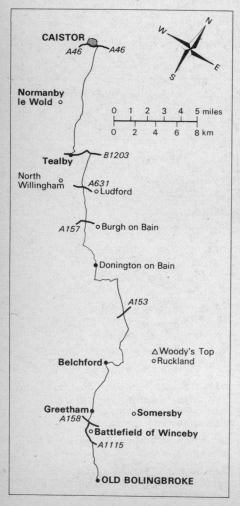

Caistor The site of this small market town was once occupied by a British hillfort, and later a Roman camp. In AD 828 King Egbert of Wessex is said to have defeated the Mercians here. Links with Route 62, 158.

Normanby Le Wold On a clear day it is possible to see the Boston Stump, Lincoln Cathedral, Selby and York from this little village set right on the edge of the Wolds.

Tealby Across the valley from this attractive village stand the ruins of Bayons Manor, once the home of Tennyson's grandfather. In earlier times it belonged to the half brother of William the Conqueror, Bishop Odo of Bayeux. A public footpath passes close to the Manor.

Belchford The village is situated in one of the most beautiful valleys in Lincolnshire.

Somersby The old rectory was the birthplace of Tennyson and the church has several memorials to him.

Greetham There is a pleasant view over Tennyson's valley.

Battlefield of Winceby In 1643 a major engagement took place here between Cromwell and his Roundheads and the Royalists who were on their way to relieve Bolingbroke Castle.

Old Bolingbroke See Route 60. Also links with Route 66.

Route 62   25 miles   41 km
EAST BUTTERWICK — CAISTOR

OS 1:250 000 no. 6
Bartholomew's 1:100 000 no. 30
OS 1:50 000 nos 112, 113 (just)

East Butterwick Links with Routes 63, 133.

Ermine Street The lane which crosses the B1206 here follows the course of Ermine Street, the Roman road built to link London and York.

Redbourne At the entrance to Redbourne Park is a grand gateway, and the

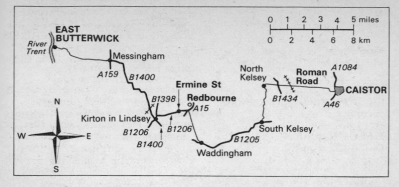

church has an imposing tower and colourful east window.

Roman Road Between North Kelsey and Caistor.

Caistor See Route 61. Also links with Route 158.

Route 63   30 miles   43 km
EAST BUTTERWICK — LINCOLN

OS 1:250 000 no. 6
Bartholomew's 1:100 000 no. 30
OS 1:50 000 nos 112, 121

East Butterwick Links with Routes 62, 133.

Gainsborough Market town with some 18th-century quayside warehouses. There is a bore on the river Trent here at certain tides. The 15th-century black and white Old Hall was the meeting place of the group who became the Pilgrim Fathers. It has a great hall, an oriel window, a complete medieval kitchen and a museum with exhibits ranging from coins to period dress (open).

Stow Still known as the Dowager Minster of Lincoln, the fine church was founded in the 7th century to mark the site of a miracle, but was rebuilt in the 11th century with help from Lady Godiva.

Roman Road This stretch of lane follows the course of one of the many Roman roads in the Lincoln area.

Lincoln See Route 64. Also links with Routes 65, 66.

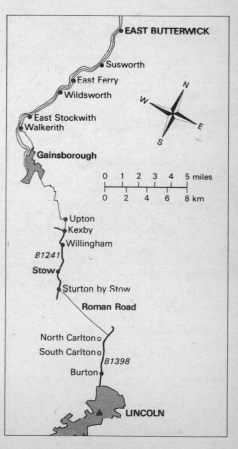

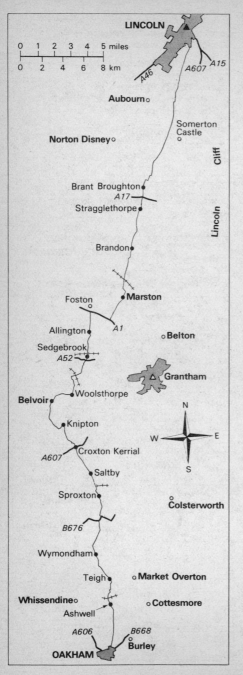

LINCOLN

0 1 2 3 4 5 miles
0   2   4   6   8 km

A46   A607   A15

Aubourn

Somerton
Castle

Norton Disney

Lincoln Cliff

Brant Broughton
A17
Stragglethorpe

Lincoln Cliff

Brandon

Foston   Marston

Allington   A1   Belton
Sedgebrook
A52

Grantham

Belvoir   Woolsthorpe

N

Knipton

W   E

Croxton Kerrial
A607
Saltby   S

Sproxton
Colsterworth

B676

Wymondham

Teigh   Market Overton

Whissendine   Cottesmore
Ashwell

A606   B668
Burley
OAKHAM

Route 64   46 miles   74 km
LINCOLN — OAKHAM

OS 1:250 000 no. 6
Bartholomew's 1:100 000 nos 25, 30
OS 1:50 000 nos 121, 130, 141 (just)

Lincoln The Romans built a camp
here, and later William the Conqueror
chose it as the site for a castle. There is
an imposing triple-towered cathedral,
and many medieval shops. The Jew's
House dates from around 1170, and is
one of the oldest inhabited houses in
Britain. Also of interest is Aaron's
House, the Bishop's Palace (DoE), and
the cathedral treasury and library
(open). Museum of Lincolnshire Life,
the City and County Museum with local
history displays, and the Usher Gallery
which has collections of antique watches
and various works of art. Links with
Routes 63, 65, 66.

Aubourn A 16th-century house with fine
woodwork.

Norton Disney In the church are monuments to the Disney family, the forebears
of Walt Disney, their name a derivation of
the Norman 'd'Isigny'.

Lincoln Cliff The low but very straight
ridge of high land running parallel to the
route and to the east is Lincoln Cliff along
which is Ermine Street.

Marston A 16th-century manor with
ancient gardens and a neo-Gothic gazebo
(open).

Belton Set in extensive grounds with
formal gardens and an orangery, the 17th-
century Wren-style Belton House
contains carvings by Grinling Gibbons,
fine carpets and paintings (open).

Grantham Standing on the old road to
the north, Grantham has several good
coaching inns. The Angel was established
by the Knights Templars, and the sign of
the Beehive Inn is a real beehive in a tree.
Fine 14th-century work in St Wulfram's
Church includes a double-vaulted crypt.
Isaac Newton was a pupil of the 15th-
century King's School. Grantham House

stands in large grounds (open). Museum of local prehistory and history, with an Isaac Newton collection.

Belvoir Originally given by William the Conqueror to his standard-bearer, the estate now consists of a medieval and 19th-century castle with state rooms, an armoury, tapestries and old masters. The beautiful grounds include a water garden (open).

Colsterworth Small but attractive, 17th-century Woolsthorpe Manor was the birthplace of Isaac Newton, and in the orchard is a descendant of the tree from which the famous apple fell (NT, open).

Market Overton Commanding wide views, the village with its Georgian hall and some pleasant houses grew beside its church, which stands within Roman earthworks. Stocks and whipping post. Isaac Newton lived here in his youth.

Cottesmore The home of a famous fox hunt.

Burley A fine 17th-century country house, standing at the end of a great avenue of trees.

Whissendine Church with an excellent screen from St John's College, Cambridge.

Oakham See Route 47. Also links with Routes 48, 54, 59.

Route 65   42 miles 68 km
CHURCH WARSOP — LINCOLN

OS 1:250 000 no. 6
Bartholomew's 1:100 000 nos 29, 30
OS 1:50 000 nos 120, 121

Church Warsop Links with Route 157.

Clumber Park Created in the late 18th century, the property comprises some 3800 acres of parkland, farmland, lake and woodlands (NT, open). Overlooking the lake is Clumber chapel (NT, open), built by the 7th Duke of Newcastle at a cost, in 1886, of £30,000.

Sherwood Forest Well known as the

domain of the legendary outlaw Robin Hood, although only a small part of the original forest remains.

Thoresby Hall Built in 1864 with state apartments and a Great Hall (open). Thoresby Hall is considered one of the most ambitious Victorian buildings of its kind in the country.

Conjure Alders The site of a Saxon ford, reached from the lane by a bridleway.

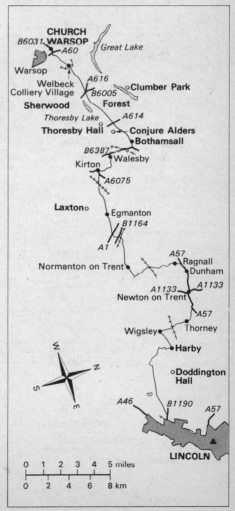

Bothamsall There are good views over Sherwood Forest from Castle Hill, just to the west of the village.

Laxton The ancient system of open field farming is still practised here. Devised originally by the Saxons, it consists of co-operatively owned one-acre strips of land. The church has 13th-century monuments.

Harby It was here in 1290 that Queen Eleanor of Castile, the wife of Edward I,

died. Her body was taken to Westminster Abbey, each resting place on the journey being marked by a cross. The last and most famous is Charing Cross in the Strand, London.

Doddington Hall This splendid Elizabeth mansion (open) contains fine furniture, porcelain, pictures and textiles and has several acres of delightful gardens.

Lincoln See Route 64. Also links with Routes 63, 66.

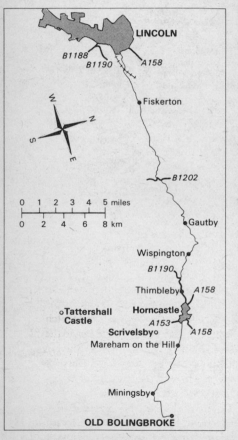

Route 66   28 miles   46 km
LINCOLN — OLD BOLINGBROKE

OS 1:250 000 no. 6
Bartholomew's 1:100 000 no. 30
OS 1:50 000 nos 121, 122

Lincoln See Route 64. Also links with Routes 63, 65.

Tattershall Castle This massive five-storey keep is one of the best examples of medieval brick building (NT, open). It has a hundred-foot high tower, stone Gothic fireplaces, and a museum in the Guard House. There are fine views from the top to Lincoln Cathedral, and the Boston Stump.

Horncastle The Romans built the town of Banovallum here, the walls of which are partly preserved. During the last century, huge ten-day horse fairs were held here, and inns such as the Fighting Cocks hint at the entertainments to be found at these fairs. St Mary's Church has pikes and scythes that were used at the Battle of Winceby during the Civil War.

Scrivelsby Traditionally the home of the Hereditary Grand Champion of England, whose duty it is to challenge anyone who disputes the monarch's right to the throne at the time of a coronation.

Old Bolingbroke See Route 60. Also links with Route 61.

SOUTH-WEST ENGLAND

Picturesque cottages set in rolling countryside: this is the theme of the south-west though with many variations. Just about every possible building material is used from warm red brick and flint to whitewash and thatch to cold grey granite. The landscape changes from low hills in the east to the sometimes daunting hills of the West Country (a term which roughly means Cornwall, Devon and the adjoining parts of Somerset and Dorset). The theme breaks altogether here and there with flat lowland or rough moorland which have characters all their own.

There is rather more to the West Country hills than their scenery: they cover some of Britain's most strenuous terrain. Not only are they often very steep, but the rolling lie of the land means that they just keep on coming at you. It is impossible to avoid hilly roads: you need low gears and you must be fairly fit to enjoy cycling here—or accept getting off the bicycle now and then, which is no hardship in such a scenic area.

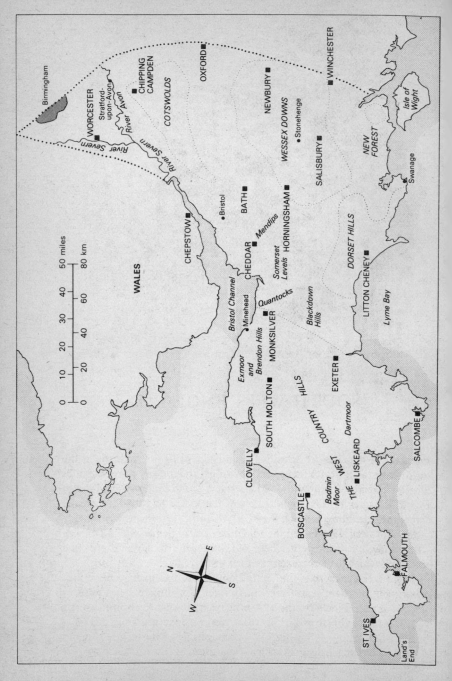

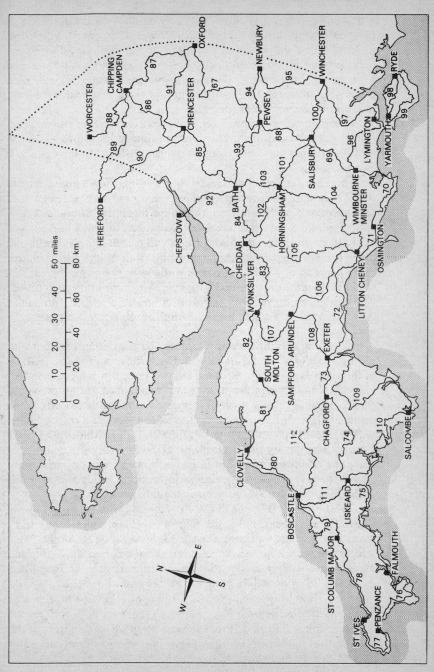

The coastline is rugged, especially in the north. A few gentler cliffs and beaches are along the south coast. From Minehead in the north right round to Land's End and as far as Swanage you will find a coast of almost unbroken but varying beauty, although you may not be so sympathetic towards the car-borne holidaymakers who are attracted to the West Country in summer. The roads can get very congested and there are a number of commercialized resorts.

An important but subtle facet to the character of the region is the evidence of prehistoric man. There are many humble clues to his passing as well as the more renowned monuments that are found in the vicinity of Stonehenge.

Cornwall is a county of hills and secluded valleys. Small green fields are edged by granite walls or lanes with high banks and hedges. The isolated farmsteads and small hamlets in the valleys often have names beginning with 'Tre', from the Celtic word for 'homestead'. Cornwall held out as a Celtic kingdom against the Saxon English till the 9th century. Prehistoric cairns and abandoned 19th-century tin mines with their slender chimneys brave more open, windswept positions. Between the grey cliffs and sea-stacks of the north coast are sandy bays popular for the surfing they afford. The south coast rugged cliffs mingle with wooded creeks, and around St Austell the brilliant white, man-made hills of china-clay waste arrest the eye from afar.

Devon continues the pattern of farmland on great rolling hills, but with more patches of wood and arable land. Ploughing exposes the rich red soil in the south-east. Proof of medieval Devon's prosperity is found in its fine churches although many people were content with their cottages of cob and thatch. Fishing villages, such as famous Clovelly, nestle in clefts in the north coast, while in the south around Salcombe wooded creeks flecked with the sails of yachts wind in among the hills. Although much of the West Country is good dairy farming land, it is in Devon particularly that you can enjoy the traditional cream tea of scones, clotted cream and strawberry jam. A friend recalls, a little guiltily, one fortnight's holiday during which fifteen cream teas helped fuel her over the hills!

Bleak Dartmoor is one of England's National Parks. Its boggy hollows and rounded moorland hills, often topped by plugs of granite called 'tors', make an apt setting for Conan Doyle's *The Hound of the Baskervilles*. Few people live on the moor now, but you can see the granite circles and standing stones of prehistory, abandoned medieval farms and tin-smelting houses. The moor stands open to the elements: exhilarating in good weather, but in wind or rain you may well think it best left to the stocky Dartmoor ponies. Bodmin Moor has much the same wild, open aspect. You will have to climb hard to get up to the moors, but once there you will find the roads quite easy. As neither moor has many roads you cannot stay cycling on them for long.

Exmoor, or Exmoor Forest as the National Park is now named, is less wild and more friendly than Dartmoor, although it still has some long, hard climbs for which low gears are needed. Neat fields give way near the summits to open expanses of heather and rough grass dotted with sheep. The steep-sided valleys (like that at Lynton) are often luxuriantly wooded, and clear rivers tumble their short distance to the sea. The moor falls quickly away to the coast, cliffs alternating with huge, steep slopes of bracken or woods.

Lying just to the east of Exmoor are the Brendon Hills, a gentler variant of the same theme. The Quantocks and the Mendips are two ridges of high land with steep slopes of woods, fields and heaths. In the broader Mendips you can explore narrow, rocky gorges, of which the Cheddar Gorge is the most famous (and the most commercialized). The Somerset Levels, lying between the Quantocks and the Mendips, were marshland in former times, but are now rich pastures divided by straight ditches or 'rhines' and willow-lined roads. The landscape is broken in places by grassy, conical hills, and the most famous one, Glastonbury Tor, is King Arthur's Avalon in legend. The Levels give way to a close knitted landscape towards Taunton, where the orchards of cider country and fields of fruit growing line the Vale of Taunton Deane.

Clean, smooth curves are the hallmark of the Wessex Downs, whether in the steeper slopes or the almost level plains. There are short hard climbs, but some of the best free-wheeling can be had riding a downland lane which snakes easily along for miles, sometimes in the company of a swift trout river, and now and then passing a string of villages of brick and flint cottages. The area is pervaded with an aura of prehistoric times, when great blocks of stone were brought from afar to build monuments such as Stonehenge and Avebury (on Routes 68 and 93); the humps of burial mounds are also seen on many skylines. Modern man has copied the ancient idea of cutting away the turf on a steep slope to make a picture in the white chalk beneath, and the Uffington White Horse and Cerne Giant have more recent companions scattered through the area.

To the south-west, stretching from Swanage past Lyme Bay to the loftier block of the Blackdown Hills, the Wessex Downs shade gradually into the higher and more expansive ridges of the Dorset hills, the Wessex of Dorchester and Thomas Hardy. Here, wide fertile valleys are dotted with villages with cottages in warm, buff-coloured stone. The cycling is quite strenuous except in the roads which follow ridge or valley, and low gears are a definite advantage. The coast has tourist resorts, but also some superbly rugged cliffs, sea-arches and coves in shimmering white rock.

South-east of the Wessex Downs is the New Forest. This low, largely flat area was declared a royal hunting reserve of the Norman kings in 1078 and there are few houses, hedges or walls there. Open rough heathland where New Forest ponies and cattle wander freely alternates with woodland of magnificent gnarled oaks and tall beeches or pine forest. There are few roads through the heart of the Forest but there are many heathland paths, and the miles of firm gravel tracks made by the Forestry Commission are officially open to walkers and horse-riders. A compass and 1:50 000 map will be needed.

The Isle of Wight has appeal as a pretty island although you will have to share it with many seaside holiday-makers. Along its backbone is airy grass downland, ending with the famed chalk stacks of the Needles in the west. To the north lies a flat plain of fields, woods and marshes, and to the south a fertile vale rises to another high downland, the coast of which is cleft by small but deep valleys called 'chines'. The summer influx of tourists has led to the opening of many interesting buildings ranging from castles to working water mills.

The Cotswolds are par excellence the area of the English village, where landscape and buildings complement each other to perfection. The uplands are divided into fields with honey-coloured stone walls, while every valley has its cottages built from the same mellow stone. Many date from medieval times when the Cotswold wool trade prospered, and you will see memorial brasses to rich merchants in the fine wool churches, such as the one at Northleach. The abrupt north-west edge of the Cotswolds is a major hill climb but the effort will be rewarded with a fine view over a wide valley to the Welsh mountains, and then with some lazy free-wheeling, perhaps back towards the south east where the Cotswolds become ever lower, with wider, shallower valleys. Lying near the Cotswolds, the city of Oxford has many fine buildings built from Cotswold stone. Towards Bath the hills become lower, but the pattern of folded valleys and beautiful villages continues.

Hemmed in by the hills of the Welsh borderlands and the Cotswolds lie the Severn and Avon valleys. Here you can revel in easy cycling in a landscape of riverside meadows, fields and orchards. Old buildings in black and white half-timbering, or timber and brick abound. Shakespeare's town, Stratford-upon-Avon, has some fine examples, but you will find others just as good in the quieter country lanes.

Route 67
OXFORD — PEWSEY
51 miles   82 km

OS 1:250 000 no. 9
Bartholomew's 1:100 000 nos 8, 14
OS 1:50 000 nos 173, 174, 164

Oxford See Route 21. Also links with
Routes 22, 87, 91.

Cumnor The church has a rare contemporary statue of Elizabeth I. Good
views from Hurst Hill, to the east.

Kingston Bagpuize The gardens (open)
of Kingston House have flowering
shrubs, bulbs and woodland.

Pusey Pusey House Gardens (open)
include a water garden, fine trees, shrubs
and roses.

Great Coxwell The Great Barn (NT,
open) dates from the 13th century and is
stone built with an interesting timber-
constructed roof.

*a   The alternative route detours to climb
the Downs and visit the Uffington White
Horse while the main route proceeds more
directly.*

Uffington A good place for viewing the
White Horse on the Down to the south.

Uffington White Horse The 360-foot
(120-metre) long horse was probably
cut in the chalk during the Iron Age.
On the hill top is Uffington Castle,
an Iron Age camp providing fine views
from its oval ramparts. The ancient
Ridge Way passes here, now a designated long distance footpath and bridleway.

Wayland's Smithy A megalithic long
barrow named after a legendary smith
who made invincible swords and armour.
Stone Age skeletons have been found in
the barrow (DoE).

*b   At this point the route crosses the desig-
nated long distance path, The Ridgeway.
Extending as far as Overton Hill in the south
west and Streatley-on-Thames to the east,
the path follows the ridge of the North
Wessex Downs, and is open to cyclists.
Beyond Streatley it is open only to walkers.*

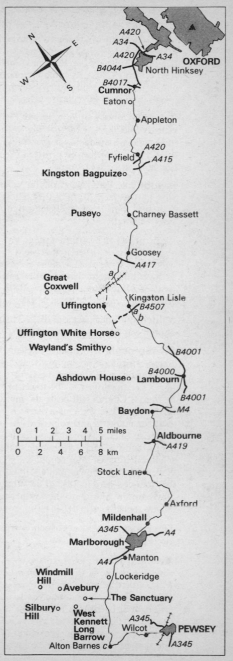

Fine rough stuff detours can be made along the path.

Lambourn The centre for well-known horseracing stables set in countryside dotted with ancient burial mounds and field systems. There are some Victorian almshouses and an old church containing good brasses and the village stocks.

Ashdown House Built in the late 17th century for Elizabeth of Bohemia, with a huge staircase and family portraits (NT, open). To the north-west is Alfred's Castle, an ancient earthwork.

Baydon Excellent views from the village which at 764 feet (233 m) is the highest in Wiltshire. Finche's Farm belonged to Isaac Newton.

Aldbourne In a beautiful setting, and once famous for its bell foundry and willow and straw plaiting industry. The 12th-century church has a fine alabaster tomb of a 15th-century vicar, two 18th-century fire engines and some brasses.

Mildenhall The interior of the Norman church was refitted with oak in 1816.

Marlborough Settled since ancient times, a former coaching town, and the scene of fierce fighting in the Civil War. The north face of the tower of St Mary's Church still bears the marks of this war. The wide main street is used for markets, and is lined with Georgian buildings and colonnaded shops, and the back streets hide many medieval cottages. Marlborough College, a well-known public school, was founded here in 1843. The White Horse on the hillside to the south was cut by schoolboys in 1804.

The Sanctuary A series of concentric circles with post holes (DoE).

Avebury The attractive village is ringed with one of the most important Megalithic ceremonial monuments in Europe, the Avebury Stone Circle (NT). Built by Bronze Age people around 1800 BC, the stone circles are enclosed by a ditch and bank, and approached by an avenue of stone by the road from West Kennett. A hundred of the great sarsen stones still stand. The Alexander Keiller Museum has Bronze Age and Neolithic objects found here and on Windmill Hill. The attractive church is partly Saxon, and Elizabethan Avebury Manor (open) has fine plasterwork, panelling, furniture and gardens.

Windmill Hill On top are remains of three concentric lines of earthworks marking a Neolithic camp (DoE).

Silbury Hill A curious conical man-made hill (DoE), 130 feet (40 m) high, and thought to have been built at around the same time as Stonehenge.

West Kennett Long Barrow This 350-foot (107 metre) long mound (DoE) covers a tomb consisting of five chambers and probably built around 2700 BC.

c If you next intend to follow Route 93 to Bath, you can turn to it here.

Pewsey See Route 68. Also links with Routes 93, 94.

Route 68   28 miles   45 km
PEWSEY — SALISBURY

OS 1:250 000 no. 9
Bartholomew's 1:100 000 no. 8
OS 1:50 000 nos 184, 173

Pewsey The exterior of the south aisle of the church rests on stones similar to those at Stonehenge, and the altar rails are taken from a ship captured by Nelson off Cape St Vincent in 1797. A statue of King Alfred looks out across the river Avon. Links with Routes 67, 93, 94.

Casterley Camp The remaining banks of a hill-fort.

Woodhenge A neolithic earthwork (DoE) consisting of a large circular bank with a ditch inside.

a For full appreciation of Stonehenge, try not to visit at peak times of day or the holiday season.

Stonehenge One of the country's most

famous monuments (DoE), dating from around 2000 BC. More than eight blue-stones were probably dragged and carried by boat from the Prescelly Mountains, over 200 miles (320 km) away in south Wales, and later a further eighty huge sarsen stones were brought from the Marlborough Downs. The purpose of Stonehenge is still a mystery. Some believe that it was used for sun-worship, at its axis is aligned with the sunrise on the longest day of the year. Others believe that it was a detailed calendar because of the large number of astronomical align-ments.

Amesbury The town has a five-arch Palladian style bridge, an abbey, and an interesting church. The outlines of pre-historic earthworks, known as Vespasian's Camp, can be seen west of the abbey.

Heale House An early Carolean manor house with a river garden, roses, and authentic Japanese tea house (open).

Old Sarum A 56-acre earthwork whose site has been occupied by Iron Age people, Romans, Anglo-Saxons and Danes. The stones from the cathedral on this site were used in the building of the new cathedral at Salisbury.

Salisbury See Route 69. Also links with Routes 100, 101.

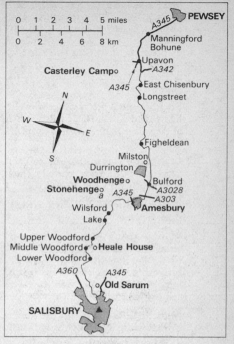

Route 69   29 miles   47 km
**SALISBURY —
WIMBORNE MINSTER**

OS 1:250 000 no. 9
Bartholomew's 1:100 000 no. 5
OS 1:50 000 nos 184, 195

Salisbury The city was planned in the 13th century when the cathedral was moved here from Old Sarum. The streets, which still show tne plan, have many interesting buildings dating from all following eras. The cathedral is Early English with 14th-century spire. Cathedral Close, where the graves were removed in the 18th century, has Queen Anne houses including Malmesbury House with baroque and rococo plaster-work (open), and Mompesson House with Georgian plasterwork (NT). There is a museum of Salisbury and South Wiltshire. Links with Routes 68, 100, 101.

Coombe Bissett Roman tiles are in-corporated in the church walls.

Duck's Nest Barrow A bridleway leads to this fine long barrow.

Knap and Grans Barrow Over 300 feet (91 m) long and reached by bridleway from the lane.

Whitsbury Ancient earthworks just north of the village.

Breamore House An Elizabethan manor house (open); countryside and carriage museums.

Breamore Most of the houses date from Tudor times and there is an excellent Anglo-Saxon church.

Miz Maze Cut in the turf, measuring about 90 feet (30 m) across, this curious feature may have been associated with religious rituals or dances. It is situated on Breamore Down, one mile north-west of Breamore House by bridleway, and one mile north-east of Whitsbury by foot-path.

Rockbourne A pretty village with old houses and thatch. Half a mile south-east of the village is the excavated site of a Roman villa.

Cranborne This was once the seat of the Chase Court, the body controlling hunting rights in the forest of Cranborne Chase. Manor gardens (open).

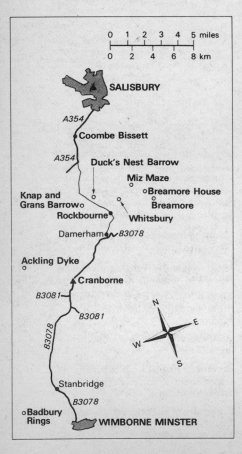

Ackling Dyke Crossing the B3081, just south-east of where it crosses the A354, is the Roman road that used to run between Badbury Rings and Old Sarum. Close by, running in a north-east–south-west direction is the Dorset Cursus, thought to have been a neolithic processional way.

Badbury Rings A massive Iron Age fortification enclosing a wood. It is at the intersection of two important Roman roads, from Bath to Poole Harbour, and Dorchester to Old Sarum, and according to legend a great battle took place here between the Britons under King Arthur, and the invading Anglo-Saxons.

Wimborne Minster See Route 70. Also links with Route 96.

Route 70   44 miles   70 km
**WIMBORNE MINSTER —
OSMINGTON**

OS 1:250 000 nos 9, 8
Bartholomew's 1:100 000 no. 4
OS 1:50 000 nos 194, 195

This route offers many opportunities for walking parts of the long distance Dorset coast path which runs between Poole and Lyme Regis. There is a break in the path between Kimmeridge and Lulworth Cove which is a restricted Ministry of Defence area. The route also requires the use of a ferry between Sandbanks and South Haven Point.

Wimborne Minster Unusual minster church in a mixture of styles, with a 14th-century clock and a chained library. Museum of local history in the Tudor Priest's House. Links with Routes 69, 96.

Poole Dorset's largest town, with a huge natural harbour which was once a haven for smugglers and later one of the main ports for the Newfoundland trade. There are many Georgian houses and old inns; the Old Customs House was built in 1813. It is a great yachting centre. Scaplen's Court accommodates a museum of Poole's history, while the Maritime Museum illustrates the town's association with the sea. The Guildhall Museum

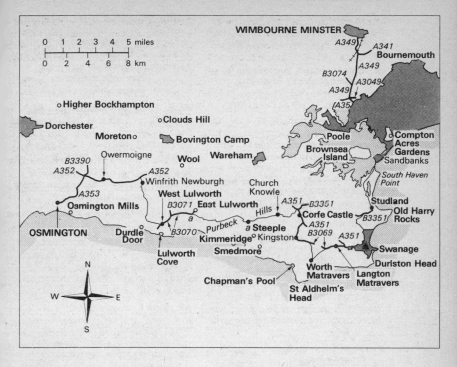

portrays Poole in the 18th and 19th centuries; it is in a two-storey Georgian market house.

Compton Acres Gardens Comprises seven secluded gardens of different styles (open) with valuable bronze and marble statuary. There are fine views over the harbour.

Bournemouth A holiday resort with beaches, piers, parks and museums.

Brownsea Island An island of heath and woodland with beaches, glades and good views of the Dorset coast (NT, open). Nature reserve, lagoon. Boats run from Poole Quay and Sandbanks.

Studland Excellent Norman church, and to the west, the Agglestone rock. There is good bathing here.

Old Harry Rocks Crumbling chalk stacks that can be viewed from the Dorset Coast Path.

Swanage Once a Saxon port, and now a quiet holiday resort with a good bathing beach. On the sea front is a column commemorating the defeat by King Alfred of a Danish fleet out in the bay in 877. The facade of the town hall was designed by Wren, and the clock tower near the pier originally came from the southern end of London Bridge.

Durlston Head Portland stone model of the world, weighing 40 tons. To the south are the Tilly Whim Caves, an old cliff quarry, a smuggler's hide and source of fossils.

Langton Matravers An old quarry-men's community.

Worth Matravers The famous Purbeck marble came from around here, and the village was once an important quarrying centre.

St Aldelm's Head A well-defined public bridleway from Renscombe Farm, west of Worth Matravers, leads to the coast-guard station on the Head, where there is a Norman chapel and a magnificent viewpoint.

Chapman's Pool A lovely valley leads to this little cove.

Corfe Castle The spectacular ruined castle has an eventful history including the murder of the eighteen-year-old King Edward by his stepmother in 978, the starving to death in the dungeons of twenty-two French nobles by King John, and a prolonged and destructive siege during the Civil War. Much of the stone was used to build cottages in the village.

Wareham A market town and resort for small boat enthusiasts. In the Saxon Church of St Martin is a fine sculpture of Lawrence of Arabia and in North Street there is a small museum containing Lawrence relics. The coffin of Edward the Martyr, killed at Corfe Castle, is in the church. The bridge has an old sign which threatens transportation to anyone who should deface it.

Kimmeridge Famous for soft clay, used by the Romans and Celts.

Smedmore A 17th–18th century manor house (open) with a collection of antique dolls and a walled garden.

Steeple In the church are the interlocking arms of the Lawrence and Washington families who intermarried in the 14th century; the latter produced the first President of the United States.

a The road between Steeple and East Lulworth crosses Ministry of Defence land, and is sometimes closed, in which case you have to make a substantial detour to the north.

East Lulworth A pretty village, with a large castle, burnt down in 1929.

West Lulworth The chapel was built by imported Italian craftsmen.

Lulworth Cove A famous tourist spot best seen out of season and created by the erosion of softer rock behind harder bands of Portland and Purbeck stone.

Durdle Door Reached by the Dorset Coast Path from Lulworth Cove, this is a huge natural limestone arch jutting out into the sea. Adjacent is Man o' War Bay, a sheltered bathing lagoon of great beauty. Westwards, the Dorset Coast Path follows spectacular coast scenery.

Wool A charming village with a fine 17th-century bridge. Woolbridge Manor and the grounds of Bindon Abbey half a mile east are associated with Thomas Hardy's *Tess of the D'Urbervilles*.

Bovington Camp The Royal Armoured Corps Tank Museum and Royal Tank Regiment Museum has over 140 examples of armoured fighting vehicles.

Clouds Hill A gamekeeper's cottage bought by T. E. Lawrence (Lawrence of Arabia) when he rejoined the RAF in 1915; it contains his furniture and other relics (NT, open).

Moreton Lawrence of Arabia was killed in a motor cycle accident near here in 1935 and was buried in the churchyard of the small church, which has sand blasted windows. There is a pleasant ford through the river.

Osmington Mills Little inns look out over the sea.

Higher Bockhampton A thatched cottage where Thomas Hardy was born (NT).

Dorchester Dorset's county town. In 1685 the Bloody Assize took place, at which Judge Jeffreys condemned seventy-four men to be hanged and cut up. In 1834 the trial of the Tolpuddle Martyrs took place in a court room now owned by the TUC as a memorial. There is a County museum and a Military museum. Thomas Hardy was assistant to the restorer of St Peter's church, and lived his last years in the town. Maumbury Rings are the remains of a Roman amphitheatre built on the site of a Bronze Age stone circle. The place was used in later centuries for 'hanging fairs' at which the public could witness executions.

Osmington See Route 71.

Route 71   20 miles   32 km
OSMINGTON — LITTON CHENEY

OS 1:250 000 no. 8
Bartholomew's 1:100 000 no. 4
OS 1:50 000 no. 194

Osmington The artist Constable spent his honeymoon here. Links with Route 70.

White Horse The figure of King George III on a horse is cut in the chalk hillside.

Preston The floor of a Roman temple has been preserved (DoE, open).

Weymouth An ancient port with an attractive sea front of Georgian and early Victorian houses. It is claimed that this is where the first bathing machine was used in 1763; in 1789 King George III came to try one out while a band played 'God Save the King'. No. 3 Trinity Street was once Tudor Cottages (open); Weymouth Local History Museum illustrates local transport, bygones and shipwrecks.

a Ferries run from Weymouth to Cherbourg in France.

Portland Castle Built by Henry VIII in 1520 (DoE, open).

Isle of Portland Much disfigured by the quarries that produced the Portland Stone for many well-known buildings, including St Paul's Cathedral. The massive harbour and breakwater were started in 1872 and took 23 years to build; today they shelter a major naval base. The Portland Museum has items of local, historical and folk interest.

Chesil Beach A huge wall of shingle, 10 miles (16 km) long, swept up by sea currents. The pebbles increase in size from west to east along the bank, and were used as ammunition by the Iron Age defenders of Maiden Castle.

Abbotsbury One of the best tithe barns in the country is here, 276 foot (84 m) long, built by Benedictine monks in the 15th century, who established the famous

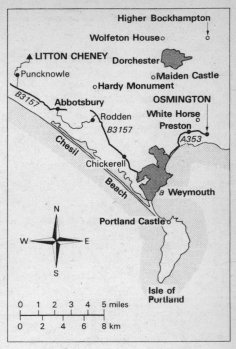

swannery that still exists. The ruins of a 12th-century abbey remain (DoE, open), and on the hill to the south is St Catherine's Chapel (DoE, open) a seamen's chapel built in the 15th century. A public footpath leads north to White Hill; fine views.

Wolfeton House Medieval and Elizabethan manor house with excellent stone and woodwork, a great hall, and a cider house (open).

Maiden Castle One of Britain's most impressive prehistoric earthworks, Maiden Castle consists of a flat plateau about half a mile long surrounded by ramparts and ditches some of which reach a depth of 90 feet (30 metres). Its population built it before the Roman era, and lived on the plateau in huts. Most tourists visit it from Dorchester, but the south-west corner can be reached from the lane to the south, and is likely to be quieter.

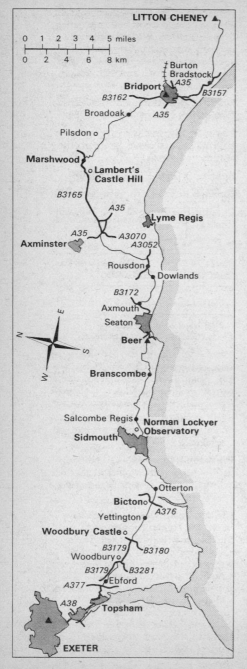

Hardy Monument A monument commemorating the Hardy who fought beside Nelson and was present at his deathbed.

Higher Bockhampton and **Dorchester** See Route 70.

Litton Cheney Links with Routes 72, 104, 105, 106.

Route 72   55 miles   88 km
LITTON CHENEY — EXETER

OS 1:250 000 no. 8
Bartholomew's 1:100 000 nos 2, 4
OS 1:50 000 nos 192, 193, 194

Litton Cheney Links with Routes 71, 104, 105, 106.

Bridport A very old ropemaking town, the wide pavements were used in the craft. A market and holiday centre; there is a local museum. Coastal walk to the west, over Golden Cap.

Marshwood The town is set in an area of small fields in Dorset's best dairy and cheese country.

Lambert's Castle Hill On the hill are an Iron Age fort and barrow. There are wide views from the top, including to Chesil Beach and as far as Dartmoor.

Axminster A market town with an attractive centre and coaching pubs. Here is the Axminster and Wilton carpet factory.

Lyme Regis Ancient port and cloth town which became a fashionable resort in the 18th century; favourite place of Jane Austen. Famous for the 19th-century fossil-hunter, Mary Anning; ammonites are easy to fine on the seashore rocks.

Beer The many nearby caves were once the haunts of smugglers.

Branscombe There is a Norman church with fine woodwork. Nearby is NT land with cliff walks and old farm buildings.

Norman Lockyer Observatory Astronomical and geophysical observatory.

Sidmouth A select resort in the 19th century. It still has some Regency and 'cottage orné' architecture.

Bicton The grounds of Bicton House include an Italianate garden and a countryside museum. Rides on steam and diesel trains.

Woodbury Castle A prehistoric hillfort.

Topsham Once a busy port, until ships became too large to reach it. The Strand boasts 18th-century 'Dutch' houses.

Exeter See Route 73. Also links with Routes 108, 109.

Route 73   17 miles   28 km
EXETER — CHAGFORD

OS 1:250 000 no. 8
Bartholomew's 1:100 000 no. 2
OS 1:50 000 nos 191, 192
1 inch:1 mile tourist map of Dartmoor

Exeter A town may have existed here as early as the 3rd century BC; it was certainly a large Roman settlement. The cathedral began as a monastic church built by Athelstan in 932 and was rebuilt by Canute in 1017; it contains fine stone and woodwork. The porticoed guildhall is believed to be the oldest municipal building in the country (the timber roof dates from 1468–70); the Hall of the Tuckers (15th century) is a reminder of the wool trade. The ship canal was the first in England (now much deepened and widened from the Elizabethan original). The quay area has port buildings dating from several centuries and a maritime museum. Medieval underground aqueducts which gave Exeter a constant supply of fresh water are open. Links with Routes 72, 108, 109.

Fingle Bridge A steep side road leads to Fingle Bridge, a riverside beauty spot.

Castle Drogo Granite Castle Drogo is England's newest castle, built early this century by Lutyens (NT).

Spinster's Rock A large cromlech.

Gidleigh Ruins of a Norman castle.

Chagford See Route 74. Also links with Route 112.

Route 74   50 miles   80 km
CHAGFORD — LISKEARD

OS 1:250 000 no. 8
Bartholomew's 1:100 000 no. 2
OS 1:50 000 nos 191, 201, 202 (just)
1 inch:1 mile tourist map of Dartmoor

For some 15 miles (25 km) this route crosses the open country of Dartmoor. There is very little shelter. While some like the bleakness of the moor, in inclement weather you may wish to wait and cross it when the skies are clearer.

Apart from the section over Dartmoor, much of the route passes through an exceptionally complex maze of lanes and patience with map-reading is necessary.

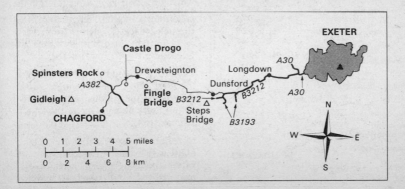

Chagford One of Dartmoor's four stannary towns in the middle ages, where all tin won from the moor had to be brought for assessment and taxation. It

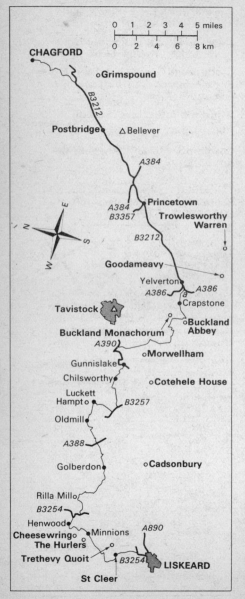

has a 15th-century granite church, with a processional cross made of metal from the first zeppelin brought down in England. The Three Crowns porch is said to be haunted by a poet who was shot there in the Civil War. Links with Route 73, 112.

Grimspound The remains of a pre-historic village. Between it and the main road to the west lies an area rich in old tin workings.

Postbridge The clapper-bridge is said to be 13th-century.

Princetown Here is the famous Dartmoor Prison, originally built in 1806 for Napoleonic War prisoners. The prisoners of war built the church.

Goodameavy Lands with the remains of a hill-fort and Bronze Age hut circles (NT).

Trowlesworthy Warren A large area with many minor prehistoric artefacts. There is also a small, ancient farmhouse, originally the warrener's house (NT).

a The lane between Yelverton and Crapstone is not shown on the Bartholomew's map of 1975.

Buckland Abbey A 13th-century monastery with gardens and a medieval tithe barn. It later belonged to Francis Drake, and now contains a museum about him (NT, open).

Buckland Monachorum The garden house is open.

Morwellham An important port in the 19th century, and now an industrial archaeology museum. Barges were lifted through 240 feet (73 metres) from river to canal up an inclined ramp by means of a huge water wheel (now restored).

Tavistock Called the 'Gothic Town of the West' e.g. the 14th-century parish church and the guildhall. Remains of 10th-century abbey. One of the stannary towns.

Cotehele House A medieval granite house with extensive collections and gardens on many levels. There is a manorial water mill. Cotehele Quay has picturesque 18th- and 19th-century buildings (NT, open).

Cadsonbury An important, probably early Iron Age hill-fort (NT).

The Hurlers A stone circle said to be a group of men petrified for playing the game of hurling on the sabbath (DoE).

Cheesewring Impressive rock formation with fine views.

St Cleer Holy well and chapel.

Trethevy Quoit A prehistoric chambered tomb, regarded as one of Cornwall's two finest.

Liskeard See Route 75. Also links with Routes 110, 111.

Route 75　　51 miles　83 km
LISKEARD — FALMOUTH

OS 1:250 000 no. 8
Bartholomew's 1:100 000 no. 1
OS 1:50 000 nos 201, 204, 200 (just)

Two ferries are included in this route, running from Falmouth to St Mawes and from Fowey to Polruan.

Certain of the seaside villages are picturesque but much visited by tourists, notably Looe, Polperro and Mevagissey. If a visit can be timed for a quiet time of day, so much the better.

Liskeard One of Cornwall's four stannary towns. The town prospered for long on the nearby copper mines. The old town is in the dip below the main road. Links with Routes 74, 110, 111.

St Keyne Collection of large musical instruments (open).

St Keyne's Well This holy well is said to give the mastery to whichever one of a couple of newlyweds first drinks its water.

Looe There are three guildhalls: one each for East and West Looe, and a newer one built after the two towns were united. Museum of Cornish culture. St Nicholas' church has interesting stories attached to it. Boat trips and shark fishing.

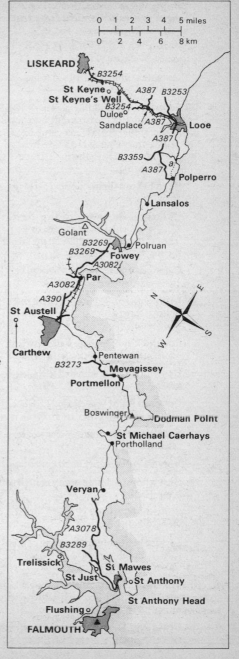

a An easily followed way links Polperro to the bay to its east. There is no defined right of way.

Polperro A quaint village in a steep valley. Walks on NT cliff-top lands.

Lansalos Church with good wood-carving.

Fowey A ship-building port in earlier times (ships for the Crusades were fitted out here), and now a china-clay port. The 14th-century church has a fine 16th-century tower. St Catherine's Castle (DoE, open).

Par A purpose-built shipping harbour for china-clay.

St Austell The town grew large after 1755, when china-clay was discovered. The prominent white 'hills' in the area are the slag from the industry.

Carthew Wheal Martyn Museum of china-clay industry.

Mevagissey A fishing port with some unusual three storey cottages, a few of them slate-hung.

Portmellon From here a cliff footpath goes south-east to Bodrugan's Leap.

Boswinger Rock arch on Hemmick beach.

Dodman Point Gorse-clad NT lands, with an Iron Age promontory fort.

St Michael Caerhays A 19th-century castle and gardens.

Veryan Five unique round cottages.

St Anthony A 13th-century church with central belfry.

St Anthony Head NT land with good views. Lighthouse.

St Just in Roseland Beautiful church-yard, with subtropical shrubberies started by a 19th-century rector.

Trelissick NT grounds including park-land, farmland, woods and gardens with rare plants (open).

St Mawes The castle is one of a pair of fortresses built by Henry VIII to defend the Fal estuary, the other being Pendennis Castle.

Flushing A village of rows of simple but pretty cottages, founded by Dutch families.

Falmouth See Route 76.

Route 76   59 miles   95 km
FALMOUTH — PENZANCE

OS 1:250 000 no. 8
Bartholomew's 1:100 000 no. 1
OS 1:50 000 nos 203, 204

In this narrow part of Cornwall it is not always possible to keep away from main roads. There are many dead-end roads and rights of way leading short distances from the route to the coast. The 1:50 000 map shows many opportunities for exploration. This route uses a ferry at Helford Passage. It operates at high water only.

Falmouth The natural harbour of Falmouth is said to be the world's third largest and one of England's finest. The town divides into the resort to the south and the port to the north, where the older buildings are to be found. Boat trips, yachting and oyster beds. Pendennis Castle, built by Henry VIII in 1543 to defend the Fal estuary, withstood a five month siege by Roundheads in the Civil War (DoE, open). The castle drive is a pleasant ride. Links with Route 75.

Port Navas The Duke of Cornwall's oyster beds.

Glendurgan NT lands with walled and water gardens, and a maze (open).

Helford Picturesque village clustered either side of a creek (cars are excluded). Nearby is Frenchman's Creek, the smugglers' haunt made famous in Daphne du Maurier's novel.

St Keverne An unusual Cornish village with a large square. The church has fine woodwork, e.g. the Jacobean pulpit.

Lowland Point Cliffs and a raised beach formed by an ice age.

Manacle Rocks Dangerous rocks which have claimed many wrecks.

Coverack A fishing village with a classic harbour and thatched cottages. The village has a long history of lifeboat rescues from wrecks on the Manacles.

Goonhilly Down The underlying serpentine rocks of the Lizard peninsula and the exposure to wind make this an area of little vegetation. On the hill is Goonhilly earth satellite radio station, where in 1962 the first live TV signals from America were received.

Cadgwith A fishing village with a clifftop chasm called The Devil's Fryingpan.

Lizard Point These high cliffs are England's most southerly mainland point. Lighthouse built in 1752.

a Several tracks cross the open land of the Lizard peninsula. A right of way for cyclists links the A3083 to Kynance Cove, which can also be reached by coastal path from Lizard Point.

Kynance Cove From the cove with its shaped rocks and caves, the best views of the multi-coloured, serpentine rock formations can be had.

Mullion Church with a tower made in part of serpentine rock. It has interesting bench ends.

Mullion Cove A famed, cliff-girt cove.

Poldhu Point The Marconi Memorial marks the place where the first transatlantic morse signals were transmitted and received in 1901.

b A track over the golf course links Poldhu and Church Coves. No defined right of way.

Helston A port until the Looe Bar formed, and a stannary town in Elizabethan times. It is famed for the Furry Dance. Charles Kingsley attended the grammar school. Folk museum.

Rinsey Ruins of tin and copper mines.

St Michael's Mount A 14th-century castle stands on the off-shore rock site formerly occupied by a Benedictine priory (NT, open).

Penzance Cornwall's first resort town. Victorian and Regency promenade. Statue of Humphry Davy who invented the safety lamp for miners, and who lived here. Museums of local interest; boat trips, including to Scilly Isles. Links with Route 77.

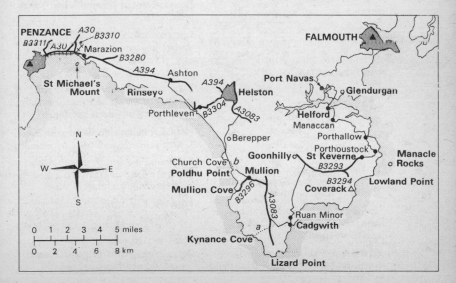

Route 77   37 miles   59 km
ST IVES — PENZANCE

OS 1:250 000 no. 8
Bartholomew's 1:100 000 no. 1
OS 1:50 000 no. 203

St Ives A prosperous pilchard port in the 19th-century, the resort of St Ives has long been popular with artists. Barbara Hepworth Museum; Barnes Museum of cinematography. Wide sands and surfing beach. Links with Route 78.

Zennor Quoit In Cornwall the term 'quoit' is applied to the remaining stone uprights and roof-slabs of prehistoric burial chambers, the earth coverings of which have long since gone. Of all such structures in England, Zennor Quoit is said to have the largest roof slab.

Zennor Head Impressive cliffs (NT).

Zennor Folk museum.

Men An Tol A prehistoric, upright, disc-shaped stone with a hole through it. It used to be the practice to pass children through the hole to cure them of diseases.

Lanyon Quoit which is unusually accessible, being directly by the road.

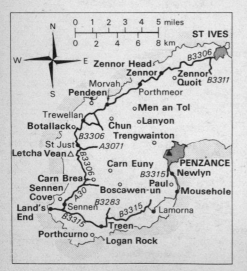

Chun A quoit and Chun Castle, the best surviving example of a Cornish hill-fort.

Pendeen A stone-lined fogou or underground burial chamber on private land.

Botallack The coastal area near Botallack has Cornwall's greatest concentration of abandoned mine engine houses, including the Botallack 1000-foot (300-m) mine shaft and 500-foot (150-m) tunnel reaching under the sea. Beware of open shafts in this area.

Letcha Vean Land's End YH.

Carn Euny Remains of prehistoric village.

Carn Brea Bronze Age barrows, with a good view from the summit.

Sennen Cove Fishing village with a round windlass house, and good beach.

Land's End A haunt of tourists. Views from the cliffs to the two lighthouses: the Longships, about a mile (1.5 km) away; the Wolf, some 8 miles (13 km) off-shore.

Porthcurno White sand strand. The Minnack is an open-air amphitheatre carved into the granite cliffs; performances in summer.

Boscawen-Un Cornwall's best-known stone circle.

Logan Rock A 66 ton rock, apparently named from the Cornish 'log', to move.

Treen The focus of a typical Cornish fishing community, with scattered granite cottages. There is an Iron Age promontory fort above the village (NT).

Paul The church has a rare epitaph in Cornish.

Mousehole Burnt by the Spaniards in 1595; the Keigwin Arms was almost the only surviving building.

Newlyn The Ordnance Survey tidal observatory is here—all heights above sea-level in Britain are given relative to Newlyn. Also a gallery of local art.

Trengwainton Parklands and gardens where sensitive plants, unable to grow elsewhere in the UK, are grown out of doors (NT, open).

Penzance See Route 76.

Route 78 39 miles 62 km
ST COLUMB MAJOR — ST IVES

OS 1:250 000 no. 8
Bartholomew's 1:100 000 no. 1
OS 1:50 000 nos 200, 203, 204

In this narrow part of Cornwall it is not always possible to keep off the main roads. However, the majority of them on this route are B roads and not too busy. Many places of interest in this area are prehistoric or associated with industrial architecture and lie distant from modern roads. You are better able to discover them on tracks and rights of way with a 1:50 000 map.

St Columb Major Slate-hung houses. A church with a semi-detached tower, brasses and carved bench-ends. Links with Route 79.

Castle an Dinas An Iron Age hill-fort with wide views from the hill summit.

Trerice A 16th-century manor house with good fireplaces and plaster ceilings (NT, open). Nearby Lappa Valley miniature railway.

Cubert Common NT land. One of England's few enclosed commons, still grazed by the commoners' stock.

St Piran's Oratory In an area of sand-dunes is the 'lost' church of St Piran, patron saint of tin miners. Built between the 7th and 10th centuries, it was buried by sand and recovered in the 19th-century.

St Piran's Round Ancient theatre; mystery plays sometimes performed.

Perranporth A good bathing beach.

St Agnes A tin-mining town till the 19th century. Functional cottages line steep slopes.

Wheal Charlotte One of several dis-used tin and copper mines in this area

of NT land.

Pool Cornish Engines, being two beam mine engines, an early application of steam power to industry (NT, open).

Phillack The sand-dune coast between here and Gwithian is rich in wild-life.

Trencrom Hill A hill with wide views, an Iron Age fort, and relics of tin-mining.

St Ives See Route 77.

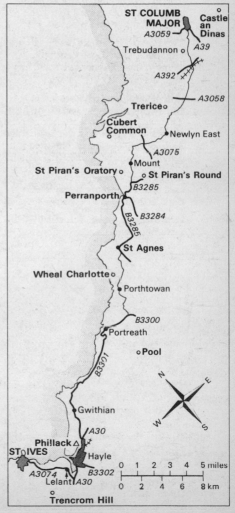

Route 79   29 miles   47 km
BOSCASTLE —
ST COLUMB MAJOR

OS 1:250 000 no. 8
Bartholomew's 1:100 000 no. 1
OS 1:50 000 nos 200, 190 (just)

Boscastle A village with some very old houses and a narrow harbour, hemmed in by cliffs, well known as a beauty spot. There is a blow-hole. Celtic farming strips are on the seaward side of the church. Links with Routes 80, 111, 112.

Tintagel Good bathing beaches near this celebrated resort. There is a 14th-century, small manor-style house now used as a post office (NT, open).

'The Island' This is Tintagel Head, a rocky promontory 300 feet (91 m) high. There was a Celtic monastery on it before the building of the Norman castle (ruins; DoE, open). The site is connected with Arthurian romances, and King Arthur is said by some to have held his court here. Views to the slate cliffs and caves of the mainland.

Penhallick Point Fine views down the coast to the south-west.

Delabole Just east of the village is one of England's largest slate quarries, which has been in use constantly since at least the reign of Henry VII.

St Kew Church with beautiful late medieval glass and carved slate monuments.

Walmsley Bird sanctuary, rich in geese and waders.

Wadebridge One of Britain's best medieval bridges.

Castle an Dinas See Route 78.

St Columb Major See Route 78.

Route 80   42 miles   68 km
CLOVELLY — BOSCASTLE

OS 1:250 000 no. 8
Bartholomew's 1:100 000 nos 1, 3
OS 1:50 000 no. 190

Between Boscastle and Hartland this route is frequently only a mile or so distant from superb coastal scenery, which can be reached and enjoyed by dead-end lanes, tracks and footpaths.

The area within a few miles of Hartland is particularly rich in farm roads and other tracks which are enclosed on both sides but which can have the appearance of lanes. Extra care with navigation is necessary.

Clovelly A famed, picturesque village, whose steep and cobbled streets are car-free. Links with Route 81.

Gallantry Bower Splendid 400-foot (130-metre) cliffs. To the west are NT lands with several old farm buildings.

Hartland The town clock dates from 1622.

Stoke Hartland's parish church of St Nectan, with a rood screen and fine tower, which may be climbed for wide

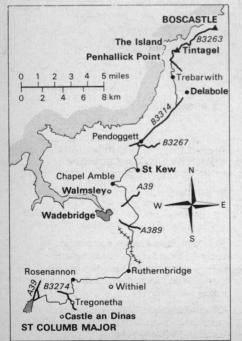

views. The parish of Hartland is vast, lying in some of the most sparsely populated farming country of the west country.

Hartland Quay Dramatic cliffs and jagged off-shore rocks.

Hartland Point Lighthouse.

a A way which is enclosed on both sides crosses the very steep-sided valley between Welcombe and Gooseham, thus linking the coastal lanes to the north and south. No defined right of way.

Morwenstow Church with fine Norman carving. Buried in the church-yard are many sailors, drowned in wrecks on the notorious rocks nearby. A past vicar, the eccentric Reverend R. S. Hawker, penned 'And shall Trelawney die', and built the vicarage with its unusual chimneys.

Hennacliff Cornwall's highest sheer cliffs, at 450 feet (140 m).

Coombe The valley stretching east-wards from the village is a beauty spot.

Poughill Church with 15th-century wall paintings and 16th-century bench ends.

Stratton An attractive small town with narrow streets and some thatched houses. The 14th-century church has brasses and a Burne-Jones window.

Launcells A 14th-century church, hardly touched by restorers.

Bude The early 19th-century canal, which extended to Launceston, carried beach-sand inland, where it was valued as a fertilizer because of its high lime content. The first Surf Life Saving Club was formed here. Ebbingford Manor (12th century) is open.

Penfound Manor Said to be one of Britain's oldest surviving inhabited manor houses, Penfound Manor once belonged to Edward the Confessor's wife. Although the building is mostly Eliza-bethan, there is still a 6-foot (2-metre) wide Anglo-Saxon wall.

Boscastle See Route 79. Also links with Routes 111, 112.

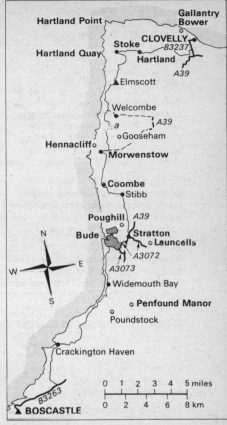

Route 81   37 miles   59 km
SOUTH MOLTON — CLOVELLY

OS 1:250 000 no. 8
Bartholomew's 1:100 000 no. 3
OS 1:50 000 nos 180, 190
1 inch:1 mile tourist map of Exmoor

South Molton This once-important coaching town has a square with many Georgian buildings. The church has a fine carved stone pulpit. Local museum. Links with Route 82.

Chittlehampton Village square with thatched cottages. The church tower is acclaimed as Devon's finest.

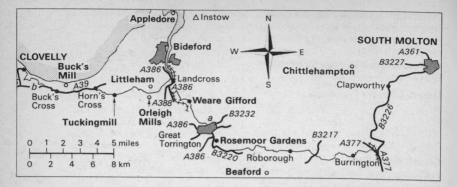

Beaford The Beaford Centre, set up in a Georgian house during this century, promotes many enterprises in arts and crafts. It has a theatre and exhibition gallery (open).

Rosemoor Gardens Started in 1959, this garden has many unusual plants, including eucalyptus and scree and alpine beds (open).

a Seasonal ferries from Great Torrington via Ilfracombe to Wales and Lundy Island via the B3232 to Barnstaple, and thence the B3230.

Weare Gifford The 15th-century Hall is now a private hotel. The village is renowned for strawberry teas.

Bideford An important port during the 16th to 18th centuries, Bideford still has some rich 17th-century merchants' houses. The bridge has twenty-four different-sized arches.

Appledore Museum of North Devon maritime history.

Littleham Church with a medieval wall-painting and a 19th-century rood screen.

Orleigh Mills A grist mill still powered by water.

Tuckingmill The village name is derived from the 15th-century fulling mill that stood here.

Buck's Mill A picturesque village reached by a very steep descent.

b The lane (Hobby Drive) is privately owned though the public may use it.

Clovelly See Route 80.

Route 82   32 miles   51 km
MONKSILVER — SOUTH MOLTON

OS 1:250 000 no. 8
Bartholomew's 1:100 000 no. 3
OS 1:50 000 nos 180 and 181

Monksilver Links with Routes 83, 107.

Cleeve Abbey The remains of a Cistercian monastery, including a 13th-century dormitory and a 15th-century refectory with a fine timber roof (DoE, open).

Dunster This town was once an important cloth centre, and still has its yarn market (DoE). The church has some good woodwork and an adjoining walled garden with dovecot and medieval tithe-barn. Dunster Castle (13th century) was remodelled in the 19th century (NT, open).

a The detour shown on the route map takes the rider through some of Exmoor's superb scenery. The A39 in the north is very scenic, affording views on the one side over wooded cliffs to the sea and on the other over a classic Exmoor valley to the moors beyond. It is, however, a major road, much used by traffic so try to avoid it at busy times.

Exford A Burne-Jones window in the small chapel.

Culbone Church This church is a likely

contender for the title 'England's smallest complete parish church'. It is in a lovely site, a stream-side glade above wooded cliffs, inaccessible by car. Coleridge wrote 'Kubla Khan' in a farmhouse near the church.

Doone Country A pleasant, river-side path leads from the village of Malmsmead deep into the moor, to an area which is associated with events in R. D. Blackmore's *Lorna Doone*.

Countisbury There are opportunities for exhilarating walking with views over land and sea on Countisbury Common to the north of the A39.

b Countisbury Hill, dropping westwards into Lynmouth, is renowned for its steepness and length. The danger is compounded by the busy traffic.

Lynmouth Lynton YH. Popular as a resort since the time of the Napoleonic Wars, Lynmouth has now recovered from its disaster of 1952, when an over-night deluge brought boulders down the river and wreaked havoc. Thatched cottages by the harbour.

Watersmeet A famed beauty spot. There is a NT shop in a 19th-century fishing lodge, and a long-established tea-garden beside the river.

North Molton The local lord was the 'mining landlord' of iron and copper mines in the area, now long since closed. There is an alabaster monument to him and his family in the church, which also has a beautiful medieval pulpit.

South Molton See Route 81.

Route 83   37 miles   59 km
CHEDDAR — MONKSILVER

OS 1:250 000 no. 8
Bartholomew's 1:100 000 no. 7
OS 1:50 000 nos 181, 182

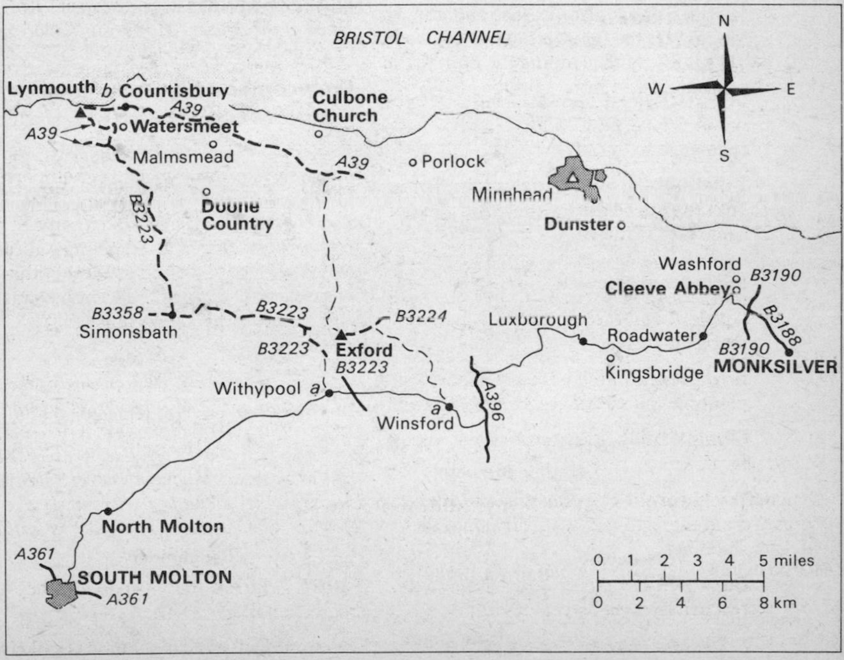

Cheddar Some 'real' Cheddar cheese is still made here; motor and transport museum. Links with Routes 84, 102, 105.

Cheddar Gorge A commercialized limestone gorge, with caves containing limestone formations, in which have been found bones of prehistoric Man and Roman coins (guided tours). The NT lands above the gorge are a nature reserve.

Axbridge Previously a base from which the Anglo-Saxon and Norman kings hunted the Mendip Hills, Axbridge still has some of its ancient atmosphere. King John's Hunting Lodge, actually a Tudor merchant's house, contains a museum (NT, open).

a If you next intend to follow Route 105 to Litton Cheney, turn to it here.

Chedzoy The church walls have grooves said to be from the sharpening of weapons in preparation for the Battle of Sedgemoor.

Sedgemoor Near the village of Weston Zoyland is the site of England's last major battle. It took place in 1685 and was fought by the followers of two of Charles II's heirs, both claiming the right to the throne.

Bridgwater In medieval times Bridgwater was an important river port. A tidal bore comes up the River Parrett twice daily. Architecturally, the best part of the town is now west of the river, Castle Street in particular being almost entirely early 18th-century. King's Square is on the site of a castle which was destroyed by Roundheads. The church contains fine woodwork and a Renaissance altar painting. Museum of Cromwellian Admiral Blake and the Battle of Sedgemoor.

Bridgwater Bay Nature Reserve Centred around the mouth of the River Parrett is an area of mud-flats and salt-marshes, now designated as a national nature reserve. It is rich in geese, ducks, waders and rare plants.

Barford Park A Georgian mansion in miniature (open).

Fyne Court The pleasure grounds of the pioneer electrician, Andrew Gosse (NT, open). Headquarters of the Somerset Trust for Nature Conservation.

Nether Stowey Coleridge wrote *The Rime of the Ancient Mariner* in 'Coleridge Cottage' (NT, open).

Crowcombe A 13th-century market

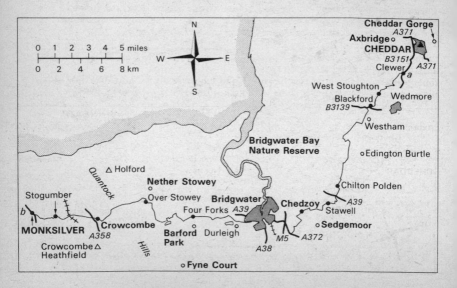

cross. The 16th-century church house is particularly well-preserved. The church has interesting bench-end carvings with pagan themes.

b The village of Monksilver is marked on Bartholomew's map no. 7 (1975) but is not named. It is by the edge of the map, some 1.5 miles (2.5 km) west of Stogumber.

Monksilver Links with Routes 82, 107.

Route 84   29 miles   47 km
BATH — CHEDDAR

OS 1:250 000 no. 8
Bartholomew's 1:100 000 no. 7
OS 1:50 000 nos 172, 182

Cheddar Gorge lies at the extreme western end of this route. It is considered by many to make a better ride if approached from the top (east), rather than from Cheddar itself.

Bath The Roman city of *Aquae Sulis*. The Roman baths, which made use of the natural hot waters, still have some of the original plumbing in working order (open). In the 18th century, and during the 'reign' of Beau Nash, it became fashionable to take the waters at Bath, and the city has many fine buildings of that era. Pultney Bridge has shops on it. The Pump Room where waters may yet be taken. The Bath Assembly Rooms house a museum of costume (NT, open). No. 1 in the Palladian Royal Crescent is furnished in the style of Bath's heyday as a spa (open). The abbey is from an earlier time, being one of the finest examples of the perpendicular style. Edgar of the

house of Wessex was crowned the first king of all England here in 973. Towpath walks beside the Kennet and Avon canal. Links with Routes 85, 92, 93, 103.

Claverton Claverton Manor, a Greek Revival house, contains an American museum, with complete American rooms of the 17th, 18th and 19th centuries.

Stony Littleton Long barrow (DoE, open).

Paulton Various gravestones in the churchyard document 19th-century cholera plagues.

Compton Martin Church with some of the best Norman architecture in the West Country.

Priddy Circles In an area with many barrows and tumuli, are these four aligned, large earthwork circles.

a If you next intend to follow Route 102 to Horningsham, you can turn off to Priddy to join it there.

Charterhouse Site of a Roman lead mining settlement to the north.

The Mendips Earlier centuries have seen lead mining in these hills, and traces of 'scruffs', or mining trenches, can still be seen. Several of the isolated pubs on top of the Mendips began in order to serve the needs of the miners.

Cheddar Gorge and **Axbridge** See Route 83.

Cheddar See Route 83. Also links with Routes 102, 105.

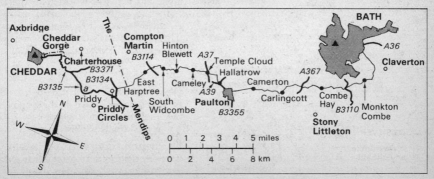

Route 85   42 miles   67 km
CIRENCESTER — BATH

OS 1:250 000 nos 8, 9
Bartholomew's 1:100 000 nos 7, 13
OS 1:50 000 nos 172, 173, 163

Cirencester This town claims to be the capital of the Cotswolds, and in Roman times it was the second most important town in Britain. The Corinium Museum has a fine collection of Roman antiquitie from the Cotswold area. The Parish Church of St John is one of the greatest and most beautiful 'wool churches' in Britain, and has many fine brasses. The Park of Cirencester House is open. Link with Routes 86, 90, 91.

Severn — Thames Canal Tunnel
The impressive entrance to the tunnel can be reached via Coates.

Source of the Thames Accessible by footpath from Coates.

Kemble Clement collection of horse-drawn, dairy and domestic items.

Oaksey The church has wall paintings and fine glass.

Tetbury An Elizabethan market town with a well-known 17th-century town hall built on three rows of pillars. Worn steps lead to the Chipping Square, the old market place. There are some fine 18th-century houses; Gothic Revival church.

Chavenage House An Elizabethan Cotswold manor house (open) with tapestried rooms and a medieval Cotswold barn.

Malmesbury One of the oldest boroughs in England, positioned on a good defensive site. Many of the honey-coloured Cotswold stone houses were built by rich weavers in the 17th and 18th centuries. The fine abbey dates from Norman times, and has outstanding Romanesque sculptures and 12th-century arches; also the tomb to King Athelstan, grandson of Alfred the Great. In the 11th century a monk tried, unsuccessfully, to fly from the abbey tower. There are old inns, almshouses, and in the high street a fine octagonal market cross. The Athelstan Museum of local history.

Westonbirt Arboretum One of the finest collections of trees in the country, including maples, rhododendrons, birches and conifers (open).

Luckington Luckington Court (open) has a fine group of ancient buildings and a garden with ornamental trees and shrubs.

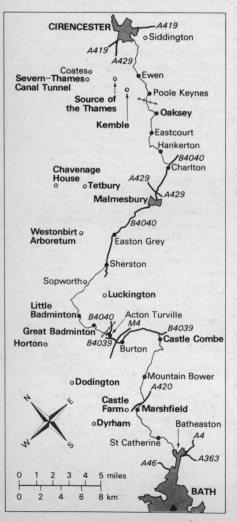

Little Badminton The Early English church is roofed with Cotswold tiles, and there is an ancient dovecot.

Horton Horton Court (NT, open) is a Cotswold manor house with a 12th-century Norman hall and an ambulatory in the grounds.

Great Badminton Grand Palladian Badminton House (open) is famous for the Three Day Event Horse Trials. This has been the home of the Dukes of Beaufort for more than three hundred years. Fine paintings and carvings (open); there are several follies and lodges in the grounds.

Dodington Splendid Dodington House (open) was designed by James Wyatt and completed in 1817. It has an enormous staircase, a museum of coaches and horse-drawn vehicles, imposing stables, a narrow gauge passenger railway and 700 acres of parkland landscaped by Capability Brown.

Castle Combe Also has claims to be Britain's most beautiful village, with its stone cottages, an arched bridge and a market cross. The castle has disappeared, but an effigy of its builder, Walter de Dunstanville, remains in the church. This was once a weaving centre, and the Weavers' House by the river was where villagers would take their woven cloth. The 17th-century manor house is now a hotel.

Dyrham The 17th-century house of Dyrham Park (NT, open) has panelling, tapestries, furniture, paintings and an ancient park with deer.

Castle Farm The farm has an old long house, once occupied by a farmer and his stock (open) and a group of 18th-century buildings containing a folk museum and craft workshop.

Marshfield Many of the houses and inns date from the time when this was the last coaching stop before arriving at fashionable Bath.

Bath See Route 84. Also links with Routes 92, 93, 103.

Route 86   39 miles   63 km
CHIPPING CAMPDEN — CIRENCESTER

OS 1:250 000 no. 7
Bartholomew's 1:100 000 no. 14
OS 1:50 000 nos 150, 151, 163

Chipping Campden A Cotswold 'wool' market town. The church has brasses and a Last Judgement window; Grevel House has a two storey bay window. Ruined

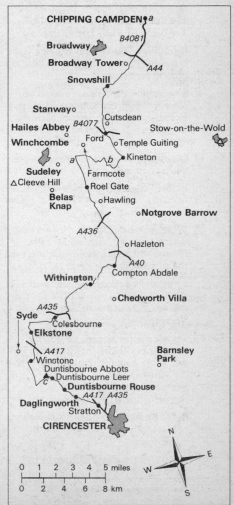

Hicks mansion was burnt by its occupants to keep it from Cromwellian hands. Links with Routes 57, 58, 87, 88 89.

a Several of the points of interest between Chipping Campden and the Winchcombe vicinity lie on or near the A46. Lying west of the route, and below the Cotswolds, the A46 is flatter but also busier than the route itself.

Broadway The 'perfect Cotswold village'. Of special interest are the Main Street, Abbot's Grange, Lygon Arms, The Tudor House, St Patrick's Tea Room and Hunter's Lodge.

Broadway Tower Built as a folly at the end of the 18th century and standing in a country park (open).

Snowshill Tudor manor with a 17th-century facade, containing collections including musical instruments, clocks, bicycles and Japanese armour (NT, open).

Stanway Tudor house with a great gate-house and a medieval tithe barn.

Hailes Abbey Set in meadowland are the ruins of a 13th-century Cistercian Hailes Abbey (DoE, NT, open).

Winchcombe In this one-time capital of the kingdom of Mercia stand St Peter's Church with its grotesque sculptures and the ancint pilgrims' George Inn.

b A short lane section here is not shown on the Bartholomew's map of 1975. The lane runs beside the river at the eastern side of Guiting Wood.

Sudeley Set in formal yew gardens stands the castle, reconstructed in 1858 but dating from the 12th century. It was the home of Katherine Parr, Henry VIII's last wife; her tomb in the chapel replaces one destroyed in the Civil War.

Belas Knap A large, neolithic long barrow, the site of many prehistoric finds (DoE, open).

Notgrove Barrow Prehistoric long barrow (DoE, open).

Withington Good church in the perpendicular style.

Chedworth Villa Mosaic pavements in one of England's best-preserved Roman villas (NT, open).

Elkstone The 12th-century church has beautifully carved Romanesque door and a dovecot over the chancel. A pagan stone by the vestry is said to be 'Ealac's Stone' from which the place name derives.

Syde Norman church. Ancient, stone-buttressed barn.

c The unusually long ford between Duntisbourne Abbots and Leer occurs where the road follows, rather than crosses, the river. There is a footpath above the river, beside the road.

Duntisbourne Rouse The beautifully simple Saxon church, stepped because of its position on a slope, contains good misericords.

Daglingworth Saxon carvings in the church.

Barnsley Park Georgian baroque mansion built in fine local stone, set in large grounds with vistas (open).

Cirencester See Route 85. Also links with Routes 90, 91.

Route 87 39 miles 63 km
CHIPPING CAMPDEN — OXFORD

OS 1:250 000 no. 9
Bartholomew's 1:100 000 no. 14
OS 1:50 000 nos 151, 164, 163 (just)

Chipping Campden See Route 86. Also links with Routes 57, 58, 88, 89.

Barton-on-the-Heath Barton House was built by Inigo Jones. Although the village is not on any county boundary now, it is in or near Gloucestershire, Warwickshire, Worcestershire and Oxfordshire, and has a four-shires stone.

Chastleton A Jacobean mansion with fine plasterwork and panelling, and original tapestries and furniture. Topiary gardens date from 1700 (open).

Rollright Stones These Bronze Age stones consist of a circle called the 'King's Men', a smaller group called the

'Whispering Knights', and a single dolmen called the 'King Stone'. They are thought to have been used in funeral ceremonies.

Great Rollright Church with a 15th-century painted rood screen, and a macabre carving on the typanum.

Great Tew A very picturesque village with thatch cottages. The trees were planted by Loudon two centries ago. The church contains brasses.

Sandford St Martin A beautiful village in Cotswold stone.

Woodstock An attractive market town, once the residence of kings, and scene of the romantic tale of Henry II and Fair Rosamund. Oxford County Museum, with stocks outside, is situated here.

Blenheim Palace John Churchill, Duke of Marlborough's defeat of Louis XIV in 1704 at Blenheim was rewarded by a gift of Woodstock Manor from Queen Anne, and government money with which to build a palace. Wren's design was rejected and John Vanbrugh's was used. The grounds, originally by Wise, were modified by Capability Brown who created the lake. The palace contains a wealth of superb treasures. It was Sir Winston Churchill's birthplace (open).

a The main road between Woodstock and Oxford has a cycle-track alongside it.

Bladon Sir Winston Churchill's grave.

b If you next intend to follow Route 91 to Cirencester, you can turn to it here.

Oxford See Route 21. Also links with Routes 22, 67, 91.

Route 88   32 miles   51 km
WORCESTER —
CHIPPING CAMPDEN

OS 1:250 000 no. 7
Bartholomew's 1:100 000 nos 14, 18
OS 1:50 000 nos 150, 151 (just)

Worcester The beautiful cathedral has a Norman crypt, cloisters, and in the centre of the fine chancel, the tomb of King John. There is a good view from College

Green. A number of interesting houses can be found in Fish Street, New Street and Foregate Street, and just outside St Peter's Gate is a 15th-century timber-framed Commandery (NT). The guild-

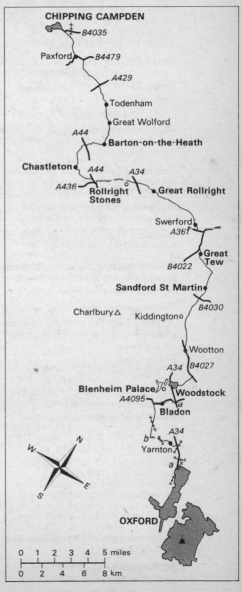

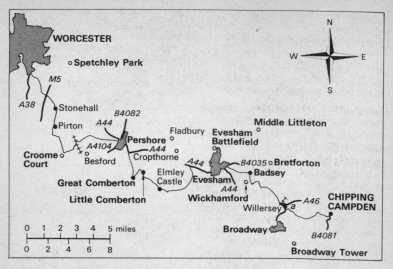

hall is built in the style of Wren and the 15th-century timber-framed and tiled Greyfriars is open (NT). The finest collection of Old Worcester porcelain in the world can be seen in the Dyson Perrins Museum of Worcester Porcelain. City Museum and Art Gallery; Tudor House Museum. Links with Route 234.

Spetchley Park The grounds are open, and feature trees, shrubs, plants, water fowl and deer.

Croome Court Built by Capability Brown. The Park has several derelict structures and is crossed by public footpaths. There is a wooden font in the Gothic revival church.

Pershore A prosperous Georgian town set in an area known for its plum orchards. There are some interesting houses, and the remains of a once magnificent abbey, destroyed during the Dissolution.

Great Comberton The round dovecot has 3-foot (1-metre) thick walls and more than 500 nesting holes. The square dovecot has 1425 holes.

Little Comberton The 17th-century Nash's Farm has a medieval dovecot.

Evesham A fruit market town. There are many fine houses and old inns, including Booth Hall and Dresden House. Two churches and a superb bell tower share the same churchyard, and there are ruins of a Benedictine abbey. The Almonry Museum contains much of local historic interest.

Evesham Battlefield Here stands an obelisk commemorating the terrible battle between Henry III's son Edward and Simon de Montford in 1265, in which 4000 perished.

Badsey The manor house was once an infirmary for the monks of Evesham.

Middle Littleton A 140-foot (43-m) long tithe barn (NT, open).

Bretforton The 14th-century Fleece Inn has a pewterware collection. There are many dovecots.

Wickhamford The church has the 'stars and stripes' tomb of one of the ancestors of George Washington.

a   If you next intend to use Route 89 to Hereford, turn to it here.

Broadway and **Broadway Tower** See Route 86.

Chipping Campden See Route 86. Also links with Routes 57, 58, 87, 89.

Route 89   56 miles   90 km
HEREFORD—
CHIPPING CAMPDEN

OS 1:250 000 no. 7
Bartholomew's 1:100 000 nos 13, 14
OS 1:50 000 nos 149, 150, 151 (just)

Hereford The cathedral was founded by King Offa of Mercia, and has fine Norman work, brasses, misericords, and an ancient fireplace. The Mappa Mundi, a rare map of the flat world drawn in the 13th century, is here, and the cathedral has the largest chained library in the world. The 14th-century church of All Saints has another chained library, and misericords. The Old House, built in 1621 and now preserved as a Jacobean period musem is open, and there is a panelled and timbered roofed hall in what is now the restaurant of the Booth Hall Hotel. The site of the house where Nell Gwynne was born is marked in Gwynne Street, and you can walk the high ramparts of Castle Green. A fine collection of Roman remains and displays of local history can be seen in the City Museum and Art Gallery, and the Churchill Gardens Museum has an extensive costume collection. Hereford is the home of the world's biggest cider factory (open). Links with Routes 90, 217, 218, 223.

Bosbury The village is the centre for the surrounding hop growing area.

Ledbury The town has several interesting buildings, including Market House, the Feathers Hotel and Talbot Inn. Two other delights are the cobbled Tudor Church Lane and the magnificent Church of St Michael.

Eastnor Pretty cottages. The 19th-century castle has pictures, armour and an arboretum (open).

Hereford Beacon An impressive Iron Age hill-fort with medieval castle earthworks within.

Midsummer Hill A 'contour' hill-fort from the Iron Age (NT); Bronze Age barrows to the south.

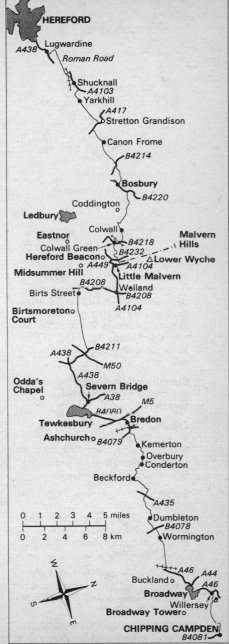

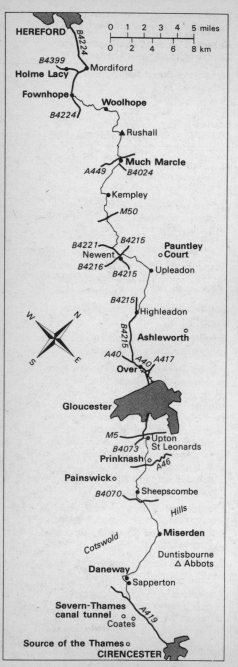

Malvern Hills There are fine walks along the ridge with excellent views.

Little Malvern The 15th-century Little Malvern Court incorporates the remains of the 12th-century Benedictine Abbey (open).

Lower Wyche Malvern Hills YH.

Birtsmoreton Court A perfect example of a medieval manor house (open).

Severn Bridge Built by Thomas Telford in 1793–96.

Tewkesbury The many old inns include Nodding Gables, the Black Bear, The Hop Pole of *Pickwick,* and the Bell Inn which was once a monastery guest house. There are good views from the tower of the abbey and a priest's hiding hole in Tudor House. King John's Bridge is medieval. There is a museum.

Odda's Chapel Saxon chapel at Deerhurst (DoE, open).

Bredon There is an interesting church, 17th-century stone almshouses, and a 14th-century tithe barn with fine porches (NT, open).

Broadway and **Broadway Tower** See Route 86.

If you next intend to use Route 88 to Worcester turn to it at Willersey.

Chipping Campden See Route 86. Also links with Routes 57, 58, 87, 88.

Route 90　　　　52 miles　83 km
HEREFORD — CIRENCESTER

OS 1:250 000 no. 7
Bartholomew's 1:100 000 no. 13
OS 1:50 000 nos 149, 162, 163

Hereford See Route 89. Also links with Routes 217, 218, 223.

Holme Lacy A pretty village with an interesting church, set in meadows.

Fownhope A village of half-timbered cottages and a church with a good Norman tympanum.

Woolhope Home of the Woolhope Society of Naturalists and Archaeologists, of much significance to geologists, and set in an area where Silurian limestone outcrops occur on the hills of red sandstone. The fine church has associations with Lady Godiva, and she is portrayed in one of the windows.

Much Marcle The beautiful church has interesting monuments and effigies. Hellens (open) is a manorial house lived in since 1292, with several superb period rooms.

Pauntley Court The fabled 14th-century Lord Mayor of London, Dick Whittington, was born in the village, and his coat of arms can be seen in the church window.

Ashleworth Tithe barn (NT).

Over Telford's bridge (DoE).

Gloucester The town was originally an important Roman fort, finds from which are in the City Museum and Art Gallery. Ancient inns include the Ravern Tavern, and two with galleried courtyards. There is an outstanding Norman and perpendicular cathedral with cloisters, monastic gardens, and a library. An excellent folk museum is in Bishop Hooper's Lodging, a 16th-century timber-framed house. There is also a Transport Museum, and a City Wall and Bastion exhibition off Kings Walk. Greyfriars Church (DoE).

Prinknash (Pronounced Prinnage) Old and 20th-century abbeys, a pottery and tea rooms.

Painswick Wool town with many 14th to 18th-century houses. Jacobean Courthouse (once a court room and bed chamber of Charles I); Lovedays, Yew Tree House; and the Little Fleece (NT); Palladian Painswick house has Chinese wallpaper (open). The churchyard is famed for its 99 clipped yews planted in 1792.

Miserden An attractive estate village with views over the valley.

Daneway A lovely pub which used to serve boatmen and 'leggers'. There is a

pleasant walk east along the towpath to the entrance of the canal tunnel.

Severn–Thames Canal Tunnel and Source of the Thames See Route 85.

Cirencester See Route 85. Also links with Routes 86, 91.

Route 91   47 miles   76 km
OXFORD — CIRENCESTER

OS 1:250 000 no. 9
Bartholomew's 1:100 000 no. 14
OS 1:50 000 nos 163, 164

Oxford See Route 21. Also links with Routes 22, 67, 87.

a If you next intend to follow Route 87 to Chipping Campden, turn to it here.

Cassington Stone and thatch cottages. Sombre Norman church with very old pews, screen and wall paintings.

South Leigh Church with medieval paintings.

North Leigh Villa Roman villa remains with a mosaic floor (DoE, open).

Witney Famed for blankets, this town has long been associated with the processing of wool from the Cotswolds, using power from the river Windrush. Two mills were mentioned in the Domesday survey. Interesting buildings include merchants' houses, the Butter Cross and the 18th-century Old Blanket Hall. Riverside Cogges hamlet boasts a church and manor house built by French monks.

Minster Lovell The ruined hall and dovecot belonged to the Lovell family, two of whom were tragically incarcerated and starved. (DoE, open).

Swinbrook Church famed for its storied tombs.

Widford A path from Swinbrook church leads to the tiny medieval church of Widford in its riverside setting.

Burford A lovely market town in mellow

stone. Many 15th-century buildings, including the Bear and Crown Inns. The church has fan vaulting and five medieval screens. Tolsey Museum has historical regalia, bygones and a Regency dolls' house.

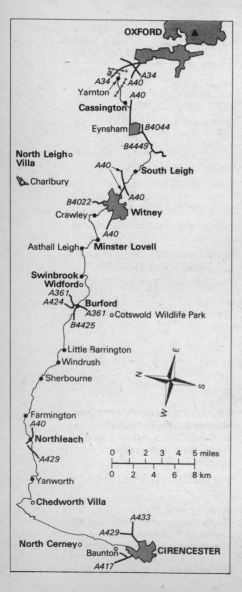

Northleach The church, said to be the 'cathedral of the Cotswolds', contains many fine brasses of rich medieval wool merchants. There are 16th-century alms-houses.

Chedworth Villa Mosaic pavements in one of England's best-preserved Roman villas (NT, open).

North Cerney A pretty village, with mill, inn and fine 18th-century houses. Delightful church with work from many periods.

Cirencester See Route 85. Also links with Routes 86, 90.

Route 92   28 miles   46 km
CHEPSTOW — BATH

OS 1:250 000 no. 8
Bartholomew's 1:100 000 no. 7
OS 1:50 000 no. 172

The merits of this route lie in its usefulness as a link between the West Country and Wales rather than in its scenic value. Several busy roads will be encountered.

Chepstow Severn Bridge YH. This town of steep, winding streets derives its name from the Anglo-Saxon for 'market place'. The river ford site was probably used by the Romans, and defended by the Norman castle, in which Henry Marten, the regicide, was captive for twenty years (DoE, open). Town walls (DoE). Bridge Street buildings have 19th-century bow windows; Beaufort Square has stocks; 17th- and 18th-century almshouses; an iron bridge of 1816, and Brunel's railway bridge. There is a museum of antiquities and photographs. At the south end of the town is Bulwarks, the ramparts of an Iron Age fort (DoE). Links with Routes 196, 208, 209, 217.

a There is a cycle path between the two roundabouts.

b When approaching the bridge look out for signs directing you to the cycle path which you have to follow to the other side of the Severn. Be wary for any maintenance vehicles that might also be using the cycle path.

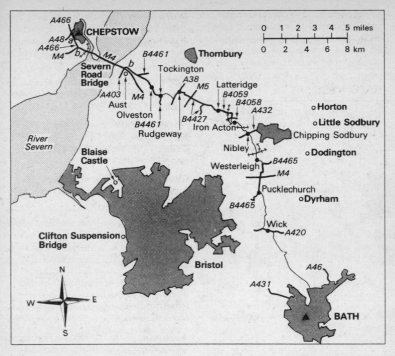

Severn Bridge Good views from this dramatic suspension bridge. It was completed in 1966, and has a central span of 3240 feet (988 m).

Thornbury The Tudor castle was built by the Duke of Cumberland, who was executed in 1521, before its completion.

Little Sodbury The 15th-century manor house (open) has a fine great hall and was where William Tyndale the 16th-century biblical translator, did much of his work.

Horton, Dodington and **Dyrham** See Route 85.

Bristol A historic city and commercial centre. It grew up around the harbour on the river Avon and was a major commercial port from the 10th century onwards. From here John Cabot sailed in 1497 to discover Newfoundland and North America; a tower commemorates his journey. The cathedral dates from the 12th century and has an organ case carved by Grinling Gibbons; the theatre Royal is the oldest existing theatre in England. John Wesley's Chapel is the oldest Methodist chapel in the world and fine St Mary Redcliffe Church dates from the 13th century. Outside the 18th-century Exchange Building are four bronze pillars known as 'nails' where merchants settled accounts, hence the phrase 'paying on the nail'. The huge ship 'Great Britain', designed by Brunel, and the first to rely primarily on screw propulsion, is being restored here (open). The first American consulate in Europe opened in Queen Street in 1792. Overlooking the Clifton Suspension bridge is St Vincent's Priory (open). Bristol City Art Gallery, Bristol City museum with archaeology, industrial and natural history displays, and St Nicholas Church and City Museum.

Clifton Suspension Bridge Built by Brunel in 1864, it spans spectacularly the Avon Gorge, and offers fine views.

Blaise Castle An 18th-century house

(open) with a folk museum and extensive woodlands.

Bath See Route 84. Also links with Routes 85, 93, 103.

Route 93   36 miles   57 km
BATH — PEWSEY

OS 1:250 000 nos 8, 9
Bartholomew's 1:100 000 nos 7, 8
OS 1:50 000 nos 172, 173

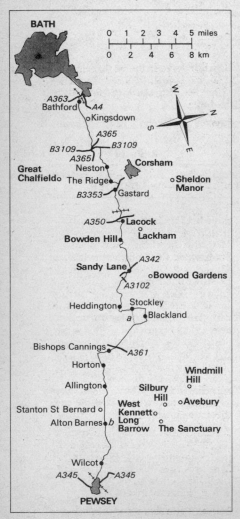

Bath See Route 84. Also links with Routes 85, 92, 103.

Corsham Old weavers' cottages, 17th- and 18th-century stone house and the Hungerford Almshouses. Corsham Court (open) is an Elizabethan mansion of 1582, with park and grounds laid out by Capability Brown and Repton.

Sheldon Manor A Plantagenet manor house (open) with a 13th-century porch, 15th-century detached chapel, and gardens containing ancient yews.

Great Chalfield A 15th-century moated manor house with a great hall (NT).

Lacock One of the most beautiful villages in England, all its buildings dating from before 1800. The 13th-century Lacock Abbey (NT, open) has medieval cloisters, sacristy and chapter house, a 16th-century stable court and a Gothic hall built in 1754. By the abbey gates is the Fox Talbot Museum with displays of early photography.

Lackham At the College of Agriculture is a museum of agricultural implements and tools.

Bowden Hill Good views across the Avon valley to Lacock.

Sandy Lane Timber-framed St Nicholas's Church was built in 1842 and is unusual for its thatched roof.

Bowood Gardens A large garden (open) with an arboretum, pinetum, rose garden, Italian garden, lake, waterfalls, caves, a Doric temple, picture gallery and chapel.

a The alternative route follows a public bridleway, while the main route detours to the north on lanes.

Silbury Hill, West Kennet Long Barrow, The Sanctuary, Avebury and **Windmill Hill** See Route 67.

b If you next intend to follow Route 67 to Oxford, you can turn to it here.

Pewsey See Route 68. Also links with Routes 67, 94.

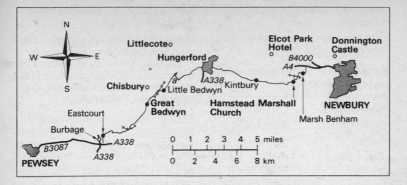

Route 94   24 miles   39 km
NEWBURY — PEWSEY

OS 1:250 000 no. 9
Bartholomew's 1:100 000 no. 8
OS 1:50 000 nos 173, 174

Newbury See Route 20. Also links with
Routes 19, 95.

Donnington Castle See Route 19.

Hamstead Marshall Church Rustic,
with a three decker pulpit.

Elcot Park Hotel A large garden laid out
in 1848 (open) with extensive views,
lawns and woodland.

Hungerford Situated on the old London
to Bath road, the Kennet and Avon canal
and the river Kennet, the last being
famous for its fish. On the Tuesday of
Easter week there is a celebration marking the award of fishing rights to the town
by John of Gaunt in the 14th century.

Littlecote A historic Tudor manor
associated with a gruesome legend concerning 'Wild' Darell, and the baby that
he cast onto a fire. It has a fine great hall,
panelled rooms, a good example of Cromwellian chapel, and splendid armour
(open).

*a A short section of lane here is not shown on
the Bartholomew's map of 1975.*

Chisbury There is an Iron Age camp
covering 15 acres and offering fine views.
Close by is a 14th-century flint chapel.

Great Bedwyn In the old flint church is
a monument to Sir John Seymour, father
of Jane Seymour who was Henry VIII's
third wife.

Pewsey See Route 68. Also links with
Routes 67, 93.

Route 95   37 miles   59 km
NEWBURY — WINCHESTER

OS 1:250 000 no. 9
Bartholomew's 1:100 000 no. 8
OS 1:50 000 nos 174, 185

Donnington Castle See Route 19.

Enborne There is Norman work in the
church, and a fine 14th-century painting
of the Annunciation.

Hamstead Marshall Church See Route
94.

*a The route follows a rough track over the
top of Walbury Hill. It can be avoided by
using a lane which drops down to the north.*

Walbury Hill At 974 feet (297 m), this is
the highest chalk down in England, and
offers superb views.

Combe Gibbet Standing on Inkpen
Hill, the hanging place of highwaymen
and felons until the early 19th century.
Close by is a neolithic long barrow, and
just to the south-west, the 954 foot
(290 m) summit of Inkpen Hill.

Combe The manor is said to have been a

haunt of Charles II and Nell Gwynn. There are good views.

Hurstbourne Tarrant A pretty village with an interesting flint church.

Wherwell A showpiece village of timbered and thatched cottages. There is part of an Anglo-Saxon cross in the church.

Stoke Charity The church has monuments and brasses.

Kings Worthy The Coach and Horses inn dates from the 16th century.

Headbourne Worthy The Anglo-Saxon church has an 11th-century rood screen.

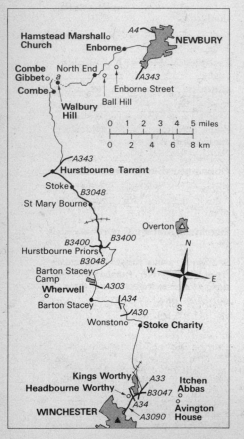

Itchen Abbas and **Avington House** See Route 9.

Winchester See Route 1. Also links with Routes 9, 97, 100.

Route 96   30 miles   49 km
WIMBORNE MINSTER — LYMINGTON

OS 1:250 000 no. 9
Bartholomew's 1:100 000 no. 5
OS 1:50 000 nos 195, 196
1 inch:1 mile tourist map of the New Forest

Wimbourne Minster See Route 70. Also links with Route 69.

Ringwood Architecture of many eras and some thatch.

Ellingham The church contains a 15th-century screen, barrel roof, handwritten tympanum and a reredos said to have been carved by Grinling Gibbons.

Arnewood Hidden from the road is Arnewood Manor, the newer counterpart of that immortalized in Marryat's *The Children of the New Forest*.

Sway Tower When cement was a new, criticized building material, this tower was built by an enthusiast to prove the strength and attractiveness of Portland cement.

a This track is almost entirely a wide, gravel farm road except for a woodland path at the southern end. The track passes Batchley Farm.

Hurst Castle Reachable either by ferry from Keyhaven, or by the long walk over the gravel spit is Hurst Castle. Within the Napoleonic fortifications is a smaller castle built by Henry VIII and in which Charles I was imprisoned (DoE, open).

b The track over Pennington Marsh is a clearly-defined one of firm earth, but there are large ruts in places so take care. At the eastern end it passes beside the corporation dump, and at the western end it starts at the quayside road. It is signposted as 'unsuitable for motors', and is not a defined right of way.

Pennington Marsh This area is also

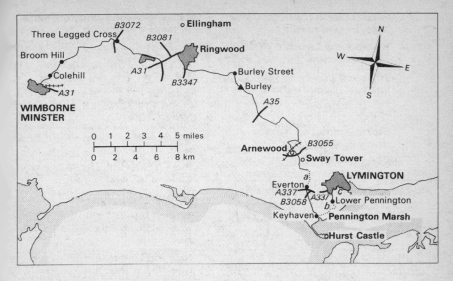

called 'the Salterns' and here the making of salt by the evaporation of sea-water was an important industry for Lymington before the exploitation of the Cheshire salt-mines. The area is now a bird sanctuary.

c Ferries to Yarmouth on the Isle of Wight.

Lymington An attractive yachting port with Georgian and 19th-century buildings. The French names on churchyard stones bear witness to the French Revolution refugees who decided to stay. Links with Route 97.

Route 97   43 miles   69 km
WINCHESTER — LYMINGTON

OS 1:250 000 no. 9
Bartholomew's 1:100 000 no. 5
OS 1:50 000 nos 185, 195, 196, 184 (just)
1 inch:1 mile tourist map of the New Forest

Winchester See Route 1. Also links with Routes 9, 95, 100.

Romsey The town grew around the Abbey. Mainly Norman, it contains old treasures and a modern door-hanging. King John's House is 13th century.

East Wellow Florence Nightingale's tomb.

Rufus Stone A much-visited memorial marking the spot where in Norman times Walter Tyrell's arrow killed William Rufus. A visit to it involves a ride along the very busy A31.

Lyndhurst The 'capital' of the New Forest where the verderers who care for the rights and animals of the commoners hold the Court of Swainmote in the Verderers' Hall. Queen's House. Venison can often be bought in the town. The churchyard is the burial place of Lewis Carroll's 'Alice'.

Beaulieu A pretty village on the estuary of the Beaulieu river. Ruined Cistercian abbey; the abbey refectory is now the parish church. Other parts are incorporated in the stately home of the Montague family (open); large motor museum.

Bucklers Hard Planned as a sugar-refining town, it remained a village of a single wide town street when the land-owner lost his sugar supply as a result of a political treaty. Later famed for ship building, some of Nelson's ships were built here; ship museum.

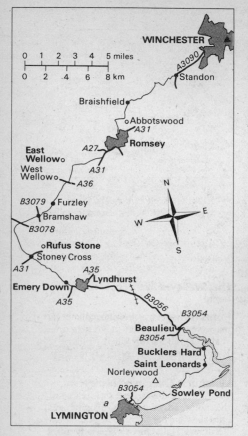

The Isle of Wight divides roughly into a backbone of chalk hills in its southern half and a low, flat area in the north. This rout passes through the flat country, with just o; foray into the hills around Downend. Rou 100 explores the island's chalk hills.

The island is immensely popular with British holiday-makers, and there are man; tourist attractions. These two Routes show just a selection of the places of interest, so visit the local information offices to discove more.

Ryde A resort with a half-mile long pier Links with Route 99.

a Ferries from Ryde to Portsmouth.

Arreton Manor A 17th-century manor with collections and a museum of childhood (open).

Newport Chief town of the island, on the river Medina. The Old Grammar School was King Charles' lodging. Buildings of note are 17th-century Chantry House, 18th-century God's Providence House and a Roman Villa. Albany steam and industrial museum.

Carisbrooke Castle A good medieval castle, housing the Isle of Wight county museum, with England's oldest working organ (DoE, open).

Newtown The Old Town Hall is 18th-century (NT, open). There are walks in the estuarine nature reserve.

Calbourne Water mill and rural museum.

b Ferries from Yarmouth to Lymington.

Yarmouth The castle was built by Henry VIII (DoE, open). Links with Route 99.

Saint Leonards The gable ends of the tithe barn belonging to the Abbey of Beaulieu, which fell out of use at the Dissolution, can be seen.

Sowley Pond The pond was created as a fish pond for the monks of Beaulieu.

a Ferries to Yarmouth on the Isle of Wight.

Lymington See Route 96.

Route 98   23 miles   37 km
RYDE — YARMOUTH

OS 1:250 000 no. 9
Bartholomew's 1:100 000 no. 5
OS 1:50 000 no. 196

Route 99   40 miles   65 km
RYDE — YARMOUTH

OS 1:250 000 no. 9
Bartholomew's 1:100 000 no. 5
OS 1:50 000 no. 196

See comments Route 98.

Ryde See Route 98.

a Ferries from Ryde to Portsmouth.

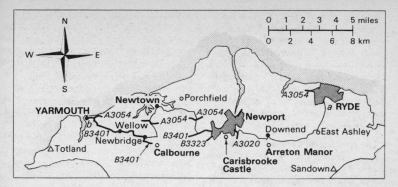

Bembridge The windmill contains much of its old wooden machinery (NT, open).

Brading This is the island's oldest house, built in the 13th century, and containing a waxwork museum. Site of a Roman villa with mosaic pavements. Nunwell House contains medieval documents and furniture (open).

Sandown Museum of the island's geology.

Appuldurcombe House The ruins of a baroque house set in grounds landscaped by Capability Brown (DoE, open).

Godshill A pretty village, but very commercialized, with a miniature village model.

St Lawrence Old Park A tropical bird park takes advantage of the sub-tropical climate of the south-facing cliffs.

St Catherine's Tower Oratory (DoE, open).

Yafford Watermill and collection of rare livestock.

b The track route is a strenuous one along the ridge of the hills, but it affords panoramic views over the island to the sea to both sides. If you are following this route towards

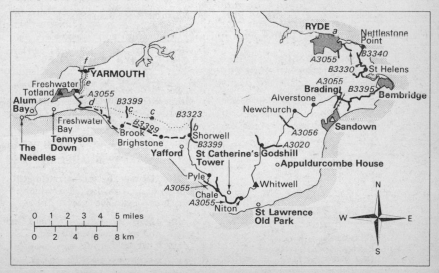

Yarmouth, turn off the B3323 onto the 'Bridle road to Freshwater', After the summit, descend along the left edge of the woods. Go right for a very short distance on the lane, then left onto a track on NT land, keeping left of Brighstone Forest. Cross the B3399 to follow the bridleway 'To Five Barrows and Freshwater'. Take the steeper track, climbing onto the ridge. Emerge through the golf course to join the A3055.

c The middle section of the track route, between the intersections of the track with the B3399 and the lane to its east, is the hardest part, with only a relatively short flat section between the uphill and downhill slopes. It is possible to use an alternative route on roads to the south for this middle section alone.

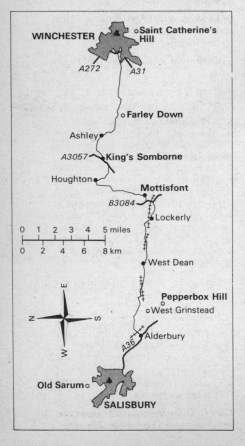

d The track route is a strenuous one along the ridge of the hills, but it affords panoramic views over the island to the sea on both sides. If you are following this route towards Ryde, follow the A3055 past the golf club entrance, then soon fork left onto a path by a NT 'Afton Down' sign. Gradually climb to the ridge-top through the golf course, then continue along it. Cross the B3399 to follow the 'Bridle road to Newport, Brightstone and Shorwell'. At a fork in the woods go left. On reaching the tarmac lane, go right onto it for a short distance, then left onto a gravel track where the lane itself forks.

Tennyson Down An area of open downland owned by the NT. A monument commemorates Tennyson. The walk to it from Freshwater Bay is fine.

Alum Bay The cliffs of the bay are of multicoloured chalk. The bay is very commercialized.

The Needles Off-shore stacks of chalk, best seen from Alum Bay, from where there are boat trips around them.

e The track between Freshwater and Yarmouth follows the course of an old railway, and is surfaced with cinder. Defined as a footpath only.

f Ferries from Yarmouth to Lymington.

Yarmouth See Route 98.

Route 100   27 miles   44 km
WINCHESTER — SALISBURY

OS 1:250 000 no. 9
Bartholomew's 1:100 000 no. 5
OS 1:50 000 nos 184, 185

Winchester See Route 1. Also links with Routes 9, 95, 97.

St Catherine's Hill See Route 9.

Farley Down The unusual monument on the summit was erected in memory of a racehorse; extensive views.

King's Somborne John of Gaunt's Deer Park, and the remains of his palace. The church has notable brasses.

Mottisfont Abbey converted during the

dissolution of the monasteries into a fine house by Henry VIII's chancellor. Rex Whistler designed the drawing room (NT, open).

Pepperbox Hill Views from the hill, which is named from the appearance of 17th-century Eyre's Folly. There are junipers; the land is NT.

Old Sarum See Route 68.

Salisbury See Route 69. Also links with Routes 68, 101.

**Route 101   23 miles   36 km
HORNINGSHAM — SALISBURY**

OS 1:250 000 nos 8, 9
Bartholomew's 1:100 000 nos 7, 8 or 5
OS 1:50 000 nos 183, 184

Horningsham A group of lime pollards by the inn is known as 'The Twelve Apostles'. The Scotland chapel was built for the Scottish artisan builders of Longleat. Links with Routes 102, 103, 104.

Stockton Pretty cottages, almshouses, and a 14th-century church.

Wylye The chequer-work stone and flint cottages are typical of the area. There are some Georgian buildings, and a restored Perpendicular church with a fine carved Jacobean pulpit.

Dinton Philipps House (NT, open) is a neo-Grecian house designed in 1816, and set in a park. The village is delightfully situated and has a Tudor manor house called Little Clarendon, and 17th-century Lawes Cottage, which belonged to the composer friend of John Milton, William Lawes.

Great Wishford Old cottages, alms-houses, and a church with interesting tombs. On the east wall of the churchyard is a record of the price of bread since 1800. On the hill to the south west is Grovely Wood where villagers have an ancient right to collect free firewood.

Wilton Once the capital of Saxon Wessex, and famous for carpet making

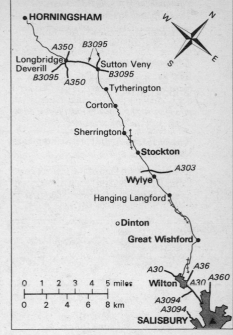

since the 17th century. There is an 18th-century market house and a Gothic church restored by the former American ambassador, Robert Bingham, in 1937. Wilton House (open) was reconstructed after a fire in 1647 by Inigo Jones and is notable for its single and double cube rooms, state rooms, furniture and fine collection of pictures. There is an exhibition of seven thousand model soldiers.

Salisbury See Route 69. Also links with Routes 68, 100.

**Route 102   32 miles   51 km
CHEDDAR — HORNINGSHAM**

OS 1:250 000 no. 8
Bartholomew's 1:100 000 no. 7
OS 1:50 000 nos 182, 183

Cheddar Gorge lies at the extreme western end of this route. It is considered by many to make a better ride if approached from the top (east), rather than from Cheddar itself.

Cheddar See Route 83. Also links with Routes 84, 105.

Cheddar Gorge See Route 83.

The Mendips, Charterhouse and **Priddy Circles** See Route 84.

a If you next intend to follow Route 84 to Bath, you can turn to it here.

Ebbor Rocks An impressive limestone cleft (NT).

Wookey Hole One of the major cave complexes in Britain (open), once occupied by Stone Age hunters. The first

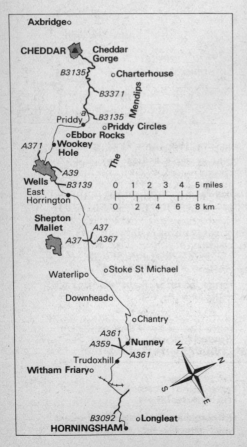

three chambers are now floodlit, revealing stalagmites and stalactites, and the river Axe. The Wookey Hole Museum has human and animal remains that were found in the caves, and is the storeroom of Madame Tussaud's famous waxworks. It also has Lady Bangor's fairground collection—the greatest collection of fairground carvings of its kind—and a paper mill, making handmade paper.

Wells The 12th-century cathedral has a fine west front and north porch, chapterhouse, cloisters, and lady chapel. In the north transept is a remarkable 14th-century clock, across the face of which knights joust on the hour. Through the nearby Chain Gate is Vicar's Close, a street of 14th-century houses. The Bishop's Palace (open) dates from the 13th and 15th centuries and is enclosed by 14th-century fortifications. There is an ancient guildhall and many old pubs; the City Arms used to be the city gaol. The Wells Museum has prehistoric finds from Wookey Hole, local bygones and historic displays, and fossils and rocks from the Mendips. Between the cathedral green and market place is Penni-Less Porch where beggars would collect money.

Shepton Mallet Once an important wool centre, now an agricultural town known for its cheese making. The church has a fine carved ceiling and a stone pulpit. There is a good market cross and remains of the medieval Shambles (meat market). North west of the market place is a maze of interesting little lanes.

Nunney A pretty village surrounds the shell of a 14th-century moated castle destroyed by Cromwell in the Civil War (DoE, open).

Witham Friary Parts of the church and a dovecot are all that remain of the first Carthusian monastery to be founded in England. Crossing the lane to the north is the course of a Roman road which probably once led to the Roman lead mines in the Mendips.

Longleat Renaissance-style Elizabethan house sumptuously decorated in the Italian style, with ornate ceilings; it has state rooms and Victorian kitchens. The grounds were landscaped by Capability Brown, and include a safari park (open).

Horningsham See Route 101. Also links with Routes 103, 104.

Route 103   24 miles   39 km
BATH — HORNINGSHAM

OS 1:250 000 no. 8
Bartholomew's 1:100 000 no. 7
OS 1:50 000 nos 172, 173, 183

Bath See Route 84. Also links with Routes 85, 92, 93.

a The main route between Bath and Bradford-on-Avon is, for the most part, easy going along a river valley, but it does make some use of the busy A4. The alternative is quieter, but involves the ascent and descent of a hill. If you wish to visit Claverton Manor you should in any case follow the alternative route.

Claverton See Route 84.

Bradford-on-Avon This town has prospered for centuries, and consequently its narrow, winding streets have many pleasant buildings of different eras and styles. There is an almost complete 8th-century, Anglo-Saxon church, a medieval bridge with a chapel, later used as a lock up; and a fine, large, 14th-century tithe barn (DoE, open). The 12th-century church contains the first English bible ever to be used in a church.

Great Chalfield Manor A 15th-century moated manor house with a great hall (NT, open).

The Courts On the outskirts of Holt lies The Courts, gardens with a topiary and arboretum. Centred on an 18th-century house, the gardens are open to the public (NT, open).

Westwood A 15th-century stone manor house with Gothic and Jacobean windows; modern topiary (NT).

Farleigh Hungerford The castle contains a museum of arms and armour, especially of the civil war era, and

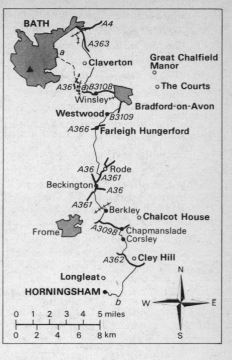

medieval stained glass (DoE, open).

Chalcot House A small, 17th-century Palladian manor (open).

Cley Hill A chalk hill surmounted by an Iron Age hill-fort with two bowl-barrows (NT).

Longleat See Route 102.

b If you next intend to follow Route 101 to Salisbury, you can turn to it here.

Horningsham See Route 101. Also links with Routes 102, 104.

Route 104   58 miles   93 km
HORNINGSHAM — LITTON CHENEY

OS 1:250 000 no. 8
Bartholomew's 1:100 000 nos 4, 7
OS 1:50 000 nos 183, 194

Horningsham See Route 101. Also links with Routes 102, 103.

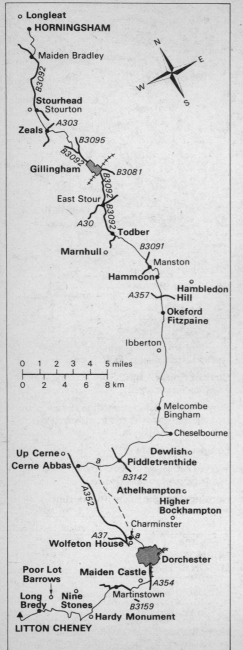

Longleat See Route 102.

Stourhead An 18th-century Palladian house set in landscaped garden with temples and lakes. (NT, open).

Zeals A pretty village with thatch, affording good views.

Gillingham Old silk mill.

Todber Celtic cross in the churchyard.

Marnhull This is supposed to be 'Marlott' where Tess in Thomas Hardy's *Tess of the d'Urbervilles* was born. The church has a Burne-Jones window.

Hammoon The manor of William de Moion, who brought forty-seven knights to the Battle of Hastings. The church has a 15th-century stone reredos rescued from a London junk-heap.

Hambledon Hill Earthworks of a neo-lithic camp with long barrows.

Okeford Fitzpaine Good church pulpit.

Dewlish Queen Anne house (open).

Piddletrenthide A long, narrow valley-bottom village of yellow stone. The church has interesting gargoyles.

a Alternative to the main route which follows a valley-bottom A road, is a quieter lane over a spur of high land. If you wish to ride the alternative route but also visit the Cerne Abbas Giant, you must drop down from the spur to the village, and climb up the same road again.

Cerne Abbas During, or even before, Roman times the picture of a man was cut into the turf of a hillside. Called The Giant, it can now best be seen from the main road at the north end of the village. Cerne Abbas village incorporates a gatehouse, tithe barn and guest house remaining from an abbey founded in the 10th century. The church has 14th-century wall-paintings and a Jacobean pulpit.

Up Cerne A pretty hamlet with a manor house.

Wolfeton House, Maiden Castle and **Hardy Monument** See Route 71.

Dorchester and **Higher Bockhampton** See Route 70.

Athelhampton One of England's finest medieval manors, set in large grounds (open).

Nine Stones Prehistoric stone circle (DoE).

Poor Lot Barrows Barrows in an area of many tumuli (DoE).

Long Bredy Just south-east of the village lies Kingston Russell House, in medieval times the seat of the Duke of Bedford's ancestors. The impressive 18th-century frontage can be seen down its drive.

Litton Cheney Links with Routes 71, 72, 105, 106.

Route 105   52 miles   84 km
CHEDDAR — LITTON CHENEY

OS 1:250 000 no. 8
Bartholomew's 1:100 000 nos 4, 7
OS 1:50 000 nos 182, 183 (just), 193, 194

Cheddar See Route 83. Also links with Routes 84, 102.

a If you next intend to follow Route 83 to Monksilver, you can turn to it here.

Wedmore It is thought that this is where King Alfred reached a treaty with the Danes.

Godney In earlier times a marshy lake lay between what are now Godney and Meare. A village of huts on stilts and brushwood mounds existed on and around the lake.

Glastonbury In legend, Joseph of Arimathaea buried the chalice used at the Last Supper below a spring on Glastonbury Tor. He stuck his staff into the ground, and it grew into the winter-flowering Glastonbury Thorn. There are wide views to be seen from the Tor summit. Also in legend, King Arthur and Queen Guinevere were reburied in the abbey (open). From the 13th to the 19th centuries Glastonbury was a wool centre. Glastonbury Tribunal (DoE) houses a museum of local interest, including

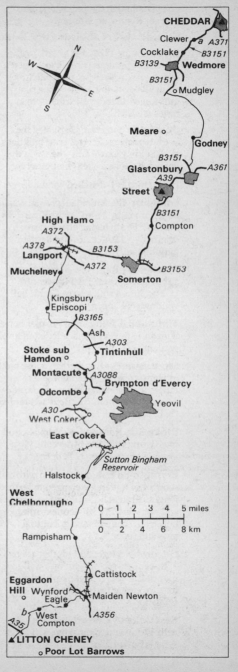

objects found in the prehistoric lake village; Rural Life Museum.

Meare Abbot's Fish House (DoE, open).

Street In the 1820s a Mr Clark made modest beginnings with a shoe concern which rapidly grew, as then did Street from village to town. There is a shoe museum with footwear from Roman times onwards.

Somerton Somerset's capital in the West Saxon era. Several good buildings are built in yellow Ham stone, and the church has an excellent tie-beam roof.

High Ham NT thatched windmill.

Langport The settlement grew in Anglo-Saxon times by a ford on the River Parrett. The 'hanging chapel' was originally a 15th-century tradesmen's guildhouse.

Muchelney Ruins of a Benedictine abbey (DoE, open). A 14th-century priests' house with a large Gothic hall window (NT, open).

Tintinhull A 17th-century manor house with an 18th-century facade, set in lovely gardens (NT, open).

Montacute An Elizabethan house built in Ham stone, with heraldic glass, tapestries, panelling and furniture and portrait collections. Gardens and topiary (NT, open).

Stoke Sub Hamdon A group of buildings dating from the 14th century, intended for priests (NT, open).

Brympton d'Evercy Mansion with state rooms and a staircase claimed to be the longest straight one in England. Gardens and vineyard. A 13th-century priests' house now contains an agricultural museum (open).

Odcombe A legend holds that a son of a 17th-century rector went on a walking tour of Europe, returning with the first fork for eating with to be used in England.

East Coker A lovely Ham stone village with 17th-century almshouses. T. S. Eliot is buried here.

West Chelborough Charming hamlet.

Eggardon Hill An impressive Iron Age hill-fort, with grain storage pits.

b   If you next intend to follow Route 106 to Sampford Arundel, turn to it here.

Poor Lot Barrows See Route 104.

Litton Cheney Links with Routes 71, 72, 104, 106.

Route 106   62 miles   100 km
SAMPFORD ARUNDEL —
LITTON CHENEY

OS 1:250 000 no. 8
Bartholomew's 1:100 000 no. 4
OS 1:50 000 nos 193, 194

Sampford Arundel Links with Routes 107, 108.

Wellington Hill On NT land stands a Wellington monument.

Forde Abbey A 12th-century Cistercian monastery possessing the famed Mortlake tapestries and set in large, attractive grounds (open).

Pilsden Pen Dorset's highest hill, surmounted by an Iron Age earthwork. It affords superb views over fertile Marshwood Vale to the south.

Broadwindsor A plaque on a cottage commemorates a stay by Charles II. The church has a fine 16th-century pulpit.

Stoke Abbott A pretty village.

Beaminster Although much of the town was rebuilt after Civil War fires, it is architecturally pleasing with its warm, golden stone. Almshouses date from 1603. The church has a tower with interesting sculptures, and within is an unusual monument with figures dressed as Romans.

Parnham A Tudor manor house, now used as a school for craftsmen in wood. There are large grounds with formal and water gardens. House, grounds and workshop are open.

Mapperton Terraced and hillside gardens including a classical orangery and an 18th-century summerhouse (open). The village that once surrounded the manor was wiped out by the great plague of 1660.

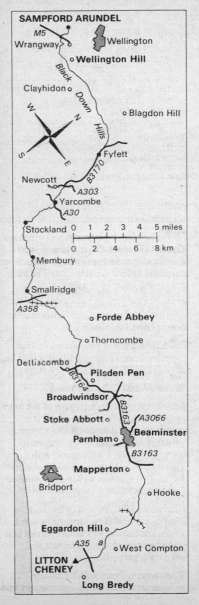

SAMPFORD ARUNDEL

M5
Wrangway
Wellington
o Wellington Hill
Black Down Hills
Clayhidon o
o Blagdon Hill
Fyfett
Newcott
B3170
A303
Yarcombe
A30
Stockland

0 1 2 3 4 5 miles
0 2 4 6 8 km

o Membury
o Smallridge
A358
o Forde Abbey
o Thorncombe
Detliscombe
B3164
Pilsden Pen
Broadwindsor
B3162
Stoke Abbott o
A3066
Parnham o
Beaminster
B3163
Mapperton o
Bridport
o Hooke
Eggardon Hill o
A35 a
o West Compton
LITTON CHENEY
Long Bredy

Eggardon Hill See Route 105.

a If you next intend to follow Route 105 to Cheddar, you can turn to it here.

Long Bredy See Route 104.

Litton Cheney Links with Routes 71, 72, 104, 105.

| **Route 107** | 42 miles | 67 km |
MONKSILVER —
SAMPFORD ARUNDEL

OS 1:250 000 no. 8
Bartholomew's 1:100 000 no. 3
OS 1:50 000 no. 181

This route swings considerably to the west in order to take in some of the exhilarating scenery of high, open hills and deep river valleys to be found at the eastern edge of Exmoor and in the Brendon Hills. It is consequently a fairly strenuous route. A more direct route between Monksilver and Sampford Arundel would cross the lower but nevertheless hilly area where the hills start to rise out of the Vale of Taunton Deane to the east.

Monksilver Links with Routes 82, 83.

a Between the points marked 'a' on the route map, the main route runs along a spur of high land between two deep river valleys. The alternative follows one of these winding, wooded valleys, but uses an A road which might be busy at times.

Dulverton This town has served as a centre for south-east Exmoor for several centuries, and has thus acquired buildings of many architectural styles. It has a clapper bridge and is a hunting centre, with salmon and trout rivers.

Combe Head Arboretum with unusual trees and shrubs, and collections of climbers and roses (open).

Bampton The town is well known for its fair in late October, when Exmoor ponies are rounded up and sold.

Knighthayes A 19th-century house containing collections of Old Master paintings. Grounds with woodlands, shrub and formal gardens (NT, open).

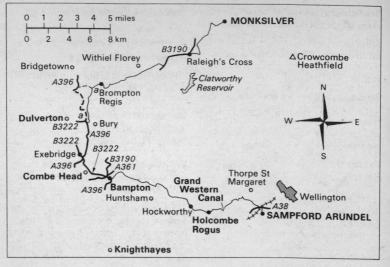

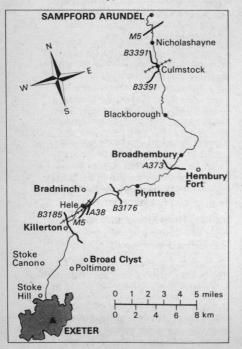

Holcombe Rogus Holcombe Court is a fine Tudor house. It was built for the Bluett family, who have monuments and a family pew in the adjacent 15th-century church.

Grand Western Canal At this point the route crosses the canal which was intended to link the Bristol and English Channels. Parts of it were constructed early in the 19th century, but it was never completed.

Sampford Arundel Links with Routes 106, 108.

Route 108   27 miles 44 km
SAMPFORD ARUNDEL — EXETER

OS 1:250 000 no. 8
Bartholomew's 1:100 000 no. 3
OS 1:50 000 nos 192, 193

Sampford Arundel Links with Routes 106, 107.

Broadhembury A classic example of a thatched village.

Hembury Fort The earthworks of a fort in use during the first two centuries BC and the first century AD. The hill-top site affords superb views.

Plymtree Church with a 15th-century rood screen adorned with painted panels.

Bradninch This was an important town in the heyday of the Devon wool industry.

Killerton An 18th-century house, with a theatrical costume collection. Large grounds with views and rare trees and shrubs (NT, open).

Broad Clyst Many of the buildings in this village belong to the NT. There is a restored river mill, a church with a red and grey tower and fine Jacobean monuments.

Exeter See Route 73. Also links with Routes 72, 109.

Route 109   90 miles   144 km
EXETER — SALCOMBE

OS 1:250 000 no. 8
Bartholomew's 1:100 000 no. 2
OS 1:50 000 nos 192, 191, 202

This route requires the use of a ferry between East Portlemouth and Salcombe. The main part of the route loops to the north-west, exploring Dartmoor. There are several ways of omitting this loop, for example by using coastal roads between Dawlish and Dartmouth, although these will be busy.

Exeter See Route 73. Also links with Routes 72, 108.

Powderham Medieval Powderham Castle (open) is the seat of the Earls of Devon, with rich furnishings, a music room by Wyatt, a picture collection and a park with deer.

Dawlish The town developed as a resort in the 18th century, and has associations with Jane Austen. It is notable for the Lawn, a fine landscaped garden, and the seafront railway was partly designed by Brunel.

Ashcombe Pleasant church.

Chudleigh A small market town. To the south-west are Chudleigh Rocks, a limestone outcrop with prehistoric caves.

Moretonhampstead There is a 15th-century granite church and row of 17th-century almshouses.

Cranbrook Castle An Iron Age hill-fort.

Castle Drogo, Gidleigh and **Fingle Bridge** See Route 73.

North Bovey A thatched village well known for its prettiness. The church dates from the 15th century.

Grimspound See Route 74.

Hamel Down There are some Bronze Age barrows on the west side of this hill.

Widecombe in the Moor An attractive moorland village usually overrun with tourists. The 14th-century church has a fine tower paid for by local tin miners and an interesting story associated with the collapse of a pinnacle during a storm in 1638 with fatal results. Widecombe Fair, which takes place here each September, has been made famous by the song about Uncle Tom Cobleigh's grey mare.

Dartmeet The confluence of the rivers East Dart and West Dart, a famous beauty spot, where a typical clapper bridge crosses the East Dart.

Holne The 13th-century church has a medieval screen. Charles Kingsley, the Victorian writer, was born at the vicarage.

Ashburton Once a stannary town and coaching stop on the Exeter to Plymouth road. The church has a fine tower, and Ashburton Museum has local antiquities and bygones.

Buckfast The abbey was built by Benedictine monks, and completed in 1938.

Buckfastleigh The northern terminus of the Dart Valley Railway, owned by steam train enthusiasts, which runs to Totnes through delightful scenery.

Dartington Hall A medieval estate bought in 1925 by a rich American lady and her English husband, who rebuilt the Hall using local labour (open). It has developed into a centre of research, education and crafts, Dartington glass being well known.

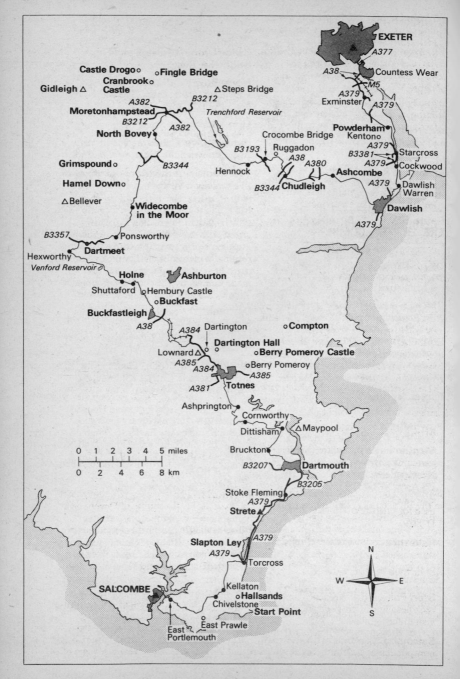

Totnes In medieval times this was a rich cloth town. Walls and keep remain of the 13th-century castle (DoE, open).
St Mary's Church has a fine rood screen, the guildhall is 16th-century, and in the high street is the arcaded Butterwalk. This is the southern terminus of the Dart Valley Railway, run by steam train enthusiasts on a scenic line up to Buckfastleigh. Elizabethan House museum of period furniture, costumes and local history; Devonshire Collection of period costume.

Berry Pomeroy Castle Magnificent ruins dating from the 14th century standing in woods above a ravine.

Compton A fine example of a medieval fortified manor house (NT, open) with a restored great hall.

Dartmouth A historic port in a fine setting, now a holiday resort. The 15th-century castle (DoE, open) guarded the estuary. Arcaded houses, known as the Butterwalk, date from the 17th century; one is the Town Museum. Close by is the Engine House with the first effective steam engine, invented by Thomas Newcomen. Also of interest are St Saviour's Church, another castle at Bayards Cove (DoE, open), Agincourt House and the customs house. Just to the north of the town is the Royal Naval College.

Strete Start Bay YH.

Slapton Ley A nature reserve. Reeds for thatching grow around the fringe. Nearby is a memorial presented by the US Army to local people who had to evacuate their homes while the beach was used for practice landings prior to D-Day.

Hallsands In 1903 and 1917 the village was washed away following the dredging of protective shingle. The ruined houses can still be seen.

Start Point A fine walk out along this rock headland offers good views and a visit to the lighthouse.

Salcombe A beautifully situated town, now popular as a yachting centre. It has a mild climate and an almost Mediterranean atmosphere. Near North Sands beach is a ruined Tudor castle. Links with Route 110.

Route 110   58 miles   92 km
LISKEARD — SALCOMBE

OS 1:250 000 no. 8
Bartholomew's 1:100 000 no. 2
OS 1:50 000 nos 201, 202

This route involves the use of a ferry between Cremyll and Plymouth.

Liskeard See Route 75. Also links with Routes 74, 111.

St Germans A pretty village overlooking a small harbour. It was a cathedral city until the 11th century. The priory church remains, and has a fine Norman doorway. The east window was designed by Burne-Jones. There is a memorial to Edward Eliot, whose family house can be seen from the churchyard. To the west of the village are some almshouses, and to the east an old stone shipping quay.

Anthony House A grand 18th-century house (NT, open) with fine furniture, panelling, china, needlework and extensive grounds. Half a mile away by the river Lynher is the Bath Pond House, built in 1784.

Mount Edgcumbe The fine gardens and park (open) have good views over Plymouth Sound. The house was bombed in 1941.

Plymouth The largest city in, though not the capital of, the county of Devon, on a fine site between the estuaries of the Tamar and Plym. It has been an important port since the 13th century and has associations with many famous seafarers: Hawkins, Raleigh, and Frobisher sailed from here and Sir Francis Drake played his famous game of bowls on the Hoe before setting out to destroy the Spanish Armada. The Pilgrim Fathers in 'The Mayflower' left from here in 1620 for America and so also departed James Cook and Sir Francis Chichester on voyages of

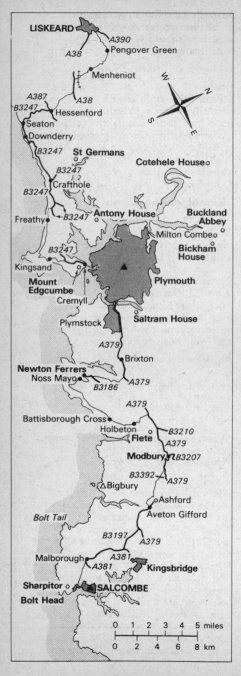

world circumnavigation. The Citadel was built by Charles II in the 17th century, and on the Hoe is Smeaton's Tower, the lighthouse that once stood on the Eddystone Rocks. It is also a good viewpoint. There are excellent views from the top of the Civic Centre. At 32 New Street is Elizabethan House (open), a 16th-century house with period furnishings. The City Museum and Art Gallery has paintings, porcelain, ships' models and local history displays.

Bickham House A shrub garden (open) with good views.

Buckland Abbey and **Cotehele House** See Route 74.

Saltram House Originally a Tudor House, with two fine rooms by Robert Adam, period furniture, china and pictures, and a garden with an orangery and octagonal summer house (NT, open).

Newton Ferrers The waterfront is attractive, and the estuary is a popular anchorage.

Flete The house is built around an Elizabethan manor (open).

Modbury A picturesque market town with Georgian and slate-hung houses. The Exeter Inn has been used since Elizabethan times, and the church has a medieval spire.

Kingsbridge A small market town which until the 19th century was a commercial port. The Shambles is an 18th-century arcaded building and St Edmund's Church has a 13th-century tower. The Cookworthy Museum in the old Grammar School describes local history and the life of William Cookworthy, who discovered china clay in Cornwall and made the first true porcelain in England.

Sharpitor The Overbecks Museum has collections of local interest, bygones, and a section on local shipbuilding (NT). The garden overlooks the entrance to Salcombe Harbour and has many rare plants.

Bolt Head Fine coastal scenery between here and Bolt Tail can be explored using footpaths which form part of the designated long distance South Devon Coast Path.

Salcombe See Route 109.

Route 111   28 miles   44 km
BOSCASTLE — LISKEARD

OS 1:250 000 no. 8
Bartholomew's 1:100 000 no. 1
OS 1:50 000 nos 200, 201, 190 (just)

Boscastle See Route 79. Also links with Routes 80, 112.

a If you next intend to follow Route 79 to St Columb Major, turn to it here.

The Island, Tintagel, Penhallick Point and **Delabole** See Route 79.

Lanteglos This was once a Celtic settlement, and there are two large Iron Age hill-forts to the north-west.

Helsbury Castle An earthwork with a ruined chapel associated with a Celtic saint. Good views.

Blisland The part Norman church has a coloured and finely carved screen, a Jacobean pulpit, carved roof beams and a brass. The village has a green—an unusual feature in Cornwall.

b The main route is fairly direct and skirts the south of Dodmin Moor, while the alternative route explores part of it and passes several places of interest.

Brown Willy At 1375 feet (419 m) this is the highest hill on Bodmin Moor.

Stripple Stones This circle of standing stones is one of the most impressive prehistoric monuments on the moor.

Temple The Knights Templars had a chapel here in the Middle Ages.

King Arthur's Hall An enclosure thought to have been built in about 2000 BC as a shelter for livestock.

Bolventnor A tiny hamlet. Jamaica Inn is the title and setting of Daphne Du Maurier's famous novel about smugglers.

Dozmary Pool This is, according to legend, the bottomless pool into which King Arthur's sword Excalibur was flung.

St Cleer and **Trethevy Quoit** See Route 74.

St Neot The church has exceptional stained glass, much of which dates from the 15th and 16th centuries. One of the windows describes the extraordinary St Neot, who according to legend was only 15 inches (38 cm) high. There is a holy well in the village.

Liskeard See Route 75. Also links with Routes 74, 110.

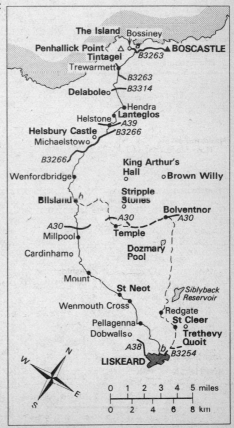

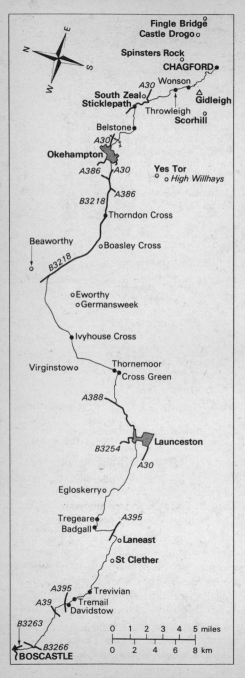

Route 112   52 miles   83 km
CHAGFORD — BOSCASTLE

OS 1:250 000 no. 8
Bartholomew's 1:100 000 nos 1, 2, 3 (just)
OS 1:50 000 nos 190, 191, 201

Chagford See Route 74. Also links with Route 73.

Fingle Bridge, Castle Drogo, Spinsters Rock and **Gidleigh** See Route 73.

Scorhill A fine stone circle.

South Zeal Once a copper mining village with an early 16th-century manor house which became a pub and is said to be haunted.

Sticklepath Museum of rural industry with a 19th-century iron foundry.

Yes Tor This and High Willhays are the two highest tors of Dartmoor, offering superb views. Use by the military sometimes prohibits access.

Okehampton To the west of this market town are castle remains dating back to Norman times (DoE, open).

Launceston An old market town. The unusual Church of St Mary Magdalen has carvings covering the outside walls and 12th-century St Thomas's Church has the largest font in Cornwall. There are two 16th-century bridges, and the remains of a 12th-century Augustinian priory. There are good views from the remains of the 13th-century castle. The impressive South Gate, spanning the main street, was once part of the town wall. Lawrence House (NT) contains the borough museum.

Laneast A beautiful little church with a delightful interior. The bench ends are all carved and there is a 16th-century pulpit. Outside is a Celtic wheel cross.

St Clether Reached by footpath to the north west of the village is a 15th-century holy well chapel consisting of granite slabs.

Boscastle See Route 79. Also links with Routes 80, 111.

NORTHERN ENGLAND AND SOUTHERN SCOTLAND

This region contains half the National Parks of England and Wales, so it is not surprising to learn that it offers plenty of the wilder sort of beauty, although there are no vast, remote areas. Even in the most rugged parts, the haven of a green and pleasant valley is rarely far away, and the moderate sprinkling of villages will allow scope for buying food given just a little forethought.

Running from the Peak District northwards almost to the Scottish border, the Pennines form the backbone of northern England. Sometimes rising to over 2000 feet (650 metres), their broad moorlands divided by long valleys continue and widen out to become the Scottish Southern Uplands. In stark contrast to the scenic heights of this region, there are large industrial areas and flat farmlands, the latter around the Pennines and Southern Uplands, and across to the splendid heights of the Lake District and North York Moors. The heavily built-up and industrialized areas

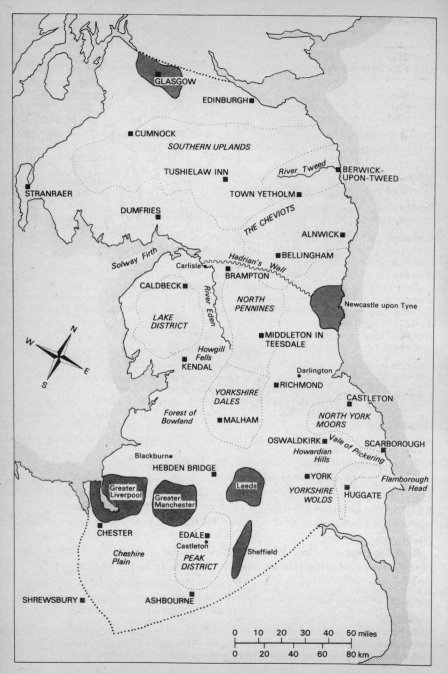

GOUROCK 188
LARGS
187
GLASGOW 193
194
EDINBURGH
192 123 HADDINGTON
186 CUMNOCK 122 124
BARR 190
BIGGAR
185 195 MENNOCK 191 BERWICK-UPON-
STRANRAER 146 TWEED
184 TUSHIELAW 147
NEWTON STEWART INN 144
183 DUMFRIES 189 121 TOWN YETHOLM 145 125
CARTER BAR 143
LANGHOLM 141 148
KIRKCUDBRIGHT 182 181 142 126 ALNWICK
120
140 BELLINGHAM
137
BRAMPTON GREENHEAD
CALDBECK 180 139 127
175 119 HEXHAM
BRAITHWAITE 174 176 136 138
SANTON BRIDGE SKIRWITH 128
ELTERWATER POOLEY
173 177 178 BRIDGE
172 118
FAR SAWREY MIDDLETON IN TEESDALE
171 KENDAL KIRKBY STEPHEN
179 129
117 135 RICHMOND
170 130 162
161 CASTLETON
164 167 160
OSMOTHERLEY 165
SLAIDBURN MALHAM 131 RIPON PICKERING
116 OSWALDKIRK 188
169 134 SCARBOROUGH
115 ILKLEY HARROGATE 166
HEBDEN BRIDGE 132 159
163
114 YORK
HUGGATE
133 158
CHESTER
154
SIDDINGTON EDALE 156 EAST
152 155 EYAM BUTTERWICK
HIGHTOWN 151 113 CAISTOR
153 157
150 149 CHURCH WARSOP
SHREWSBURY STONE ASHBOURNE

N
W   E
S

0   10   20   30   40   50 miles
0   20   40   60   80 km

— Scotland-England Border

around Manchester and Liverpool, Leeds, Newcastle upon Tyne, Edinburgh and Glasgow are for the most part a cyclist's nightmare, although a few reasonable routes (such as Nos 123, 193 and 194) have been picked out. Some of these routes are useful ways into interesting cities, rather than scenic.

The Peak District gives a foretaste of the Pennine scenery as a whole for it includes both gritstone moors and limestone country. The latter, called the 'White Peak', lies south of Castleton. Grassy hills, patterned with straight drystone walls and grazing sheep, are divided by winding, hidden valleys, some with clear rivers, small cliffs and caves. Dovedale is a beautiful example and there are many others. Villages are compact and sturdy, but there is elegance to be found in some 18th-century spa towns.

North of Castleton you will find the wilder 'Dark Peak', with its brown hues of bracken, heather and peat, shaggy sheep and few villages huddling in the valleys. England's millstones used to be cut from the long cliffs of dark rock called 'edges', where great blocks of stone seem poised to fall at any moment. As for cycling in the Peak District as a whole you can learn from this hard-won first experience. The cyclist exhausted himself almost to the point of throwing the bike in the nearest ditch after tackling hills that seemed to crowd one another with deliberate malice and then realized that the Peak District hills have a 'grain'. Life is made much easier by going along the valleys and ridges. However, even if you wisely 'go with the grain' (as Route 113 takes care to do), you will be glad of low gears.

The Pennines become even more desolate in the area between Blackburn and Leeds. The farmsteads and villages stick to the valleys, some of which, like the Hebden Bridge valley, are quite packed with terraced cottages reminding you of their first tenants, the early cotton and wool workers. Most of the few roads are busy with traffic plying between the cities on the Pennine flanks, and Route 114 picks out virtually the only reasonable way through.

A little further north rise the Yorkshire Dales, a National Park and a more magnificent, but less cosy, version of the White Peak. The limestone is white against the grass in long cliffs called 'scars' and in flat rocky areas called 'limestone pavements', there being fine examples of both near Malham. The rock has been used to build cottages, farms, lonely field barns and long straight walls, some of which originally marked the sheepwalks of powerful medieval monasteries. You will enjoy easy riding along the long, broad valleys or 'dales', but you will have to climb hard to get from one dale to the next.

The north Pennines present moorland heights divided by deep valleys of green pastures and grey houses, although many of the cottages of Teesdale are whitewashed. Long, gradual slopes or short but very steep roads will take you through sparsely populated hills, some bearing the scars and ruins of old mineral workings, but most left to the heather and the grouse.

The Cheshire Plain fills the south-west corner of this region with a gentle countryside of dairying pastures, the lanes wandering between hedges and reed-fringed waters called 'meres'. As you cycle easily along, you can admire houses of timber and brick or the black and white half-timbering of which there is such a wealth in Chester. Where the plain rises to higher land near the Peak District, swift streams once provided water-power and there are several early industrial mill villages.

North of Manchester and Liverpool, in a belt of varying width following the coast all the way up to Carlisle, lie the lowlands of Lancashire and Cumbria. By and large it is an area of dairying pasture and is reasonably pleasant in Cumbria despite a few working ports, but too busy and built-up in Lancashire for enjoyable cycling. The Forest of Bowland (where there are few trees) is an extension of the moorland Pennines and juts out, a welcome refuge, into the busy lowlands. The Vale of Eden is part of the Cumbrian lowlands, but with the difference that it could almost have been designed for cyclists. Here you can wend a leisurely way along lanes through a rural foreground contrasting with the skyline of the Lake District mountains to the west. To the east the great wall of the Pennines falls to the Vale with steep slopes of rough grass while to the south it is hemmed in by the moorland Howgill Fells, a block of highland split into long spurs by deep valleys.

The Lake District boasts England's most rugged scenery with gaunt, craggy mountains and steep bracken covered slopes cut by jagged lines of streams. In the valleys are pastures, clumps of trees and cottages of whitewash and slate, the whole scene often featuring a long, deep lake. The lie of the land allows only few roads through the area which can be busy with tourist traffic as well as having very steep, long gradients such as the Hardknott and Wrynose Passes. Using tracks or bridleways could add a lot of interest in this terrain, but you need to be very fit and equipped with low gears to tackle the Lake District even if you keep to the roads.

Much of the area lying to the east of the Pennines is the flat Vale of York, a monotonous patchwork of arable fields. Between Leeds and Sheffield lie the large industrial towns of the Yorkshire coalfields. The area between Darlington, Newcastle upon Tyne and the coast is also fairly built-up.

The Yorkshire Wolds are a small but attractive range of rounded hills. Villages nestle in the valleys which will give you miles of easy riding although there are steep roads climbing out of them. Small patches of rough pasture and woodland are left where the valley sides are too steep for farming. Route 159 passes a great number of ancient abandoned villages, many of which are just scant bumps in the ground today. The Wolds and the coast enclose an area of flat farmland, the chief attractions of which are the chalk cliffs and seabird colonies of Flamborough Head.

Hemmed in by and in stark contrast with the Wolds, the North York Moors and the low, wooded Howardian Hills is the Vale of Pickering. It is very flat, with even a few patches of marsh though most of it is intensively farmed.

The North York Moors National Park is a great block of bracken and heather moorland carved into long ridges and wide valleys. Along the broad summits wild land stretches for miles, while in the valleys are grey stone walls, hamlets and farmsteads. It is hard work climbing some of the roads on to and over the North York Moors (you will be glad of those low gears), but the reward comes in the shape of fairly level ridge and valley roads. The coast has some fine cliffs, and Robin Hood's Bay and the one-time whaling port of Whitby are both famed for their picturesque groupings of houses climbing the hillside behind the harbours.

The Cheviot Hills in Northumberland have rounded moorland summits and winding valleys penetrated by few roads and some strenuous tracks. To their south lies a great undulating expanse of forestry plantation and boggy, heathery wasteland. This in turn is bounded to the south by Hadrian's Wall and you can easily imagine the Roman soldiers patrolling the ramparts of the grey stone stretches of wall. The east coast has fine sandy beaches to tempt you to inactivity, fishing villages and the islands of Farne and Lindisfarne. The superb castles of Warkworth, Alnwick, Bamburgh and Dunstanburgh, along with many lesser fortifications, show that Northumberland was in the thick of border clashes for centuries.

The valley of the river Tweed lies mostly in Scotland, although the history of Berwick-upon-Tweed is a fascinating one of a border town that changed its nationality many times. The lush scenery of the fertile farmlands is made all the more attractive by a scattering of fine ornamental woodlands. Old houses are built in dusky red stone, as are some of the great abbeys, now in ruins, but still hinting at the prosperity of their builders.

The Southern Upland hills are mostly very high and rounded. You will find that the few roads which follow the deep valleys are only moderately strenuous, but some of them are very busy with traffic plying between England and the cities of Glasgow and Edinburgh (especially the A74). In the west are more rugged hills with bare rocks and crags. Throughout there are simple, stone-built houses clustered into hamlets, but in the east are the border towns such as Peebles and Selkirk which grew up where fast rivers provided water-power for the working of wool from the Tweed valley sheep.

Between the Southern Uplands and the Solway Firth is a low, undulating land of pastures and fields, level peat mosses and estuarine marshes rich in bird life. There are whitewashed farms, and port towns which have grown quiet with the silting of their rivers.

Southern Scotland as a whole has been enjoyed briefly by many on their way to or from grander northern Scotland, but its varied attractions reward exploration in their own right.

Route 113 35 miles 56 km
EDALE — ASHBOURNE

OS 1:250 000 no. 6
Bartholomew's 1:100 000 nos 24, 29
OS 1:50 000 nos 119, 110
1 inch:1 mile tourist map of the Peak District
with OS 1:50 000 no. 119 (just)

Edale This is the southern end of the
Pennine Way long distance footpath, and
is a popular centre for walkers. There are
fine walks with views up Mam Tor, Lose

Hill and Kinder Scout. Links with
Routes 114, 155, 156.

Rowland Cote Edale YH.

Mam Tor The largest Iron Age hill fort in
the Peak District is on the top of this hill.
The hill is sometimes called 'Shivering
Mountain' because of the frequent land-
slides that occur.

Castleton The impressive remains of
Norman Peveril Castle (DoE, open)
dominate the village. There are several
famous caves in the area. Below the castle
is Peak Cavern (open), once used by the
village population as a refuge from
northern raiders. West of the village
exciting excursions can be made into the
Speedwell Cavern, Treak Cliff Cavern
and Blue John Cavern, the only place in
the world where the mineral Blue John is
found.

Bradwell Famous Bagshawe's Cavern
has fine rock formations and can be
visited; there is a rocky dale by the
village.

Tideswell The fine church of St John the
Baptist with its eight pinnacle tower has a
good collection of pre-Reformation
monuments and brass.

Miller's Dale Walks down Chee Dale
and Wye Dale can be made from here.

Bakewell This small market town has a
seven arch medieval bridge and some
interesting buildings including the old
Town Hall, St John's Hospital, the Bath
House and the Rutland Arms Hotel, from
where Bakewell Tarts are said to have
originated. Parts of the Parish Church of
All Saints date from the 12th century.
The Old House, a Tudor building,
contains a museum of costume and
domestic items.

Arbor Low A fine henge monument with
ditches, fallen stones and a Bronze Age
barrow (DoE).

*a The main route follows the Tissington
Trail, the course of the old railway that used
to link Buxton to Ashbourne. It has been
specially adapted as a way for walkers, horse
riders and adventurous cyclists, and has a*

rough but rideable surface. The alternative route includes the delightful Manifold Valley, Hartington and Ilam, and is fairly hilly.

Hartington The small village is centred

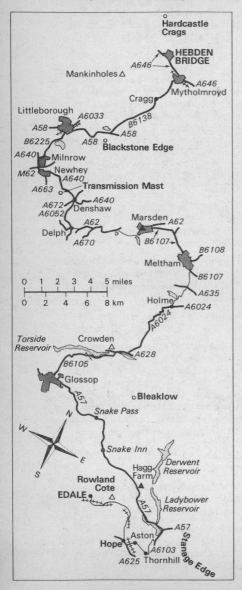

on an open market place surrounded by Georgian buildings. There is an attractive Town Hall, and the church has some curious gargoyles. This is a good centre for visiting the many delights of the surrounding countryside. There is a path to Beresford Dale, once the fishing ground of Izaak Walton (who wrote *The Compleat Angler*) and the location of Cotton's fishing temple. Footpaths lead further south through Wolfscote Dale to Dove Dale.

Tissington In this beautiful old village originated, in about 1350, the tradition of well dressing that is celebrated each Ascension day. There is Norman work in the church and a Jacobean Hall.

Ilam A model village rebuilt during the last century. Part of the stately Hall (NT, open) is the YH. The stream in the Park is where Dr Samuel Johnson experimented with marked corks to prove that the stream is the river Manifold, which disappears underground 4 miles north. William Congreve, the Restoration playwright, wrote *The Old Bachelor* in Ilam.

Dove Dale This wooded limestone gorge, with its many strange rock formations, provides two miles of magnificent scenery and a superb walk. Footpaths lead from here to Hall Dale, Milldale, Wolfscote Dale and the delightful Manifold valley.

Ashbourne See Route 49. Links with Routes 50, 149, 151.

Route 114   67 miles   108 km
HEBDEN BRIDGE — EDALE

OS 1:250 000 nos 5 or 6
Bartholomew's 1:100 000 nos 29, 32
OS 1:50 000 nos 109, 110; 103, 104 (just)

Only the Pennines prevent the large towns and cities to the east and west from joining together. This route picks its way through and over the hills, avoiding some of the worst built-up areas but inevitably involving many main roads. Care should be taken as traffic may be heavy in places.

Hebden Bridge Weaving as a small

cottage industry ended here with the arrival of steam power and the building of large mills. Workers were housed in rows of terraced cottages with a boss's house at the end of each row. Links with Routes 115, 169.

Hardcastle Crags A pine clad glen with rocky scenery, known as 'Little Switzerland'.

Blackstone Edge The best surviving section of Roman road in the country runs over this hill. It is thought to have been part of a road which linked Manchester and Ilkley and has a depression down its middle which was either worn by chariots or used as a base for turf, which would have helped the horses to grip.

Transmission Mast Good view.

Bleaklow This lonely moor is one of the largest areas in England still uncrossed by road.

Stanage Edge This grit stone outcrop is a favourite training ground among rock climbers.

Hope There are some interesting gargoyles on the church.

Rowland Cote Edale YH.

Edale See Route 113. Also links with Routes 155, 156.

Route 115   36 miles   58 km
ILKLEY — HEBDEN BRIDGE

OS 1:250 000 no. 5
Bartholomew's 1:100 000 no. 32
OS 1:50 000 nos 103, 104

Large towns occupy the valleys and flanks of this part of the Pennines. Between Riddlesden and Haworth this route follows some of the busy main roads that grew with the Industrial Revolution.

Ilkley A spa town and health resort. The small 16th-century Tudor manor house is built on the site of a Roman fort, and now accommodates a museum illustrating the history of Ilkley. Links with Routes 116, 134.

Swastika Stone This ancient marked stone is the only one of its kind in Britain, and may have been used for fire worship.

Ilkley Moor The subject of the Yorkshire national anthem 'On Ilkla Moor baht 'at'.

Riddlesden East Riddlesden Hall is a 17th-century manor house (NT, open) with a magnificent tithe barn.

a The alternative route crosses Ilkley Moor involving a sharp ascent and descent, which on the north-east side is by means of a track. This is not a defined right of way. The main route uses lanes which skirt the eastern edge of Ilkley Moor.

Keighley The art gallery and museum at Cliffe Castle has among other exhibits a pre-Industrial Revolution hand-loom. Trips on the Keighley and Worth Valley Light Railway to Oxenhope.

Haworth A small manufacturing town made famous because it was the home of

the Bronte family. The Bronte Parsonage Museum has many of the family's articles on display. The town's traditional industry of spinning and weaving is now supplemented by tourism. Workshops and museum of the Keighley and Worth Valley Light Railway at the station (open).

a   The alternative route here is to take the A6033. The main route avoids the A road by following lanes over the moors.

Wycoller Hall The house that Charlotte Bronte made into Ferndean Manor in *Jane Eyre*.

Hardcastle Crags See Route 114.

Heptonstall Originally a village of stone weavers' cottages. The 17th-century Grammar School has a museum.

Hebden Bridge See Route 114. Also links with Route 169.

Route 116   27 miles   43 km
MALHAM — ILKLEY

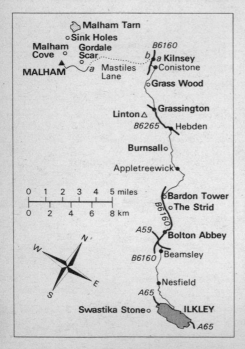

OS 1:250 000 no. 5
Bartholomew's 1:100 000 no. 32
OS 1:50 000 nos 104, 98

Malham A popular centre for exploring the surrounding wild limestone scenery. Links with Route 117.

Malham Tarn A natural lake dammed by glacial moraine during an ice age.

Sink Holes Holes in the limestone down which the River Aire disappears.

Malham Cove This 240-foot (75-metre) sheer white cliff was a waterfall before the Ice Age.

Gordale Scar A winding gorge with splendid plunging waterfalls. It forms part of the 22-mile (35-km) long Craven Fault.

a   Between Malham and Kilnsey the route follows Mastiles Lane, an old drovers' road and favourite among rough-stuff cyclists. At the Kilnsey end the track is a continuation of a surfaced road which passes a quarry, and at the Malham end the track leaves the road at a corner just south east of Malham Tarn. Mastiles Lane has a reasonable surface and can be ridden for much of its length. Only part of the Lane is a defined right of way.

b   If cycling this route from south to north, then at this point you have the option of continuing on the B6160 via Skirfare Bridge and Kettlewell, joining Routes 117 and 130. The main route, as described above, will take you along the rough-stuff track, Mastiles Lane, and through the famous limestone scenery around Malham.

Kilnsey The jutting limestone scar of Kilnsey Crag provides an imposing landmark and plenty of scope for rock climbers. Monks from Fountains Abbey once used the village as their headquarters for manor courts and sheep rearing. The Upper Wharfedale Show is held annually here, one of the events being the crag race to the top of the hill and back.

Grass Wood A nature reserve.

Grassington Once a lead mining centre. The bridge was built in the 17th century and Old Hall in the 13th. An Iron Age village once stood on Lea Green. There are footpaths beside the river between here and Bolton Abbey.

Linton A delightful little village with three bridges: a packhorse bridge, a clapper bridge and a modern road bridge. The Georgian hospital was originally seven almshouses for poor women. St Michael's church is set in a charming location down by the river Wharfe, and has some Norman features.

Burnsall The interesting church has the village stocks in its churchyard. A five-arch bridge spans the Wharfe; pleasant walks along its banks.

Bardon Tower Built in the 15th century, but now in ruins.

The Strid Here the Wharfe surges through a defile formed by limestone ledges. 'Strid' comes from the old English word 'turmoil'.

Bolton Abbey The lovely ruins of a 12th-century priory stand among meadows, woods and waterfalls. There are riverside paths going upstream to the Strid, the Strid Wood nature trail, and eventually to Grassington.

Swastika Stone See Route 115.

Ilkley See Route 115. Also links with Route 134.

Route 117   50 miles   80 km
KIRKBY STEPHEN — MALHAM

OS 1:250 000 no. 5
Bartholomew's 1:100 000 nos 32, 35
OS 1:50 000 nos 98, 91

Kirkby Stephen Old market town. Fountain Cafe is 17th century. Links with Routes 118, 135, 179.

Wharton Hall A 15th-century building, now a farm house.

Tan Hill England's highest inn, and a haunt of Pennine Way walkers.

Thwaite The area around here is very rich in field barns, a relic of the Norse farming system.

Buttertubs The local name given to a number of limestone shafts, situated 60–90 feet (20–30 m) east of the road, which resemble butter tubs or churns.

Buttertubs Pass The famous link between Swaledale and Wensleydale, with fine views from the top.

Hardrow The impressive 100-foot (30–metre) waterfall known as Hardrow Force is just north of the village.

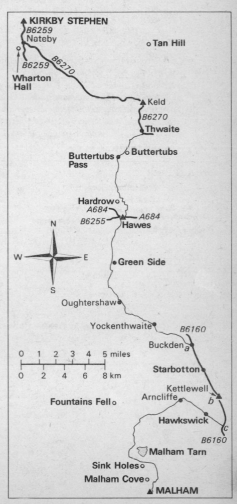

Hawes A lovely Dales village. There are factories making Wensleydale cheese, and some of the thinnest and smoothest stone slates for traditional Dales roofs have come from here for centuries.

Green Side Views from the top of the pass.

a If you next intend to follow Route 130 to Richmond, you can turn to it here.

Starbotton There was tragedy here in 1686 when the River Wharfe flooded and carried away villagers and houses.

b If you next intend to follow Route 130 to Ripon, you can turn to it at this point.

c If cycling this route from north to south, then at this point you have the option of continuing on the B6160 to Kilnsey, and joining Route 116. The main route, as described below, will take you through the famous limestone scenery around Malham, and along a well-known rough-stuff track, Mastiles Lane.

Hawkswick Isaac Trueman, who is reputed to have lived for 117 years, lies buried in the churchyard.

Fountains Fell So called because it belonged to Fountains Abbey in medieval times.

Malham Tarn, Sink Holes and **Malham Cove** See Route 116.

Malham See Route 116.

Route 118   24 miles   38 km
SKIRWITH — KIRKBY STEPHEN

OS 1:250 000 no. 5
Bartholomew's 1:100 000 nos 34 or 35
OS 1:50 000 no. 91

Skirwith Links with Routes 119, 136.

Kirkland To the south-east are the Hanging Walls of Mark Anthony.

Cross Fell Summit At 2930 feet (893 m), this mountain has the highest summit in the Pennines.

Acorn Bank Garden A walled garden with herbaceous plants and a herb garden (NT, open).

Temple Sowerby Sometimes referred to as the 'queen' of east Cumbrian villages, with an interesting old church.

Kirkby Thore Situated at the junction of two Roman roads, and the site of the Roman fort Bravoniacum. The church is partly built from stones taken from the fort.

Knock Gold used to be mined in Great Rundale, the valley stretching to the east.

Dufton A good centre for hill walking. Tracks lead up to Cross Fell and the dramatic valley of High Cup Nick.

Appleby in Westmorland The county town of former Westmorland. There is a 12th-century motte and bailey castle and a 16th-century moot hall. The Church of St Lawrence was rebuilt in the 12th century after the Scots burnt the original, and the Church of St Michael has a Scandinavian hog-back gravestone built into the north wall. St Anne's Hospital

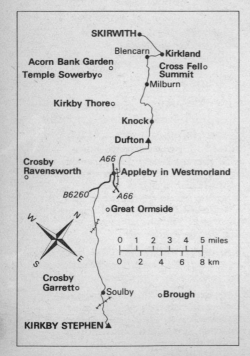

was once an almshouse. A famous horse fair takes place here every June.

Crosby Ravensworth There is a delightful church in the village, and many Iron Age settlement sites and burial mounds in the surrounding countryside.

Great Ormside The Norman church has an Anglo-Saxon tower that was probably once used for defence.

Brough The castle has a 12th-century keep (DoE, open), and is built on the site of the Roman fort of Verterae. There is a medieval church, and Musgrave Fell (NT) to the north is known for its limestone pavements and interesting plants.

Crosby Garrett Norman church. To the south are three ancient village settlement sites with remains of huts, paths and boundaries.

Kirkby Stephen See Route 117. Also links with Routes 135, 179.

Route 119   22 miles   35 km
BRAMPTON — SKIRWITH

OS 1:250 000 nos 5, 4 or 3
Bartholomew's 1:100 000 no. 38
OS 1:50 000 nos 86, 91, 90 (just)

Brampton Links with Routes 120, 137, 180, 181.

a The lane immediately south of Cumrew is not marked on the Bartholomew's map of 1977.

Kirkoswald This pleasant village of red sandstone has an unusual church in that the tower stands 200 yards away. Only the turret and dungeons remain of a castle that was occupied for five hundred years. A building of particular note is the College, which has been the home of the Featherstonhaugh family since 1613. Here also is the cottage of Souter Johnny, who was Burns' 'Tam O'Shanter'.

Long Meg and her Daughters An 18-foot (5-metre) standing stone with a circle of other stones, 350 yards in diameter. Nearby is the Little Meg Stone Circle. Both are thought to have been used for worship in the Bronze Age.

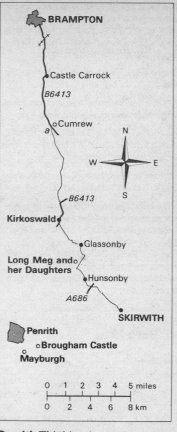

Penrith This historic town has a ruined castle (DoE, open) built originally as a defence against the Scots, and an interesting church with the Giant's Grave and Giant's Thumb in its yard. The Gloucester Arms is reputed to have been the residence of Richard III, and bears his coat of arms. The town has connections with William Wordsworth.

Mayburgh Arthur's Round Table (DoE, open) and the Mayburgh Henge (DoE, open) are prehistoric monuments.

Brougham Castle These imposing ruins (DoE, open) date from the 12th century. By the castle is the site of the Roman fort Brocavum, situated at the junction of two Roman roads.

Skirwith Links with Routes 118, 136.

Route 120   22 miles   35 km
LANGHOLM — BRAMPTON

OS 1:250 000 nos 3 or 4
Bartholomew's 1:100 000 no. 38
OS 1:50 000 nos 79, 85, 86

Langholm An old planned town in which the original street plan still exists. There are tweed mills and it is the centre of a large area of sheep and cattle farming. Langholm Castle is the remains of a Border tower. Links with Routes 121, 189.

Whita Hill The obelisk on top of the hill commemorates Sir John Malcolm, a Knight of Eskdale.

a If you next intend to follow Route 181 to Dumfries, you can turn to it here.

Brampton Links with Routes 119, 137, 180, 181.

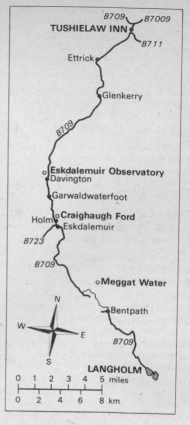

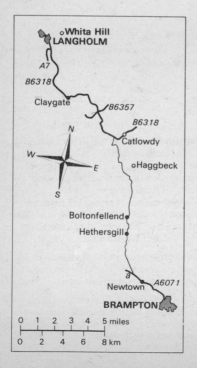

Route 121   28 miles   45 km
TUSHIELAW INN — LANGHOLM

OS 1:250 000 nos 3 or 4
Bartholomew's 1:100 000 nos 38, 41
OS 1:50 000 no. 79

Tushielaw Inn Links with Routes 122, 141, 146, 147.

Eskdalemuir Observatory An important meteorological station and magnetic institute. This is also the area of a Handfast Fair, at which, until the 18th century, couples were 'hand-fasted' for a trial marriage until the next year's fair, when the desirability of their marrying permanently was considered.

Craighaugh Ford This ford is part of an

ancient route. The Roman road, in parts 24 feet (7·5 m) wide, which goes northeast from the ford over Craik Cross is an astonishing example of road engineering in difficult terrain. To the east of the ford and footbridge is the site of the Roman fort of Raeburnfoot.

Meggat Water This valley is where Thomas Telford was born and bred.

Langholm See Route 120. Also links with Route 189.

Route 122   47 miles   75 km
EDINBURGH — TUSHIELAW INN

OS 1:250 000 nos 3 or 4
Bartholomew's 1:100 000 nos 41, 46
OS 1:50 000 nos 66, 73, 79 (just)

Edinburgh The capital of Scotland. For an overall view of the city climb Arthur's Seat 823 feet (251 m), a rugged plug of volcanic rock, or cycle the Queen's Drive around it. Notable are the Royal Palace of Holyrood House, with the abbey ruin beside it; Edinburgh Castle on Castle Rock, with the 11th-century St Margaret's Chapel on the highest part; here also Tattoo performances may be seen. At Old Parliament Hall the Scottish parliament met until the Union in 1707; St Giles Cathedral (late Gothic) contains the ancient cross of Edinburgh; also in Parliament Square stands the grave of John Knox, the 16th-century leader of the Scottish Reformation. Famous streets are Princes Street, George Street and Queen Street in the new town, and in the old town the Royal Mile which was the route along which royalty and those going to their executions often rode. In the Royal Mile is Gladstone's Land, a restored tenement (NTS); Georgian House (NTS, open) is in elegant Charlotte Square. Lamb's House (NTS, open) in Leith is a restored merchant's dwelling. The Edinburgh International Festival has been held annually since 1947. Museums include the National Gallery, the Royal Scottish Museum; the National Portrait Gallery and Museum of Antiquities in Queen Street; and a Highland Dress

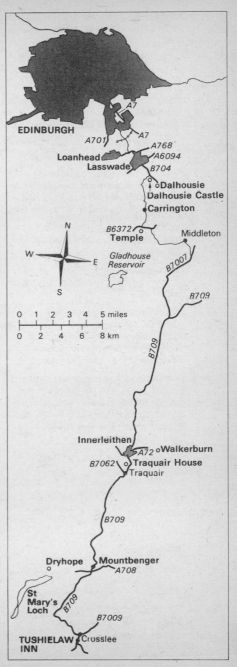

Museum in Canongate Tolbooth. There are two YHs. Links with Routes 123, 192, 193, 236, 283.

Loanhead The colliery, opened in the 1950s, produces millions of tons yearly.

Lasswade The river here is a good source of water-power and Lasswade has long been a milling town. Paper, meal and gunpowder have all been produced here.

Dalhousie Castle Dalhousie Castle, dating from the 12th-century, is now a hotel.

Dalhousie The ruin of a 13th-century church, where relatives of John Knox, the 16th-century leader of the Scottish Reformation, were ministers.

Carrington The church tower has been converted into a dovecot.

Temple Picturesque village with an ancient church of the Knights Templars in the valley.

Innerleithen A hamlet till 1790, after which the town grew both on account of its spa-waters and its woollen mills. Border Games are held here annually. The church had right of sanctuary.

Walkerburn The village was created in the 19th century by the establishment of a completely vertical wool mill, which processed the material right from raw wool to finished cloth. The Scottish Museum of wool textiles is here.

Traquair House This is claimed to be

Scotland's oldest inhabited house; 27 Scottish and English monarchs have stayed here. There is an 18th-century brewhouse still making ale. According to a vow of Prince Charles Edward, the one-time Earl, the main drive gates may not be opened until a Stuart is once again on the throne (open).

Mountbenger Yarrow Dale (through which runs the A708) is 'ballad country', praised by poets including Wordsworth.

St Mary's Loch A renowned beauty spot.

Dryhope Dryhope Tower is a strong peel-tower and the birthplace of Mary Scott, 'the Flower of Yarrow' and ancestor of Sir Walter.

Tushielaw Inn Links with Routes 121, 141, 146, 147.

Route 123   24 miles   39 km
EDINBURGH — HADDINGTON

OS 1:250 000 nos 3 or 4
Bartholomew's 1:100 000 no. 46
OS 1:50 000 no. 66

Edinburgh See Route 122. Also links with Routes 192, 193, 236, 283.

a In finding your way to Duddingston, it is helpful to remember that it lies below the south-east corner of Arthur's Seat.

Duddingston A village now absorbed into Edinburgh, yet still retaining its individuality. It has a Norman church.

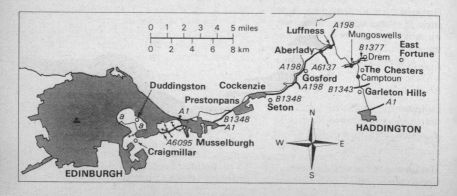

Craigmillar The 14th-century Craigmillar Castle (open) has many historic associations. Mary Queen of Scots frequently took refuge here.

Musselburgh An important port in Roman times, and an old fishing burgh. The triple-arch bridge has traces of a defensive gate, from the days when the bridge was on the main road between south-east Scotland and Edinburgh. There is a 16th-century tolbooth. Now a part of Musselburgh, Inveresk was a military camp and civil settlement in the Roman era. The 17th-century Inveresk Lodge and gardens (NTS) are open. An ancient golf-links is situated here.

Prestonpans The town previously prospered by the making of salt in salt-pans, started in the 12th century by the Newbattle monks. A coastal open-air social history museum centres on a giant colliery beam pumping engine. At Preston there is some good Scottish country architecture: 17th-century Hamilton House (NTS, open); Preston House, a 15th-century fortress house, now ruinous but with a dovecot for a thousand birds; Northfield is a 16th-century tower house. The mercat cross has a unicorn and a criers' platform.

Cockenzie An ancient fishing village, once a centre for the herring and whaling industries. The vast power station, with chimneys 500 feet (170 m) high, has a promenade around its sea wall.

Seton Seton Collegiate Church (DoE).

Gosford Note the trees growing at an angle of thirty degrees, caused by wind-blow behind the Gosford estate wall.

Aberlady Once the port to Haddington, it has some attractive cottage rows. Aberlady Bay is a nature reserve.

Luffness The 16th-century castle is on the site of a Norse raiders' camp.

East Fortune Museum of Flight with many historic aircraft.

The Chesters The earthworks of Chesters fort (DoE).

Garleton Hills Monument to the Earl of Hopetoun, a hero of the 18th-century Peninsular War.

Haddington See Route 124.

Route 124   41 miles   65 km
HADDINGTON —
BERWICK-UPON-TWEED

OS 1:250 000 no. 4
Bartholomew's 1:100 000 no. 46
OS 1:50 000 nos 66, 67, 74, 75 (just)

It is possible to link Haddington and Berwick-upon-Tweed by a 'coastal' route some miles east of this route. Such a route would involve much use of A roads including the A1, and would generally be at some distance from the sea, which could be reached by the use of dead-end side roads. However, the coast is attractive, with cliffs and off-shore rocks and stacks.

Haddington A town of great architectural interest. There are 129 protected buildings, and an architectural trail is marked on the wall of the Town House. The town preserves its medieval street plan. St Mary's Kirk, where John Knox worshipped as a boy, once had a steeple, but it was removed and the church fortified when held by an English garrison. There is a dovecot with 568 nesting holes. The 18th-century Poldrate corn-mill is an arts and community centre. St Martin's church is notable (DoE). Links with Route 123.

Lennoxlove The estate was previously called 'Lethington', and was once owned by Mary Queen of Scots' secretary and councillor. Later it became known as 'Lennoxlove' after the then owner, Duchess of Lennox, mistress of Charles II.

Gifford Fine views of Lammermuir Hills. Reverend Witherspoon, the first president of what is now Princeton University, USA, was a Gifford man.

Yester The estate has belonged to the Gifford family since at least the 12th-century. The house is by William Adam. Sir Hugo Gifford was reputedly a wizard, and he built the underground 'Goblin Ha'.

a The route between Duns and the Yester area crosses open moorland. B roads to the north follow a more sheltered and slightly less strenuous river valley route.

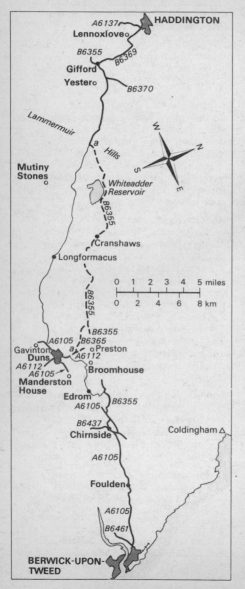

Mutiny Stones A long cairn, reached following a track starting at the roadsi

Duns The town used to be on the hill ju to the north, until it was destroyed by English in the 16th-century. It used al to be the county town of Berwickshire, since the county was Scottish but the town of Berwick lay in England. A charming 'new' town. Birthplace of the 13th-century John Duns Scotus, and o racing driver Jim Clark. Duns Castle grounds are a bird sanctuary with fine walks (open).

Manderston House One of Britain's finest Edwardian houses with charming group of farm buildings (open).

Broomhouse The town was barbarica burned by the English in 1544. The Sco had their revenge in the Battle of Ancru Moor, when 'Remember Broomhouse' was their battle cry.

Edrom At the north end of the village is church with a Norman arch (DoE).

Chirnside A 'Lang Toon', of two long streets. There is a memorial to Jim Clark the champion racing driver, at Cross Hill

Foulden A tithe barn with crow-stepped gables (DoE).

Berwick-upon-Tweed See Route 125. Also links with Route 144.

Route 125   49 miles   78 km
**BERWICK-UPON-TWEED —
ALNWICK**

OS 1:250 000 no. 4
Bartholomew's 1:100 000 no. 42
OS 1:50 000 nos 75, 81

Berwick-upon-Tweed An ancient and picturesque border town which has changed hands between the Scottish and English several times, but is now England's most northerly town. Because of its uncertain allegiance, special acts of Parliament were passed for it, resulting in some odd situations: for example, on paper it is still engaged in the Crimean War! Virtually only the ruins of the watchtower remain of the 13th-century castle (DoE, open). The town walls are of 13th-century origin but were strengthened by Elizabeth I. There is a 17th-century fifteen-arch bridge, and a local museum. Links with Routes 124, 144.

Ancroft The fortress-like tower of St Anne's church is a fine example of a peel tower. These towers were built as a refuge for villagers during the frequent border clashes.

a A causeway links Lindisfarne to the mainland at low tide.

Lindisfarne Also known as Holy Island. In the 7th century monks from Iona settled here, giving birth to English Christianity. The ruined 11th-century Benedictine priory (DoE, open) has a museum containing Anglo-Saxon sculptures and a reproduction of the Lindisfarne Gospels. There is a small but impressively sited castle which was built in the 16th century and restored in the 20th century (NT, open).

Belford Moor From the highest point on the lane over Belford Moor are fine views of the Cheviots.

Belford An old coaching stop on the A1 road. Many of the buildings were destroyed during border raids.

Bamburgh The village is dominated by the imposing red sandstone mass of the castle (open), once the seat of the first kings of Northumbria. This was the birthplace of Grace Darling, who on a stormy night in 1838 rowed out with her father in a small boat to rescue five people from a wrecked steamship. There is a small museum, with some of her relics. The fine church of St Aidan's has a memorial to Grace Darling, and a Saxon sundial.

Seahouses Once a small port, and now a resort.

a Boats from Seahouses take visitors to the Farne Islands.

Farne Islands Owned by the NT, these thirty or so islands are the breeding place for seals, and some twenty species of sea-

birds. Inner Farne has a 14th-century chapel, and an old light-tower. St Aidan and St Cuthbert lived here in the 7th century. The lighthouse on Longstone Rock was where Grace Darling and her father set forth from to rescue survivors of the steamship 'Forfarshire' which was aground on Big Harcar Rock.

Beadnell The Craster Arms is built around a 14th-century peel tower.

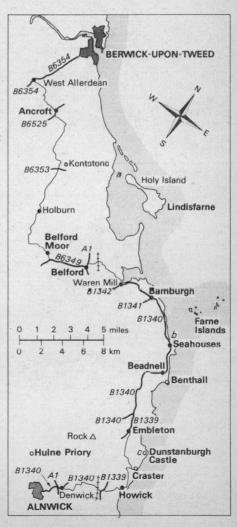

Benthall The harbour walls are built without concrete or mortar, in drystone fashion. There are some lime kilns owned by the NT. Sandy Beadnall Bay can be reached from here.

Embleton Striking views of Dunstanburgh Castle.

c There are pleasant coast footpaths linking Dunstanburgh Castle to Embleton and Craster.

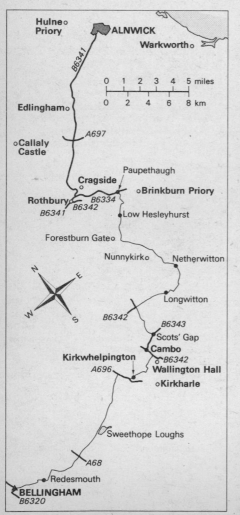

Dunstanburgh Castle This dramatic and extensive castle was painted by Turner three times (DoE, open). Although much damaged during the Wars of the Roses, the curtain walls, towers and gatehouse remain, and stand on cliffs that rise 100 feet (35 m) from the North Sea. On the shoreline is a cavern called Rumbling Churn, earning its name from the strange noises created by boulders rolling in the water.

Craster This fishing village is famous for its oak-smoked kippers, crab and lobster. The very hard local rock, known as Whinstone, used to be shipped from here.

Howick The lovely flower, shrub and rhododendron gardens of the Hall are open.

Hulne Priory Built in the 13th century, now in ruins. There are good views from Brizlee Tower, in the Park.

Alnwick See Route 126. Also links with Route 145.

Route 126   46 miles   73 km
ALNWICK — BELLINGHAM

OS 1:250 000 no. 4
Bartholomew's 1:100 000 no. 42
OS 1:50 000 nos 80, 81

Alnwick This historic border town has a great Norman castle (open) which is still the seat of the Percys. Its fine grounds were designed by Capability Brown. The tenantry column was erected by one thousand grateful tenants after the Percys had reduced their rents. Also notable are 15th-century St Michael's Church and the 15th-century Hotspur Tower.
Links with Routes 125, 145.

Hulne Priory See Route 125.

Warkworth The medieval castle (DoE, open) was once one of the most important in northern England, and was mentioned by Shakespeare in Henry IV. In the 14th-century a hermit constructed a refuge and chapel in the side of a bluff known today as the Hermitage (DoE, open).

Edlingham The sturdy looking church, set above the ruins of a 14th-century castle, provided protection during the border raids. This is the home of an alleged 17th-century witch, Margaret Stothard.

Callaly Castle A 17th-century mansion incorporating a 13th-century peel tower and with Georgian and Victorian additions (open).

Cragside Once the home of Lord Armstrong, the inventor of the Armstrong rifle-bored breech-loading gun. The 19th-century mansion was one of the first houses in Britain to be lit by electric light. The extensive gardens (NT, open) are famous for their magnificent trees, rhododendrons and artificial lakes.

Rothbury The village was established here long before the Norman conquest. It is now a busy market town.

Brinkburn Priory Only a church, set in delightful surroundings, remains of the 12th-century priory which was founded here by Augustinian canons.

Cambo A model village built in 1740 with an attractive bridge, and a post office that was once a fortified vicarage.

Wallington Hall The Hall was built in 1688 and has grounds laid out by Capability Brown (NT, open). On display are fine porcelain and needlework exhibits, a dolls' house collection and a small museum.

Kirkwhelpington Pleasant, mainly 13th-century church. The inventor of the steam turbine, Charles Parsons, is buried in the churchyard.

Kirkharle In this tiny hamlet, Capability Brown was born in 1716. The church, which has to be approached by farm track, contains a memorial stone to Robert Lorraine, who was killed by Scots raiders.

Bellingham See Route 127. Also links with Routes 140, 141, 142, 148.

Route 127   34 miles   55 km
BELLINGHAM — HEXHAM

OS 1:250 000 no. 4
Bartholomew's 1:100 000 no. 42 or nos 39, 42 (just)
OS 1:50 000 nos 80, 87

Bellingham Market town. St Cuthbert's church has a unique ribbed stone roof, erected after two fires destroyed wooden roofs. A path behind the church leads to St Cuthbert's Well, whose water is said to have healing powers. Enquire locally about the bloody legend of the pack-shaped tombstone. Links with Routes 126, 140, 141, 142, 148.

Wark The name of the village means 'earthworks' and defences from a Norman castle remain. This was once the capital of Tynedale, where Scottish kings held court. The iron bridge over the stream affords a pretty view of the village.

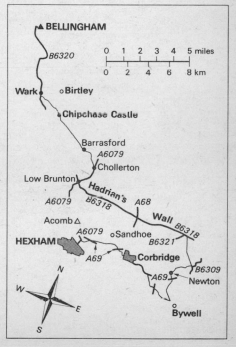

Birtley The Norman Church of St Giles has the remains of a peel tower and a notable war memorial. Legend attaches to the Devil's Stone above Holy Well.

Chipchase Castle A 17th-century mansion incorporating a medieval tower.

Hadrian's Wall The stretch of the B6318 on this route follows the course of the wall itself which is consequently no longer extant. Large sections of both ditch and vallum, which were subsidiary defences to the wall, run alongside the road.

Bywell A settlement which thrived on ironworking in the 16th century, and is now virtually dead but very picturesque.

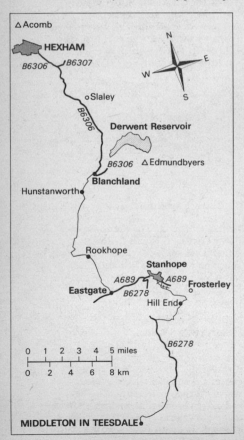

Set beside the river, it has some pleasant domestic buildings, the ruin of a 15th-century castle and two churches, one of which has the county's finest Saxon tower.

Corbridge This was the Roman settlement of Corstopitum, and a Roman Station houses a museum of Roman finds (DoE, open). A royal burgh in Saxon times and important in medieval times when it had a mint, Corbridge was thrice burnt in border clashes. The Saxon Church of St Andrew incorporates Roman stones and has a Roman gateway as an interior tower arch. Fortified vicarage. Market cross.

Hexham See Route 128. Links also with Route 139.

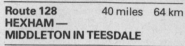

Route 128   40 miles   64 km
HEXHAM—
MIDDLETON IN TEESDALE

OS 1:250 000 nos 4, 5
Bartholomew's 1:100 000 no. 39
OS 1:50 000 nos 87, 92

Hexham A centre for the local sheep and cattle farmers with a 15th-century Moot Hall and a fine open space, the Seal, offering views of the town. The church is particularly interesting, and has a fine Saxon crypt and ornaments including Bishop Acca's Cross, and the monument to a Roman standard bearer. The frith stool (throne) is believed to have once been used for Northumbrian coronations, and was later the centre of a circle of medieval sanctuary within which fugitives from justice could claim protection of the Church. Some of the stone used in the church came from the nearby Roman camp of Corstopitum. The market place has a small colonnaded shelter, and the 14th-century Manor Office used to be a gaol. Links with Routes 127, 139.

Blanchland Much of this picturesque village was built in the 18th century from the ruins of an abbey. The village centre was probably once the outer monastery yard, and the Lord Crewe Arms incorporates parts of the old abbey guest house. The church dates from the founding of the abbey in the 12th century, and has three medieval coffin lids. Medieval gatehouse.

Derwent Reservoir The recently constructed, 1000-acre reservoir is a nature reserve.

Eastgate This village and Westgate mark the sites of the entrances to the one-time hunting park of the Bishops of Durham. Waterfalls on Rook Hope Burn are of geological and botanical interest. The church has a massive Frosterley 'marble' font.

Stanhope This was the 'capital' of the old lead-mining area of Weardale. The Church of St Thomas has two Flemish carved oak plaques, a Roman altar, a Frosterley 'marble' font and a fossil tree-stump near the churchyard.

Frosterley Nearby are quarries for Frosterley 'marble', a fossil-rich limestone which goes black with polishing. There is some fine use of the stone in St Michael's Church.

Middleton in Teesdale See Route 129. Also links with Routes 136, 138.

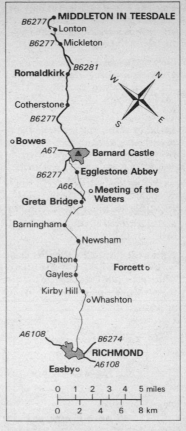

Route 129   25 miles   40 km
MIDDLETON IN TEESDALE
RICHMOND

OS 1:250 000 no. 5
Bartholomew's 1:100 000 no. 35
OS 1:50 000 no. 92

Middleton in Teesdale This was once the centre of a flourishing lead-mining industry. The church has some medieval gravestones in the wall and a 16th-century detached belfry. Links with Routes 128, 136, 138.

Romaldkirk The village, considered one of the prettiest in Teesdale, has an ancient church and almshouses.

Bowes This was the Roman Lavatrae, thus probably a bath station for troops. There is a 3rd-century Roman dedication stone in the church. The Norman keep of Bowes Castle was built with Roman stones (DoE, open). Dickens' Dotheboys Hall is now a café. His fictional school was substantially modelled on the local Shaw school, which closed after the publication of *Nicholas Nickleby*.

Barnard Castle Ruins of the 12th-century castle, including a 14th-century round tower (DoE, open). Tudor Blagraves House; and an 18th-century Market Hall. There are 18th-century houses in Thorngate which have long weavers' lights on the top floors. They, and old sandstone-built factories, show that the town was once a textile and carpet centre. Bowes museum, housed in a 19th-

century chateau built for the purpose,
contains thousands of European works of
art. Riverside walks to Egglestone
Abbey.

Egglestone Abbey Riverside ruin of a
12th-century abbey (DoE, open). Nearby
are a stone bridge over the River Tees and
an old packhorse bridge over Thorsgill
Beck.

Meeting of the Waters From the angle
in the lane, a footpath leads beside the
river through Rokeby Park (where
Walter Scott was often a guest) to the confluence of the two rivers, a spot painted
by J. M. W. Turner.

Greta Bridge Romantic bridge of 1776,
also much loved by painters such as John
Sell Cotman.

Forcett South of the village lies Stan-
wick Camp (DoE). The great earthworks,
which enclose 850 acres, were the base
from which King Venutius led the last

substantial resistance against the Rom
in AD 74.

Easby Picturesque remains of Easby
Abbey (DoE, open). St Agatha's Chur
has medieval wall paintings and the cas
of an outstanding Anglo-Saxon cross.

Richmond See Route 130. Also links
with Routes 135, 162.

Route 130   66 miles   106 km
RICHMOND — RIPON

OS 1:250 000 nos 5 or 6
Bartholomew's 1:100 000 no. 35
OS 1:50 000 nos 99, 98, 92 (just)

Richmond The town has had military
associations since the time when the
Romans occupied nearby Cataractonium
Present day Richmond is the garrison
town to Catterick Camp. Impressive
Norman castle and Scollards Hall, whic
is perhaps the oldest domestic building i
Britain (DoE, open). The Georgian

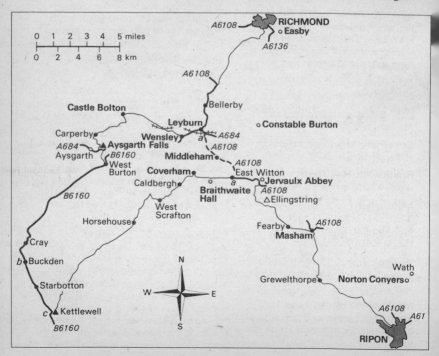

Theatre Royal of 1788 is open. The regimental museum of the Green Howards can be visited. Links with Routes 129, 135, 162.

Easby See Route 129.

Leyburn There is a fine view of Wensleydale from the 'Shawl', named after a shawl dropped here by Mary Queen of Scots following her escape from Castle Bolton.

a The 38-mile (61-km) ride around the lovely Dales can be cut out by using the A 6108 via Middleham.

Constable Burton The Hall has large informal gardens, and is open.

Wensley This small village was once a market town. The church has been described as the best in the Dales.

Castle Bolton The castle has a great chamber, which is now a folk museum. Mary Queen of Scots was imprisoned here for six months.

Aysgarth Falls Aysgarth Force waterfall, and footpaths to the middle and lower falls. The church has two fine screens and a desk that probably came from Jervaulx Abbey.

b If you next intend to follow Route 117 to Kirkby Stephen, turn to it here.

c If you next intend to follow Route 117 to Malham, turn to it here.

Coverham Abbey mill, miller's house and restored church.

Braithwaite Hall The 17th-century hall is now a farmhouse (NT, open).

Middleham Castle ruins (DoE, open). The monks of Jervaulx made this a horse-breeding and racing centre, and it became the capital of Wensleydale.

Jervaulx Abbey The sparse ruins of a Cistercian abbey in beautiful surroundings (open).

Masham The market square has a maypole and a cross, and there is the shaft of an Anglo-Saxon cross in the churchyard.

Norton Conyers A Jacobean house with a walled garden (open).

Ripon See Route 131.

Route 131   15 miles   25 km
RIPON — HARROGATE

OS 1:250 000 nos 5 or 6
Bartholomew's 1:100 000 no. 32
OS 1:50 000 nos 104, 99

Ripon Once a cloth and lace making centre, now a market town. The great cathedral has a Saxon crypt and examples of fine craftsmanship. Each night at 9 pm a Hornblower sounds his horn, a tradition said to be a thousand years old. There is a 90-foot (27-metre) obelisk in the market square and a small folk museum in the medieval Wakeman's House. There is also a town museum. Old Hall Dower House was built in the 18th century. Links with Route 130.

Newby Hall One of the most famous Adam houses, containing tapestries and sculptures, and with 25 acres of gardens (open).

Studley Roger Pretty cottages. Entrance to Studley Park.

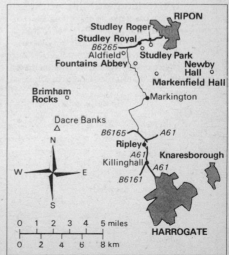

Studley Park A large park with deer, lakes, woods, towers, temples, statues, views, and a canal (open). Entrance is via Studley Roger or Fountains Abbey.

Studley Royal The 18th-century mansion has fine chimneys, mirrors and pictures (open).

Fountains Abbey Wonderful ruins of the greatest abbey in England. The lavish construction of the abbey was due largely to the wealth that the Cistercian monks accumulated through sheep farming. Both the abbey and Fountains Hall are open (DoE). Entrance to Studley Park.

Markenfield Hall A remarkable example of a fortified manor house (open). Accessible by bridleway from just north of Markington and from Ripon.

Brimham Rocks Grotesquely eroded outcrops of millstone grit. The 200-ton Idol Rock rests on a stem only 12 feet (4 metres) thick.

Ripley The village was modelled to resemble an Alsatian community. The 'Weeping Cross' in the churchyard is claimed to be the only one in England. The village also has a cross, stocks, and a castle with gardens (open).

Knaresborough Good views from the 14th-century castle ruins, and the Court House has a museum (among its items is armour worn at the Battle of Marston Moor). The oldest chemist's shop in England is in the market place. Other places of interest include the medieval Old Manor House, Georgian Knares-borough House, 18th-century Coyningham Hall, Fort Montague, St John's parish church and Sir Robert's Chapel in Abbey Road. Boats can be hired on the river. The caves of Mother Shipton (a 16th-century prophetess) and the Dropping Well (a petrifying spring) are also popular sights.

Harrogate See Route 132. Also links with Route 134.

Route 132   24 miles   38 km
HARROGATE — YORK

OS 1:250 000 nos 5 or 6
Bartholomew's 1:100 000 no. 32
OS 1:50 000 nos 104, 105

Harrogate Once a popular spa town, and now a conference centre, Harrogate is characterized by dignified Victorian architecture, banks of flowers, and well planned open spaces. The Royal Pump Room houses a museum of local history and the town has an art gallery. In Harlow Car Gardens are ornamental displays and woodland. There are good views from the tower (open) on Harlow Hill in Otley Road. Links with Routes 131, 134.

a The main route follows lanes while the alternative visits picturesque Knaresborough using busier A roads.

Harewood Harewood House (open) is a beautifully sited 18th-century mansion containing fine furniture and paintings, and with grounds designed by Capability Brown.

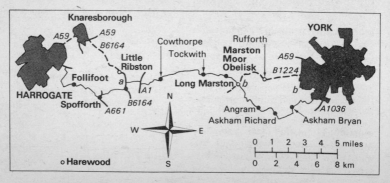

Knaresborough See Route 131.

Little Ribston The wooded park on the other side of the River Nidd was the first English home of the Ribston Pippin apple tree.

Follifoot Rudding Park (open) has a fine example of a Regency building.

Spofforth Ruin of a 14th-century manor house (DoE, open).

Marston Moor Obelisk North of the obelisk is the field where in 1644 the Parliamentarian army under Oliver Cromwell defeated the Royalist army of Charles I in the most decisive battle of the Civil War. The battle lasted three hours, during which 4000 Royalists and 300 Parliamentarians died.

Long Marston The parents of General James Wolfe, who won Canada for England, were married in All Saints Church.

b The main route uses a B road; the alternative route is longer and follows quieter lanes.

York See Route 133. Also links with Route 163.

Route 133   42 miles 69 km
YORK — EAST BUTTERWICK

OS 1:250 000 nos 5 or 6
Bartholomew's 1:100 000 nos 33, 30 (just)
OS 1:50 000 nos 105, 112

This route crosses the flat area lying between important ports and Yorkshire's industrial towns, and commercial traffic plying between the two can make the unavoidable short stretches of main road very busy.

York This fascinating city has occupied its present site for nearly two thousand years, and its rich history is reflected in the streets. The most striking feature is the grand 13th-century Minster, with its huge lantern tower and magnificent stained glass. Interesting views of the Minster and city can be had from the 2½-mile (4-km) walk around the well-preserved city walls. Both the Shambles and Stonegate are preserved medieval streets, and there are numerous buildings worth a visit. These include the Treasurer's House (NT, open), 14th-century Merchant Adventurers' Hall and

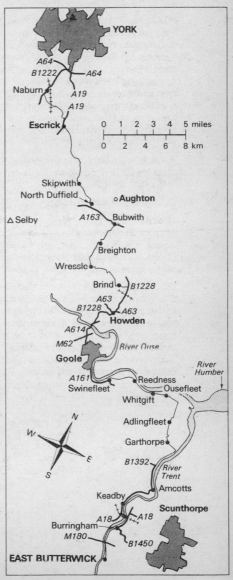

Merchant Taylors' Hall, Assembly Rooms, St Williams College, Kings Manor, Mansion House, St Anthony's Hall, Guildhall, Judges' Lodgings, St Mary's Abbey, Church of All Saints, the Debtors' Prison and Female Prison. The multi-angular tower is a surviving relic of the Roman legionary fortress. Micklegate and Bootham have a number of Georgian town houses. The Yorkshire museum has displays of natural history and archaeology. The York Story at the Hermitage Centre is a useful guide to the city, and there is an art gallery. The city is the home of the National Railway Museum, and the Castle Museum is an outstanding folk museum of Yorkshire life. Links with Routes 132, 163.

Escrick Mid-Victorian gothic revival church with fine marble work and interesting monuments.

Aughton Norman church.

Howden Surrounded by pleasant terraces stands a splendid 14th-century church, partly in use and partly ruined (DoE). Among its interesting possessions are effigies and churchwarden's chests.

Goole This busy port was established as the terminus of the Aire and Calder canal for the export of Yorkshire's textiles and coal in the 19th century. It is the meeting point of the rivers Don and Ouse, by way of the Dutch River, built by Cornelius Vermuyden, a Dutch engineer. St John's church has memorials to ships and seamen.

Scunthorpe An industrial town which has grown since the discovery of local ironstone beds in the 1860s. Good modern planning around the civic centre. Borough museum of local interest has a John Wesley collection. Regency Normanby Hall has a costume exhibition, and a centre for craft, pottery and blacksmiths' work in its grounds (open).

East Butterwick Links with Routes 62, 63.

Route 134   18 miles   29 km
HARROGATE — ILKLEY

OS 1:250 000 nos 5 or 6
Bartholomew's 1:100 000 no. 32
OS 1:50 000 no. 104

Harrogate See Route 132. Also links with Routes 131.

Harewood See Route 132.

Knaresborough See Route 131.

John of Gaunt's Castle Only a few remains are visible.

Fewston The poet Edward Fairfax lived here. Near the porch of the church are the gravestones of Joseph Ridsdale and his son, who are both recorded as having died on days that did not exist.

Denton Park Home of the Fairfaxes.

Swastika Stone See Route 115.

Ilkley See Route 115. Also links with Route 116.

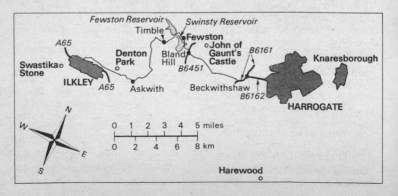

Route 135   34 miles   54 km
KIRKBY STEPHEN — RICHMOND

OS 1:250 000 nos 5 or 6
Bartholomew's 1:100 000 no. 35
OS 1:50 000 nos 92, 98, 91, 99 (just)

Kirkby Stephen See Route 117. Also
links with Routes 118, 179.

Wharton Hall and **Tan Hill** See Route
117.

*a The short stretch of road which crosses the
stream north of Rookby is not marked on the
1977 edition of the Bart's Map.*

Reeth A market town in the 17th and
18th centuries, which grew to be the
centre for the area's lead miners. The
lovely green is lined with 18th-century
inns and shops.

*b The alternative route is a detour of 14
miles (22 km) up beautiful Swaledale, and
involves a section of track north-east of
Crackpot which is not a defined right of way.*

Grinton In the days when the church had
a vast parish, the corpses had to be carried
for miles over the moors before being
buried in the churchyard.

Gunnerside Gill The bridleway up this
steep sided valley takes you past the
ruined building and 'hushes' of the old
mine workings.

*c The main route, along the valley, is
scenically very beautiful but may have heavy
traffic. The alternative route along the lanes
is quieter but very hilly.*

Richmond See Route 130. Also links
with Routes 129, 162.

Route 136   38 miles   60 km
SKIRWITH—
MIDDLETON IN TEESDALE

OS 1:250 000 no. 5
Bartholomew's 1:100 000 no. 39
OS 1:50 000 nos 91, 86

Skirwith Links with Routes 118, 119.

Ousby The church has 13th century
work.

Melmerby The village is sometimes
affected by the curious Helm Wind which
can reach speeds of 80 mph when the air a
few miles away is still.

Hartside Cross Good views.

*a This is a difficult road in snowy or icy
conditions.*

Alston The highest market town in
England, and until the early 19th century
one of the richest mineral areas in Britain.
Buildings of especial interest are the
church, Gaytes House, and Quaker
Meeting House. Many of the buildings
date from mining days.

Whitley Castle Mounds and ditches can
still be seen.

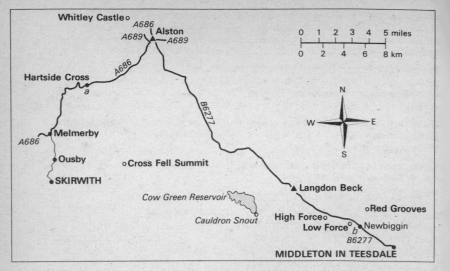

Cross Fell Summit At 2930 feet (893 m), this is the highest summit in the Pennines.

Langdon Beck There are many fine walks to be enjoyed from here, including one to Cauldron Snout waterfalls.

High Force This spectacular waterfall is created where the River Tees drops 70 feet (21 m) over the black cliffs of the Great Whin Sill, an outcrop of volcanic rock.

Low Force Waterfall on the River Tees. To the north of the road are more falls and Gibson's Cave.

Red Grooves These were caused by the ancient practice of 'hushing'. Lead prospectors would dam up water on a hillside, then release it suddenly allowing it to wash away the surface and expose the bedrock.

b If you next intend to take Route 138 to Greenhead, you can turn to it here.

Middleton in Teesdale See Route 129. Also links with Routes 128, 138.

Route 137　　　　11 miles　17 km
GREENHEAD — BRAMPTON

OS 1:250 000 no. 4
Bartholomew's 1:100 000 no. 38
OS 1:50 000 no. 86

Greenhead On the hill to the north east of the village is the Roman fort of Carvoran. Also links with Routes 138, 139, 140.

Thirlwall Castle Built with stone taken from the Roman Wall.

Gilsland The spa to the north of the village was visited by Sir Walter Scott.

a If you next intend to follow Route 140 to Bellingham, you can turn to it here.

Upper Denton The Saxon and Norman

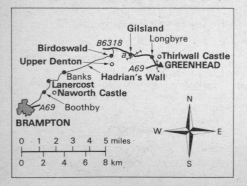

church was built using stones taken from Hadrian's Wall, and the chancel arch is probably the reconstruction of a Roman arch taken from Birdoswald.

Birdoswald Parts of walls, towers and a gateway can still be seen on the 5-acre site of the Roman fort Camboglanna (DoE, open).

Hadrian's Wall Between Birdoswald and Banks the route follows the line of the Wall, passing sites of several turrets.

Lanercost The priory, now in ruins, was founded in about 1166, and has past associations with Edward I, Queen Eleanor, and Robert Bruce. Interesting features include the Lanercost Cross, cloisters, memorials and tombs (DoE, open). A fine medieval bridge crosses the river Irthing.

Naworth Castle This 14th-century castle was used in a novel by Sir Walter Scott.

Brampton Links with Routes 119, 120, 180, 181.

Route 138   41 miles   66 km
GREENHEAD —
MIDDLETON IN TEESDALE

OS 1:250 000 nos 4, 5
Bartholomew's 1:100 000 no. 39
OS 1:50 000 nos 86, 87 (just) and 91 or 92

Greenhead See Route 137. Also links with Routes 139, 140.

Blenkinsopp Castle Built in part with stones from Hadrian's Wall.

Lambley Attractively sited railway viaduct over the River South Tyne.

Allendale Town At one time a market town for the surrounding lead-mining area, this claims to be the geographical centre of Britain, as witness the interesting sundial on the church wall. Pagan celebrations are held on New Year's Eve.

Burnhope Reservoir The dam of the reservoir, which serves Sunderland, South Shields and Jarrow, was built of local stone in the 1930s.

a If there is busy traffic on the A689 you may prefer to follow the parallel lanes between Cowshill and Daddry Shield, although they have much harder gradients.

Westgate This village and Eastgate mark the sites of the entrances to the one-time hunting park of the Bishops of Durham. Old watermill.

Red Grooves, High Force and **Low Force** See Route 136.

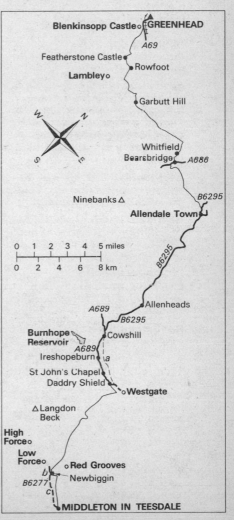

b If you next intend to follow Route 136 to Skirwith, you can turn to it here.

c The lane between Newbiggin and Middleton in Teesdale climbs high up the hillside to descend again. The B6277 is easier, following the river valley, but can be busy.

Middleton in Teesdale See Route 129. Also links with Routes 128, 136.

Route 139   24 miles   39 km
GREENHEAD — HEXHAM

OS 1:250 000 no. 4
Bartholomew's 1:100 000 no. 39
OS 1:50 000 nos 87, 86 (just)

For its whole length this route runs just south of Hadrian's Wall and there are many opportunities for making short detours to it. This famous example of military building will be appreciated best by walking along sections of it.

Greenhead See Route 137. Also links with Routes 138, 140.

Walltown Crags There are fine views from the Wall here (DoE).

Military Road This part of the route follows the course of the military road built after the 1745 uprising of Scottish Jacobites to link Newcastle and Carlisle. The building of this road was the greatest single cause of stone removal from the Wall.

Cawfields Milecastle A small lane crosses the Wall here, providing access to the fortifications on either side. These castles were constructed by the Romans at intervals of one Roman mile (1620 yards).

Once Brewed There is a National Park information centre here.

a From the point where the Wall crosses the lane 0.5 mile (1 km) north of Once Brewed a footpath leads east to Housesteads Fort along one of the most dramatic sections of the Wall above Crag Lough. It passes a milecastle and offers fine views.

Vindolanda The site of a 'behind the lines' fort (DoE), with a small museum of finds. Parts of the ramparts, gateways and central buildings remain.

Housesteads Fort The finest fort (DoE, open) on the Wall, commanding fine views. It once housed a thousand soldiers, and the ramparts, gateways, granaries, latrines, headquarters and barracks remain visible. Outside the south gate is evidence of a subsequent settlement, and the 'murder house', so called because the skeleton of a man with a sword in his ribs was found here. There is a small museum containing Roman pottery, sculpture, and small objects. There is an exciting walk westwards along the Wall, past the ruined milecastle and above Crag Lough.

Sewing Shields A milecastle and the Wall (DoE).

Stanegate This was the communications artery for the Wall which linked together the forts, garrisons and various other military posts.

Carrawbrough The reconstruction of a Roman Temple of Mithras (DoE).

Black Carts A section of the Wall (DoE).

Chesters The site of a large Roman fort (DoE, open) which once housed five hundred troops. Excavations have revealed sophisticated bath houses, rooms with underfloor heating and an aqueduct designed to bring spring water to the fort. There is also a museum containing inscriptions, tools, weapons and ornaments.

Hexham See Route 128. Also links with Route 127.

Route 140   27 miles   44 km
BELLINGHAM — GREENHEAD

OS 1:250 000 no. 4
Bartholomew's 1:100 000 nos 38, 42
OS 1:50 000 nos 80, 86

In order to ride this route it is necessary to obtain permission to use the tracks from the Conservancy Office of the Forestry Commission. Some 9 miles (15 km) of the route go through a network of untarmacadamed forestry roads, and should not be attempted without a 1:50 000 map and compass, plenty of time, good ability at map reading, and permission from the Forestry Commission (see Appendix 7).

The section of the route between Gilsland and Churnsike Lodge is over a very quiet, dead-end lane. It makes an excellent 'there and back' detour from Gilsland over open, desolate countryside, as an alternative to following the route in its entirety.

Bellingham See Route 127. Also links with Routes 126, 141, 142, 148.

a If you next intend to follow Route 141 to Tushielaw Inn, turn to it here.

b There is a gate near each end of the track section of this route which may be locked, so you must be prepared to lift your cycle over.

c If the ford over the River Irthing is in flood, use the footbridge at Butterburn.

d Parts of the land to the west of the

Churnsike Lodge to Gilsland lane constitute a danger zone, and it is unwise to go walking in the area.

Gilsland, Birdoswald and **Thirlwall Castle** See Route 137.

e If you next intend to follow Route 137 to Brampton, you can turn to it here.

Greenhead See Route 137. Also links with Routes 138, 139.

Route 141   62 miles   99 km
TUSHIELAW INN — BELLINGHAM

OS 1:250 000 no. 4
Bartholomew's 1:100 000 nos 38, 41, 42
OS 1:50 000 nos 79, 80

The stretch of this route between Bellingham and Kielder is changing due to the construction of the Kielder Reservoir. However, the reservoir is to have roads around it, and so the route will remain

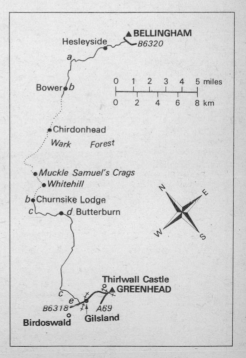

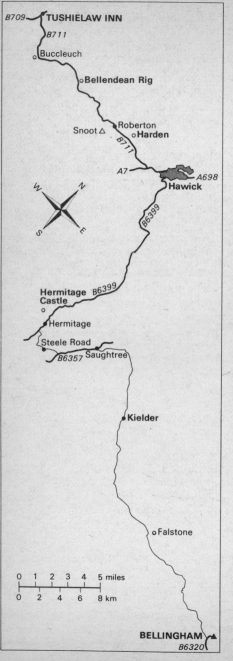

navigable although the roads will be shaped differently.

Tushielaw Inn Links with Routes 121, 122, 146, 147.

Bellendean Rig Bellendean is the highland gathering-ground of the Scott clan, and the cry they used in battle too.

Harden The 16th-century Harden House was the home of Watt Scot, a famous cattle-reiver.

Hawick The largest of the border towns, Hawick used to be called a 'women's town' as so many women worked in the hosiery mills. The town made fine underwear which was boasted to 'enjoy the patronage of many of the crowned heads of Europe'. It has Britain's oldest livestock auction market, where over a quarter-million head change hands yearly. There is a museum of local history and hosiery machinery.

Hermitage Castle This border castle was once owned by the Earl of Bothwell, the lover and third husband of Mary Queen of Scots. It has 14th-century curtain-walls (DoE, open).

Kielder A forestry village, created for the workers of the Kielder Forest, much of which was planted for timber this century. In the valley to the south-east is the site of the Kielder Reservoir.

Bellingham See Route 127. Also links with Routes 126, 140, 142, 148.

Route 142   19 miles   31 km
CARTER BAR — BELLINGHAM

OS 1:250 000 no. 4
Bartholomew's 1:100 000 nos 41, 42
OS 1:50 000 no. 80

Carter Bar Viewpoint on the English–Scottish border. On the hillside just to the north east is Redesmire Fray, the site of the last of the great border battles which took place in 1575 between the Scottish Jeddarts and the men of Redesdale. Links with Route 143.

Catcleugh Reservoir On the open hillsides you are likely to see the white-faced, hardy sheep called Cheviots, named after this area of hills for which they were bred.

Byrness This is a 20th-century village, developed for workers in the surrounding forests.

a The tracks used in this route are over easy gradients and though without tarmac have good surfaces. They follow a forest road and a farm track over open country. As there are several track junctions within the forest, not all of them shown on the Bartholomew's map, a 1:50 000 map and compass are necessary for navigation in the forest. The track over open country is not a defined right of way. You may have to lift your cycle over a locked gate between the forest and open country. The alternative route uses the A68 which can be busy at times.

b If you are following the tracks from north to south, you should turn off the A68 through a small car-park for the public, over a bridge crossing the River Rede, then fork left at a track junction with a building in the angle. On emerging from the forest, do not turn left to skirt the woods, but go straight ahead into open country.

Bellingham See Route 127. Also links with Routes 126, 140, 141, 148.

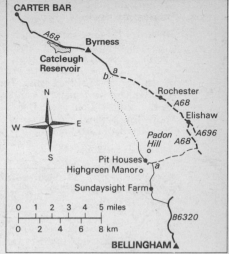

wildfowl and rare marsh-plants.

a If you next intend to follow Route 148 to Bellingham, you can turn to it here.

Woden Law Views, a hill-fort and Roman siege works. The multivallate defences that can be seen are thought to have been thrown up during a training exercise by the local garrison.

Route 143   21 miles   33 km
TOWN YETHOLM — CARTER BAR

OS 1:250 000 no. 4
Bartholomew's 1:100 000 no. 41
OS 1:50 000 nos 74, 80

Town Yetholm According to tradition, several of the Scottish nobles killed at Flodden are buried here. The town was for a long time the headquarters of Scottish gypsies. Links with Routes 144, 145, 146, 147, 148.

Kirk Yetholm This is the northern end of the walkers' Pennine Way to Edale in the Peak District. The neighbourhood has many fine tracks and paths into the Cheviot Hills.

Yetholm Loch Yetholm Loch and marsh form a nature reserve, rich in migrating

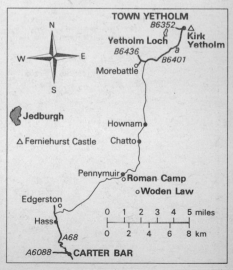

Roman Camp The banks of this large camp are still visible.

Jedburgh The town has rich historic associations with monarchs and poets. There is a museum in the Georgian County Jail, on the site of a castle which was often occupied by the English. The abbey (ruined) was founded as a priory in the 12th century (DoE, open). Queen Mary's House, where Mary Queen of Scots stayed, contains a museum (open).

Carter Bar See Route 142.

Route 144   31 miles   50 km
BERWICK-UPON-TWEED — TOWN YETHOLM

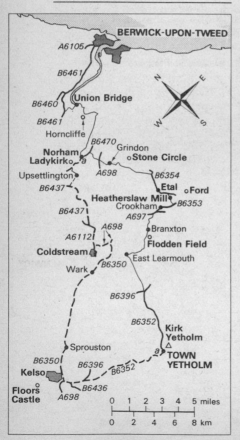

OS 1:250 000 no. 4
Bartholomew's 1:100 000 no. 41
OS 1:50 000 nos 74, 75

Berwick-upon-Tweed See Route 125. Also links with Route 124.

Union Bridge So called because the bridge geographically marks a union between England and Scotland. The border follows the river Tweed here.

Norham The ruined Norman castle (DoE, open) withstood many sieges by the Scots, and is immortalized in Sir Walter Scott's poem 'Marmion'.

a The main route follows quiet lanes and B roads through the foot hills of the Cheviots while a part of the alternative route uses the valley of the river Tweed.

Ladykirk The village church was built by James IV in gratitude following an incident in which he nearly drowned in the Tweed.

Coldstream For centuries a fording place on the Tweed, and also the first headquarters of the Coldstream Guards, raised by General Monk for Cromwell's Army in 1650.

Kelso Described by Scott as beautiful and romantic, the town has the ruins of a once great abbey (DoE, open) founded by David I in 1128. It became important as a fording point of the river Tweed and the bridge was a model for the old Waterloo Bridge over the Thames in London.

Floors Castle An immense mansion with fine tapestries, furniture, porcelain, paintings and extensive grounds and gardens (open). There is a theatre built by Napoleonic prisoners, and a holly tree in the grounds marks the place where James II was killed in 1460 by an exploding cannon.

Stone Circle Constructed of red sandstone, this is Northumberland's best megalithic monument.

Etal Thatched roofs and the ruins of a castle which was destroyed by the Scots before their defeat at Flodden in 1513.

Ford A model village with a 13th-century

castle destroyed by the Scots but with three original towers surviving. It was substantially altered in the 18th and 19th centuries. Biblical paintings by Lady Waterford decorate the walls of the old village school.

Heatherslaw Mill A restored mill standing by the river Till.

Flodden Field A terrible battle took place here in 1513 between the Scots under James IV, and the English under the Earl of Surrey. A simple monument commemorates the dead, and is said to mark the spot where James IV was killed.

Kirk Yetholm See Route 143.

Town Yetholm See Route 143. Also links with Routes 145, 146, 147, 148.

Route 145   34 miles 54 km
TOWN YETHOLM — ALNWICK

OS 1:250 000 no. 4
Bartholomew's 1:100 000 no. 42
OS 1:50 000 nos 74, 75, 81

Town Yetholm See Route 143. Also links with Routes 144, 146, 147, 148.

Kirk Yetholm See Route 143.

Branxton Just south of the village is Flodden Field—see Route 144.

a The lane (which turns into a track) leading south from here follows the lovely valley of College Burn deep into the Cheviots, to the foot of the Cheviot itself. The surrounding hills should only be ventured into in good weather, and if you are properly equipped for hill walking.

The Cheviot The highest in the range, with an extensive peat bog covering its 2676 foot (816 m) summit. Excellent views from the top.

Kirknewton The primitive structure of the Church of St Gregory suggests that it was once used as a refuge and there is a very early carving of the Adoration of the Magi. Here also is the tomb of Josephine Butler, a fighter for women's education and legal rights.

Yeavering Bell The site of a 14-acre hill-fort with foundations of many huts still visible, and a superb viewpoint.

Yeavering It is believed that King Edwin of Northumbria had a palace here. By the roadside not far away is a cairn which marks the site of the old royal township known as Gefrin.

Wooler The market town for a large

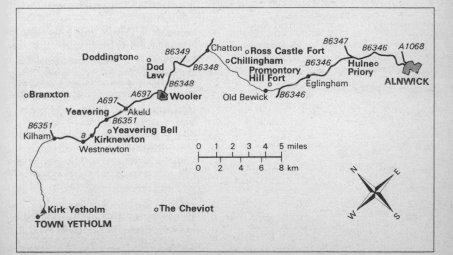

sheep farming and forestry area. Few of the original old buildings survived the medieval raids and fires. A plaque in Queen's Road commemorates Josephine Butler and the mound of a Norman castle can be seen south of the market place.

Doddington Here is one of the last peel towers to be built before England and Scotland were united. There is a 19th-century watch tower built in the churchyard to guard against body snatchers.

Dod Law On the summit are the earthworks of an Iron Age hill-fort and some rock outcrops inscribed with strange cup and ring shapes thought to date from the Bronze Age. In good weather there are excellent views.

Chillingham The park (open) surrounding the castle has a herd of white cattle which are descendants of prehistoric wild oxen. They are said to have survived because they were walled in when the park was created in 1220, and thus escaped future outbreaks of cattle disease. The Wildlife park is also open. The church has an interesting 15th-century monument in the crypt.

Ross Castle Fort The outlines of an ancient hill-fort (NT) can still be seen, and there are superb views. This was probably a beacon hill in prehistoric and border fighting times.

Promontory Hill-Fort A large and complex site, the west section having the foundations of circular huts while the east was probably once used for livestock.

Hulne Priory See Route 125.

Alnwick See Route 126. Also links with Route 125.

Route 146   48 miles   77 km
TOWN YETHOLM — TUSHIELAW INN

OS 1:250 000 no. 4
Bartholomew's 1:100 000 no. 41
OS 1:50 000 nos 73, 74, 79 (just)

Both this route and Route 147 link Town

Yetholm to Tushielaw Inn, and indeed they are the same between Town Yetholm and point a on the route map, and between Tushielaw Inn and point b on the route map.

This route makes significant use of A roads in order to visit many of the features of architectural interest in the area, whereas Route 147 passes fewer points of interest but is on quieter roads.

Town Yetholm See Route 143. Also links with Routes 144, 145, 147, 148.

Kirk Yetholm and **Yetholm Loch** See Route 143.

Kelso and **Floors Castle** See Route 144.

a Routes 146 and 147 diverge at this point.

Smailholm Tower This tower, which was probably built in the 16th century, has walls well over 7 feet (2 m) thick and five storeys still intact. It affords magnificent views (DoE, open).

St Boswells Site of the gruesome gravestone of Maiden Lilliard, who joined the Battle of Ancrum after her lover was slain, and fought valiantly even after mutilation.

Dryburgh A 12th-century border monastery in a lovely setting and having good cloisters. It is the burial place of Walter Scott and Earl Haig (DoE, open).

Bemersyde The estate has been in the hands of the Haig family at least since the 12th century. An old prophecy has it that, 'Tyde what may, whate'er betyde, Haig shall be Haig of Bemersyde'. The family now run a pottery and showroom (open).

Scott's view This view over the River Tweed was beloved by Walter Scott. On the opposite side of the river is Old Melrose, where there was a monastery from the 7th century until the 12th when it became inadequate for the Cistercians, who built the 12th-century abbey at Melrose.

Trimontium On this riverside bluff was Trimontium, a complex of Roman forts and camps where 'Dere Street' crossed the River Tweed.

Melrose The ruins of the 12th-century Cistercian abbey, founded by David I, where Robert the Bruce's heart is supposedly buried (DoE, open). Remains of beautiful traceried windows; abbey museum. Priorwood Gardens has Lutyens wrought-iron work (NTS, open). There is a 17th-century mercat cross in the square. The town invented 'sevens' Rugby.

Bowden One of Scotland's earliest surviving churches, built in the 12th century by the monks of Kelso. Some of their work can still be seen.

Abbotsford The celebrated home of Sir Walter Scott (open).

Galashiels In Waukrigg Mill is the Bernet Klein Exhibition of paintings and photographs. The Scottish College of Textiles is situated in the town and is the headquarters of the country's tweed manufacture.

Selkirk The town was once a royal burgh; in 1204 King William the Lion held his parliament here. Selkirk was a centre of border wars for three hundred years. When it was burnt by the English in 1513 there was only one survivor. Walter Scott was once the sheriff. It is now a mill town. There is a museum of Mungo Park, the explorer, and also of local crafts.

Philiphaugh Nearby is the site of the decisive battle against Charles I's cause in Scotland.

Bowhill The long-standing and splendid seat of the Dukes of Buccleugh. The house contains fine collections (open).

Foulshiels The birthplace of Mungo Park, African missionary and explorer.

Newark The 15th-century ruin of Newark Castle, which was once a royal hunting seat. It bears the Arms of James I.

b Routes 146 and 147 diverge at this point.

Tushielaw Inn Links with Routes 121, 122, 141, 147.

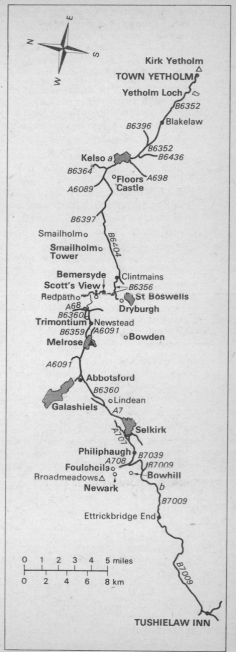

Route 147   48 miles   77 km
TOWN YETHOLM — TUSHIELAW INN

OS 1:250 000 no. 4
Bartholomew's 1:100 000 no. 41

OS 1:50 000 nos 73, 74, 79 (just), 80 (just)

See comments Route 146.

Town Yetholm See Route 143.
Also links with Routes 144, 145, 146, 148.

Kirk Yetholm and **Yetholm Loch** See Route 143.

Kelso and **Floors Castle** See Route 144.

a Routes 146 and 147 diverge here.

Peniel Heugh The 'Waterloo' monument on the hill is reputed to have been built by French prisoners of war.

Jedburgh See Route 143.

Ancrum Moor The battle site of a great 16th-century victory of the Scots over the English.

Ashkirk The Ashkirk lands were long held by the Glasgow bishops, who used to have their country palace here.

Hawick See Route 141.

a Routes 146 and 147 diverge here.

Tushielaw Inn Links with Routes 121, 122, 141, 146.

Route 148·   43 miles   69 km
TOWN YETHOLM — BELLINGHAM

OS 1:250 000 no. 4
Bartholomew's 1:100 000 no. 42
OS 1:50 000 nos 74, 80.

The track section of this route has no road alternative, and is very strenuous. It rises to about 1800 feet (550 metres) over rough ground, with some long and steep ascents and descents which normally necessitate the separate carrying of the bicycle and the pack. You should attempt the route only if equipped with a 1:50 000 map, compass and spare food and clothing, and if you are fit. Good map reading ability, good weather and plenty of time are essential.

Town Yetholm See Route 143. Also links with Routes 144, 145, 146, 147.

Kirk Yetholm and **Yetholm Loch** See Route 143.

a If you next intend to follow Route 143 to Carter Bar, you can turn to it here.

b If you are following the route from north to south, you should leave Cocklawfoot on the track south-east, which climbs and then follows the spur between Kingseat and Kelsocleuch Burns. At the head of the spur continue generally south-east to cross the main ridge of high land, which is the England–Scottish border and also the Pennine Way. Veer south to Hebden Burn, and thence south-west on the track to Trows Burn and Rowhope.

c If you are following the route from south to north, you should turn right off the lane 3.5 miles (5.5 km) north-west of Shillmoor, onto a track passing Rowhope, to reach Trows. From there veer north-east to pass south of Ward Law. On descending to Hebden Burn, turn left off the track to climb steeply with Hazely Law on your right. Go generally north to cross the main ridge of high land at the head of the spur, the ridge being also the English–Scottish border and the Pennine Way. From the ridge proceed to Cocklawfoot along and down the spur of land between Kingseat and Kelsocleuch Burns.

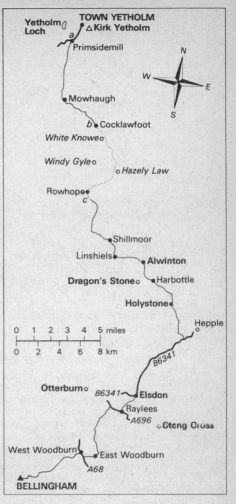

Alwinton Near the unusual split-level church stands a stone-roofed stable for the parish hearse, whose wheels are large enough to cope with travelling through fords and in snow. Sir Walter Scott worked on *Rob Roy* in the Rose and Thistle.

Dragon's Stone Reached by a footpath south of West Wood is the rock formation known as the Dragon's Stone, which has seen the performance of Druidic rites, and which was believed to cure the ills of children.

Holystone Lady's Well, traditionally associated with SS Ninian and Paulinus, is Anglo-Saxon or older (NT).

Elsdon The large village green was used as a cattle pound in times of danger. The church contains a Roman tomb, and is the site of a mass grave of some hundred people, thought to have been English soldiers killed at the

Battle of Otterburn. There is a 14th-century peel house.

Otterburn This was the site of the Chevy Chase, a famed border clash between the Scots and English in 1388. Tweeds and rugs are made at water-powered Otterburn Mill.

Steng Cross The summit is the site of an ancient gibbet.

Bellingham See Route 127. Also links with Routes 126, 140, 141, 142.

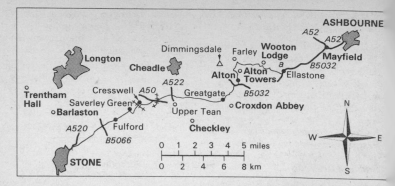

Route 149   23 miles   37 km
ASHBOURNE — STONE

OS 1:250 000 nos 6 or 7
Bartholomew's 1:100 000 nos 24, 23 (just)
OS 1:50 000 nos 128, 127, 118 (just)

Ashbourne See Route 49. Links with
Routes 50, 113, 151.

Mayfield and **Wooton Lodge** See
Route 50.

*a If you next intend to use Route 151 to
Hightown you can turn to it at Ellastone.*

Alton A village with steep lanes and a
windowless lock-up. Pugin's Alton
Castle, set above a valley cliff with the
remains of a Norman castle in its
grounds, has earnt Alton the nickname
'Rhineland of Staffordshire'.

Alton Towers The shell of a vast house
with towers and battlements in extensive
landscaped gardens. This 19th-century
creation is now a pleasure ground with
entertainments (open).

Croxden Abbey The ruins of a 12th-
century abbey (DoE, open).

Cheadle An outstanding Roman
Catholic church with brass lions, and rich
colours within.

Checkley An impressive church with
Anglo-Saxon cross shafts, medieval glass,
effigies and a sundial.

Longton The Gladstone pottery
museum and works.

Barlaston The Wedgwood museum ha
a comprehensive collection of Wedgwoo
pottery, a cinema and craft demonstra-
tion area.

Trentham Hall Italianate gardens, a 60
acre park and lake (open). All that
remains of the once great 17th-century
mansion is the ballroom and a hall.

Stone See Route 150.

Route 150   35 miles   56 km
STONE — SHREWSBURY

OS 1:250 000 no. 7
Bartholomew's 1:100 000 no. 23
OS 1:50 000 nos 126, 127

Stone Named after the cairn of stones
that once stood above the graves of two
7th-century Mercian princes, killed by
their father because they embraced
Christianity. A pleasant high street.
Links with Route 149.

Barlaston and **Trentham Hall** See
Route 149.

Eccleshall A market town. The town has
associations with the bishops of Lichfield, six of them lying buried in the
magnificent Norman and Gothic church
and its yard. There are rare carved Anglo-
Saxon stones in the tower of the church.
The bishops used to live in the castle, the
remains of which can be seen.

Longdon Upon Tern Thomas Telford
built the first cast iron viaduct here in
1794.

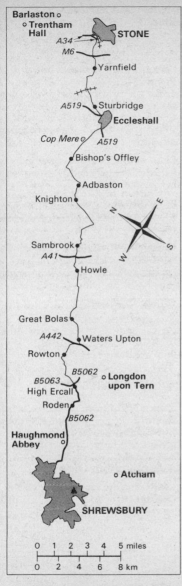

Roman Wroxeter. Attingham Park (NT, open) is famous for its interior decoration, and has a fine drawing room and picture gallery.

Shrewsbury See Route 219. Also links with Routes 153, 220, 233, 235.

Route 151   29 miles   47 km
HIGHTOWN — ASHBOURNE

OS 1:250 000 nos 5 or 7
Bartholomew's 1:100 000 nos 24, 28
OS 1:50 000 nos 118, 119

Several places of interest lie south-west of the route in or near the deep valley of the river Churnett. All of them involve steep rides down and back up again.

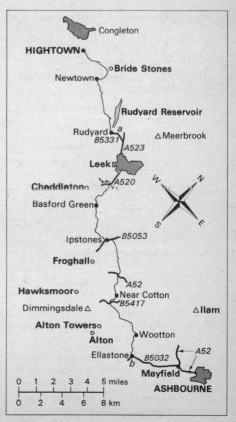

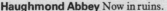

Haughmond Abbey Now in ruins.

Atcham The seven-arch bridge was built by a founder member of the Royal Academy, and the unique Church of St Eata contains stones from nearby

Hightown Links with Route 152.

Bride Stones A group of megalithic stones, thought to have been erected as a burial chamber by contemporaries of the Stonehenge builders.

Rudyard Reservoir The parents of the author Rudyard Kipling were so fond of this place that they named their son after it. It is a feeder reservoir for the Trent and Mersey Canal, and walks are laid out around it.

a The B5331 is shown as a lane on the 197 Bartholomew's map.

Leek A settlement since at least the Roman era, Leek enjoyed a heyday during the early industrial revolution as silk and textile town, as is reflected in th housing and the mill by Brindley. There are 17th- and 18th-century inns, and an art gallery.

Cheddleton A water-powered mill and museum of pottery milling, with a narrov boat on the canal.

Froghall The end of the Cauldon Canal which took water-mill products to Stoke on Trent; a canal pub.

Hawksmoor Nature reserve and bird sanctuary.

Alton and **Alton Towers** See Route 149.

b If you next intend to follow Route 149 to Stone, you can turn to it at this point.

Mayfield See Route 50.

Ilam See Route 113.

Ashbourne See Route 49. Also links with Routes 50, 113, 149.

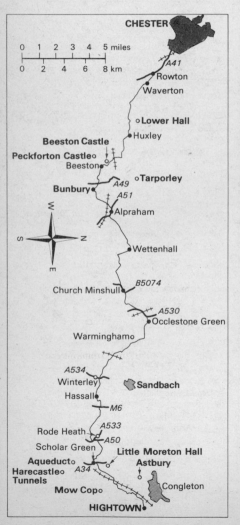

CHESTER

0 1 2 3 4 5 miles
0 2 4 6 8 km

A41
Rowton
Waverton
○ **Lower Hall**
● Huxley
Beeston Castle
Peckforton Castle○
Beeston○
○**Tarporley**
A49
Bunbury●
A51
●Alpraham
W
N
S
m
● Wettenhall
B5074
Church Minshull
A530
●Occlestone Green
Warmingham○
A534
Winterley
Sandbach
Hassall●
M6
Rode Heath *A533*
Scholar Green *A50*
Aqueduct○
Little Moreton Hall
Harecastle○ *A34*
Astbury
Tunnels
○
Mow Cop○
Congleton
HIGHTOWN●

Route 152   41 miles   65 km
CHESTER — HIGHTOWN

OS 1:250 000 nos 5 or 7
Bartholomew's 1:100 000 no. 28
OS 1:50 000 nos 117, 118

Chester Occupied by the Romans in the 1st century AD, who laid out the rectangular walled town. The city was important until the 15th century when the port declined through silting up of the Dee. It is now one of the most interesting old cities in England, and is rich in archaeological and architectural treasures, dominated by the cathedral (begun 11th century, but mainly 14th-century). The church of St John the Baptist is also notable. The castle (DoE) contains a museum, and the well-preserved city walls provide a fine walk. The Roman amphitheatre (DoE, open) is the largest discovered in Britain. Eastgate with its Victorian clock, the King Charles Tower with its museum of the Civil War and the Water Tower with its exhibition of medieval Chester are all interesting. There are many half-timbered Tudor and Elizabethan buildings, e.g. Stanley Palace, the Bishop Lloyd House and Abbey Square. The 14th-century arcades, known as the 'Rows' are unique to Chester. Grosvenor Museum has Roman antiquities. The Zoo is noted for keeping animals in natural surroundings. Links with Routes 153, 154, 225, 226.

Lower Hall This 17th-century manor house is the ancestral home of Thomas, Aldous and Julian Huxley.

Tarporley The church of St Helen has vivid stained glass and monuments.

Beeston Castle On the hill summit, which gives wide views, stand the ruins of 13th-century Beeston Castle which was destroyed after the Civil War (DoE, open).

Peckforton Castle Impressively sited on a hill is the 19th-century castle.

Bunbury In the village of old cottages stands the 14th-century collegiate church of St Boniface with 16th-century oak doors and monuments.

Sandbach The old timbered houses and cobbled market place testify to Sandbach's past prosperity. It was and is a salt and silk town. The 17th-century Old Hall is now a hotel. There are two tall Anglo-Saxon crosses with carvings (DoE).

Aqueduct Near Kidsgrove the Macclesfield Canal crosses an aqueduct over the Trent and Mersey Canal.

Harecastle Tunnels Brindley's 1.5-mile (2.5 km) long tunnel for the Trent and Mersey Canal has no towpath and the boats had to be legged through. Later, Telford built another tunnel beside it, which had a towpath to speed up the traffic.

Little Moreton Hall An outstanding black and white half-timbered hall. Built in the 15th and 16th centuries, it has a moat, elaborate gables and a great hall (NT, open).

Mow Cop On the summit of what was a beacon hill in Tudor times stands an 18th-century folly built in the shape of a ruined castle. In 1807 it was the scene of the Primitive Methodists' first large gatherings.

Astbury The church has good woodwork and effigies, but was damaged in the Civil War when horses were stabled in the pews.

Hightown Links with Route 151.

Route 153 45 miles 72 km
CHESTER — SHREWSBURY

OS 1:250 000 no. 7, or *Wales and the Marches*
Bartholomew's 1:100 000 nos 23, 28
OS 1:50 000 nos 126, 117

Chester See Route 152. Also links with Routes 154, 225, 226.

Maiden Castle An ancient earthwork thought to date from the Iron Age.

Malpas An attractive town with timbered houses, almshouses and old inns. The town is also the centre for surrounding dairy farms and the famous Cheshire cheeses can be bought here. The fine Church of St Oswald was built in the 14th and 15th centuries.

Whitchurch The market town was once a Roman settlement; finds from this era are seen in the local museum. There is a pleasant selection of old streets, shops and Georgian houses. The heart of the 1st Earl of Shrewsbury, who was killed aged 80 while fighting with the English army against Joan of Arc, lies buried in an urn beneath the church porch.

Tilstock Fine church.

Wem Most of the buildings of this market town were destroyed in a great fire in 1667. The notorious 17th-century Judge Jeffreys, whose home was Lowe

Hall, was once Baron of Wem. Interesting buildings include the market hall, town hall, cheese hall and the church. William Hazlitt, essayist and critic, grew up in a small white house in Noble Street.

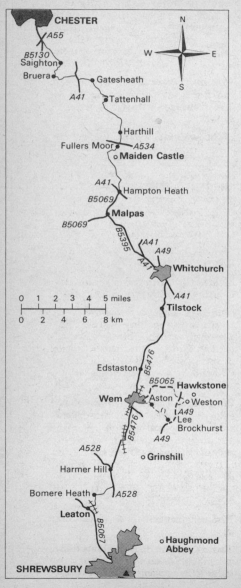

Hawkstone House House and park are described as the most romantic and beautiful in Salop.

Grinshill Stone from the sandstone quarry here was used to build Roman Wroxeter, and copper was once mined on the nearby ridge. The church is of local stone.

Leaton Victorian church and vicarage.

Haughmond Abbey Ruins (DoE).

Shrewsbury See Route 219. Also links with Routes 150, 220, 233, 235.

Route 154   33 miles   53 km
SIDDINGTON — CHESTER

OS 1:250 000 nos 5 or 7
Bartholomew's 1:100 000 no. 28
OS 1:50 000 nos 117, 118

This route links North Wales with the Pennines, and to do this while avoiding conurbations has to take a tortuous line through the busy West Midlands. It does however necessitate crossing and using short stretches of A road, and on these extra care should be taken.

If you intend to use both this route and Route 155, you should read the comment at the head of the latter.

Siddington Links with Route 155.

Nether Alderley Alderley Old Mill is a 15th-century corn-mill (NT, open) which has been restored to full working order.

Capesthorne Hall A grand Victorian building containing furniture, pictures and Americana (open).

Jodrell Bank This famous radio telescope was built for Manchester University in 1957, and is used to record the movements of extra-terrestrial bodies. The Concourse Building has exhibitions and can be visited.

Peover Hall The house dates from 1585 and has Tudor stables with fine ornamental plasterwork ceilings (open). The grounds have topiary work and an Elizabethan summer house.

Knutsford A pleasant town with old black and white houses. This was the Cranford of Mrs Gaskell's novel of the same name. It was also the meeting place of Sir Henry Royce and Charles Stewart Rolls which led to the forging of the famous Rolls Royce partnership.

Tatton Park The Hall, built in about 1800, has a fine collection of furniture, pictures, china, silver and glass (NT, open). There are 54 acres of formal gardens and a 1000-acre deer park (NT, open), nature trails and a medieval village trail.

Lower Peover Several old cottages, an old water-mill and a fine church with pews designed to keep the draughts out.

Great Budworth An attractive village with a church that has interesting monuments and woodwork.

Delamere Forest The 4000 acres of dense forest is interspersed with small lakes known locally as meres.

Tarvin The town is set on the A51 road, the old Roman Watling Street. In the Civil War it was an important Parliamentarian garrison.

Chester See Route 152. Also links with Routes 153, 225, 226.

Route 155 30 miles 48 km
EDALE — SIDDINGTON

OS 1:250 000 nos 5 or 7
Bartholomew's 1:100 000 no. 29
OS 1:50 000 nos 110, 118, 109 (just)

In order to avoid busy roads and built up areas, this route uses lanes which in places require diligent map reading.

If you intend to use both this route and Route 154, read the comment at the head of the latter.

Edale See Route 113. Also links with Routes 114, 156.

Rowland Cote Edale YH.

Mam Tor and **Castleton** See Route 113.

a If you next intend to follow Route 113 to

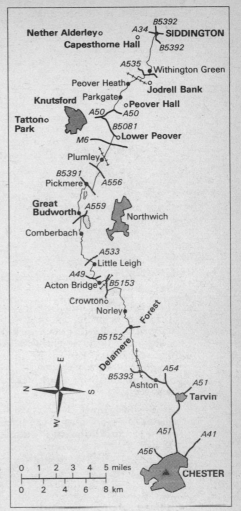

Ashbourne, you can turn to it here.

Chapel-en-le-Frith This place used to be situated on the edge of the once extensive Peak Forest, hence its name 'Chapel-by-the-forest'. There are several old inns, a 17th-century market cross, and the town stocks.

Lyme Park The House is Elizabethan, with a fine Palladian exterior, and carvings by a student of Grinling Gibbons

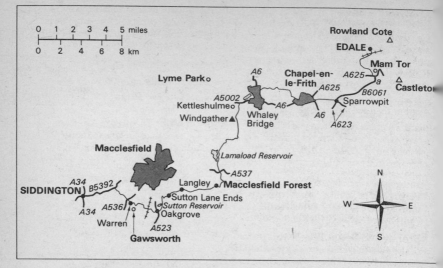

(NT, open). There is also a large garden and extensive deer park.

Macclesfield A silk manufacturing town of character, with black and white timbered houses, and a church reached on one side by 108 steps. The West Park Museum and Art Gallery has an important collection of Egyptian exhibits, paintings, and sketches by Landseer.

Macclesfield Forest The crags and valleys of the surrounding moors were once the haunt of highwaymen and brigands.

Gawsworth Tudor Gawsworth Hall is an attractive half-timbered manor house (open) with an orangery, tilting ground and walled park. This was the home of Mary Fitton, Maid of Honour to Elizabeth I, and possibly 'Dark Lady' of Shakespeare's sonnets.

Siddington Links with Route 154.

Route 156   13 miles   20 km
EDALE — EYAM

OS 1:250 000 nos 6, 5 or 7
Bartholomew's 1:100 000 no. 29
OS 1:50 000 nos 119, 110
1 inch:1 mile Peak District tourist map

Edale See Route 113. Also links with Routes 114, 155.

Rowland Cote Edale YH.

Mam Tor, Castleton and **Bradwell** See Route 113.

Eyam Moor Fine views and a Bronze Age stone circle (DoE).

Eyam See Route 157.

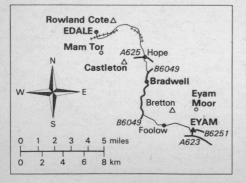

Route 157   33 miles   53 km
EYAM — CHURCH WARSOP

OS 1:250 000 nos 6 or 5
Bartholomew's 1:100 000 no 29
OS 1:50 000 nos 119, 110, 120

Eyam The village is known for tragic but courageous events which overcame the community during the Great Plague of 1665–66. The Plague was brought to Eyam in a box of infected clothes, and rather than see it spread to neighbouring districts, the villagers cut themselves off from the world, under the leadership of their resolute rector William Mompesson. Five out of every six inhabitants died. Mompesson's Well, where money and goods were exchanged during the Plague can be visited. Saxon cross and unusual 18th-century sundial in the churchyard. Links with Route 156.

Stoney Middleton The village is the site of the August well dressing, a tradition common in this part of the country, and there is an unusual octagonal church.

Edensor The village was destroyed and rebuilt in its present position to suit the landscaped views from Chatsworth for the benefit of its eccentric owner, the 6th Duke of Devonshire.

Chatsworth House Built in 1707 for the 1st Duke of Devonshire, this is one of England's greatest stately homes. The house contains famous collections of paintings, sculptures and furniture; there is a great park, and gardens with elaborate waterworks (open).

Bakewell See Route 113.

a The detour around Stanton Moor uses mostly quiet roads, and links together several places of interest.

Stanton Moor The Bronze Age monuments on this moor include the Nine Ladies, the King Stone and Doll Tor.

Birchover The Heathcote Museum contains finds from the Bronze Age barrows on Stanton Moor, and there are two 'rocking stones'.

Winster A late 17th- or early 18th-century market house (NT, open).

Haddon Hall This is perhaps the most complete and authentic example of a manorial home in England. Much of the interior and furnishing is original and there is a small museum of items discovered during restoration work. The delightful gardens have terraces and masses of roses (open).

Rowsley The Peacock Hotel was originally a stone manor house, built in the 17th century.

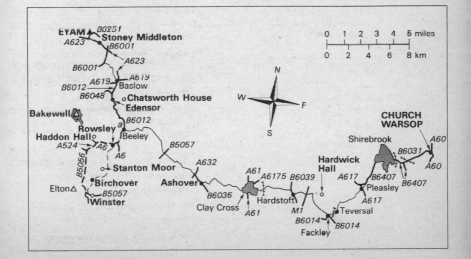

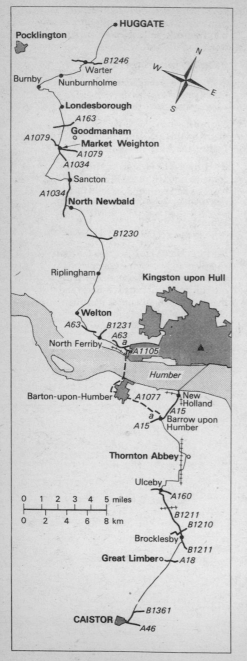

Ashover In 1814 over-enthusiastic bell ringers cracked the church bell while ringing out the news of Napoleon's defeat. The church also has a rare Norman lead font and an early 16th-century rood screen. To the east of the village stand the ruins of Eastwood Hall, an Elizabethan manor house destroyed by Parliamentarians.

Hardwick Hall Bess of Hardwick built this imposing hall (NT, open) in the last decade of the 16th century, and had the initials of her name built into the top of each tower. Many of the original contents remain, among them tapestries, elaborate plasterwork, and furniture. There is also a walled garden and a herb garden.

Church Warsop Links with Route 65.

Route 158   53 miles   85 km
HUGGATE — CAISTOR

OS 1:250 000 no. 6
Bartholomew's 1:100 000 nos 30, 33
OS 1:50 000 nos 106, 112, 113

This route uses a British Rail ferry between New Holland and Hull.

Huggate North of the village are the unusual earthworks called Huggate Dikes. Links with Routes 159, 166.

Pocklington Burnby Hall Gardens have fine lily ponds and a museum of hunting and fishing (open).

Londesborough Traditionally this was the site of King Edwin of Northumbria's palace, and the place of his conversion to Christianity.

Market Weighton William Bradley, the Yorkshire Giant, is buried in the churchyard.

Goodmanham The site where, in 627, King Edwin of Northumbria smashed his pagan temple after his conversion to Christianity.

North Newbald Church with four Norman doors.

Welton Dick Turpin was arrested in the inn.

a Eventually the new Humber Bridge will provide a means of avoiding the busy city of Hull.

Kingston upon Hull Nowadays often called simply Hull, this city gained its longer name by its origin as a 12th-century settlement on lands of Edward I. Hull is England's third port and its largest fishing port. It has mostly modern buildings because of severe bombing in the Second World War. Maister House has a Palladian hall and good ironwork (NT, open). Wilberforce's birthplace houses a museum of slavery (open). The Georgian Houses museum consists of furnished 17th- and 18th-century merchants' houses. Transport and archaeology museum; Town Docks museum with whaling collection. Hull is Britain's only city with its own telephone system.

Thornton Abbey Abbey with an excellent 14th-century gatehouse (DoE, open).

Great Limber An 18th-century mausoleum, built over a tumulus where Roman artefacts have been found.

Caistor See Route 61. Also links with Route 62.

Route 159　　　　50 miles　80 km
SCARBOROUGH — HUGGATE

OS 1:250 000 no 6
Bartholomew's 1:100 000 nos 33, 36
OS 1:50 000 nos 101, 106

Part of the fascination of this route lies in the

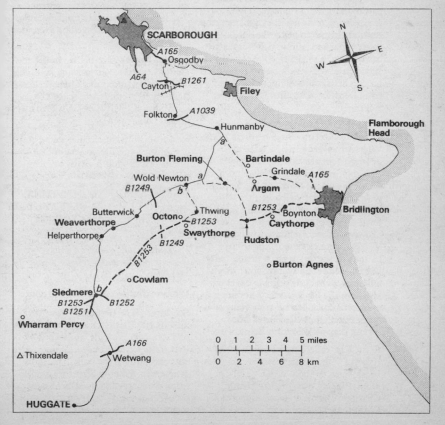

many deserted village sites, as described below. If you are particularly interested in them, you will find a 1:50 000 map helpful as their locations are generally not immediately obvious.

Scarborough A holiday resort and early spa town. According to the old sagas, Scarborough was founded by the Norse (Escardeburg or Skardeburge). The site of the 12th-century castle has been occupied intermittently since the Bronze Age (DoE, open); remains of the Roman signal station can be seen. Anne Bronte is buried in the churchyard of St Mary's. The church of St Martin was built in the 19th century, and has much pre-Raphaelite decoration. There is a superb view from Oliver's Mount, and there are many old pubs in the medieval fishing part of the town. Londesborough Lodge is a museum of Scarborough history, the Rotunda Museum has archaeological collections, and paintings by local artists can be seen in the Crescent Art Gallery. Wood End, once the home of the Sitwell family, houses Sitwell memorabilia and a natural history museum. Links with Routes 160, 168.

Argam, Bartindale, Caythorpe, Cowlam, Octon, Swaythorpe and **Wharram Percy** are all sites of deserted villages close to the route. Although many areas of England have 'lost' villages, this area of the Yorkshire wolds is especially rich in sites with visible remains, which usually take the form of ridges and depressions over the one-time house foundations and streets. Villages were deserted for various reasons in the past, but a prime cause was the reduction of England's population by a third during medieval outbreaks of the black death. They are too numerous for all to be archaeologically investigated, but there have been several digs at Wharram Percy.

Filey The mile-long coralline rocky ridge of Filey Brigg serves as a natural breakwater to the old fishing village, around which a resort has grown. Charlotte Bronte was a frequenter of Cliff House.

a The main route provides a fairly direct link between Scarborough and the more typical Wold scenery of steep, winding valleys. The alternative passes further points of interest in gentler hill scenery.

Bridlington A seaside resort with long sands, which has developed around an old, still active, fishing port. St Mary's Church, incorporating the nave of a 12th-century priory, has a fine north porch and west doorway. The priory's 14th-century Bayle Gate has served many purposes, but is now a museum. Georgian Sewerby Hall, set in gardens of botanical interest, houses a museum with an exhibition about Amy Johnson, the first woman to fly from England to Australia.

Flamborough Head The chalk cliffs of the head, formed where the Yorkshire Wolds meet the sea, are England's most important mainland breeding ground for sea-birds.

Burton Agnes Elizabethan house containing carved woodwork and paintings of old master and impressionist schools, standing in grounds landscaped by Capability Brown (open). Norman manor house (DoE, open).

Rudston Both the circular shape of the churchyard and the presence of a huge prehistoric monolith testify to the antiquity of the church site.

Burton Fleming The area is rich in square burial barrows, which are peculiar to Northumbria and the Yorkshire Wolds.

b The main route follows a valley bottom, whereas the alternative follows a ridge of higher land.

Weaverthorpe Good Norman church.

Sledmere The Georgian house has a famous 100-foot (30-metre) long library, and stands in grounds landscaped by Capability Brown (open). A fine modern church stands in the park. The 18th-century Sir Sykes of Sledmere transformed the previous open-field scenery of the Wolds to its present aspect by planting hedges, making roads, pioneering rops and so forth. A war memorial to the Wold Waggoners' in the village.

Muggate See Route 158. Also links with Route 166.

Route 160   41 miles   65 km
CASTLETON — SCARBOROUGH

OS 1:250 000 nos 5, 6
Bartholomew's 1:100 000 no. 36
OS 1:50 000 nos 94, 101
1 inch:1 mile North York Moors tourist map

Castleton Links with Routes 161, 164, 167.

a This rough moorland track can be used in good weather as an alternative to the surfaced lane further down the hillside. The track runs between Beacon Hill and a point just to the south west of the village of Stonegate. It is not a defined right of way.

Beacon Hill Views from near the triangulation point.

b The route follows a lane which is not marked on the Bartholomew's map of 1977, but which runs west from Hutton Mulgrave towards Alder Park.

Whitby The dramatically sited abbey was founded in the 7th century and was an important centre of learning in early times. It is now in ruins (DoE, open). St Mary's Church is Norman with a Georgian interior and has 199 steps leading up to it. Whitby was a whaling centre in the 18th century, and is now a fishing town and quiet resort. The area is well known for its jet (fossilized wood), and there are still some jet craftsmen in the town. The home of James Cook can be seen in Grape Lane. The Whitby Museum has a fine collection of fossils, Captain Cook relics and much of local interest. There is also an art gallery.

c There are two routes between Scarborough and High Hawsker. The coastal route follows the line of a disused railway between Robin Hood's Bay and Ravenscar. This has a reasonable surface but is not a defined right of way. The inland

route goes via Broxa Forest and does not involve rough stuff.

Robin Hood's Bay An old fishing village beloved of tourists and artists. Every house once had a hiding place for contraband.

Boggle Hole A smugglers' cove.

Scarborough See Route 159. Also links with Route 168.

Route 161   27 miles   44 km
CASTLETON — OSMOTHERLEY

OS 1:250 000 nos 5 or 6
Bartholomew's 1:100 000 no 36
OS 1:50 000 nos 93, 94, 99 (just), 100 (just)
1 inch:1 mile North York Moors tourist map

Castleton Links with Routes 160, 164, 167.

Cook's Monument On a hill summit commanding extensive views, stands a monument to Captain James Cook, navigator and explorer.

Ingleby Greenhow Church with interesting carvings and effigies.

a   The main route penetrates a particularly impressive part of the North York Moors at the cost of some strenuous hill-climbs. The alternative follows the foot of the Moors.

Botton Head The highest point of the Cleveland Hills. A triangulation pillar surmounts a great stone burial mound,

which marks the end of Thurkilsty, the ancient trackway from York to Cleveland.

Cringle Moor At the summit are a stone seat and a plaque indicating the other peaks around and their names.

Carlton This pretty village with its manor house and small Palladian villa had an unusual vicar in Canon Kyle at the turn of the century. Besides rebuilding the church, he rode to hounds and kept the pub.

Whorlton Hill There are old jet workings on the north-west face of the hill, which was a legendary dragon's lair.

Whorlton At this now tiny place are the entrenchments which enclosed a medieval market and village, and the gatehouse of a castle.

Mount Grace Priory The most important Carthusian ruin in England (DoE, NT, open). The start of the strenuous Lyke Wake Walk is nearby.

Osmotherley See Route 165. Also links with Route 162.

Route 162   26 miles   42 km
RICHMOND — OSMOTHERLEY

OS 1:250 000 nos 5 or 6
Bartholomew's 1:100 000 no 35
OS 1:50 000 nos 99, 93, 92 (just)

Richmond See Route 130. Also links with Routes 129, 135.

Easby See Route 129.

Scotch Corner Now an uninspiring road junction, but in the past the place where Scottish drovers handed over herds of Scottish cattle, destined for London and other markets, to their English counterparts. The A1 road still follows much of the droving route between Scotland and London.

Moulton Rebuilt in about 1650, Moulton Hall has a fine carved wooden staircase (NT, open).

Brompton Fine examples of Anglo-Danish hogback tombstones, probably a

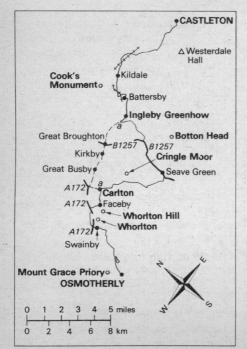

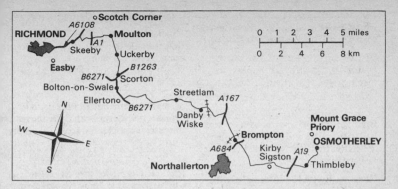

thousand years old, can be seen in the churchyard, where there are also portions of Anglo-Saxon crosses and shafts.

Northallerton An old posting town, with many inns still remaining.

Mount Grace Priory See Route 161.

Osmotherley See Route 165. Also links with Route 161.

to York Minster. Small classical church with a cupola giving unusual light. Wood-carver's shop.

Crayke In this hill-top village are the remains of the one-time castle of the bishops of Durham.

Sheriff Hutton The ruin of a castle, which was prominent in the Wars of the Roses, stands on the site of an earlier

---

Route 163   24 miles   39 km
OSWALDKIRK — YORK

OS 1:250 000 nos 5 or 6
Bartholomew's 1:100 000 nos 33, 36
OS 1:50 000 nos 100, 105

Oswaldkirk Links with Routes 164, 165, 166.

Gilling East Castle with a Norman keep and later additions including a hall and great chamber (open).

Ampleforth The abbey and Roman Catholic public school were founded by monks. Good views south-east to Gilling Castle.

Byland Abbey Ruins of a 12th-century Cistercian abbey, sited by farmlands which were drained from the marsh by the monks (DoE, open).

Coxwold Shandy Hall, which was first built in the 15th century as a timber-framed open hall, was the home of Laurence Sterne and where he wrote *Tristram Shandy* (open).

Brandsby Views over the plain of York

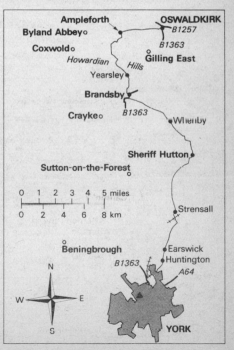

castle built by the Sheriff of Yorkshire, which gave the village its name. Church with several monuments and good pews.

Sutton-on-the-Forest The 18th-century house with its beautiful furnishings stands in grounds landscaped by Capability Brown, with a Georgian ice house and temple (open).

Beningbrough An early 18th-century hall with friezes and panelling, housing a collection from the National Portrait Gallery (open).

York See Route 133. Also links with Route 132.

Route 164   44 miles   71 km
CASTLETON — OSWALDKIRK

OS 1:250 000 nos 5 or 6
Bartholomew's 1:100 000 no. 36
OS 1:50 000 nos 94, 100 (just)
1 inch:1 mile North York Moors tourist map

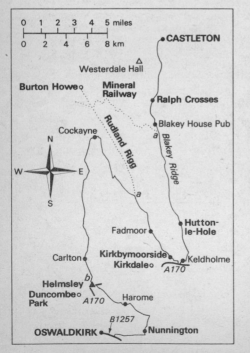

Castleton Links with Routes 160, 161, 167.

Ralph Crosses The roadside crosses are examples of the stones erected on the North York Moors long ago for a variety of reasons. Many were way markers, some erected by monks for the guidance of pilgrims, and others were boundary stones. At a short distance, by the road to the east, is another old stone, Fat Betty.

a Depending on your interests, you may like to explore either the mineral railway or Rudland Rigg (both dead-end detours). If you are tempted to use both to join the two points marked 'a' on the map, you will need plenty of time to cover so much distance on rough tracks.

Mineral Railway This disused mineral line has had its sleepers removed and cinders put down. Often used by walkers, it is part of the Lyke Wake and Cleveland Way long distance walks. It takes a lofty course above Farndale, and makes a traffic-free detour for cyclists. No defined right of way.

Burton Howe Four huge Bronze Age cairns.

Hutton-le-Hole Founded by Quakers in the 17th century, this village is a renowned beauty spot. The Ryedale Folk Museum has exhibits ranging from pre-historic to 19th-century craft tools, and has complete buildings.

Kirkbymoorside Market town with several blacksmiths.

Kirkdale The church, which was St Gregory's minster, can be dated at circa 1060 by the inscription on its Anglo-Saxon sundial. It contains Anglo-Saxon coffin lids, one of which is possibly 7th century. Mesolithic flint tools and the remains of prehistoric animals have been found in Kirkdale Cave.

Rudland Rigg Clearly following a ridge of high land, this rough track passes through a moorland area rich in tumuli and old pits.

b If you next intend to follow Route 165 to Osmotherly, you can turn to it here.

Helmsley This lovely market town has a square with several old inns, including the 16th-century Black Swan. The ruined 13th-century castle withstood a three-month siege in the Civil War (DoE, open). The Church has 20th century murals.

Duncombe Park The house by John Vanbrugh is now a school. The formal gardens with their 18th-century temples can be visited.

Nunnington Large 17th-century manor house with a panelled hall and stairs (NT, open).

Oswaldkirk Links with Routes 163, 165, 166.

Route 165   20 miles   32 km
OSMOTHERLY — OSWALDKIRK

OS 1:250 000 nos 5 or 6
Bartholomew's 1:100 000 no. 36
OS 1:50 000 nos 99 (just), 100
1 inch:1 mile North York Moors tourist map

Osmotherley The name of this village was derived from 'Oswy by his mother lay', following his death caused by a rock collapse at Roseberry Topping. Fish are sold from a stone table in the market place on Sundays. In the 19th century this was a centre of linen industry. Links with Routes 161, 162.

Rievaulx Magnificent ruins of a 12th-century Cistercian abbey (DoE, open). Rievaulx Terrace is an 18th-century landscaped walk affording fine views over the valley and abbey, and is provided with two temples (NT, open).

a The lane to Rievaulx climbs steeply into and back out of the Rye valley. If you do not wish to visit it you may prefer to continue on the B1257.

b If you next intend to follow Route 164 to Castleton, you can turn to it here.

Helmsley and **Duncombe Park** See Route 164.

Oswaldkirk Links with Routes 163, 164, 166.

Route 166   29 miles   47 km
OSWALDKIRK — HUGGATE

OS 1:250 000 nos 5, 6 (just)
Bartholomew's 1:100 000 nos 33, 36
OS 1:50 000 nos 100, 106

Oswaldkirk Links with Routes 163, 164, 165.

Gilling East See Route 163.

Hovingham The village of stone cottages is set around an 18th-century hall in local stone, which is the scene of music and cricket festivals.

Castle Howard This splendid stately home was designed by Vanbrugh, architect of Blenheim. It possesses fine statuary, furniture and paintings (including Holbein's 'Henry VIII'), and houses a costume museum. Set in the beautiful grounds are the Temple of the Four Winds and a huge mausoleum (open).

Malton This busy market town was the Roman settlement of Derventio; Roman-British, prehistoric and medieval relics can be seen in the museum. Old Malton was deliberately burnt in 1138 to drive out the Scots. Cross Keys Inn has a medieval crypt. St Mary's incorporates

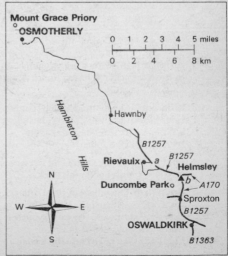

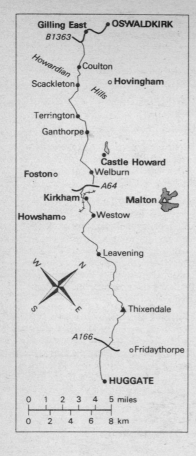

Gilling East   • OSWALDKIRK
B1363

Howardian   • Coulton
Scackleton •   o **Hovingham**
            Hills

Terrington •
Ganthorpe •

            • Castle Howard
Foston o   • Welburn
        A64
Kirkham •   **Malton**
Howsham o   • Westow

            • Leavening

            ▲ Thixendale

A166
            o Fridaythorpe

            • HUGGATE

0 1 2 3 4 5 miles
0   2   4   6   8 km

Huggate See Route 158. Also links with Route 159.

Route 167   30 miles   49 km
CASTLETON — PICKERING

OS 1:250 000 nos 5 or 6
Bartholomew's 1:100 000 no. 36
OS 1:50 000 nos 94, 100 (just)
1 inch:1 mile North York Moors tourist map

Castleton Links with Routes 160, 161, 164.

Danby Castle A present-day farmhouse incorporates ruins of a 14th-century castle, which was the home of Catherine Parr, Henry VIII's last wife. Not far to the north is Duck Bridge, a 14th-century packhorse bridge.

Beggar's Bridge The elegant, single-arch bridge is said to have been built by a man returning with a fortune to claim his sweetheart.

Egton Bridge Together with Egton, its neighbour, this village is noted for salmon fishing and the August Gooseberry Fair. This was the home of the last English martyr, Nicholas Postgate, who was hanged in 1679 at the age of 82 for baptizing a child.

Grosmont Station for the North Yorkshire Moors steam railway which runs to Pickering.

High Bride Stones Remains of two standing stone circles.

Rosedale Abbey The nunnery founded here in the 12th century was demolished by Scots in the 14th, after which many of its stones were used for building cottages. Iron-working was carried out here till quite recently, and in the 13th to 16th centuries for Byland Abbey; the old iron-works chimney is a landmark.

Wheeldale Roman Road A fine stretch of Roman road (DoE).

Lastingham St Mary's Church has a superb 11th-century crypt which was built as a shrine to St Cedd.

Pickering Attractive market town. The

parts of a 12th-century priory church. St Leonard's church has an unusual iron-founder's monument.

Kirkham On an entrancing site stand the ruins of a 12th-century priory, including a 13th-century gatehouse and a fine lavatorium (DoE, open).

Foston The 19th-century Old Rectory is built in Flemish bond pink brick.

Howsham This village of stone cottages, with its Elizabethan hall, was the home of George Hudson, an early railway tycoon who at one time owned a third of England's lines but eventually died in poverty.

astle, the ruins of which stand on a high
motte, was founded by William the
Conqueror (DoE, open). The Church of
SS Peter and Paul has superb 15th-
century murals, 14th-century knight
effigies and a monument to the surveyors
of Washington. Beck Isle is a Georgian
house, now used as a folk museum.
Station for the North York Moors steam
railway. Links with Route 168.

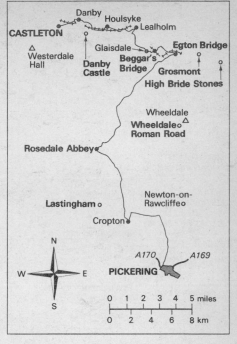

Route 168   24 miles   39 km
SCARBOROUGH — PICKERING

OS 1:250 000 no. 6
Bartholomew's 1:100 000 no. 36
OS 1:50 000 nos 100, 101
1 inch:1 mile North York Moors tourist map

Scarborough See Route 159. Also links
with Route 160.

Hackness Misericords in the church.

Bride Stones Interesting rock
formations.

Levisham Water mill.

Hole of Horcum This natural amphitheatre, which was eroded by glaciers and
springs, almost encloses an area of
meadowland.

Thornton Dale Pretty, stone-built
village. Tudor Thornton Hall, now a
hotel, has an 18th-century facade. There
are 17th-century almshouses; a 17th
century grammar school; market cross
and stocks.

Pickering See Route 167.

Route 169   32 miles   51 km
SLAIDBURN — HEBDEN BRIDGE

OS 1:250 000 no. 5
Bartholomew's 1:100 000 no. 32
OS 1:50 000 no. 103

Slaidburn A pretty village set in the
heart of the Forest of Bowland, with an

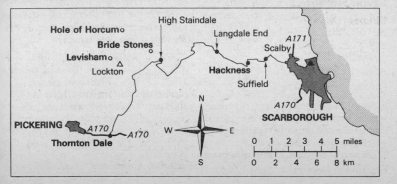

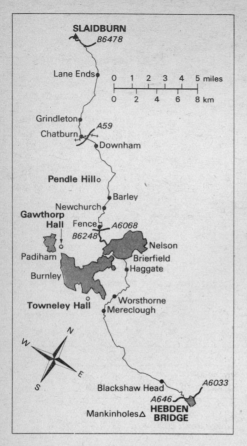

14th-century, and contains fine collections of paintings, period furniture, ivories, glassware, Chinese ceramics and natural history (open).

Hebden Bridge See Route 114. Also links with Route 115.

Route 170   33 miles   53 km
KENDAL — SLAIDBURN

OS 1:250 000 no. 5
Bartholomew's 1:100 000 nos 32, 34 or 31
OS 1:50 000 nos 103, 98, 97

Kendal The town has many fine buildings of grey limestone, and a Norman castle where Katherine Parr, the last wife of Henry VIII, was born. The Dairy is a good example of Tudor domestic architecture. In Abbot Hall, an 18th-century mansion, is a museum of lakeland life and industry and an art gallery. The Kendal Museum has outstanding collections of local history. Links with Routes 171, 178, 179.

Sizergh Castle The impressive 14th-century peel tower rises to 60 feet (20 m) and still has some original windows, floors and fireplaces. There is also a great hall, and fine paintings, ceilings, panelling and furniture (NT, open).

Levens Hall A large Elizabethan mansion incorporating a 14th-century tower built for protection against the Scots (open). Inside there is some notable furniture, plaster work and panelling; famous topiary garden and collection of working steam engines.

a If you next intend to follow Route 179 to Kirkby Stephen, turn to it here.

Kirkby Lonsdale A beautiful town overlooking the river Lune. The 13th-century Devil's Bridge which spans the river is one of the finest ancient bridges in England. There are several Georgian buildings, old inns and a Norman church. From the lovely footpath by the river to the north of the town there are good views.

old church that has a three-decker pulpit. Links with Route 170.

Pendle Hill Records survive of the trials of the Witches of Pendle who aided the 'respectable' Alice Nutter in her evil intentions in return for favours. Hence the insult 'nutter'.

Gawthorp Hall An early 17th-century manor house, restored in the 1860s, with some fine panelling, moulded ceilings and a Jacobean long gallery (NT, open). Inside is the Kay-Shuttleworth Collection of textiles and embroidery, and the Ryder Collection of early European furniture. There is a craft shop in the stable block.

Towneley Hall The house dates from the

b The alternative route follows tiny roads

through the superb scenery of Barbondale, Dentdale and Kingsdale and passes through the delightful village of Dent. It involves two ascents, while the main route remains in the valley.

Casterton There is a prehistoric stone circle 0.5 mile (1 km) north of the village.

Dent The narrow cobbled main street has a timeless atmosphere. A large granite slab in the street is a memorial to Adam Sedgewick, who became famous as a pioneer geologist.

Ingleton A tourist centre amid excellent walking country. Paths lead to the summits of Whernside and Ingleborough Hill.

White Scar Caves Fascinating underground rock formations, lakes and rivers, which can be visited by the public.

Slaidburn See Route 169.

Route 171   31 miles   49 km
FAR SAWREY — KENDAL

OS 1:250 000 no. 5
Bartholomew's 1:100 000 no. 34
OS 1:50 000 no. 97

Faw Sawrey Links with Route 172.

a Although this route is both interesting and attractive, if you wish to link Kendal to the mountainous Lake District quickly, you may prefer the alternative route, which involves a frequent ferry.

Lake Windermere This is England's largest lake, now much used for pleasure boating, and thought to be the setting of A. Ransome's *Swallows and Amazons.*

Graythwaite Hall There are 7 acres of landscaped gardens (open).

Newby Bridge A pretty village with an unusual arched bridge.

Fell Foot A recreational park on NT land offering yacht hire.

Cartmel The gatehouse of a 14th-century priory is now a local craft

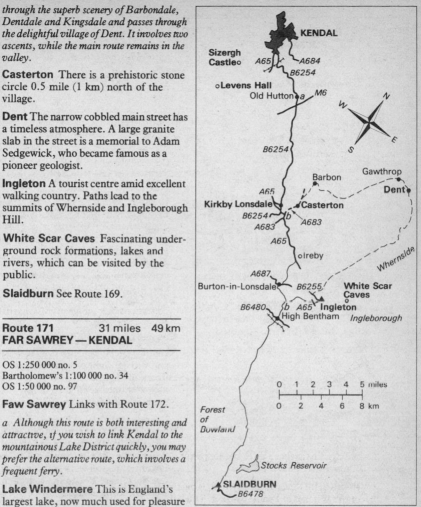

centre (NT, open). The priory church of St Mary has excellent Renaissance screens, good glass and misericords. There is a market cross.

Cark At the north end of the fishing village lies 16th-century Holker Hall with 19th-century additions. Set in gardens and a deer park, it houses collections and exhibitions (open).

Grange-Over-Sands A seaside resort

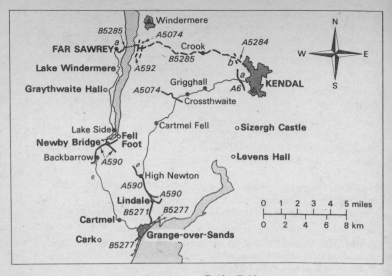

with parks and gardens and a Lakeland Rose Show in July.

Lindale Monument to 18th-century John Wilkinson, who launched the first iron ship in the nearby river Winster.

Sizergh Castle and **Levens Hall** See Route 170.

b   If you next intend to follow Route 178 to

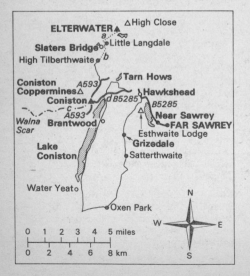

Pooley Bridge, you can turn to it here.

Kendal See Route 170. Also links with Routes 178, 179.

Route 172   30 miles   48 km
ELTERWATER — FAR SAWREY

OS 1:250 000 no. 5
Bartholomew's 1:100 000 no. 34
OS 1:50 000 nos 90, 96 or 97
1 inch:1 mile Lake District tourist map

Elterwater This area was formerly one of much slate production. Links with Routes 173, 176, 177.

a   The lane has a firm but bumpy surface of natural rock, which cannot be ridden in parts. No defined right of way.

Slaters Bridge A pretty, arched, foot-bridge built of slates.

b   North of the river, which can be crossed on a footbridge, this track is a surfaced lane. South of the river it is unsurfaced, and follows the west side of the Pierce How Beck valley. If you are following the route towards Far Sawrey you should keep right at the track fork just after crossing the river.

Coniston Museum of John Ruskin, eminent 19th-century art critic and champion of the beauty of hand rather than machine-made objects. Churchyard cross, in the Celtic style, to Ruskin.

Coniston Coppermines An area strongly scarred by mining and quarrying.

c The Walna Scar road links this route with Route 173 near Seathwaite. The unsurfaced track is firm but bumpy, and long stretches have to be walked, but it rises high to good views. Some 4 miles (6.5 km) long and involving hard climbing, it should not be attempted without a 1:50 000 or 1 inch:1 mile map, spare clothing, food and plenty of time. No defined right of way.

d The loop of roads passing Tarn Hows must be taken anticlockwise, as one of the roads is one-way.

Tarn Hows A famed beauty spot on NT land, being a lake with softly wooded banks and views to distant mountains.

Brantwood The one-time home of John Ruskin (open).

Lake Coniston In 1967 Donald Campbell died on this lake in an attempt on the water speed record.

Grizedale A Forestry Commission nursery and wildlife centre, with nature trails laid out. The Theatre in the Forest.

Hawkshead Old lanes and cottages. The 16th-century grammar school, now a museum, was attended by William Wordsworth who carved his name on one of the desks, and lodged at Anne Tyson's cottage. North of the village lies Hawkshead Courthouse, the remains of medieval manorial buildings now a local folk museum (NT, open).

Near Sawrey The 17th-century house called 'Hill Top' where Beatrix Potter lived and wrote, and which contains her furniture, pictures and other possessions (NT, open).

Far Sawrey Links with Route 171.

Route 173   36 miles   57 km
ELTERWATER — SANTON BRIDGE

OS 1:250 000 no. 5
Bartholomew's 1:100 000 no. 34
OS 1:50 000 nos 89, 90, 96
1 inch:1 mile Lake District tourist map

Elterwater See Route 172. Also links with Routes 176, 177.

Dungeon Ghyll The pub lies in Great Langdale, the steep sides and flat bottom of which are typical of a valley created by

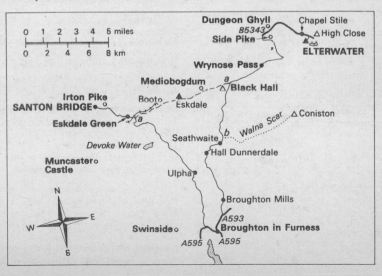

a glacier. A steep footpath beside Dungeon Ghyll Force climbs to the lovely, cliff-backed Stickle Tarn.

Side Pike A relatively short climb on foot to the summit gives good views.

Wrynose Pass This and Hardknott are notoriously strenuous passes. By the road stands the Three Shire Stone, marking the meeting of the three old counties of Cumberland, Lancashire and Westmorland.

a   The alternative route passes a different choice of points of interest than the main route. Although shorter, it climbs over the strenuous Hardknott Pass.

Black Hall Duddon YH. The Duddon valley inspired some thirty-five of Wordsworth's sonnets.

b   The Walna Scar road links this route with Route 172 at Coniston. The unsurfaced track is firm but bumpy, and long stretches have to be walked, but it rises high to good views. Some 4 miles (7 km) long, involving hard climbing, it should not be attempted without a 1:50 000 or 1 inch:1 mile map, spare clothing, food and plenty of time. No defined right of way.

Broughton in Furness An old market town; St Mary's church has a Norman doorway.

Swinside A large circle of some fifty stones from the 1st millennium BC.

Muncaster Castle A 13th-century family seat in gardens (open).

Mediobogdum A large Roman fort with remains of ramparts, walls and gateways (DoE).

Eskdale Green Station for the miniature railway from Ravenglass to Boot, now giving rides to the public but originally for the transport of ore from the mines.

Irton Pike Wide views from the summit encompass Lake District mountains to the east and fertile lands and the sea to the west.

Santon Bridge Links with Route 174.

Route 174   39 miles   62 km
BRAITHWAITE — SANTON BRIDGE

OS 1:250 000 no. 5
Bartholomew's 1:100 000 no. 34
OS 1:50 000 no. 89

Braithwaite Links with Route 175.

a   A short-cut between Braithwaite and Portinscale on Route 175 uses the A66.

Cockermouth Wordsworth House is an 18th-century merchant's house with original woodwork, where William and Dorothy Wordsworth were born (NT, open). There is a 12th-century ruined castle with a good oubliette dungeon.

b   On the alternative route, the section of track between Black Sail and Ennerdale Water is easy to ride, being a firm forestry road. The section between Black Sail and Wasdale Head is extremely strenuous, taking a rough path over a high, steep pass. Many riders will find it necessary to take the

*pack from their cycles and carry each up
separately. This alternative route should be
attempted by the fit only, fully equipped with
1:50 000 map, spare food and clothing and
plenty of time.*

Calder Abbey On a fine riverside site
stand the ruins of a 12th-century abbey,
including the nave, aisles, cloisters and
13th-century Chapter House.

Scafell At 3210 feet (978 m) this is
England's highest mountain.

Wastwater England's deepest lake.

Wasdale Hall Wastwater YH.

Santon Bridge Links with Route 173.

Route 175   43 miles   69 km
CALDBECK — BRAITHWAITE

OS 1:250 000 no. 5
Bartholomew's 1:100 000 nos 34, 38
OS 1:50 000 no. 90
1 inch:1 mile Lake District tourist map

Caldbeck In the yard of the old church
are buried the Maid of Buttermere and
the celebrated huntsman, John Peel.
Links with Routes 176, 180.

*a The lane east of Bassenthwaite is not
shown on the Bartholomew's map of 1976.*

*b The B5292 joins Braithwaite to the A66,
forming a short cut for those not wishing to
cycle the Crummock and Honister loop with
its steep pass at Honister Hause.*

Keswick This market town with narrow
lanes and grey stone houses was a haunt of
poets including Coleridge, Southey,
Lamb, Shelley and Wordsworth. The
Royal Oak Hotel was patronized by Scott,
Tennyson and R. L. Stevenson. The
19th-century moot hall has a one handed
clock. Fitz Park museum and gallery have
collections of local interest and literary
manuscripts. Crosthwaite church has rare
consecration crosses and 15th-century
effigies.

Castlerigg Circle A large prehistoric
circle of 38 stones on a site commanding
wide views (DoE).

Lingholm Large formal and woodland
gardens with fine views of Borrowdale
(open).

*c The main route passes scenery of lakeside
and secluded vale and involves the use of a
steep track. The direct alternative route keeps
to the valley road.*

Lodore Cascade A waterfall beauty
spot.

Friar's Crag This lakeside bluff was
bought by the NT in memory of Canon
Rawnsley, one of its three founders.
Memorial to John Ruskin.

Watendlath A NT hamlet of stone-
roofed houses. Curious Devil's Punch
Bowl formation at Watendlath Tarn
outflow. Scenes in Hugh Walpole's
'Rogue Herries' novels are set in this area.

*d Although only 1.5 miles (2.5 km) long,
this track involves a steep ascent and descent
each of several hundred feet. It should be
attempted by the fit only, who may even so*

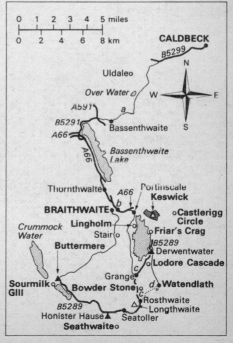

*have to carry their cycles and packs up
separately, and who should be equipped with
1:50 000 map, spare food and clothing and
plenty of time.*

Bowder Stone A seemingly pre-
cariously balanced boulder of some 2000
tons (NT).

Seathwaite Once employed in the
mining of graphite for pencils, Seathwaite
has England's highest recorded rainfall.

Buttermere Wordsworth related the
local tale of the Maid of Buttermere in
'The Prelude'; lake (NT).

Sourmilk Gill A waterfall beauty spot.

Braithwaite Links with Route 174.

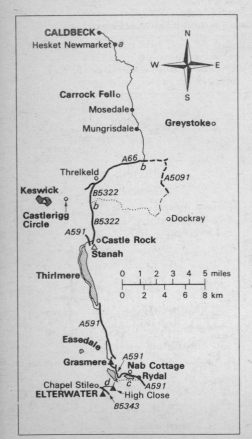

Route 176   32 miles 52 km
CALDBECK — ELTERWATER

OS 1:250 000 no. 5
Bartholomew's 1:100 000 nos 34, 38
OS 1:50 000 no. 90
1 inch:1 mile Lake District tourist map

Caldbeck See Route 175. Also links with
Route 180.

*a If you next intend to follow Route 180 to
Brampton, you can turn to it here.*

Carrock Fell Stone fort, possibly dating
from the early Iron Age. The stiff climb to
the summit should not be attempted in
bad weather.

Greystoke Collegiate church with
superb 15th-century glass, effigies, brass
and carved woodwork. The castle was
restored in the 19th century, and has eye-
catching follies in its grounds.

*b The alternative road involves the use of
the Old Coach Road track. Although it
keeps below the hills, it crosses bleak,
open country, and should be attempted
only if you have a 1:50 000 or 1 inch :
1 mile map, spare food and clothing, and
plenty of time.*

Castlerigg Circle and **Keswick** See
Route 175.

Castle Rock This is the rock in Walter
Scott's *The Bridal of Triermain*. It is used
for rock-climbing.

Stanah Thirlmere YH.

Thirlmere Previously two smaller lakes,
Thirlmere was flooded in the 19th
century to provide water for Manchester.

Grasmere Dove Cottage, the one-time
home of Wordsworth and meeting place
of poets, is near the Wordsworth
museum. St Oswald's churchyard has the
graves of William and Dorothy Wordsworth. The famed Grasmere Sports are
held in August.

Easedale The entire Grasmere area
abounds in fine walks, but those in
Easedale enjoy fine scenery whilst being
relatively easy.

Nab Cottage The one-time home of De Quincey and Hartley Coleridge.

Rydal Rydal Mount was Wordsworth's last home, where he designed the garden. The house contains possessions and first editions of his works (open). Wordsworth bought Dora's Field (NT).

c The track, called Loughrigg Terrace, is virtually flat and offers fine lake-side views.

d The lane between High Close and Chapel Stile is not shown on the Bartholomew's map of 1976.

Elterwater See Route 172. Also links with Routes 173, 177.

Route 177   22 miles   36 km
POOLEY BRIDGE — ELTERWATER

OS 1:250 000 no. 5
Bartholomew's 1:100 000 no. 34
OS 1:50 000 no. 90
1 inch:1 mile Lake District tourist map

Pooley Bridge Links with Route 178.

Dalemain Gardens and a house dating from medieval to early Georgian times, incorporating museums of agriculture and yeomanry (open).

Dacre Tradition associates the signing of a treaty between the Scots and the English king in the 10th century with Dacre. Farmhouse incorporating parts of a 14th-century castle.

Hutton Hutton John manor house centres on a peel tower, built for protection against 14th- and 15th-century Scottish raiders. Hutton-in-the-Forest 14th-century peel tower (open).

a The main route explores a quieter area of the Lake District which requires care and time as it follows the steep shore of the lake, and parts of it are too rough to be cycled. A 1:100 000 or larger scale map should be carried. The alternative route uses an easy but busy road, and passes different points of interest.

Martindale Church with 17th-century woodwork.

Hallin Fell The summit of the relatively low fell affords fine views.

Deer Forest Wild red deer may sometimes be glimpsed in the area south of Martindale.

Gowbarrow Park NT land with Lyulphs Tower, the high Aira Force waterfall, and Wordsworth's daffodils.

Glencoyne Wood NT land with some ancient oaks.

Greenside Helvellyn YH.

b Kirkstone Pass has a long, steep, section north of the inn.

c The alternative route involves some use of busy roads in order to pass points of interest.

Town End A 17th-century yeoman's family home with period furniture, books and papers, and carved woodwork (NT, open).

Broad Oaks Windermere YH.

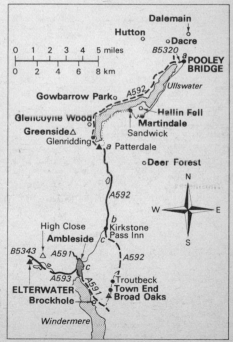

Brockhole A national park information centre, with exhibits about many aspects of the Lake District and its life.

Ambleside This tourist resort has attractive houses by the parish hall. St Mary the Virgin's Church has a Wordsworth chapel. The stone Bridge House, said to have been built over the river to avoid payment of ground rent, is a NT information centre. The town is associated with literary figures such as Keats, Charlotte Bronte and George Eliot. Other interests are the old mill; remains of the 2nd to 4th century Roman fort of Galava (NT); and Stock Ghyll Force in the park. South of the town lies Stagshawe woodland garden (open).

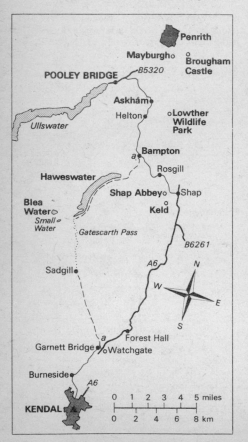

Elterwater See Route 172. Also links with Routes 173, 176.

Route 178   29 miles   46 km
POOLEY BRIDGE — KENDAL

OS 1:250 000 no. 5
Bartholomew's 1:100 000 no. 34
OS 1:50 000 nos 90, 97

Pooley Bridge Links with Route 177.

Mayburgh, Brougham Castle and **Penrith** See Route 119.

Askham On the north side of this pretty village is Askham Hall, a 14th-century fortified tower. To the west is grand Lowther Castle.

Lowther Wildlife Park An extensive Park (open) with many species of animals and birds wandering freely.

Bampton The church is interesting, and the free library here was one of the first in Britain. There are the remains of several ancient British settlements in the area.

a The main route uses the A6, which skirts around the eastern edge of the Lake District, while the alternative route traverses Gatescarth Pass, a very strenuous rough stuff ascent and descent which reaches an altitude of about 1900 feet (579 m). It should only be attempted in good weather, with a 1:50 000 map and suitable equipment.

Shap Abbey Much of the stone from the abbey has been used for local buildings, but the impressive 16th-century tower (DoE, open) can still be seen.

Keld An interesting small pre-Reformation chapel (NT, open).

Haweswater In 1940 a dam was built and this valley flooded, submerging the village of Mardale. When the waters are rough it is said that the bells of the church can be heard.

Blea Water The deepest tarn in Lakeland.

Kendal See Route 170. Also links with Routes 171, 179.

Route 179   26 miles   42 km
KIRKBY STEPHEN — KENDAL

OS 1:250 000 no. 5
Bartholomew's 1:100 000 no. 34
OS 1:50 000 nos 91, 97, 98

Kirkby Stephen See Route 117. Also links with Routes 118, 135.

Wharton Hall See Route 117.

Ravenstonedale A delightful little village. The church has a three-tiered pulpit with a seat in it for the parson's wife. Elizabeth Gaunt, who was the last woman to be executed in England for a political offence, was born here. She had sheltered a follower of the rebel Duke of Monmouth, and was burnt at Tyburn in 1685.

Sedbergh This busy market town has a boys' public school founded in 1525. There are some good brasses in Norman St Andrew's church.

Brigflatts An early Quaker meeting house, and the remains of a yew tree under which George Fox, the 17th-century founder of the Society of Quakers, once preached.

Kendal See Route 170. Also links with Routes 171, 178.

Route 180   27 miles   43 km
BRAMPTON — CALDBECK

OS 1:250 000 nos 3 or 5, 4 (just)
Bartholomew's 1:100 000 no. 38
OS 1:50 000 nos 90, 85, 86

Brampton Links with Routes 119, 120, 137, 181.

Low Geltbridge A footpath leads south east to the Written Rock of Gelt, inscribed by a Roman standard bearer.

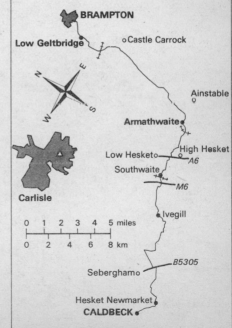

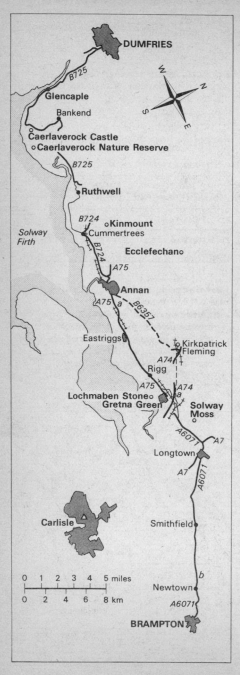

Carlisle Although the town has an industrial character today, there are several interesting old buildings. The castle (DoE, open) has a 12th-century keep and a 13th-century gatehouse, and houses a regimental museum. Rich collections of archaeology, natural history and art can be seen in Tullie House, a Jacobean town house. There is an imposing cathedral with a fine Early English choir and east window. The Guildhall dates from the 14th century and a market cross from 1682. A typical border city, Carlisle lies at the western end of Hadrian's Wall.

Armathwaite This pretty village has a church that was rebuilt in the 17th century having been used as a cattle shed for some time.

Caldbeck See Route 175. Also links with Route 176.

Route 181   47 miles   75 km
DUMFRIES — BRAMPTON

OS 1:250 000 nos 3 or 4
Bartholomew's 1:100 000 no. 38
OS 1:50 000 nos 84, 85, 86

Dumfries This historic town, on the site of a Bronze Age settlement, first became a Royal burgh in 1186. Robert Burns died in Dumfries, 1796 (mausoleum in St Michael's churchyard). Relics of Burns, Carlyle and Scott in the burgh museum. Devorgilla Bridge is a stone footbridge c. 1450, named after the founder of Sweetheart Abbey. Mid-steeple, a tolbooth in High Street, has a plan of the town as it was in Burns' day, and a standard for the old Scottish length measurement called the 'ell'. The Observatory and the Town Hall designed by Adam both house museums of local interest. Links with Route 182.

Glencaple Once a busy fishing and shipping port, Glencaple lost its importance in the 1930s through the silting of the river.

Caerlaverock Castle Ruins of the castle, built in 1290 and dismantled in

1640 (DoE, open).

Caerlaverock Nature Reserve An area of salt-marshes, rich in geese.

Ruthwell Church with one of Britain's two best preserved runic crosses surviving from the Anglo-Saxon period (DoE).

Kinmount Rock garden and woodland walks (open).

Annan Once a fishing and shipbuilding centre, where the 'Queensberry' tea-clipper was built. The area still sees some fishing by old methods. The Moat House contains a museum of local interest and shipping.

Ecclefechan Carlyle's birthplace, with mementoes (NTS, open).

a If the A75 is busy, the quieter alternative route between Gretna Green and Annan can be used.

Lochmaben Stone A weighty 7-foot tall stone which has been used as an important meeting place for many centuries. Initially it may have been connected with a stone circle, or with a shrine to the ancient god of youth and music.

Gretna Green Famous as a place where, in the 18th century especially, eloping couples from England came to be married in accordance with Scots law. Bonnie Prince Charlie is said to have stayed a night in 'Prince Charlie's Cottage' by the Kirk.

Solway Moss The site of a battle in 1542, in which the Scots were defeated.

Carlisle See Route 180.

b If you next intend to follow Route 120 to Langholm, you can turn to it here.

Brampton Links with Routes 119, 120, 137, 180.

Route 182   46 miles   73 km
DUMFRIES — KIRCUDBRIGHT

OS 1:250 000 no. 3
Bartholomew's 1:100 000 nos 37, 38 (just)
OS 1:50 000 no. 84

Although this is a 'coastal' route, it is generally a mile or so from the shore-line. Those with the time and inclination can explore the coast more thoroughly by exploring lane side-loops and dead-ends.

Dumfries See Route 181.

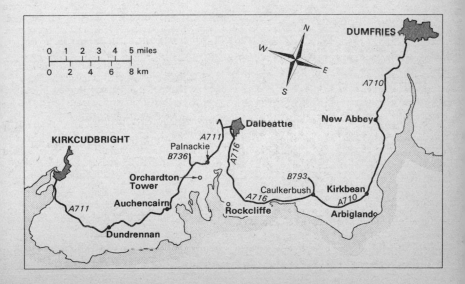

New Abbey A pretty village with an old smithy, an Abbey House and a water mill. Sweetheart Abbey (founded 1275) is considered one of Scotland's most beautiful monastic remains (DoE, open). The last abbot, Gilbert Brown, is believed to be the original of Scott's *The Abbot*.

Kirkbean US Navy memorial font in the church. Smuggling was once rife in the area.

Arbigland Cottage where Admiral Paul Jones was born. Arbigland Gardens, with woods and formal and water gardens, where Paul Jones worked in his youth (open). The shore is rich in fossils.

Rockcliffe A village noted for its rock gardens. Nearby is the Mote of Mark, a Dark Ages fort (NTS). At low tide it is possible to walk to Rough Island, which is a bird sanctuary.

Dalbeattie A granite town which grew on the export of its rock, part of which was used on the Thames embankment. Now granite road chips are produced.

Orchardton Tower A 16th-century round tower house (DoE, open).

Auchencairn A pretty village which was the scene of a famous poltergeist haunting

in 1690. There are several Dark Ages forts in the vicinity.

Dundrennan Ruins of a 12th-century Cistercian abbey with a 13th-century chapter house (DoE, open). The village buildings are partly built out of stones 'recycled' from the abbey. Mary Queen of Scots spent her last night in Scotland here.

Kircudbright An active port in earlier centuries, Kircudbright is now popular amongst artists. There are streets of 18th-century buildings; a 17th-century tolbooth; Maclellans Castle (DoE, open); Broughton House, surrounded by fine gardens, houses a museum including Robert Burns' mementoes; Stewartry museum has displays of Galloway life. Links with Route 183.

Route 183   31 miles   50 km
NEWTON STEWART — KIRCUDBRIGHT

OS 1:250 000 no. 3
Bartholomew's 1:100 000 no. 37
OS 1:50 000 no. 83

Newton Stewart For centuries an area in which agricultural and forestry techniques have been pioneered. Since

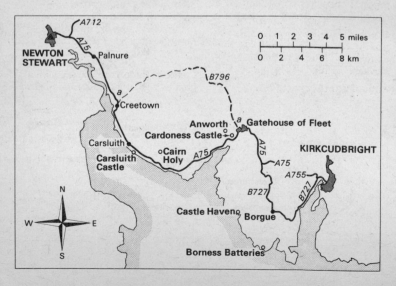

the 18th century, boggy land in the estuary has been reclaimed to give the fertile landscape of today. Links with Routes 184, 195.

Carsluith Castle A 16th-century tower house (DoE, open).

Cairn Holy Two great neolithic court-yard cairns (DoE).

Anworth Dark Age cross in the church-yard.

Cardoness Castle A fine 15th-century castle with four storeys, good fireplaces and a vaulted basement (DoE, open).

a Although much of this route is unavoid-ably on A roads, the stretch between Gate-house of Fleet and Newton Stewart on the A75 is particularly likely to be busy. It is possible to avoid part of it, and to see an inland valley as a change from the coastal lands, by the alternative shown.

Gatehouse of Fleet Before about 1800, Gatehouse was small. It prospered and grew around successful light industry; the ruin of a cotton factory still remains.

Castle Haven A fine Iron Age strong-hold.

Borness Batteries A good promontory fort in an area generally rich in Iron Age and early medieval forts.

Borgue The village is named after a nearby prehistoric fort which was later occupied by Vikings, the nordic 'borg' meaning 'fortress'.

Kircudbright See Route 182.

Route 184   29 miles   47 km
NEWTON STEWART — STRANRAER

OS 1:250 000 no. 3
Bartholomew's 1:100 000 no. 37
OS 1:50 000 nos 82, 83

The Wigtownshire peninsula which lies south of the line between Newton Stewart and Glenluce is particularly rich in pre-historic remains, several being designated ancient monuments in the care of the DoE. If particularly interested in them you might like to explore the peninsula with the aid of 1:50 000 maps.

Newton Stewart See Route 183. Also links with Route 195.

Cascreugh Castle Sir John Dalrymple built the castle in 1680. It was the betrothal and marriage of his daughter, Janet, which gave Sir Walter Scott the theme for his novel, *The Bride of Lammermoor.*

Glenluce Abbey The ruins of Cistercian Luce Abbey, founded in 1190, including the abbey church and a fine 15th-century vaulted chapter house (DoE, open). The abbey is traditionally linked with Michael Scott, a 13th-century wizard who supposedly lured the plague then raging to the abbey, to shut it up in the vault. Mary Queen of Scots visited the Abbey in 1563.

Castle of Park A castellated mansion built in 1590, using stone from Glenluce

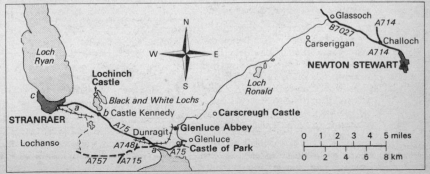

Abbey after its dissolution (DoE, grounds open).

a The busyness of the A75 hereabouts varies according to the times of sailing and arrival of the Stranraer ferries. If it is busy, the alternative but longer route is quieter.

b If you next intend to follow Route 185 to Barr, you can turn to it here.

Lochinch Castle This 19th-century castle is famed for its magnificent grounds, which were inspired by Versailles, and which contain the ruins of Castle Kennedy (grounds open).

c Ferries run from Stranraer to Larne in Northern Ireland.

Stranraer A seaport and resort centred on an attractive old town. The 16th-century castle was once occupied by Claverhouse, a persecutor of the Covenanters. North West Castle was the home of Sir John Ross, the Arctic explorer. There is a museum of local interest. Links with Route 185.

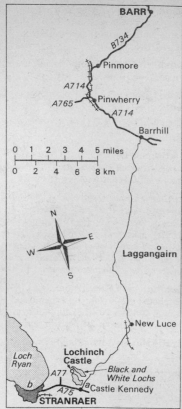

Route 185   34 miles   54 km
BARR — STRANRAER

OS 1:250 000 nos 3 or 4
Bartholomew's 1:100 000 no. 37
OS 1:50 000 nos 76, 82

Barr The centre of an area of sheep-farming and forestry. It used to be the scene of the famed Kirkdandie Fair, which was used as an occasion for meeting by the Ballantrae smugglers as well as the local hill men and shepherds. Links with Route 186.

Laggangairn Deep in the moors lies Laggangairn, which means 'hollow of the cairn'. There are standing stones (DoE) with Dark Age crosses carved upon them. Local superstitions are attached to the stones, which can be reached by a long track and path route from New Luce. The attempt should not be made in bad weather, and a 1:50 000 map and compass should be carried.

c If you next intend to follow Route 184 to Newton Stewart, turn to it here.

Lochinch Castle See Route 184.

d Ferries run from Stranraer to Larne in Northern Ireland.

Stranraer See Route 184.

Route 186   32 miles   51 km
CUMNOCK — BARR

OS 1:250 000 nos 3 or 4
Bartholomew's 1:100 000 nos 37, 40
OS 1:50 000 nos 70, 71 (just), 76, 80

Cumnock The town once prospered on the manufacture of snuff-boxes. There is an old market cross; the churchyard has some Covenanters' graves. The Bank is a pretty, wooded, riverside walk. Links with Routes 187, 190, 194, 195.

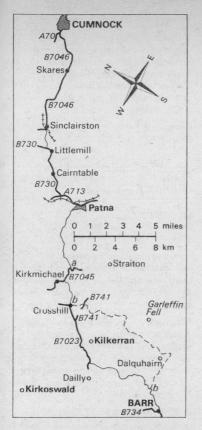

Route 187   41 miles   66 km
LARGS — CUMNOCK

OS 1:250 000 nos 3 or 4
Bartholomew's 1:100 000 nos 40, 44
OS 1:50 000 nos 63, 70, 71 (just)

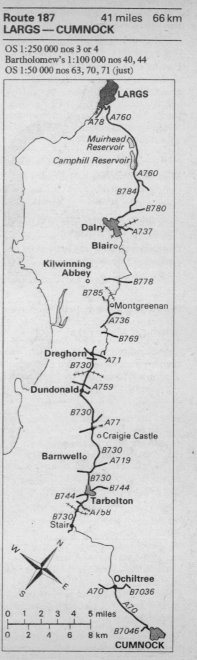

Patna A mining village.

a If you next intend to follow Route 195 to Newton Stewart, you can turn off on the B7045 in the south-easterly direction to join it at Straiton.

b The alternative route passes through wilder, lonelier country than the main route, but it is also hillier.

Kilkerran The mansion house has been the seat of the Fergussons of Kilkerran for more than five hundred years.

Kirkoswald Thatched Souter Johnnie's Cottage was the home of Burns' Souter in 'Tam O'Shanter'; Burns relics (NTS, open).

Barr See Route 185.

Together with Route 188, this route is a means of linking areas north and south of the Firth of Clyde avoiding the alternative option of passing through Glasgow.

Largs In 1263 Alexander III annihilated the Viking fleet here. Now Largs is a resort. Douglas Park gives views of islands, mountains and shipping. Skelmorlie Aisle is a 17th-century mausoleum (DoE, open). Steamer cruises. Links with Route 188.

Dairy An 18th-century weaving town.

Blair The Blair estate, containing a 15th-century keep, has been in the hands of the family of that name for 700 years.

Kilwinning Abbey Remains of a 12th-century abbey (DoE, open).

Dreghorn Dunlop, the inventor of the pneumatic tyre, was born here.

Dundonald Ruins of Dundonald Castle (DoE).

Barnwell A hill-top tower commanding wide views commemorates the 'Burning of Barns of Ayr' in 1297.

Tarbolton In 1780 Robert Burns, who then lived nearby, founded the Bachelors Club in a 17th-century thatched cottage,

now housing a museum (NTS, open).

Ochiltree Set in an area of both coal-mining and dairy-farming, this was the birthplace of George Douglas Brown who wrote *House With The Green Shutters*, 1901, a controversial book describing Scottish provincial life in an unromanticized fashion.

Cumnock See Route 186. Also links with Routes 190, 194, 195.

Route 188   14 miles   23 km
GOUROCK — LARGS

OS 1:250 000 nos 3 or 4
Bartholomew's 1:100 000 no. 44
OS 1:50 000 no. 63

Although this route (together with Route 187) provides a quieter means of linking areas north and south of the Clyde than going through Glasgow, it does pass through built-up areas and a maze of A and B roads.

Gourock A Clyde-side resort. 'Granny Kempock's Stone' is of prehistoric origins, and has long been linked with local superstitions. In 1688 Britain's first ever cured herring was produced here. Clyde ferries, including that to Dunoon. Links with Route 259.

a Between Gourock and Largs you can choose to follow the coastal roads which give frequent views of the busy shipping, or the quieter, but hillier inland alternative route.

Greenock Clyde-side ship-building. James Watt, the pioneer of steam power, was born here. The McLean museum has collections concerning Watt, shipping and local interest.

Cloch Point The lighthouse built in 1796 is preserved as a private house.

Inverkip The village was previously called 'Auldkirk', as the Greenock people came here to church before their own was built. An infamous centre of witch mania in the 17th century, and of smuggling in the 18th century.

Wemyss Bay A recent town with a 19th-century mansion called 'Castle Wemyss'

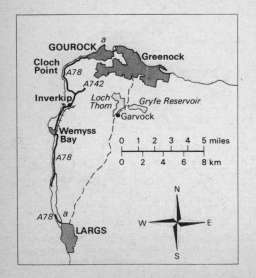

where Trollope wrote *Barchester Towers*.
Ferry to Rothesay.

Largs See Route 187.

Route 189   52 miles   84 km
MENNOCK — LANGHOLM

OS 1:250 000 nos 3 or 4
Bartholomew's 1:100 000 nos 38, 40
OS 1:50 000 nos 78, 79, 85 (just), 86

Mennock Links with Routes 190, 191.

Drumlanrig Castle A 17th-century
castle, the home of the Duke of
Buccleuch, containing Grinling Gibbons
carvings, Old Master paintings, relics of
Bonnie Prince Charlie and other collections (open).

Morton Castle A loch-side castle (DoE).

Keir Mill An inscription on the smithy
commemorates Kirkpatrick Macmillan
of this village, who invented the bicycle in
1839.

Thornhill An 18th-century monument
has the winged horse of the Queensberry family. Thomas McCall of
Thornhill was the first commercial
bicycle builder.

Crichope Linn A river beauty spot with
rock ravine, arch and cauldron.

Ae Forest The Forestry Commission has
planted exotic trees beside the public road
through the forest.

Ae A forestry village started in 1947. The
area has pioneered many techniques of
tree-planting in difficult conditions.

Elshieshields A good 16th-century
tower house which is still inhabited.

Lochmaben The town is said to have
been chartered by Bruce. The church has
the 14th-century 'Bruce Bell'.

Castle Loch Remains of a medieval
castle on a promontory, the site of a shrine
to an Iron Age god. It last withstood siege
in 1588.

Rammerscales Georgian manor with
contemporary walled gardens (open).

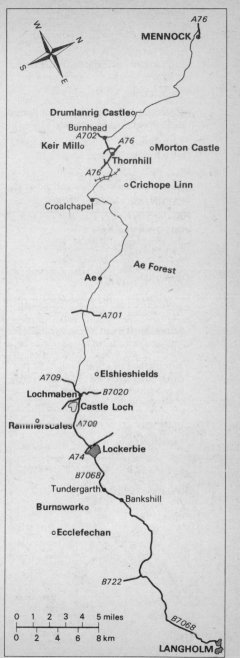

Lockerbie Set in a rich farming area, Lockerbie used to be a market for lambs and horses. The town is built with sandstone from the Corncockle quarry, which is famed for its fossilised reptile footprints.

Ecclefechan See Route 181.

Burnswark A large complex of Roman earthworks, including a fort.

Langholm See Route 120. Also links with Route 121.

Route 190   19 miles   31 km
CUMNOCK — MENNOCK

OS 1:250 000 nos 3 or 4
Bartholomew's 1:100 000 no. 40
OS 1:50 000 no. 71

Cumnock See Route 186. Also links with Routes 187, 194, 195.

a   If you next intend to follow Route 195 to Newton Stewart, turn to it here.

Sanquhar Twice Covenanters fixed their Declarations against the monarchs of their times to a cross, the site of which is now marked by a granite obelisk. The castle dates from the 15th century; there is an 18th-century tolbooth.

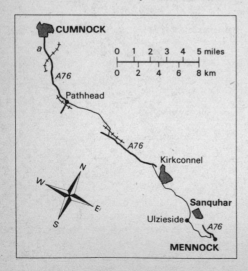

Mennock Links with Routes 189, 191.

Route 191   29 miles   47 km
BIGGAR — MENNOCK

OS 1:250 000 nos 3 or 4
Bartholomew's 1:100 000 no. 40
OS 1:50 000 nos 71, 72

Biggar North of the high street are the traces of crofts, a reminder of medieval land-tenure days. Gladstone Court museum contains a whole street with old houses, shops, a bank, a telephone exchange etc. Links with Route 192.

Coulter Motte Hill A good example of a medieval castle mound (DoE).

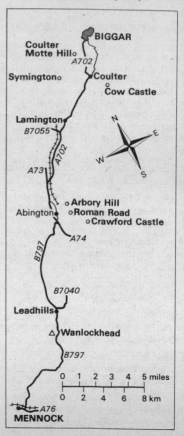

Symington The 11th-century church is noted for its openwork timber roof.

Coulter Coulter House is a typical 17th-century Scots house, and has a mile-long avenue of trees.

Cow Castle A complex of two prehistoric settlements sited on a ridge which, in prehistoric times, stood above marsh. The area has many cultivation terraces and prehistoric remains.

Lamington The church has a fine Norman arch.

Arbory Hill A spectacular hill-fort.

Roman Road The track which runs along the valley below Arbory Hill follows the course of a Roman road.

Crawford Castle A castle in a dominating riverside position.

Leadhills Mining has probably been carried out in the surrounding hills since at least the Roman era. Gold from these hills is contained in the crown of Scotland. Britain's first circulating library opened here in 1741. The gravestone of J. Taylor gives his life-span as 1637 to 1770!

Wanlockhead This is a strong contender for title of 'Scotland's highest village'. Lead mining has been carried out at least since 1680, and in the streams gold was actively prospected by the Mint in the time of Elizabeth I. The originators of steam navigation, W. Symington and J. Taylor, both lived here. See the beam engine (DoE, open).

Mennock Links with Routes 189, 190.

Route 192   32 miles   52 km
EDINBURGH — BIGGAR

OS 1:250 000 nos 3 or 4
Bartholomew's 1:100 000 nos 40, 45
OS 1:50 000 nos 66, 72

Edinburgh See Route 122. Also links with Routes 123, 193, 236, 283.

Fairmilehead At the west side of the village is a prehistoric monolith (NTS).

Castlelaw A prehistoric trivallate hill-fort with an underground earth house. (DoE, open).

Glencorse The barracks used to be the headquarters of Britain's oldest regiment, the Royal Scots.

Rosslyn A lovely chapel containing the famed, intricately-carved apprentice

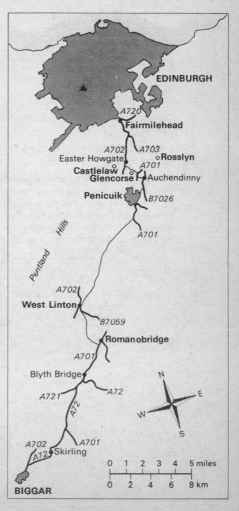

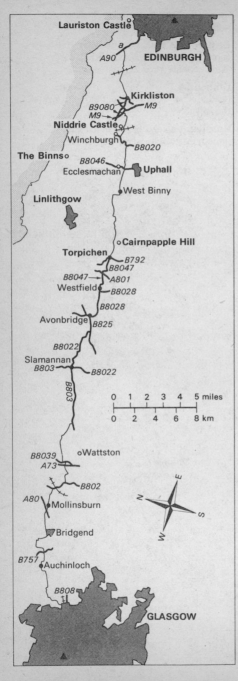

pillar. There are ruins of a 14th-century castle which has often featured in verse and song.

Penicuik This was once the 'Paper-making Town', although no mills remain active today.

West Linton This was once the grave-carving centre of the country. A sample of its stone-carving is on the 17th-century 'Lady Gifford's Well'.

Romanobridge A prettily-sited village with a narrow bridge and mill. Just south of the village are the curious Romano-bridge terraces; their origin is undecided.

Biggar See Route 191.

Route 193   51 miles 81 km
EDINBURGH — GLASGOW

OS 1:250 000 nos 3 or 4
Bartholomew's 1:100 000 no. 45
OS 1:50 000 nos 64, 65, 66 (just)

This route runs through a belt of land in which there is much industry and housing. In an area where no excellent touring route is possible, it is a relatively good route for those who specifically wish to link Edinburgh and Glasgow. However, to avoid busy roads as much as possible, the route takes many turns in the maze of roads and patient navigation is essential. A more northerly, busier route lying roughly along the line between Bo'Ness and Kirkintillach would pass close by many remains of the Roman Antonine Wall, which was planned as a defence of the Roman Empire's northern boundary in the 1st century AD.

Edinburgh See Route 122. Also links with Routes 123, 192, 236, 283.

Lauriston Castle Castle associated with John Law, the founder of France's first bank.

a If you next intend to follow Route 283 to Kincardine or Route 236 to Rumbling Bridge, turn to either here.

Kirkliston Previously this was called 'Templeliston' after the Knights

Templars who settled here. The church has a saddleback tower and Romanesque doorway.

Niddrie Castle Ruins of the 15th-century castle where Mary Queen of Scots spent her first night after escaping from Loch Leven.

Uphall Once an oil shale-mining centre, Uphall has a church with 12th-century work and an ancient bell.

The Binns A mainly 17th-century historic house (NTS, open); views.

Linlithgow On the loch promontory stands Linlithgow Palace, one of Scotland's four Royal Palaces. It was the birthplace of Mary Queen of Scots; Queen Elizabeth II has held a reception in it (DoE, open). The loch is a bird sanctuary. St Michael's church has good window tracery, and bullet holes left by Cromwellian troops can be seen. Architecturally interesting buildings in the town include numbers 44–48 High Street (NTS).

Cairnpapple Hill Prehistoric remains from many eras, including stones, henges, sanctuary and burial cairns (DoE). Knock to the south has a mountain indicator; wide views from both.

Torpichen Church incorporating remains of a preceptory and hospital of the Knights of St John of Jerusalem (DoE).

Glasgow See Route 194. Also links with Routes 281.

Route 194   36 miles   58 km
GLASGOW — CUMNOCK

OS 1:250 000 nos 3 or 4
Bartholomew's 1:100 000 nos 40, 44
OS 1:50 000 nos 64, 70, 71

It is not possible to avoid busy A roads in going into Glasgow, the price of entering an interesting, albeit often considered ugly city. Those wishing to link areas north and south of the Clyde without passing through

Glasgow and its extensive suburbs can do so by taking Routes 187 and 188.

Glasgow The city originated as an ecclesiastical settlement founded by St Mungo, c.543, when its name was the Celtic *Glesgu* meaning 'beloved green place'. It grew prosperous on tobacco, sugar and cotton trading prior to the American Revolution, after which it turned to the shipping and ship-building still practised on the Clyde today. The

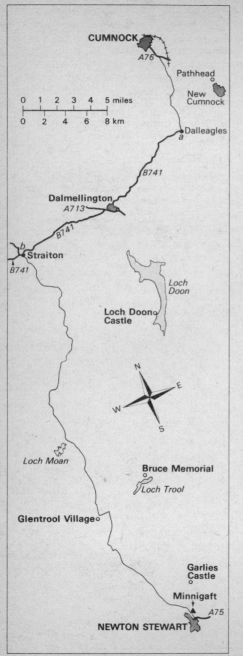

'Comet', the first commercial steamship was launched on the Clyde in 1812. The 'Queen Mary' and QEs 1 and 2 were also built here. Places to note are the 12th-century cathedral which escaped destruction in the Reformation (DoE); 15th-century Provan Hall mansion (NTS, open); Pollock House, a William Adam house, which contains collections of Spanish paintings and glass (open). The Provands Lordship is the oldest house in Glasgow (1740) and now houses collections of furniture, tapestries and paintings (open). Also Kelvingore art gallery and museum, and many other museums, including those of transport and of costume. There are two universities and the Glasgow School of Art. Zoo, botanic gardens and several parks. The Old Glasgow museum is in the People's Palace. Links with Routes 193, 281.

Eaglesham A planned town, built by the 12th Earl of Eglinton in 1796. The church has a monument to two Covenanters killed in 1685. It was near here that Rudolf Hess made his dramatic landing by air in 1941.

Galston This was once a mining town, but now the pits are exhausted. Jaspers and agates are sometimes found in Burn Anne, the town's river.

Sorn Castle A 15th-century castle with 18th-century additions.

Sorn A 17th-century church with an outside stair to its gallery.

Auchinleck A coal-mining village.

Cumnock See Route 186. Also links with Routes 187, 190, 195.

Route 195   47 miles   76 km
CUMNOCK — NEWTON STEWART

OS 1:250 000 nos 3 or 4
Bartholomew's 1:100 000 nos 37, 40
OS 1:50 000 nos 71, 77, 83

Cumnock See Route 186. Also links with Routes 187, 190, 194.

If you next intend to follow Route 190 to Mennock, turn off on the B741 and join it at Pathhead.

Dalmellington A very old mining and hill-farming town with a hill-fort.

Loch Doon Castle When the loch was raised to make a reservoir, this castle was moved from its island site and reconstructed on the shore (DoE, open). It can be reached by road from Dalmellington.

Straiton A charming farming village with a 14th-century parish church.

b If you next intend to follow Route 184 to Stranraer, you can turn off on the B7045 in a north-westerly direction to join it near Kirkmichael.

Glentrool Village A forestry village

serving the vast Galloway Forest Park. Forestry Commission booklets about the forest are available. Red deer are sometimes seen in the forest.

Bruce Memorial The memorial records a victory of Robert the Bruce over the English in 1307. Old oakwoods nearby have government protection. The Glen Trool Hoard of Bronze Age implements found in the area is now in the Edinburgh museum.

Minnigaff Newton Stewart YH.

Garlies Castle The ruins of a group of 17th-century buildings around an older tower, which was once a Stewart family seat.

Newton Stewart See Route 183. Also links with Route 184.

WALES AND THE BORDERS

Running virtually the whole length of Wales is a long spine of mountains and hills crossed by many superb and sometimes strenuous cycling roads. In contrast to this empty upland core, the coastal lands and Welsh Borders to either side have a tamer terrain, with lower hills and interesting places to visit.

On many mountain roads you will not pass a house for miles, yet on others a hamlet will be nestling just around the corner. Many of the roads show little respect for gradient and the resulting steep climbs mean that a touring cycle with low gears is a necessity. In compensation the hilly roads offer wonderful views, and after a long and winding haul to the top, you can often drift gently along enjoying the panorama of hills and forest before free-wheeling down to a valley. If you are really keen to cycle to the back of beyond, try some of the rough tracks. Wales is particularly well endowed with these, and they often have firm if bumpy surfaces and run for many miles. Some are old cattle or sheep droving roads linking valleys and towns by fairly direct routes over the hills, whereas the tarmac roads often follow a much longer detour to arrive at the same place. A 1:50 000 map and a compass will be needed to find the tracks, and special care in forests should be taken, where tracks are often unmarked on even the large scale maps.

In the hilly areas where towns and villages are some distance apart and separated by a hard ride, it is best to plan overnight stops in advance, booking ahead if necessary, rather than just turning up at a hostel or bed-and-breakfast. After one very long day we can remember struggling over those unforgiving hills towards Clun spurred on only by thoughts of hot soup and sleep. On arrival, virtually on hands and knees, we found the hostel full and ended up spending a cool night in the open, with no soup and little sleep! Give yourself a lot more time than you would allow for the same distance in East Anglia.

There is only one part of Wales which is not really suitable for touring— the industrial south. Here the coal mining valleys have attracted heavy industry and sprawling towns and the roads are very busy. Routes 196 and 197 do their best to avoid the worst and are useful routes if you want to link the port of Swansea with England. But if possible take a route further north through the more attractive Brecon Beacons.

On the edge of industrial south Wales, the Gower peninsula is a renowned scenic gem. It is a little out of the way, but if you find yourself in or around Swansea, perhaps waiting for a ferry, it is well worth the extra miles. From the Mumbles to Worms Head a succession of grey craggy cliffs plunges to rocks that have wrecked many a ship. There are several secluded sandy beaches along the Gower coast, which is best explored on foot. Being so close to Swansea, the narrow roads become choked with traffic on summer weekends and public holidays.

Straddling the Welsh–English border and stretching from the river Dee to the Severn is the area called on the accompanying map the 'Welsh Borders', also known as the 'Welsh Marches'. This is fine cycling country, with hills and vales of forest and farmland and few towns. The peace of this rural backwater belies its history: the clues to centuries of conflict are the stout castles, earthworks and defensive houses. Offa's Dyke was built in the 8th century to define the boundary of Wales and England and much of the earth bank remains; it is now the course of a designated long distance footpath. The successful Norman invasion of England heralded new assaults on Wales, and right up to the 16th century Norman 'Marcher' lords ('Marcher' comes from an old French word for 'border') penetrated deep into the country establishing many castles and towns such as Chepstow, Ludlow, Grosmont and Skenfrith.

If you have no time to explore the Borders thoroughly, then the lower reaches of the river Wye and adjacent Forest of Dean provide an excellent area for a short tour. The Wye valley is deep and winding, clothed in dense woods. It reaches its most impressive north east of Monmouth at Symonds Yat, where the river passes beneath precipitous crags. A stiff climb

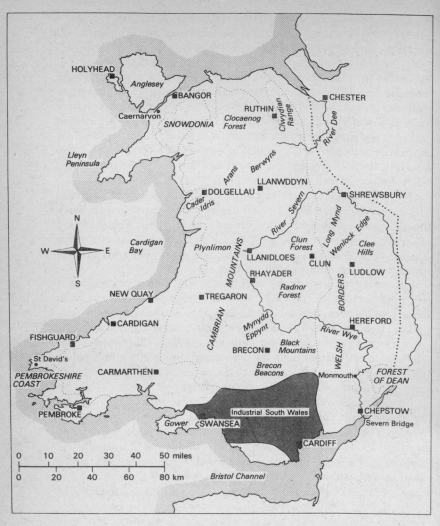

eastwards from the valley leads to the Forest of Dean, one of the few remaining primeval forests in Britain.

Cycling north you come to more typical Border landscape. Undulating hills are dotted with livestock and prosperous farms, the fields lined with stone walls and thick hedges. Here and there are higher ridges, their steeper sides often wooded. South of Shrewsbury the Long Mynd rises to over 1500 feet (500 metres) and stretches in a slim ridge for 7 miles (11 km) or so. The rough-stuff tracks along the crest give panoramic views eastwards towards the English lowlands, and westwards to the Welsh hills.

— England-Wales Border

HOLYHEAD
228
BANGOR
227
226   CHESTER
229
RHYD-
LYDAN
225
232
TRAWSFYNYDD
231
LLANWDDYN   233   SHREWSBURY
230   224   235
                                IRONBRIDGE
220
219
LLANIDLOES
CLUN   234
YSBYTY   205   206
YSTWYTH   222   221   LUDLOW
204   216   RHAYADER
NEW QUAY   TREGARON   207   218
211   210   WORCESTER
203   215   HEREFORD
FISHGUARD   GLASBURY   223
212   213   BRECON   214
202   209   208   217
CARMARTHEN
201   200   CHEPSTOW
PEMBROKE   199   GOWERTON   196
        SWANSEA
RHOSSILI   198   107   CARDIFF

N
W   E
S

0   10   20   30   40   50 miles
0   20   40   60   80 km

Close by, the ridge of Wenlock Edge is longer but lower than the Long
Mynd, while just north of Ludlow are the rounded Clee Hills. North of
Shrewsbury, the Welsh Borders taper sharply as they become sandwiched
between the flat expanse of the Cheshire Plain and the hills of North Wales.

Well served by rail, the Welsh Borders are easy to get to and are suitable
for a 'one way only' tour, but they can also be included in a longer tour of
Wales. It is worth remembering that the Borders are considerably warmer
and drier than the Welsh hills further west, and can provide an excellent
alternative touring area should you be driven eastwards by bad weather.

The greater part of inland Wales is occupied by the Cambrian Mountains and their surrounding hills—wild country supporting isolated hill farms. It is an area which can be beautiful but is often bleak, windswept and wet. It offers some of the most exciting cycling in the British Isles. Apart from the real mountain scenery of Snowdonia, the Cambrians are more a collection of bulky hill groups. The bigger of these are the Black Mountains, the Brecon Beacons, Cader Idris and the Arans and Berwyns, all of which rise over 2500 feet (800 metres). Their grassy slopes are often steep and in places there are massive rock faces. The gaps between the larger hill groups contain yet more hills, lower and crammed together: Mynydd Eppynt, Plynlimon, the Forests of Clun, Clocaenog and Radnor, and the Clwydian Range are a few, all of them with fine cycling roads. You certainly need low gears and to be fit; it can be hard work cycling here. Most of the main roads follow valleys, only climbing over the tops where necessary, and to appreciate fully the wildness of this part of Wales you must take to the narrow, switchback lanes which you will more likely be sharing with sheep than with cars.

Large areas of Wales are now commercially forested and a sea of dark conifers often dominates the landscape. With so many hills and no shortage of running water it is not surprising that Wales has some of the most spectacular waterfalls in the British Isles, many of them little known or visited. In several valleys dams have been constructed and reservoirs fill the arms of the valleys behind.

Rugged Snowdonia has some famous mountain scenery, commanded by Snowdon which at 3559 feet (1084 metres) is the highest mountain in England and Wales. The skyline is marked by rocky ridges and peaks which drop suddenly to bare grey rock faces and grassy slopes beneath. There are few passes through these mountains, that of Llanberis being the most impressive, and those that do exist contain busy main roads. But for mountain lovers the fine roadside scenery makes the traffic just tolerable and if weather conditions are good you can always pause to walk in the mountains. However, if you are tempted to go up Snowdon, take the 1:50 000 or tourist map which gives alternatives to the main tourist path. It rather spoils the atmosphere of mountain grandeur to be overtaken at 3000 feet by a steam train bursting with passengers heading for the summit café. It must be Britain's ugliest mountain top! Fortunately the concentration of people on Snowdon leaves the surrounding heights comparatively empty.

Just to the south west of Snowdon is the Lleyn peninsula which tapers to form the northern arm of Cardigan Bay. Its peaceful lanes and low hills are a pleasant contrast to neighbouring parts. Round the corner is Anglesey, an intensively farmed flattish island with many ancient monuments to explore as you make your way to or from the ferry at Holyhead,

Southwards, the graceful curve of Cardigan Bay ends with the rocky cliffs of the Pembrokeshire coast. Prehistoric man left hill-forts and monuments here and later, with the coming of the Normans, many castles were built; to this day Pembrokeshire (the county is now renamed Dyfed) is remembered as 'little England'. Rather like Devon, it has become famous for the beauty of its wild and rocky coastal scenery and if you want a day or so out of the saddle you will be well rewarded by a walk along part of the 170-mile (270-km) designated Pembrokeshire Coast Path. From the Cambrians to this corner of Wales the villages become more frequent and the fields and farms more prosperous. It is warmer and drier than inland Wales, and though hilly in places the steep gradients are not as prolonged as those of the Cambrian roads.

Route 196   30 miles   48 km
CHEPSTOW — CARDIFF

OS 1:250 000 nos 7 or 8
Bartholomew's 1:100 000 nos 12, 13
OS 1:50 000 nos 171, 162 or 171, 172

This route is intended (together with Route 197) to serve as a useful link between England and South Wales, and in so doing has to pass through industrial and built up areas. There will be heavy traffic on the A roads.

Chepstow See Route 92. Also links with Routes 208, 209, 217.

Caerwent The site of the Roman city of Venta Silurum (DoE, open). The walls and gates can still be seen, and there are relics in the church.

Earthwork Once a fort of the Silures tribe.

Gray Hill Views and stone circle.

Penhow The castle was built by the Normans to defend the border, and is the oldest inhabited castle in Wales (open).

Caerleon The 50-acre Roman fortress of Isca has an amphitheatre and small museum (DoE, open), and has been associated with the legend of King Arthur.

Newport Busy industrial town and seaport. Unusual Transporter Bridge over the River Usk, with views. The Cathedral of St Woolos has Norman arches and a medieval tower, and there is a 12th-century castle (DoE, open). Birthplace of the famous poet W. H. Davies, remembered for his lines 'What is this life if, full of care, we have no time to stand and stare?' His bust is in the Museum and Art Gallery, which also has local history displays.

Tredegar House The finest Restoration house in Wales with paintings and large grounds (open).

Cardiff The capital of Wales, with a great port that grew up in the 19th century with the export of coal and iron. The castle has a fine Norman keep and interior decorations (open). The National Museum of Wales includes important archaeological collections and the Welsh Industrial and Maritime Museum covers industrial development in Wales. Links with Route 197.

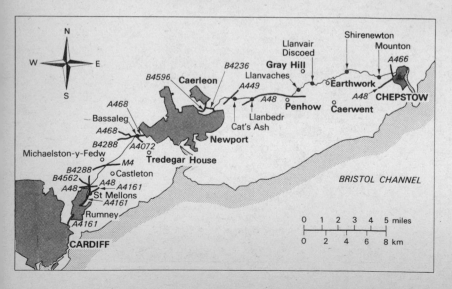

Route 197
SWANSEA — CARDIFF

58 miles · 94 km

OS 1:250 000 nos 7 or 8
Bartholomew's 1:100 000 no. 12
OS 1:50 000 nos 159, 170, 171

This route is intended (together with Route 196) to serve as a useful link between England and South Wales rather than as a scenic touring route. It does however pass through a variety of landscapes and visits several places of interest. In cycling

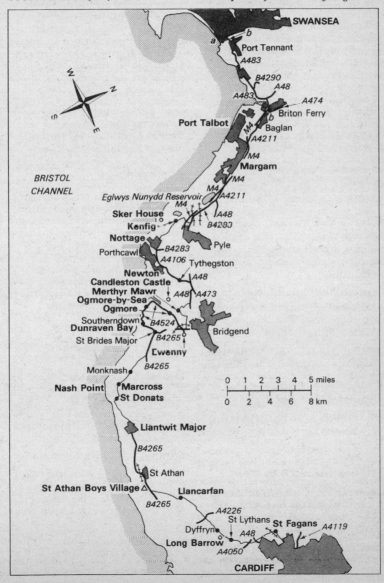

through the industrial part of South Wales, busy main roads are encountered.

Swansea This port and university town is Wales' second city, also called by its Welsh name Abertawe. Much of the architecture is 20th century, built after Second World War bombings. The town originally grew around a Norman castle; there are ruins of a 14th-century castle (DoE). The new civic building has Brangwyn murals. The birthplace of 18th-century Beau Nash. Traditional seaweed laver bread on sale. The Royal Institution of Wales is a notable industrial museum; Swansea Museum; Art Gallery attached to the public library; Glynn Vivian Art Gallery. Links with Route 198.

a Seasonal ferries from Swansea to Ilfracombe, North Devon.

b Between Swansea and the Briton Ferry roundabout the route can be followed by using a cycle path which runs parallel to the main road.

Port Talbot Once the largest steel-works in Europe, with its own port for ore carriers.

Margam The abbey was founded in 1151, and there is a country park and museum containing the Roman Margam stones (DoE, open).

Kenfig The old town of Kenfig was buried by a sandstorm in the early 16th century, and only a part of the castle remains now. Various legends are associated with the lost town.

Sker House R. D. Blackmore's novel *The Maid of Sker* was set here.

Nottage Nottage Court is a restored Tudor mansion where the author R. D. Blackmore wrote *The Maid of Sker.*

Newton The old church has a strong defensive tower, and curious St John's Well nearby has a water level that fluctuates with the tides.

Merthyr Mawr Thatched cottages and a medieval bridge. Views across the river valley to Ogmore Castle. A foot-path leads to stepping stones over the river.

Candleston Castle A ruined 15th-century fortified manor house. The high sand dunes to the west cover a rich archaeological area, which includes tumulii and possibly neolithic settlements.

Ewenny The Priory (DoE, open) is a fine example of Norman ecclesiastical architecture, and has defensive walls. Ewenny Pottery is reputed to be the oldest established pottery in Wales.

Ogmore A ruined castle (DoE, open) stands near stepping stones over the Ogmore River which join a footpath to Merthyr Mawr.

Ogmore-by-Sea Good views across the Bristol Channel.

Dunraven Bay The rocks have inter-esting geological bedding, and there is an Iron Age fort on the headland to the south.

Marcross The 12th-century church has an outsize font.

Nash Point Two lighthouses, only one of which is in use, guard a dangerous coastline. There are views over to Exmoor in north Devon. There is an Iron Age fort by the valley.

St Donats The fine castle is the home of Atlantic College.

Llantwit Major An ancient place with an old church containing crosses and memorials. This was a centre of religion in early times. There is a 15th-century town hall, tithe barn, and by the church a monastery gateway and a dovecot.

St Athan Boys Village St Athan YH.

Llancarfan The large church probably stands on the site of a 6th-century monastery. The 18th-century poet Iolo Morgannwg was born at Pennon, just to the south.

Long Barrow A burial chamber, just south east of the road (DoE).

St Fagans The Welsh Folk Museum

provides a unique insight into traditional Welsh life. It comprises St Fagan's Castle, an Elizabethan mansion with period furnishings and gardens, and a wide range of buildings that have been transported here from all over Wales and re-erected. There are several working exhibits, and craftsmen practising traditional crafts.

Cardiff See Route 196.

Route 198   26 miles   42 km
RHOSSILI — SWANSEA

OS 1:250 000 nos 7 or 8
Bartholomew's 1:100 000 no. 12
OS 1:50 000 no. 159

Much of the attraction of the Gower peninsula lies in its south and west coasts, where limestone cliffs alternate with sandy bays. Many of the associated features of beauty or interest can be reached on foot only. The cyclist can enjoy them by stopping often for short walks, or by making an extended coast walk to return to his machine by public transport. In either case, a 1:50 000 map is a great advantage. The entire coast from Mumbles through Rhossili to Burry Holms can be walked.

Rhossili Church with a Norman doorway. To the south-west of the village, the Middle Ages open field system survives. Links with Route 199.

Worms Head An island which can be reached across a rocky causeway at low tide; ask locally for safe times to cross.

Tears Point Raised beach.

Mewslade Bay Accessible by valley path from Pitton is the small but fine sand Mewslade Bay, overlooked by Thurba Head with its Iron Age hill-fort.

Paviland Paviland Yellow Top hill-fort, and nearby Goats Hole bone cave.

Llanddewi Church with nave and chancel out of line.

Porteynon Some thatch in the village.

a A track between Horton and Porteynon

avoids the retracing of some distance on the A4118.

Oxwich A 16th-century fortified mansion on a Norman castle site.

Penrice The motte of Penrice's first Norman castle.

Penrice Castle Ruins of 13th-century Penrice castle beside the new Georgian and Victorian castle.

Oxwich Burrows A nature reserve of salt-marsh, dune, pond and woods.

Parkmill Pleasant detour north-west along stream valley to Parc le Breos chambered long barrow (DoE, open). Nearby Cathole Cave, one of Gower's 'bone caves'.

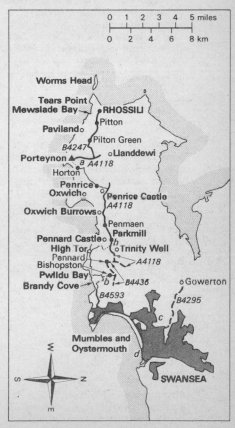

Pennard Castle The 13th-century ruins of a castle which was often threatened by blown sand.

Trinity Well Near Ilston stream, an outdoor stone pulpit marks the 17th-century foundations of Wales' first Baptist Chapel.

High Tor Mitchin Hole and Bacon Hole have yielded prehistoric finds.

Pwlldu Bay Sand and shingle beach with good walks in the NT valley behind.

b The alternative route uses A and B roads while the main route follows lanes and rough tracks. At its eastern end the track past Pwlldu Bay leaves the car park at the end of the lane from Pyle; at its western end it leaves the end of the lane by High Pennard to drop steeply, with a rocky surface, to the bay below. The other track is wide, sandy and, except at its northern end, level.

Brandy Cove Associated with smugglers' tales.

Mumbles and Oystermouth Views over the sweeping bay, popular for yachting, to the massive Port Talbot steel-works opposite. From Roman times till relatively recently the bay was noted for oyster beds. Mumbles holiday resort was served by the world's first passenger railway, built in 1804 and initially powered by horses, which ran alongside the bay from Swansea. Ruins of 13th-century Oystermouth Castle, the 'Keys of the Gower'.

c A direct route between Swansea and Gowerton, missing out the long ride on Routes 198 and 199 around the lovely Gower peninsula, is as shown on the map.

d Ferries from Swansea to Cork, Ireland. Seasonal ferries from Swansea to Ilfracombe, north Devon.

Swansea See Route 197.

Route 199   17 miles   28 km
GOWERTON — RHOSSILI

OS 1:250 000 nos 7 or 8
Bartholomew's 1:100 000 no. 12
OS 1:50 000 no. 159

Gowerton Links with Route 200.

Cil Ifor Earthworks of an 8-acre, early Iron Age camp.

a A direct route between Swansea and Gowerton, missing out the long ride on Routes 198 and 199 around the lovely Gower peninsula, is as shown on the map.

Arthur's Stone A cromlech with a 25-ton capstone, supposedly split by King Arthur's sword. It stands by the hill, Cefn Bryn.

Weobley Castle A 13th- and 14th-century fortified manor house (DoE, open).

Cheriton Church containing much woodwork done by a rector this century.

North Hill Tor Massive earthworks beside the marshes, probably the remains

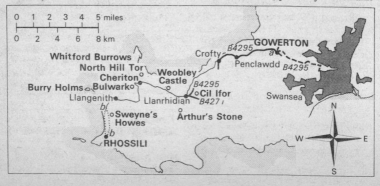

of Norman fortifications.

Bulwarks Iron Age hill-fort, with a complex of banks and ditches.

Whitford Burrows A peninsula of sand burrows and salt marshes, belonging to the NT and now a nature reserve.

Burry Holms An island beyond the dunes, which is accessible on foot for about three hours each side of low tide, and which bears traces of an Iron Age fort and a 6th-century monastic cell.

b Tracks link the north and south ends of Rhossili Down both over the top of the Down, which involves climbing but gives views over the Gower to one side and Rhossili bay to the other; and along the western foot of the Down beside the extensive sands of the bay. Alternative to both tracks is a much longer road route via Llanddewi.

Sweyne's Howes Ruined megalithic tombs, dating from about 2500 BC.

Rhossili See Route 198.

Route 200   25 miles   40 km
CARMARTHEN — GOWERTON

OS 1:250 000 nos 7 or 8
Bartholomew's 1:100 000 nos 11 or 12
OS 1:50 000 no. 159

Carmarthen Originally a Roman settlement. Remains of town walls and a castle founded by William Rufus. Edward III made this the staple town for Welsh wool. St Peter's Church (13th-century) has good glass set off by a sombre interior. There are Georgian and Victorian buildings and an 18th-century Guildhall. County museum with archaeological exhibits. Links with Routes 201, 212, 213, 215.

Abergwili The palace of the Bishop of St David's.

Llangunnor On the route of a Roman road, this was the site of Maridunum, the furthest west of the Romans' large bases.

Loughor Castle This lowest bridge-

able place on the River Loughor was on the Roman road to Maridunum and defended by a Roman station. The Norman castle built to defend the crossing was ruined by the Welsh in 1115 (DoE, open).

a A direct route between Swansea and Gowerton, missing out the long ride on Routes 198 and 199 around the lovely Gower peninsula, is as shown on the map.

Gowerton Links with Route 199.

Route 201   43 miles   70 km
CARMARTHEN — PEMBROKE

OS 1:250 000 no. 7 or 8
Bartholomew's 1:100 000 no. 11
OS 1:50 000 nos 158, 159

Carmarthen See Route 200. Also links with Routes 212, 213, 215.

Llanstephan The castle ruin, on a bluff of land by the shore, was favoured by painters of the Romantic

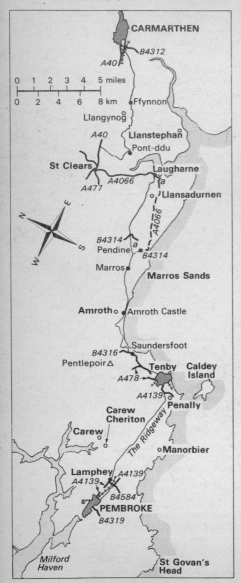

Movement (DoE, open). Nearby are prehistoric remains including an Iron Age fort.

St Clears The church was that of a Cluniac priory of Norman times, and it has good Norman carving.

Laugharne A picturesque village with Georgian houses and 'Romantic' ruins of a Tudor castle. Dylan Thomas lived in Boat House, and is buried here.

a The lane route crosses a ridge with views to the sea. The alternative, which uses an A road, passes below the steep slope of the ridge, beside the marshes and dunes to the south.

Llansadurnen The quarry is in a limestone bluff which has yielded several fossil mammals of large size.

Marros Sands Secluded beach.

Amroth This village above a lovely wooded valley has a Georgian inn.

Tenby Possibly the site of an earlier Norse settlement, Tenby was a 9th-century Welsh stronghold. An active port in the 17th and 18th centuries, it became a fashionable Georgian watering-place, and is now a resort. There is a 13th-century castle keep, and 15th-century town walls. The 15th-century Tudor merchant's house has a fine Flemish chimney and remains of wall frescoes (NT, open). St Mary's, Wales' largest parish church, has carvings and monuments. St Julian's chapel was Tenby's first bathing hut. A museum of local interest. Boat trips to Caldey Island.

Penally Fine Celtic cross.

Caldey Island Some buildings remain of a 12th-century Benedictine monastery, and there is an active Trappist monastery which came from Belgium in 1929. Ancient ogham stone.

Manorbier Secluded Norman castle with a vast gatehouse (open). King's Quoit burial chamber, lying south-west of the village, has a 15-foot (5-m) capstone.

Carew Cheriton A fine 15th-century church with Carew family tombs.

Carew Waterside ruins of a 13th-century castle, and Celtic cross.

Lamphey The Bishop's palace has a great hall with an arcaded roof (DoE, open).

St Govan's Head Near the end of the lane is a 14th-century chapel, dramatically set in precipitous cliffs.

Pembroke The imposing castle (c.1207), standing on a good vantage point for Ireland, withstood a long siege in the Civil War. It was the birthplace of Henry VII. There are old town walls and ruins of Benedictine, barrel-vaulted Monkton Priory. Pembroke Dock was created in 1814. Links with Route 202.

Route 202   52 miles 83 km
FISHGUARD — PEMBROKE

OS 1:250 000 no. 7
Bartholomew's 1:100 000 no. 11
OS 1:50 000 no. 157

Fishguard The Lower Town is an old fishing village with a quay. The great breakwater was built in anticipation of Atlantic liners whose passengers would travel on to London by train, but the liners went elsewhere. During the War of Independence the American privateer, Paul Jones, landed here to demand ransom for a captured ship. Links with Routes 203, 212.

a Ferries from Fishguard to Rosslare, Ireland.

b Between Fishguard and St David's the route passes many dead-end roads and tracks leading to the beautiful Pembroke coast where there is a designated long distance footpath.

Carregwastad Point In 1797 a French invasion ship, prevented by unfavourable winds from sailing the Bristol Channel, landed here instead. The French were repulsed, in part by Welshwomen whose red skirts and black hats they mistook for soldiers' uniforms at a distance. They were the last hostile force to land on British soil.

Garn Fawr Iron-Age hill-fort.

Longhouse A large megalithic dolmen on six supports.

Carnllidi St David's YH.

St David's Head In an area rich in prehistory is a beautifully sited promontory fort with remains of stone huts and rock shelters.

St David's Now a tourist centre, formerly a place of pilgrimage, St David founded Welsh Christianity here in the 6th century. The present 12th-century sandstone cathedral is simple without, but intricately decorated within: it contains the stone screen of Bishop Gower, the carved stalls of Bishop Tully, and fan vaulting of Bishop Vaughan. By the cathedral are ruins of the 14th-century Bishop Gower's palace with a great hall and arcaded parapet (DoE, open). Close Wall and St Non's chapel (DoE).

Wooltack Point An earthwork turns the promontory into a fort. Views to Skomer Island, which has the remains of many prehistoric huts, which probably housed a community of shipmasters. Seals are sometimes seen.

Rath A prehistoric cliff-top fort with a triple defence bank.

Gateholm Island The small island has the remains of over a hundred prehistoric huts.

Milford Haven In the sailing era it was said that a thousand ships, each hidden from the others, could have harboured in the marvellous harbour of Milford Haven. It is now used for oil-tankers.

Pembroke See Route 201.

Route 203   41 miles   66 km
NEW QUAY — FISHGUARD

OS 1:250 000 no. 7
Bartholomew's 1:100 000 nos 11, 17
OS 1:50 000 nos 145, 157 (just)

New Quay The town grew up in the 18th and 19th centuries, during the ship-building boom. There are Georgian and Victorian houses. Links with Routes 204, 211.

Aberporth Good bathing.

Pencribach An RAF missile range is on the headland summit.

Cardigan The town is thus named as it was once 'Ceredig's province'. Before the river withdrew, Cardigan was an important seaport, and tall warehouses still stand beside the ancient arched bridge. The castle incorporates the remains of a 12th-century fortress.

Cilgerran Castle The ruin of a 13th-century riverside promontory castle has been an inspiration to painters including J. M. W. Turner (DoE, NT, open).

St Dogmaels The village grew around the 12th-century abbey of the Order of Tiron, which has intricate carvings including a stone cadaver (DoE, open). Parish church with a 6th-century Ogham stone.

Moylgrove A small but pretty village in a secluded valley.

a The north-eastern side of the detour consists of a bridleway which is bounded on both sides for almost all of its length.

Pantsaeson An 18th-century country house.

Monington Church with ochre frescoes.

Llech-y-Drybedd and **Trellyfant** Fine cromlechs.

Nevern This place was the capital of the 11th-century Norman Martin of Tours' kingdom. The churchyard contains ogham stones. This was on a pilgrims' route to St David's, and some hundred yards west of the church are a pilgrims' cross and kneeling place.

Pentre Ifan A superb burial chamber with a 17-ton capstone (DoE).

Carningli Hill One of Wales' best-preserved prehistoric camps.

b If you next intend to follow Route 212 to Carmarthen, you can turn to it here.

Carregwastad Point See Route 202.

c Ferries from Fishguard to Rosslare, Ireland.

Fishguard See Route 202. Also links with Route 212.

Route 204   33 miles   53 km
YSBYTY YSTWYTH — NEW QUAY

OS 1:250 000 no. 7
Bartholomew's 1:100 000 no. 17
OS 1:50 000 nos 135, 146, 145 (just)

Ysbyty Ystwyth The 19th-century architecture dates from the time when the inhabitants worked in the Cwmystwyth mines. Links with Routes 205, 216, 222.

Llanafan Good glass in St Arvan's church.

Trawscoed The present mansion stands on the site of one sacked by the Parliamentarians.

a The alternative route is flatter than the main one but uses a coastal A road which can be busy.

Llansantffraid Fishermen's cottages.

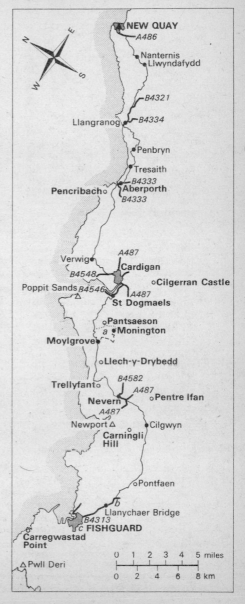

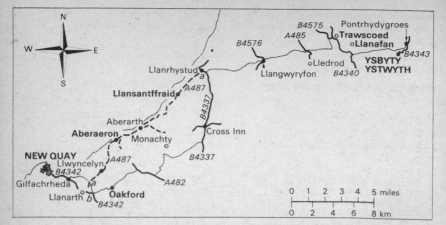

Aberaeron A trading port which lost its importance in the railway era, and is therefore 'frozen' in the Regency style.

Oakford One-storey cottages.

b If you next intend to follow Route 211 to Tregaron, you can turn to it here.

New Quay See Route 203. Also links with Route 211.

Route 205   25 miles   40 km
**LLANIDLOES —
YSBYTY YSTWYTH**

OS 1:250 000 no. 7
Bartholomew's 1:100 000 no. 17
OS 1:50 000 nos 135, 136

Llanidloes See Route 206. Also links with Routes 224, 230.

Ystumtuen Mining hamlet, now almost deserted.

Llywernog Mining museum.

Ysbyty Cynfyn Footpath into the valley to the west, to Parson's Bridge beauty spot.

Devil's Bridge When the river is in flood, there is a 550-foot (170-m) waterfall. The two newer bridges overlay an old stone one constructed by the monks of Strata Florida. A narrow gauge railway travels to Aberystwyth.

Aberystwyth A resort town with much 19th-century architecture. It is overlooked by Pen Dinas, an unusual Iron Age double hill-fort. The sea front is dominated by Edward I's (13th-century) castle ruins. Wales' first uni-

versity college opened here in a Victorian hotel; the National Library of Wales is situated here.

a If you next intend to follow Route 222 to Rhayader, you can turn to it here.

Ysbyty Ystwyth See Route 204. Also links with Routes 216, 222.

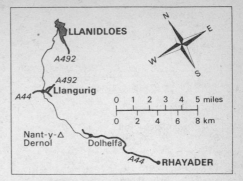

Route 206   14 miles   23 km
LLANIDLOES — RHAYADER

OS 1:250 000 no. 7
Bartholomew's 1:100 000 no. 17
OS 1:50 000 nos 136, 137

Llanidloes Timbered market hall of 1609, with a museum of local interest and industry. The town was in the thick of the Chartist disturbances of the 19th century. The church has a 13th-century arcade and hammerbeam roof. Links with Routes 205, 224, 230.

Llangurig There are traces of Roman workings in the area, but Llangurig had its peak of lead and silver mining in the 18th century. The extensive Van mines are open to the public.

Rhayader See Route 207. Also links with Routes 221, 222.

Route 207   34 miles   54 km
RHAYADER — GLASBURY

OS 1:250 000 no. 7
Bartholomew's 1:100 000 nos 13 (just), 17, 18
OS 1:50 000 nos 147, 148, 161 (just)

Rhayader Market town noted for sheep fairs. Links with Routes 206, 221, 222.

Llandrindod Wells A prosperous spa in mid-Victorian times. There is a museum of archaeology and dolls.

Builth Wells The town was entirely burnt in 1691, with the possible exception of the still existing stone wool market. The Pump Room and Old Crown Hotel are reminders of 18th-century spa days, when Builth Wells had an international clientele. The

bridge dates from this time.

Painscastle The castle site is a good example of a traditional motte and bailey.

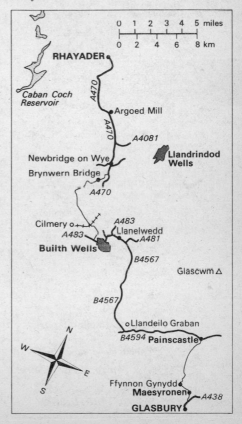

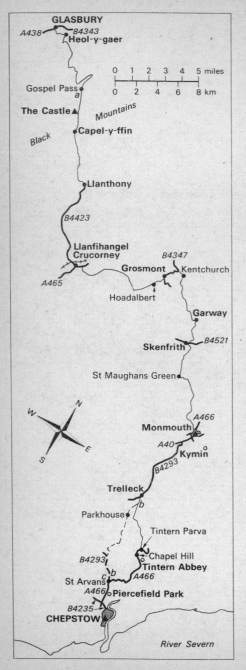

Maesyronen Dissenters' chapel of 1679.

Glasbury See Route 208. Also links with Routes 214, 223.

Route 208   53 miles   86 km
GLASBURY — CHEPSTOW

OS 1:250 000 no. 7
Bartholomew's 1:100 000 no. 13
OS 1:50 000 nos 161, 162

Glasbury The Wye valley affords a superb military entry into Wales and so there are many forts, including important Roman posts, in the area. Links with Routes 207, 214, 223.

Heol-y-Gaer The name means 'Fort on the Roadway'. Here was a Roman station large enough for a whole legion.

a The roads over Gospel Pass are not shown on Bartholomew's 1975 map.

The Castle Capel-y-ffin YH.

Capel-y-ffin The name means 'Chapel on the boundary'. The place is close to the boundaries between the old counties of Monmouth, Brecon and Hereford, and therefore also between Wales and England. A 19th-century monastery is used as a girls' school.

Llanthony Ruins of a transitional style 12th-century priory (DoE, open). The inn was the prior's lodging.

Llanfihangel Crucorney Llanfihangel Court is a gabled Tudor manor house (open).

Grosmont The size of the 14th-century church stands witness to the great importance of Grosmont in medieval times. The castle was built in the reign of Henry III (DoE, open).

Garway Foundations of a Knights Templars church. Dovecot with 666 nesting holes.

Skenfrith The castle was a Norman defence against the Welsh. It retains its 13th-century curtain walls (DoE, NT, open). The 13th-century church has a half-timbered tower.

Monmouth Castle and Great Castle House (DoE). Monnow bridge and gatehouse, with a nearby 13th-century Norman chapel of architectural merit. Remains of a priory with 14th-century glass. Museum of Admiral Nelson.

Kymin Set in NT lands on the hill summit are a Naval Temple and the Round House, a late 18th-century dining club.

Trelleck Once the capital of Monmouth, the place gets its name from three standing stones at the cross-roads. Near the church are a preaching cross and a 'druid altar'.

b The main route passes famous Tintern Abbey, but uses a valley A road which can be busy with tourist traffic, whereas the alternative forgoes the Abbey to stay on quieter roads.

Tintern Abbey The renowned romantic ruin of the 12th-century Cistercian abbey beside the meandering River Wye (DoE, open). The head of the tidal Wye is about here.

c If you next intend to follow Route 209 to Brecon, you can turn to it at this point.

Piercefield Park The race course is sited in an 18th century park, laid out by a man who bankrupted himself in so doing, and had to rebuild his fortunes in the West Indies.

Chepstow See Route 92. Also links with Routes 196, 209.

Route 209   58 miles   94 km
BRECON — CHEPSTOW

OS 1:250 000 nos 7 or 8
Bartholomew's 1:100 000 nos 12, 13
OS 1:50 000 nos 160, 161, 171, 172

Brecon The town is strategically sited at the hub of several valleys, and there are several fortifications in the area, although little of the 10th-century castle remains. The cathedral was the church of the priory founded by the Normans with monks from Battle Abbey. Beautiful lancet windows in the choir. A

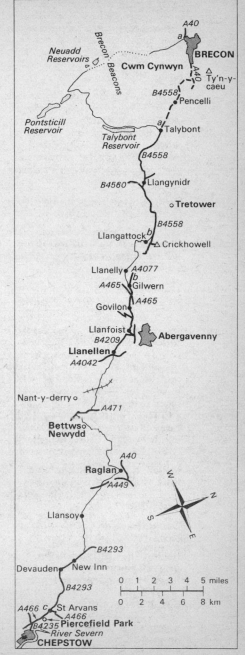

local Captain's Walk is so named from the Napoleonic officers who were prisoners-of-war here. Stories of sinners being stuck to churchyard stones centre on St David's church. Museum of the ancient Brecknock area. Links with Routes 210, 213, 214.

a The bridleway route over the pass at the head of Cwm Cynwyn valley is clear but strenuous, rising to nearly 2000 feet (over 600 metres) above sea level. It should not be attempted in bad weather, or without compass, spare food, extra clothing and plenty of time. The route enjoys mountain valley and pass scenery.

Cwm Cynwyn The bridleway follows the course of a Roman road.

b Between Llangattock and Gilwern the lanes used in the route rise and fall some 400 feet (120 m). The A4077 in the valley below is virtually flat.

Tretower Tretower Court and Castle comprise a good medieval house and ancient square keep (DoE, open).

Abergavenny The location was a strong one for invading Wales, and was possibly the site of the Roman fort, Gobannium. In Norman times it had a castle seat of ruthless Marcher lords, hated by the Welsh. The castle ruin stands in its estate, now a public park. Of a 12th-century priory, a great tithe barn and the prior's house remain, together with the church of St Mary. Castle House local interest museum.

Llanellen The Monmouthshire and Brecon Canal runs above the village, cut some 250 feet (75 m) up the hill from the river valley.

Bettws Newydd Church with a good rood screen.

Raglan The medieval castle was built for Yorkshire use in the Wars of the Roses. Henry VII, who ended the Wars, was imprisoned here. During the Civil War, the castle with its great hall and six-sided keep withstood Cromwellian attack for ten weeks (DoE, open).

c If you next intend to follow Route 208 to Glasbury, you can turn to it here.

Piercefield Park See Route 208.

Chepstow See Route 92. Also links with Routes 196, 208, 217.

Route 210   40 miles   65 km
TREGARON — BRECON

OS 1:250 000 no. 7
Bartholomew's 1:100 000 no. 17
OS 1:50 000 nos 147, 160, 146 (just)

Tregaron The church stands on an oval site, indicating great antiquity; it has some fine modern glass. Tregaron was the home town of the 16th-century scholar and scoundrel, Tom Jones. Links with Routes 211, 215, 216.

Bog of Tregaron This extensive peat bog, said to be Britain's largest, is now a nature reserve.

Abergwesyn The place grew up on a Roman metal ore route.

Llantwrydd An interesting church. The ancient inn was once used by drovers.

Llanwrtyd Wells In the 18th century this was a beautiful watering place. The vicar discovered the goodness of the waters, it is said, by observing the agility of the frogs.

Llangammarch Wells Former spa town famed for its rare barium chloride waters, efficacious against heart disease.

Y Gaer A Roman fortification of large area (DoE).

Pen-y-Crug An Iron Age hill-fort.

Brecon See Route 209. Also links with Routes 213, 214.

Route 211   25 miles   40 km
NEW QUAY — TREGARON

OS 1:250 000 no. 7
Bartholomew's 1:100 000 no. 17
OS 1:50 000 no. 146

New Quay See Route 203. Also links with Route 204.

Llanarth Earlier this century Gilfach-rheda Farm was a stud for palomino ponies used by famous circuses.

a If you next intend to follow Route 204 to Ysbyty Ystwyth, turn to it here.

Lampeter In this important market town is the early 19th-century College of Saint David. Designed for some two hundred theological students, it is modelled on Oxford and Cambridge.

Llangeitho In the 18th century this was the scene of crowds camping to hear Daniel Rowlands preaching. Ejected from the Church for his unorthodoxy,

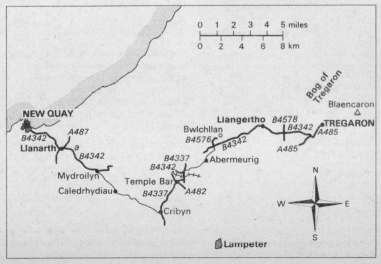

his followers built him a chapel; the back door of the present chapel was the door to his pulpit.

Bog of Tregaron See Route 210.

Tregaron See Route 210. Also links with Routes 215, 216.

Route 212   37 miles   60 km
FISHGUARD — CARMARTHEN

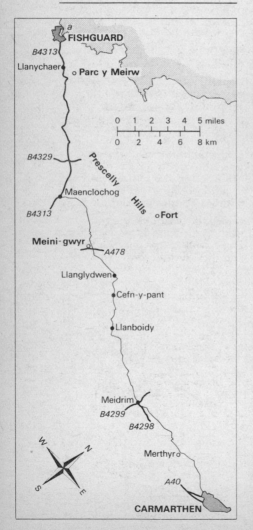

OS 1:250 000 no. 7
Bartholomew's 1:100 000 no. 11
OS 1:50 000 nos 145, 157, 159 (just)

Fishguard See Route 202. Also links with Route 203.

a Ferries from Fishguard to Rosslare, Ireland.

Parc y Meirw Standing stone row and burial chamber.

Prescelly Hills It was from quarries on these hills that Bronze Age Man cut the huge dolerite 'bluestones', to drag them to the Salisbury Plain in England, and their final famous resting place at Stonehenge. The hills are traversed by good walking tracks.

Fort An Iron Age hill-fort sited on the last of the Prescelly Hills, Foeldrygarn.

Meini-Gwyr A stone circle of unique design.

Carmarthen See Route 200. Also links with Routes 201, 213, 215.

Route 213   49 miles   79 km
BRECON — CARMARTHEN

OS 1:250 000 nos 7 or 8
Bartholomew's 1:100 000 no. 12
OS 1:50 000 nos 159, 160

Brecon See Route 209. Also links with Routes 210, 214.

Trecastle The name of this historically important place means 'town of the castle', although there are now few remains of any castle. Once an important stop on the coach route to Fishguard, Trecastle has inns with coach yards, and early 19th-century houses.

Llyn y Fan Fawr A lake associated with 'The Lady of the Lake' set in fine mountain scenery. It can be reached by track from Llanddeusant.

Carreg-Cennen One of Wales' most striking Norman castles (DoE, open).

Source of Loughor The source of the River Loughor rises in a fine limestone cavern.

Dynevor The new castle lies in its park, but the ruins of the old castle are sited on a riverside bluff, where moats are cut directly into rock.

Llangathen A 13th-century church with a good tower and monument. Aber Glasney was the home of the poet John Dyer.

Grongar Hill The summit was the site of a Roman legionary marching camp.

Drysawen Castle ruins on an earthwork beside the river.

Llangunnor and **Abergwili** See Route 200.

Carmarthen See Route 200. Also links with Routes 201, 212, 215.

Route 214   15 miles   24 km
GLASBURY — BRECON

OS 1:250 000 no. 7
Bartholomew's 1:100 000 nos 13, 17
OS 1:50 000 nos 160, 161

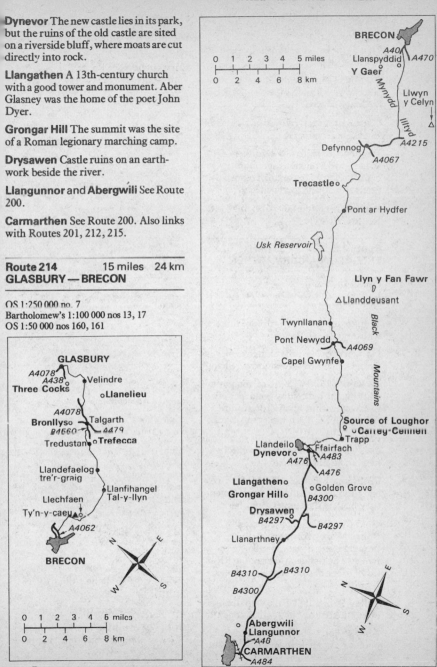

Glasbury See Route 208. Also links with Routes 207, 223.

Three Cocks A one-time important coaching stop.

Bronllys Church with a detached, fortalice tower. Bronllys Castle is a keep of the knights' type (DoE).

Llanelieu An early Welsh church with an unusual rood screen.

Trefecca H. Harris, the 'Luther of Wales', had a religious community here. Trefecca House and Tredustan Court were theological colleges.

Brecon See Route 209. Also links with Routes 210, 213.

Route 215   38 miles   62 km
TREGARON — CARMARTHEN

OS 1:250 000 no. 7
Bartholomew's 1:100 000 nos 17, 11 or 17, 12
OS 1:50 000 nos 146, 159

Tregaron See Route 210. Also links with Routes 211, 216.

Llanycrwys Near the church is the pound where stray livestock were kept.

Hirfaen A 15-foot (5-metre) monolith marking the old county boundary of Carmarthenshire and Cardiganshire. Ask locally, as it is not easy to locate.

Farmers The Drovers Arms recalls the days when cattle were herded through here to the English markets.

Pumpsaint 'Pump' is Welsh for 'five', and this place is named after the legendary birth of quintuplet saints here.

Gold Mines Originally worked by the Romans (NT). An aqueduct once brought water down the valley to the mines. The wooded valley of the River Cothi to the north-east has waterfalls near its head.

Talley Delightful village with the ruins of a 12th-century abbey (DoE, open).

Abergorlech There is an old tradition of quoit-playing here, and a delightful three-arched bridge.

Horeb Standing stones.

Merlin's Hill Univallate Iron Age hillfort.

Carmarthen See Route 200. Also links with Routes 201, 212, 213.

Route 216   9 miles   15 km
YSBYTY YSTWYTH — TREGARON

OS 1:250 000 no. 7
Bartholomew's 1:100 000 no. 17
OS 1:50 000 nos 146, 147, 160

Ysbyty Ystwyth See Route 204. Also
links with Routes 205, 222.

Strata Florida This place, whose name
means 'Way of Flowers' has also been
nicknamed 'Westminster of Wales'.
The ruins of the Cistercian monastery
(DoE, open) reflect the puritanical
ideals of the order. The monastery
possessed a healing cup said to be made
from part of the Cross, and associated
with legends of the Holy Grail.

Bog of Tregaron See Route 210.

Tregaron See Route 210. Also links
with Routes 211, 215.

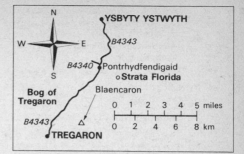

Route 217   44 miles   70 km
HEREFORD — CHEPSTOW

OS 1:250 000 no. 7
Bartholomew's 1:100 000 no. 13
OS 1:50 000 nos 149, 162

Hereford See Route 89. Also links with
Routes 90, 218, 223.

Dinedor Camp On the hill summit
scant earthworks remain on a site first
occupied by an Iron Age hill-fort and
then a Roman camp.

Hoarwithy Church with a cloister walk
and an Italianate interior.

Ross-on-Wye In the vicinity was
Ariconium, a great Roman forge for
arms. In the 17th century, John Kyrle,
philanthropic early 'town-planner', did
much to improve his town including the
provision of Britain's first public water
supply and the laying out of The
Prospect, a public walled garden. St
Mary's Church has a wealth of monuments and a plague cross in the yard.
There are 17th-century almshouses and
fourteen-arch market hall.

Goodrich The splendid ruins of

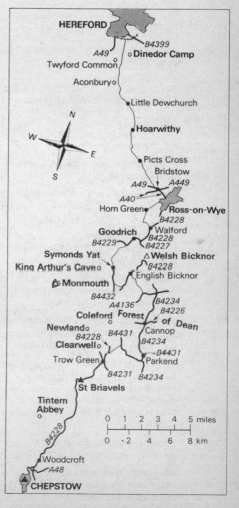

Godric's Castle, with its Norman keep and rock-cut moat, stand on a spur over the River Wye (DoE, open). Also the 14th-century Augustinian Flanesford Priory ruin. St Giles' church, where Dean Swift's grandfather was vicar, has several associations with that author. Ye Old Hostelrie is said to have been copied in the 1830s from an ancient illumination.

Welsh Bicknor The childhood home of Henry V.

Symonds Yat The renowned rock viewpoint derives its name from its position guarding the neck of land leading to a promontory, 'yat' being an old form of 'gate'.

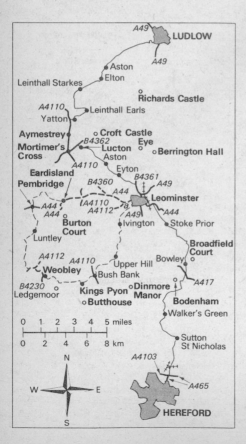

King Arthur's Cave Finds show that the caves were inhabited 20,000 years ago.

Monmouth and **Tintern Abbey** See Route 208.

Forest of Dean The fine oak timbers from this royal hunting forest were used for the navy's ships. The Spanish Armada was instructed to destroy the Forest of Dean as its first priority.

Coleford The village is sited in an area which was cleared of its trees through the burning of wood for the process of iron-smelting.

Clearwell Mock Gothic castle with a Regency interior, set in grounds with formal gardens and a bird sanctuary (open).

Newland Sumptuous 19th-century Gothic church.

St Briavels Remains of a 13th-century stronghold, built as a protection against Welsh raiders.

Chepstow See Route 92. Also links with Routes 196, 208, 209.

Route 218   34 miles   54 km
LUDLOW — HEREFORD

OS 1:250 000 no. 7
Bartholomew's 1:100 000 no. 18
OS 1:50 000 nos 137 (just), 148, 149

Ludlow Planned by the Normans, Ludlow still has a clear grid layout. Fine buildings include the Reader's House (open) and the Feathers Inn. The 11th-century castle, built for protection against the Welsh, now sees performances of Shakespearean plays in a summer festival (open). The parish church, one of England's largest, has misericords and a stained glass window showing the patron saint's life. Buttercross Museum of local history and geology. Links with Route 219.

Richards Castle A 17th-century court house with a cider mill and dovecot; church with 14th-century glass and 17th-century box pews.

Aymestrey Pretty village. Church with a good rood screen.

Mortimer's Cross An obelisk stands as a reminder of a bloody Wars of the Roses battle, in which the Yorkist leader was Edward Mortimer, who later became Edward IV. Water mill (DoE, open).

Lucton An attractive village, with an 18th-century public school built by a London merchant.

Croft Castle In the hands of the Croft family since the Domesday survey, the castle has medieval fabric, 18th-century ceilings and staircase, and is set in parkland with avenues (NT, open).

Eye Eye Manor, with its Renaissance interior, was built by a Barbados slave trader in the 17th century (open).

Berrington Hall An 18th-century hall set in Capability Brown parkland (NT, open).

Leominster Once a great wool market town, Leominster has good medieval buildings in the High Street and Drapers Row, and Georgian houses in Broad Street and Etnam Street. The fine priory church was founded by Lady Godiva's husband. There is a ducking stool.

a The optional circuit west from Leominster passes various points of interest, and explores several villages with black and white half-timbered cottages. It adds a further 24 miles (39 km) to the route.

Eardisland The showpiece of the lovely village is 14th-century Staick House, a yeoman's hall. There is a whipping post, and an unusual gabled dovecot.

Burton Court A 14th-century house with a neo-Tudor frontage, housing collections of European and Oriental dress and curios (open).

Pembridge Old half-timbered houses. Church with a detached 14th-century belfry. The New Inn and two almshouses date from the 17th century.

Weobley Many timber-framed buildings. Locally, Weobley was renowned for witches, there being fifty within two miles at one time. Preaching cross in the churchyard.

Kings Pyon The church has fine 14th-century roofs and alabaster effigies.

Butthouse An unusual house, with a gatehouse incorporating a dovecot. Nearby Black Hall has a medieval barn with cruck trusses.

Broadfield Court An attractive, gabled, medieval house.

Bodenham A lovely village with timbered cottages and stone houses; an octagonal 18th-century dovecot; a church with an unusual combination of tower and spire.

Dinmore Manor A 14th-century house with chapel, cloisters, 'music room' and rock garden (open).

Hereford See Route 89. Also links with Routes 90, 217, 223.

Route 219   29 miles   47 km
SHREWSBURY — LUDLOW

OS 1:250 000 no. 7
Bartholomew's 1:100 000 nos 18, 23
OS 1:50 000 nos 126, 138

Shrewsbury The town was founded in the 5th century, and has some of the best preserved medieval buildings in the country. Norman castle remains were refurbished by Thomas Telford. Many timber-framed houses can be found in Wyle Cop. There are three particularly interesting churches: St Mary's, the church at Meole Brace, and the unusual round church of St Chad. The Dingle gardens are the work of Percy Thrower, and are in the Quarry, a park. Ditherington malt store was built in 1796 and is the oldest surviving iron-framed building in the world. Shrewsbury School (where Charles Darwin was a pupil) now houses a museum and art gallery, and Rowley's House museum has finds from Roman Wroxeter. Clive House (open) has ceramics, art and a regimental museum. The pumping station at Coleham is open and contains preserved beam engines. Links with Routes 150, 153, 220, 233, 235.

Condover The grounds of the handsome 16th-century hall, now used as a school, are open. The church contains remarkable monuments.

Pitchford A 16th-century timber-frame mansion, with many chimneys and gables. The interesting church contains a 13th-century oaken knight effigy.

Acton Burnell In this pretty village stand the fairly complete remains of one of England's earliest fortified houses,

built in the 13th-century (DoE, open) The church has medieval floor tiles an many carved heads. The castle barn, o which two gables survive, is said to hav been the site of the first true parliamen held by Edward I.

Ruckley Ancient Langley Chapel (DoE, open).

Caer Caradoc The distinctively-shaped hill, surmounted by earthworks, affords good views of the Long Mynd. A road and track lead west from Cardington into the pretty valley to the south of the hill, and to paths ascending the hill.

Wilderhope Manor A 16th-century stone-built manor with 17th-century plasterwork (NT, open).

Acton Scott Working Farm Museum.

Aston Munslow The White House has several old buildings including a Norman dovecot and 14th-century cruck hall, and houses a country crafts museum (open).

Stokesay Castle The beautiful, early fortified and moated manor house dates from the 13th-century (open). Nearby are an interesting church and a bridge over the River Onny by Telford.

Ludlow See Route 218.

Route 220   30 miles   48 km
SHREWSBURY — CLUN

OS 1:250 000 no. 7
Bartholomew's 1:100 000 nos 18, 23
OS 1:50 000 nos 126, 137

Shrewsbury See Route 219. Also links with Routes 150, 153, 233, 235.

Stiperstones Worked for lead in the 12th century.

a The alternative route steeply ascends Long Mynd and follows lanes and tracks along the ridge which provide wonderful views. The ridge tracks have good ridable surfaces, but the track which climbs up the southern end of the Long Mynd is for the most part too steep to cycle. The main route

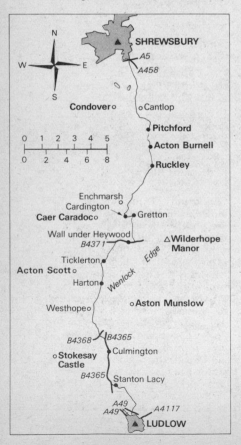

follows quiet lanes just to the west of the Long Mynd.

The Long Mynd A 10-mile (16-km) ride of moor and heath covered hills (NT) providing excellent cycling, walking and views. An ancient track, The Port Way, runs along the crest and there are many prehistoric earthworks.

Bishop's Castle The town grew up around a castle built for the Bishop of Hereford to protect his land. A bowling green stands on the remains of the castle, and there are three Tudor houses; the House on Crutches has its upper storey supported by wooden posts. The Three Tuns Inn was built in 1642.

Lydbury North The Norman church has rich medieval carving.

Stokesay Castle See Route 219.

Pen-y-Wern The ruins of Bronze Age stone circle, on the summit of a 1258 foot (383 m) hill.

Clun See Route 221.

Route 221   31 miles   49 km
CLUN — RHAYADER

OS 1:250 000 no. 7
Bartholomew's 1:100 000 nos 17, 18
OS 1:50 000 nos 137, 136

Clun Originally settled in the Bronze Age. The Norman castle was built to defend the Welsh border. There is a museum of local prehistoric relics in the town hall. The church has a double

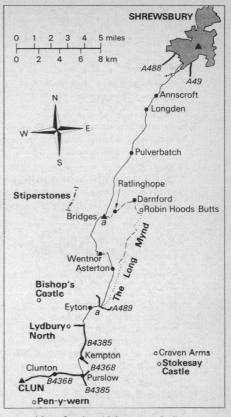

pyramid roof and an 18th-century lych gate. Links with Route 220.

Offa's Dyke Built in the 8th century by Offa, King of Mercia, to defend his

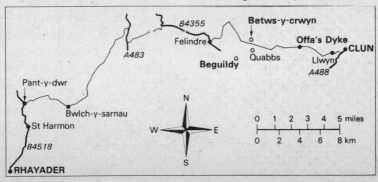

lands from the Welsh. A designated long distance footpath follows it course.

Betws-y-Crwyn The Church of the Fleeces stands on the ridge. Sheep farming area.

Beguildy This place name means 'Shepherd's House', and the church has a 13th-century rood screen.

Rhayader See Route 207. Also links with Routes 206, 222.

Route 222   26 miles   42 km
YSBYTY YSTWYTH — RHAYADER

OS 1:250 000 no. 7
Bartholomew's 1:100 000 no. 17
OS 1:50 000 no. 147

Ysbyty Ystwyth See Route 204. Also links with Routes 205, 216.

a If you next intend to follow Route 205 to Llanidloes, you can turn to it here.

Hafod An 18th-century landlord made this estate a 'Picturesque Arcadia' with a house containing a fine library set in grounds with rare trees. Coleridge visited it. The house was burnt in 1807 and only scant ruins remain.

Cwmystwyth The valley has many old lead and silver mines.

Pont Ar Elan Sheep-farming on a large scale was introduced to this area by the monks of Strata Florida Abbey.

Elan Reservoirs The main reservoirs for Birmingham.

Elan Village The poet Shelley and his young wife stayed at Cwmlan mansion near here.

Rhayader See Route 207. Also links with Routes 206, 221.

Route 223   37 miles   59 km
GLASBURY — HEREFORD

OS 1:250 000 no. 7
Bartholomew's 1:100 000 no. 13
OS 1:50 000 nos 149 (just), 161

Glasbury See Route 208. Also links with Routes 207, 214.

Clyro Beside the River Wye are the earthwork remains of a Roman camp large enough to accommodate a legion.

Hay-on-Wye This town is famed for its wealth of second-hand book shops.

Mouse Castle The ancient earthworks are sited on a spur summit, commanding good views over the Wye valley.

Dorstone Here was the last refuge of one of Thomas Becket's assassins.

Arthur's Stone Neolithic long barrow, with a huge capstone (DoE).

a The main route explores the Golden Valley, renowned for its peaceful beauty, whereas the alternative route keeps to the Wye valley, passing a different selection of points of interest.

Snodhill Large earthworks and the ruins of a 14th-century bailey on the hill, constitute the remains of a castle

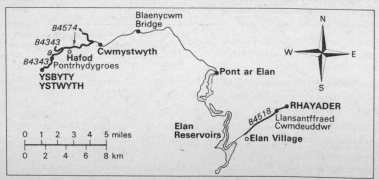

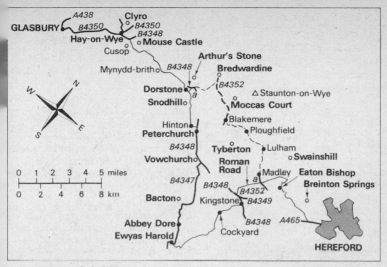

that was once a fief of Warwick the Kingmaker. In other words, he lent it to a vassal or tenant in return for knight's service when he required it.

Peterchurch The 14th-century, stone-built Wellbrook Manor.

Vowchurch The church contains fine woodwork, including an unusual wooden chalice.

Bacton A pretty village, set around the church on the hill.

Abbey Dore The church, which was originally part of a 12th-century Cistercian abbey, has good 17th-century glass and an altar which was rediscovered in a dairy. By the river, Abbey Court Garden has a walled garden and specializes in ferns (open).

Ewyas Harold This charming village is named after the Norman owner of its one-time castle.

Roman Road The lane here follows the route of one of the roads which radiated from Roman Kenchester.

Eaton Bishop Spacious church with 14th-century glass.

Bredwardine Francis Kilvert, the diarist, was vicar of the Norman church, which contains knight effigies.

Moccas Court The classical house, designed by Adam, contains panelling in the ancient mediterranean (Roman) style, and is set in parklands by Capability Brown (open). The beautiful Norman church has 14th-century glass.

Tyberton Church with an impressive reredos and monuments.

Swainshill Beside the River Wye are the Weir gardens with cliff-garden walks (NT, open)

Breinton Springs The site of a deserted medieval village (NT).

Hereford See Route 89. Also links with Routes 90, 217, 218.

Route 224   29 miles   47 km
LLANWDDYN — LLANIDLOES

OS 1:250 000 no. 7
Bartholomew's 1:100 000 no. 22
OS 1:50 000 nos 136, 125

Llanwddyn A model village built to replace the original which was drowned with the creation of Lake Vyrnwy. Links with Routes 225, 231, 232, 233.

Lake Vyrnwy Reservoir formed in

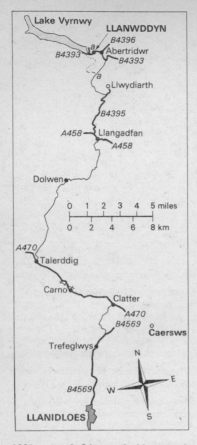

1881 to supply Liverpool with water. A public road crosses the dam.

a   The alternative route follows a rough track and lane around the flank of Craig Garth-bwlch, while the main route remains in the valley.

Caersws A former Roman military station, now the centre for a rich agricultural area.

Llanidloes See Route 206. Also links with Routes 205, 230.

Route 225   53 miles   85 km
CHESTER — LLANWDDYN

OS 1:250 000 no. 7

Bartholomew's 1:100 000 nos 22, 23, 28 (just)
OS 1:50 000 nos 125, 117, 126 (just)

Chester See Route 152. Also links with Routes 153, 154, 226.

a   If you next intend to follow Route 226 to Rhyd-Lydan, you can turn to it here.

Wrexham The industrial centre of North Wales. St Giles's Church has a majestic steeple and in the churchyard is the tomb of Elihu Yale, who crossed the Atlantic with the Pilgrim Fathers and gave his name to Yale University. There is an Exhibition Hall in the library.

Erdigg A late 17th-century House (NT, open) with much original furniture, a formal garden and domestic outbuildings including a laundry, bakehouse, sawmill and smithy.

Eglwyseg Mountain Magnificent limestone rocks above the road.

Valle Crucis Abbey Ruins of a 13th-century Cistercian abbey (DoE, open). Just to the north is Eliseg's Pillar, commemorating a battle fought in AD 603 by Eliseg, Prince of Powis, against the invading Saxons.

Castell Dinas Bran A footpath climbs to the remains of an 8th-century castle sited on a hilltop with good views.

Llangollen The home of the International Musical Eisteddfod, a contest for folk dancers and singers held here every year. There is a 14th-century stone bridge, and the church has a carved roof. Plas Newydd is an 18th-century black-and-white timbered house, for a while the home of the 'Ladies of Llangollen', two Irish aristocrats whose many guests at the house included William Wordsworth and the Duke of Wellington. The Shropshire Union Canal passes through the town, and upstream are the Horseshoe Falls, built by Telford to divert the waters of the Dee into his aqueduct.

Pont-Cysyllte Aqueduct Built by Telford, and completed in 1805, the aqueduct carries the Shropshire Union

Canal high over the valley of the Dee, and is over 1000 feet (305 m) long.

Chirk Castle Completed in 1310, this fine Marcher fortress has been inhabited ever since (NT, open). At each corner of this massive rectangle is a round 'drum' tower, and the fine wrought iron gates were completed in 1733. Inside there are interesting paintings, furniture and tapestries. Offa's Dyke can be traced in the grounds.

Llanarmon Dyffryn Ceirog There are many ancient burial sites and encampments on the hills around this village.

Wayfarers Memorial An inscribed stone memorial to W. M. Robinson, a cycling writer best known for his account of crossing the Berwyns in a snowstorm, entitled *Over the Top*. The memorial was erected by the Rough Stuff Fellowship.

Pistyll Rhaeadr This 240-foot (70-m) waterfall is the highest in Wales and can be reached by lane from Llanrhaeadr-ym-Mochnant.

Lake Vyrnwy See Route 224.

Llanwddyn See Route 224. Also links with Routes 231, 232, 233.

Route 226   47 miles   74 km
CHESTER — RHYD-LYDAN

OS 1:250 000 nos 7 or 5
Bartholomew's 1:100 000 nos 27, 28
OS 1:50 000 nos 116, 117

Chester See Route 152. Also links with Routes 153, 154, 225.

a If you next intend to follow Route 225 to Llanwddyn, you can turn to it here.

Wat's Dyke At this point the route crosses Wat's Dyke, an ancient linear earthwork and subsidiary of the better-known 8th-century Offa's Dyke.

Treuddyn Fine glass in the church.

Foel Fenlli The most impressive of the Iron Age hill-forts that were constructed along the Clwydian Range. There are good views from the 1676-

foot (511-m) summit, and a legend about a Dark Age tyrant called Benlli who was destroyed by fire from heaven because he killed a Christian who was late for work.

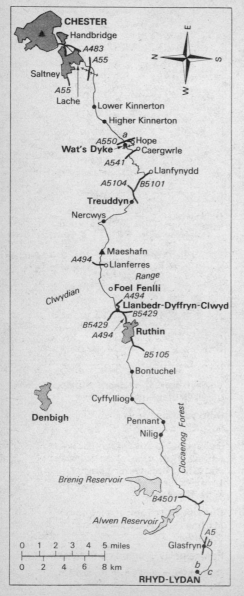

Llanbedr-Dyffryn-Clwyd Stone toll house, Griffin Inn and interesting church.

Ruthin An old market town with several interesting buildings and church. Ruins of a 13th-century strong hold remain in the grounds of the 19th century castle. Legend has it that the Maen Huail stone in the market place was the place where King Arthur executed a rival. A curfew has been rung nightly in the town since the 11th century.

Denbigh An impressive 13th-century castle overlooks this ancient market town (DoE, open). Town walls, Leicester's Church and Denbigh Friar (all DoE, open). The African explorer Stanley, who found Livingstone, was born here.

b   The lane between Glasfryn and Rhyd-Lydan is not marked on the Bartholomew's map of 1976.

c   If you next intend to follow Route 232 to Llanwddyn, you can turn to it here.

Rhyd-Lydan Links with Routes 227, 232.

Route 227   29 miles   47 km
BANGOR — RHYD-LYDAN

OS 1:250 000 nos 5 or 7
Bartholomew's 1:100 000 no. 27
OS 1:50 000 nos 115, 116

During the holiday season, the A5 between Bethesda and Pentrefoelas is particularly likely to carry heavy traffic.

Bangor University town with 19th-century cathedral and Art Gallery and Museum of Welsh Antiquities. Links with Routes 228, 229.

Penrhyn Castle Built in the 19th century, an exceptional example of neo-Norman architecture (NT, open), with lovely grounds, a walled garden, superb views, an industrial railway museum, an exhibition of dolls and a natural history display.

Llandegai Model village built by Lord Penrhyn in the 19th century.

Cochwillan The Old Hall (open) is a fine example of medieval architecture.

Bethesda Slate quarries here cut 1000 feet (300 m) into the mountainside.

Nant Ffrancon Awesome views of rugged mountains.

Idwal Cottage Situated at the head of the impressive Nant Ffrancon Pass. A footpath from near the YH leads to Llyn Idwal and the Devil's Kitchen, a huge rocky chasm on the north side of Glyder Fawr.

Capel Curig Views of Snowdon, to the south-west.

Ty-hyll 'Ugly House', a 15th-century cottage built of boulders.

a The alternative route involves a detour on a scenic lane and a B road to the interesting town of Llanrwst, while the main route continues on the A5.

Swallow Falls Pretty waterfalls, a popular tourist attraction.

Llanrwst An old market town with a beautiful three-arched stone bridge over the River Conwy. There is a 15th-century courthouse (NT, open), a 17th-century chapel, and a church with a fine rood screen. Half a mile to the west is Gwydir Castle, a historic Royal Residence (open) with magnificent Tudor furnishings and grounds with peacocks and tropical birds. Close by is Gwydir Uchaf Chapel, with a painted ceiling (DoE, open).

Betwys-y-Coed A Victorian honeymoon resort with three fine bridges, one of which, Waterloo Bridge, was built by Telford.

Capel Garmon A Bronze Age burial chamber (DoE) lies ¾ mile (1 km) south of the village, west of the lane.

Fedw Deg A 16th-century house with an arched door slab and wooden mullioned windows.

Ty Mawr The birthplace of Bishop

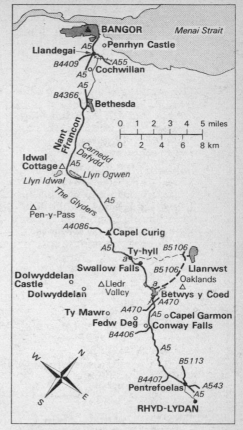

William Morgan (NT, open), the first translator of the Bible into Welsh.

Dolwyddelan An old church in original condition.

Dolwyddelan Castle Only one tower remains (DoE, open) of the stronghold said to have been the birthplace of Llywelyn the Great, most outstanding of the Welsh leaders.

Conway Falls These and the nearby Machno Falls and Fairy Glen are delightful.

Pentrefoelas Georgian coaching inn.

Rhyd-Lydan Links with Routes 226, 232.

Route 228   42 miles   67 km
HOLYHEAD — BANGOR

OS 1:250 000 nos 5 or 7
Bartholomew's 1:100 000 no. 27
OS 1:50 000 no. 114

*This route tours the Isle of Anglesey which
is very rich in prehistoric and Celtic
Christian remains. If you are particularly
interested in these, you will find that the
1:50 000 map shows many of them close
both to this route and to other lanes.*

Holyhead In Celtic and Roman times,
this was the port at the end of the
London road from where ships sailed to
Ireland, and it remains so to this day.
The 1.5-mile (2.5 km) long breakwater
was built in 1873 by the London and
North Western railway company. The
church was founded as the Celtic
St Cybi's oratory, but is now in the
medieval perpendicular style with stone
carvings including that of the Welsh
dragon. The thick churchyard wall,
with the ruins of a round tower, is the
remains of a fort built by the Romans as
a guard against sea raiders (DoE).

*a Ferries run between Holyhead and Dun
Laoghaire in Ireland.*

*b The A5 between Holyhead and Valley
may be busy or quiet, depending partly on
the timing of the ferries. If it is busy, the
quieter but fairly built up B4545 to the
south can be used.*

Holyhead Mountain Fringed by fine
cliffs, the summit affords views of the

mountains of Snowdonia, the Lake District, the Isle of Man and Ireland in clear weather. There are prehistoric remains including Caer y Twr (DoE) and hut circles (DoE) on the South Stack.

Penrhos Feilw Standing stones (DoE).

Trefignath Burial chamber (DoE).

c If you are in a hurry to get to or from the Holyhead ferry, or if you wish to make a route circuit on Anglesey, you can use the alternative route. The main route passes closer to a greater variety of scenery and interest.

Anglesey For thousands of years the island enjoyed importance as a base for travel by sea. Many Celtic Christian missionaries set out to other lands from here, and the island was sacred in the Druidic religion of Celtic times, when it was called Mon. Later the name was changed to 'Angles ea' meaning 'Isle of the English' after an Anglo-Saxon king gained it by defeat over the Welsh.

d A short stretch of lane on the route here is not shown on the Bartholomew's map of 1976.

Llanfairynghornwy The church is one of the many on Anglesey built originally in the simple, austere style of the time of the Celtic missionaries. Its site has an even older significance, as testified by the nearby standing stone.

Llyn Llygeirian The small lake is rich in trout.

e On the Bartholomew's map of 1976 Llanfflewyn is shown to be west of rather than on the route.

Parys Mountain The hill had rich deposits of copper which were worked by the Romans and in later years. After great exploitation during the Industrial Revolution, the deposits were exhausted by the mid-19th century, and the hill bears the mining remains.

Din Lligwy Remains of an ancient village (DoE). Nearby are the prehistoric Lligwy burial chamber (DoE) and the remains of Capel Lligwy (DoE).

Tregaian The church here has the single chamber plan of many of Anglesey's churches founded by Celtic missionaries.

Bodedern Similar church to Tregaean.

Presaddfed Prehistoric burial chamber (DoE).

Llangefni This market town, nowadays prominent in the affairs of Anglesey, is situated in the island's most fertile valley. Despite this, its site was not favoured by early people, who preferred to live closer to the sea in the days when the land was hard to travel over, and the 13th-century castle mound is the earliest evidence of significant settlement here.

Plas Penmynydd Owen Tudor, the grandfather of Henry, victor in the Wars of the Roses and first Tudor monarch of England and Wales, was born in this manor. It was Henry VII who first brought the Rouge Dragon of Wales into the royal heraldry.

Penmynydd There are monuments to forebears of the royal Tudors in the church. Queen Victoria contributed to its restoration in 1840.

Bryn-celli-ddu A many-sided burial chamber surrounded by four stone circles (DoE). The inscribed slab is one of two in Britain linking her Bronze Age culture with those of Brittany and Guernsey.

Plas Newydd Sited by the Menai Strait with magnificent views to Snowdonia, this 18th-century house (NT, open), designed by James Wyatt, has a spring garden, Rex Whistler's largest wall painting, and a military museum.

Llanfairpwllgwyngyll A plaque in the church of Llanfair commemorates those killed during the construction of the road bridge over the Menai Strait. The local railway station has the longest name of any in Britain: Llanfairpwllgwyngyllgogerychwyrndrobwllllantrysiliogogogoch.

Penmon Remains of ancient monastic

buildings (DoE, open). Dovecot, St Seiriol's Well and the Penmon Cross in the Deer Park (all DoE). Nearby Puffin Island was also a Celtic religious settlement.

Beaumaris The Norman name means 'beautiful flat-land'. The castle is a fine, picturesque example of medieval architecture, and it is ringed by a moat which is connected to the sea by a canal (DoE, open).

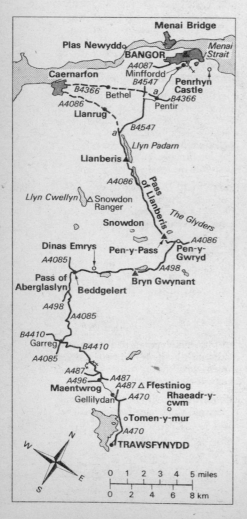

Menai Bridge The suspension bridge was completed in 1826, and built to a design by Telford. It was the first suspension structure to bear heavy traffic, and offers superb views. To the south west is the Britannia Tubular Railway Bridge. The Museum of Childhood, in the town, has toys, paintings, etc.

Bangor See Route 227. Also links with Route 229.

Route 229	39 miles 63 km

BANGOR — TRAWSFYNYDD

OS 1:250 000 no. 7
Bartholomew's 1:100 000 no. 27
OS 1:50 000 nos 115, 125

Bangor See Route 227. Also links with Route 228.

Penrhyn Castle See Route 227.

Menai Bridge and **Plas Newydd** See Route 228.

a The alternative route detours to the interesting town of Caernarfon

Caernarfon The magnificent 13th-century castle is one of the best in Britain (open), being well preserved, with thick walls and impressive towers. It is the seat of the Prince of Wales and contains the military museum of the Royal Welsh Fusiliers. St Mary's Church (13th century) and parts of the original defensive walls can be seen in the ancient town. A half mile to the east is the site of the Roman settlement Segontium (NT, open) with a museum containing relics excavated.

Llanrug To the south-east is Bryn Bras castle (open), built in the 1830s with lawns, woods, waterfalls and fine views of Anglesey and Snowdonia.

Llanberis Round peel-tower of Dolbadarn Castle (DoE, open). The North Wales Quarrying Museum has machinery and equipment associated with the local slate quarrying industry (DoE, open). A narrow gauge railway runs along the east shore of Llyn Padarn, providing good views of Snowdonia. The easiest walking ascent of Snowdon is by path from Llanberis.

Snowdon The highest mountain in England and Wales, with a summit of 3560 feet (1185 m). Its distinctive outline of steep side cwms and ridges has been carved by glacial erosion; there are several dramatic footpaths which can be followed to the top from where there are excellent views. Ascent should only be undertaken with suitable mountain-walking equipment.

Pass of Llanberis The road runs beneath the steep and rugged slopes of Snowdon and the Glyders.

Pen-y-Pass Three paths lead to the summit of Snowdon from here. The easiest is the Miners' Track, past the area once mined for copper, and Llyn Llydaw. The Pyg Track is more dramatic, passing high above the lakes. The third route, along the knife-edged ridge of Crib Goch, is dangerous for inexperienced climbers.

Pen-y-Gwryd This inn was used by Sir John Hunt's team while practising for their 1953 ascent of Everest.

Bryn Gwynant One mile south-west of the YH is the start of the Watkin Path, leading to the summit of Snowdon, the last section of which requires climbing experience.

Dinas Emrys The site of an Iron Age and also Roman hill-fort, and a 12th-century Welsh keep.

Beddgelert An 18th-century landlord invented the story about Llewellyn the Great and the dog he slew, and thousands of tourists have visited the 'Grave of Gelert' since.

Pass of Aberglaslyn Excellent views, especially from the bridge over the River Glaslyn.

Maentwrog The great stone in the churchyard probably originally marked the junction of Roman roads.

Ffestiniog Attractive village. From the station at Dduallt, two miles to the

west, the narrow gauge Ffestiniog railway runs to Porthmadog, on the coast.

Rhaeadr-y-Cwm Spectacular 200-foot (60-metre) waterfalls.

Tomen-y-Mur The site of a Roman military garrison, at the junction of two Roman roads, with remnants of an amphitheatre, bath buildings, parade ground, burial mounds and the mound of a medieval castle built by William Rufus, son of William the Conqueror.

Trawsfynydd See Route 230. Also links with Route 231.

Route 230   54 miles   86 km
TRAWSFYNYDD — LLANIDLOES

OS 1:250 000 no. 7
Bartholomew's 1:100 000 no. 22
OS 1:50 000 nos 124, 135, 136

Trawsfynydd Huge reservoir and to the north-west a hydro-electric and atomic power station. Memorial to a local shepherd-poet, Hedd Wyn, killed in Flanders in 1917. Links with Routes 229, 231.

Harlech Dramatically sited 13th-century castle built by Edward I (DoE, open), with splendid views over Snowdonia. The song 'Men of Harlech' commemorates the bravery of the Lancastrians under siege in the castle during the Wars of the Roses.

a If you next intend to follow Route 231 to Llanwddyn, you can turn to it here.

Waterfalls Two falls, the Pistyll Cain and Rhaeadr Mawddach, can be found deep in the woods at the confluence of Afon Gain and Afon Mawddach.

Llanfachreth Picturesque village clinging to the hillside.

Precipice Walk Excellent views of the Cambrian mountains including Cader Idris and the Arans, from a path which circles the hill of Foel Cynwch. There is a hill-fort of large boulders on the summit. A path leads to the hill from the Georgian manor, Nannau.

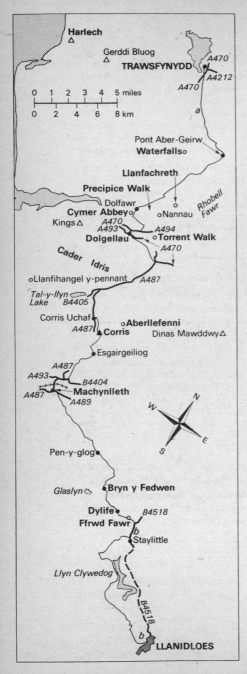

Cymer Abbey Little remains of the Cistercian abbey (DoE, open) founded in 1199.

Dolgellau Pretty town of dark local slate with an old grammar school and a graceful 17th-century bridge. Various literary associations include those with Sir Walter Scott and Thackeray.

Torrent Walk Pleasant footpath along the lower reaches of Afon Clywedog.

Cader Idris A bulky mountain with a 2927-foot (892-m) summit and steep sided cwms. It is reputed that anyone who sleeps the night on the mountain wakes either blind, mad, or a poet.

Corris A slate workers' village.

Aberllefenni Slate workings, forests, and tracks with views on the hills.

Machynlleth A delightful town where in 1404 Owen Glendower was proclaimed King in the Parliament House (Institute). Old inns and houses, including Royal House where the future Henry VII is said to have stayed in 1485; clock tower and toll house.

Bryn y Fedwen Magnificent views.

Dylife Meaning 'Place of Floods'. Old coaching stop where gallows once stood. Old mines nearby.

Ffrwd Fawr Impressive waterfall.

b The main route follows lanes past lake and forest, providing good views, and is fairly hilly, while the alternative route is more direct and uses the B4518.

Llanidloes See Route 206. Also links with Routes 205, 224.

Route 231   29 miles   47 km
TRAWSFYNYDD — LLANWDDYN

OS 1:250 000 no. 7
Bartholomew's 1:100 000 no. 22
OS 1:50 000 nos 124, 125

Trawsfynydd See Route 230. Also links with Route 229.

a If you next intend to follow Route 230 to Llanidloes, you can turn to it here.

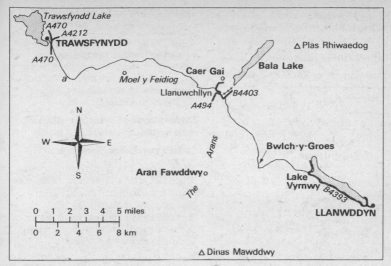

Caer Gai A 17th-century manor house built within ditches of a Roman fort.

Bala Lake The largest natural sheet of water in Wales, and the home of a mysterious white scaled salmon, the gwyniad, unique to this lake.

Bwlch-y-Groes The 'Pass of the Cross', at 1790 feet (545 m) is the highest road pass in Wales and offers beautiful views.

Aran Fawddwy At 2970 feet (905 m), the highest peak in Wales south of Snowdonia.

Lake Vyrnwy See Route 224.

Llanwddyn See Route 224. Also links with Routes 225, 232, 233.

Route 232   28 miles   45 km
RHYD-LYDAN — LLANWDDYN

OS 1:250 000 no. 7
Bartholomew's 1:100 000 nos 27, 22
OS 1:50 000 nos 125, 116

Rhyd-Lydan Links with Routes 226, 227.

a If you next intend to follow Route 226 to Chester, you can turn to it here.

Bala A centre of Methodism, and the

original home of some Welshmen who migrated to Patogonia in 1865.

Bala Lake See Route 231.

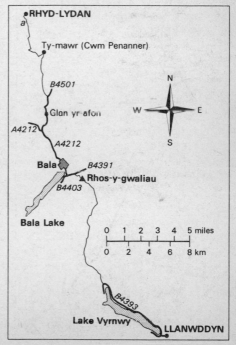

Rhos-y-Gwaliau Legends associated with Plas Rhiwaedog, a Jacobean manor house, and now a YH.

Lake Vyrnwy See Route 224.

Llanwddyn See Route 224. Also links

with Routes 225, 231, 233.

Route 233   42 miles   67 km
LLANWDDYN — SHREWSBURY

OS 1:250 000 no. 7
Bartholomew's 1:100 000 nos 23, 22 (just)
OS 1:50 000 nos 126, 125

Llanwddyn See Route 224. Also links with Routes 225, 231, 232.

Lake Vyrnwy See Route 224.

Welshpool A busy market town with much Georgian architecture. St Mary's Church has monuments and a great stone known as Maen Llog. The Powysland Museum has items of folk, archaeological, and historical interest, including an Iron Age shield.

Powis Castle Medieval castle (NT, open) with fine plasterwork, murals, furniture, paintings, tapestry and relics of Clive of India. Terraced garden and woodland with rare trees, including the tallest fir in Britain.

Beacon Ring Hill-fort on the 408-foot (124-m) summit.

Breidden Hill A range of hills caused by volcanic action. On the summit of Breidden Hill is an Iron Age hill-fort and there are superb views.

Westbury The church has an outside stair.

Shrewsbury See Route 219. Also links with Routes 150, 153, 220, 235.

Route 234   50 miles   80 km
IRONBRIDGE — WORCESTER

OS 1:250 000 no. 7
Bartholomew's 1:100 000 nos 18, 23 (just)
OS 1:50 000 nos 138; 127 and 150 (just)

An alternative, more direct route between Ironbridge and Worcester uses the B4373, B4363, B4194, B4196 and the A443, and passes the interesting towns of Bridgenorth and Bewdley.

Ironbridge Spanning the River Severn is the world's first iron bridge, designed

by Abraham Darby II, and cast in 1778.
Links with Routes 235.

Benthall Hall A 16th-century stone
hall with oak staircase and panelling
(NT, open).

Much Wenlock Medieval atmosphere.
The priory was founded in the 7th
century and has associations with Lady
Godiva. It is now in ruins (DoE, open).
The old black and white guildhall is
built on the oak arches of the butter
market. Local history museum.

Acton Round The Hall (open) was
built in the 17th century as a dower
house. There is an isolated church with
13th-century ironwork.

Shipton The Elizabethan Hall, with
stable block, walled garden and dovecot is open.

Wilderhope Manor A stone built
16th-century house with 17th-century
plaster ceilings (NT, open). Set in
remote wooded country with views
down to Corvedale.

Brown Clee Hill Three Iron Age forts
and views.

Stottesden The church has an unusual
tympanum.

Cleobury Mortimer Delightful main
street. The Talbot Hotel was once a
coaching inn, and the church has a
twisting wooden spire.

Great Witley Renowned 18th-century
rococo church, with fine glass.

Wichenford A 17th-century half-
timbered black and white dovecot (NT,
open).

Lower Broadheath Elgar's birthplace
(open).

Worcester See Route 88.

Route 235　　15 miles　24 km
SHREWSBURY — IRONBRIDGE

OS 1:250 000 no. 7
Bartholomew's 1:100 000 no. 23
OS 1:50 000 nos 126, 127

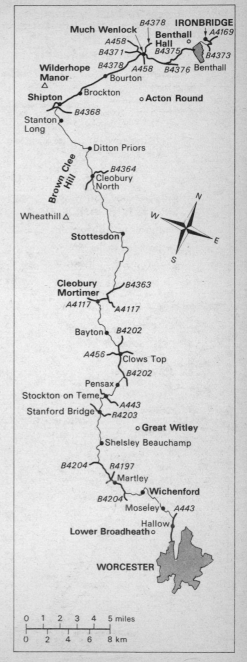

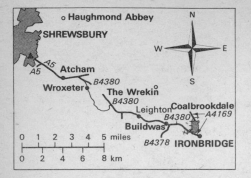

Shrewsbury See Route 219. Also links with Routes 150, 153, 220, 233.

Haughmond Abbey Ruins (DoE).

Atcham See Route 150.

Wroxter In Roman times this was the site of the fourth largest town in Britain, Viriconium (open). Extensively excavated by the DoE, there is now an excellent museum containing many of the finds. Interesting church.

The Wrekin An Iron Age fort sits on top of this hill, from where on a fine day there is a view embracing seventeen counties. This was one of the sites where a beacon fire was lit to warn of the coming of the Spanish Armada.

Buildwas The immense ruins of Buildwas Abbey are open (DoE).

Coalbrookdale Today's townscape was created by the Industrial Revolution. The Ironbridge Gorge Museum is a major open-air museum complex based on a series of industrial monuments.

Ironbridge See Route 234.

NORTHERN SCOTLAND

North of Glasgow is some of the grandest scenery in the British Isles. From the Clyde to Cape Wrath the west coast is dominated by fjord-like sea inlets and impressive mountains which can be over 3000 feet (1000 metres). Sometimes they rise straight from the still waters of a loch, dwarfing the narrow roads beneath them. Great valleys, or glens, wind their way inland to the heart of the Highlands. This area is desolate, crossed by few roads. By comparison the east coast is greener, warmer and drier with good pastures and many more villages and towns. A typical feature of northern Scotland is the straggling crofting village. Until the introduction of large-scale sheep farming, the crofter worked his small plot of arable and grazing land, often sharing his home with his animals. Today many of these low stone dwellings are roofless ruins, though in more prosperous villages they survive as modernized cottages.

Compared with the other parts of the British Isles lanes in northern Scotland are few and the routes are therefore mainly on A or B roads. South of the Great Glen this can mean sharing roads with fairly heavy traffic, although north of the Glen A roads will seldom contain another vehicle.

Many of the lanes you do see will be dead-ends, but they can make an interesting detour to an isolated crofting village or remote valley. The further north you cycle, the more common are 'single track roads'. These are generally just wide enough to take one car, but not a car and a bicycle. Passing places are provided at regular intervals and are marked with a white diamond-shaped sign. Keep a look out for frost-damaged road surfaces and pot-holes, remembering that if you do have the misfortune to buckle a wheel the nearest bike shop may be many miles distant. Generally, however, road surfaces are good and often less bumpy than those in the cities! In spite of the mountains, a tour of northern Scotland need not be specially strenuous. Many hills have gentler gradients than those of Devon and Cornwall, and with a low gear can be ascended comfortably. Distances on the map can be deceptive: what appears to be a short hop may turn out to be a very long way by the time the road has curled round lochs and mountains.

With so few roads it is particularly easy to find your way in Scotland, and the 1:250 000 map gives an adequate scale for all normal touring. If, however, you are thinking of trying some rough-stuff or hill-walking then buy the appropriate 1:50 000 maps. Northern Scotland is an ideal place to combine cycling with hill-walking so it is useful to carry a lightweight pair of walking boots. There are plenty of opportunities for enjoying rough-stuff, though you will usually find the surface of the average Scottish hill-track bumpy and rock-strewn.

Unless you have many weeks in which to explore Scotland you will probably make use of trains. For the west coast, for example, you can take a train to Oban, cycle northwards and return by train from Kyle of Lochalsh. North of Inverness where Scotland is narrow, it can take only one day to cycle across from west to east coast or vice-versa. Northern Scotland's many ferries are useful for modifying a tour while on some routes they cannot be avoided. Most are run by a company called Caledonian MacBrayne Ltd. Timetables are available at ports and tourist information centres (or by post: see Appendix 7). There are a few privately operated ferries which run on irregular schedules; the details of these and the regular services are listed in the CTC handbook. When planning a tour spend a little time looking at the ferry timetables and check that your itinerary suits the available ferries. It can be frustrating to be stranded on the wrong side of a stretch of water on a Sunday!

In all parts of northern Scotland, except the more populous east coast, there are large distances between shops so wherever you pass one be certain to get your panniers stocked. Ask locally where the nearest shop is in order to avoid inadvertently passing it by, and carry a few bars of chocolate or other iron rations just in case you do run out of food. Most Scottish hotels have a public bar which may also serve food. As there are often large distances between places with accommodation, hostelling and camping will give you the greatest flexibility. There are no YHA hostels on the Outer Hebrides but here the Gatliff Trust provides accommodation in a number of simple, hostel-style cottages (for address see Appendix 7).

Moving north from the Glasgow area past two small groups of hills, the Campsie Fells and Ochil Hills, you come to the Grampian Mountains. Extending north to the Great Glen, west to the sea and east before flattening out into eastern Scotland, they rise over 3000 feet (1000 metres). Their desolate nature has attracted few towns or villages. Very few roads cross the mountains and those that do keep to the bottoms of the largest valleys and tend to be busy A roads. The roads that link important towns, such as the A9 between Perth and Inverness, are to be avoided. However, there are good cycling routes through this area with those up the west coast and over in the east being the quietest.

The Grampians have several notable areas. Just 25 miles (40 km) north of Glasgow are the Trossachs, a small area by Loch Katrine of mountain, lochs, river and wood. It became popular with tourists in the 19th century, and is one of the most accessible and visited of Scotland's beauty spots. Just to the west is Loch Lomond, Scotland's largest lake, and further north the impressive defile of Glencoe, where the famous Massacre took place. At the western edge of the Grampians is the highest mountain in the British Isles, Ben Nevis, which rises 4406 feet (1343 metres) above the town of Fort William. The Grampian's own 'Gateway to the Isles' is the fishing port of Oban, a rail terminus and tourist resort from where ferries may be taken to the Inner and Outer Hebrides. South from Oban, reaching halfway across the water to Ireland is the long peninsula of Kintyre, much of which is little visited. At the heart of the Grampians are the desolate Cairngorm Mountains, with rounded peaks reaching heights of over 4000 feet (1200 metres). Roads skirt the edge of this range which is penetrated by just a few tracks.

To the east, between the Grampians and the North Sea, are the fertile lowlands of eastern Scotland and several interesting towns and castles. A good choice of lanes provides routes which largely avoid main roads. The terrain is much gentler than that found in the Grampians. Pretty fishing villages are found in sheltered bays along the coast and the area's main town is Aberdeen, a fishing port and centre for the North Sea oil industry.

Beyond the Grampians and the Great Glen, are the western Highlands, the most spectacular part being the west coast. South of Ullapool steep-sided mountains stand shoulder to shoulder, penetrated by narrow valleys and indented from the sea by long, thin lochs. Often rising straight from the water's edge and topped by abrupt ridges, these mountains are among the grandest in the British Isles. The roads are quiet and wind tortuously around lochs and mountains. Highlights on this section of coast are the Ardnamurchan peninsula, the most western point of mainland Britain, and the detour over the Applecross peninsula. Upper Loch Torridon has

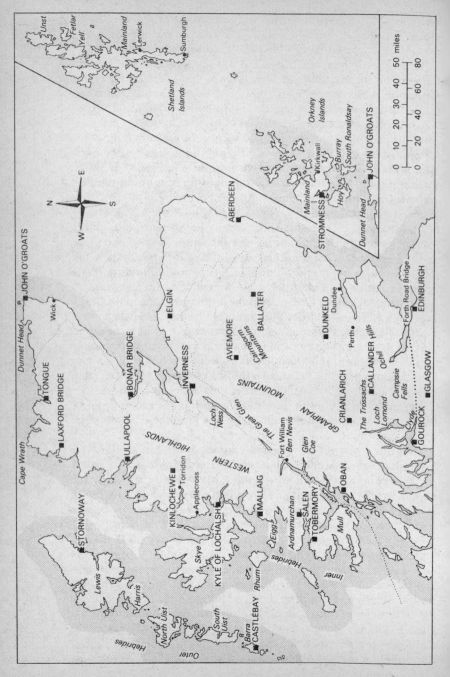

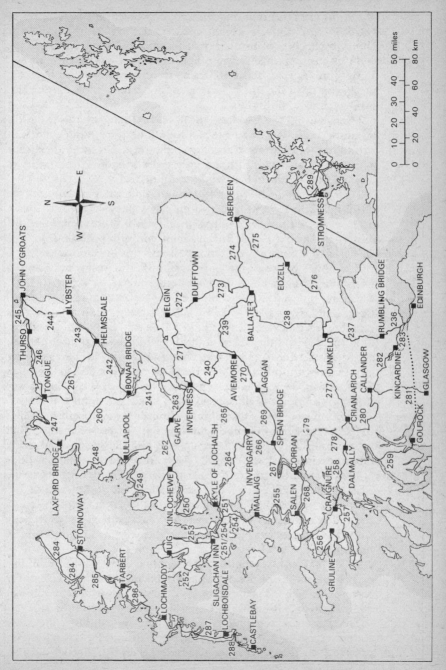

one of the most beautiful combinations of mountain and loch. North of Ullapool the mountains are less cramped and tend to stand singly as impressive hulks over undulating moorland dotted with lochans and the odd rock outcrop, while the low coastline looks across to bays and islands. Villages are far apart and there are no towns between Ullapool and the north-west tip of the British mainland, Cape Wrath, marked by a lighthouse high above sheer cliffs.

The mountains of the western Highlands stretch right across to the less scenic east coast. Valleys tend to have a north-west, south-east grain, with roads along the larger ones. Very few people live in the centre, a landscape dominated by mountain, loch and moor, and it is one of the bleakest places in Scotland to be caught in if the weather turns bad.

The north-east tip of Scotland is strangely different from the rest of the Highlands. It is flat and tree-less with long stone walls dividing square fields, while villages straggle along straight roads. There is some fine cliff scenery at Dunnet Head, Britain's most northerly point, and John o' Groats has fine views past the Orkney Islands to the Atlantic beyond.

Few people can resist the temptation to visit an island, and Scotland offers a bewildering choice; the options can, however, be narrowed a little. There are four main groups off the Scottish mainland: the Inner Hebrides, Outer Hebrides, Orkneys and Shetlands. Of these, the Inner Hebrides are easiest to reach and they have grander mountain scenery than the others. Mull and Skye are the largest of these inner islands, and involve only a short ferry trip from the mainland. Both can be used as stepping stones for a further ferry trip to the Outer Hebrides. Mull is a fine addition to a Scottish tour, the road along its beautiful western coast winding its way through a landscape of cliffs, rocky bays, islands and heather. It is much greener and more fertile than Skye and its main town, Tobermory, clings colourfully to the edge of a fine natural harbour. Off the western tip of Mull is the small island of Iona, the cradle of British Christianity, with many monastic remains. Skye is generally wilder. Here and there are small fields of grass but the island is mostly rough moorland and abrupt mountains: the rounded Red Cuillins, jagged Black Cuillins and lower, but no less impressive, inland cliffs of Trotternish being the most splendid. It does seem to rain a lot on Skye but there are compensations—such as being treated to a stirring bagpipe lament while sheltering under the eaves of an unsuspecting piper's house!

While Mull and Skye are large enough to provide many miles of fine cycling, the smaller islands of the Inner Hebrides are best seen on foot. Try leaving your bike and taking the ferry out to visit Eigg with its magnificent Sgurr Rock, or to Rhum with its nature reserve and towering peaks.

The time and expense needed to make the ferry crossing to the Outer Hebrides means that it is only worth going if you intend to stay at least two or three days. The long string of islands is generally flat, although there is a small range of mountains on North Harris rising to around 2500 feet (800 metres) and some scattered hills of around 1500 feet (500 metres) on South Harris. The contorted coastline has hundreds of small inlets and lochs, and inland the rough moorland is sprinkled with small lochans. The islands do not have enough roads to make a circular tour, and unless you retrace your way you have to start either at the south or the north end and use the appropriate ferry links. There are now causeways between some of the Outer Hebridean islands and the ride from Castlebay on Barra to Stornoway on Lewis involves only two inter-island ferries. The famous standing stones at Callanish and the Iron Age fort of Dun Carloway hint at the rich prehistoric past, and several places have associations with the flight of Bonnie Prince Charlie after his defeat at Culloden.

Just across the stormy Pentland Firth from John o' Groats are the Orkneys, a cluster of seventy or so islands, about twenty of which are inhabited. Low, undulating and tree-less, they were occupied in the Stone Age when the village of Skara Brae and tomb of Maes Howe were built. Many other prehistoric remains survived later visits by the Romans and Norsemen. Few of the Orkney folk are fishermen; most of them work the small but productive farms which specialize in beef cattle and eggs. Mainland, the largest of the islands, offers the greatest scope for cycling. Its convoluted coast circles farms, moors and several lochs, while causeways link it to two further islands, Burra and South Ronaldsay. The two main towns are picturesque Kirkwall and Stromness, both with ferry services to the other islands. If you are thinking of island hopping in the Orkneys, visit Hoy first. It is the hilliest, rising to just over 1500 feet (500 metres), and is rich in bird life. On its west side is the Old Man of Hoy, a spectacular rock-stack.

We have not suggested any routes for Shetland because the small number of roads gives little choice. It takes twelve hours by ferry from Aberdeen (eight from the Orkneys) to reach this group of a hundred or so islands, less than twenty of which are inhabited. Deeply indented, fjord-like sea lochs (called 'voes') are backed by rock and heather hills rising at their highest to around 1500 feet (500 metres). There are a few freshwater lakes. The strong winds that have discouraged trees from growing on Shetland can make cycling hard work, though luckily the warm sea currents which brush the west coast mean that the climate is fairly mild. Shetland fishing boats that used to crowd the harbours at Lerwick, Scalloway, Whalsay and Burra are fewer now and the islands are responding to the North Sea oil industry, most noticeably in the building of a huge terminal at Sullom Voe. Like the Orkneys, Shetland has been occupied since early times. Short ferry journeys take you to Yell and Unst, off which is Muckle Flugga, the most northerly point of the British Isles. To the east, Fetlar is known for the breeding of tiny Shetland ponies. These islands are so far north that the summer sun never fully sets.

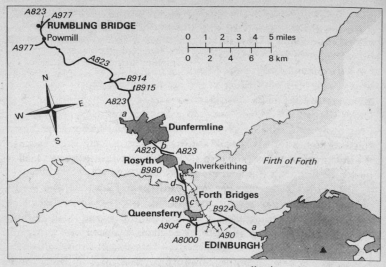

Route 236   28 miles   46 km
RUMBLING BRIDGE —
EDINBURGH

OS 1:250 000 nos 3 or 4
Bartholomew's 1:100 000 no. 45
OS 1:50 000 nos 58, 65, 66

Rumbling Bridge So called because of
the noise created by water rushing
underneath when the river is full. An
earlier bridge, built by a local stone
mason in 1713, lies beneath the present
bridge. Dramatic gorge and several
waterfalls. Links with Route 237.

*a The roads between Dunfermline and
Edinburgh are likely to carry heavy traffic,
and extra care should be taken.*

Dunfermline For six centuries this was
the capital of Scotland, and is the birthplace of several monarchs. Andrew
Carnegie, the famous industrialist and
philanthropist, was born in the cottage
which is now a museum devoted to his
life and works. The Abbey (DoE, open)
was founded in 1072 by Margaret, wife
of Malcolm III, and contains the remains of Robert the Bruce. Also of
interest is the Palace (DoE, open). Set
in a beautiful park given to the town by
Carnegie, Pittencrieff House has a fine

costume collection, while the Dunfermline museum has exhibits of local
and natural history.

*b Between Dunfermline and Rosyth the
A823 dual-carriageway has a cycle track
down its centre on a former tram track.*

Rosyth Rosyth Castle (DoE).

*c When approaching the Forth Road
Bridge, look out for signs directing you to
the cycle-path which runs alongside the
motor road on the bridge, and which you
must use.*

*d If you next intend to follow Route 283 to
Kincardine, you can turn to it here.*

Forth Bridges When the road bridge
was built in 1964 it was the largest in
Europe. The rail bridge was built in
the years 1883 to 1890, and was one of
the greatest engineering feats of the
time.

Queensferry Queensferry cannot be
reached directly from the A90 but the
B924 leads to it. The place has long been
an important river crossing point, and
the Romans had a ferry here. It takes its
name from the 11th-century Queen
Margaret, who often used the ferry in
travelling between the palaces of
Edinburgh and Dunfermline. Places of

interest are: Plewlands House (NTS); Hawes Inn near the old ferry slipway, which features in R. L. Stevenson's *Kidnapped*; Hopetoun House (open).

e If you next intend to follow Route 193 to Glasgow, you can turn to it here.

Edinburgh See Route 122. Also links with Routes 123, 192, 193, 283.

Route 237   35 miles   57 km
DUNKELD — RUMBLING BRIDGE

OS 1:250 000 no. 3
Bartholomew's 1:100 000 no. 49
OS 1:50 000 nos 53, 58

Dunkeld A monastery was founded here before AD 700. Later, Dunkeld

was the joint capital of the Picts and Scots. Notable are ruins of a 14th-century cathedral (DoE, open); a bridge by Thomas Telford and some good domestic architecture in Cathedral Street and High Street. Links with Routes 238, 276, 277.

a The main route involves some steep climbs, whereas the slightly longer alternative route has gentler gradients.

Inver Neil Gow, the celebrated Scots fiddler and composer, lived here and his cottage is preserved.

The Hermitage An 18th-century folly (NTS, open), with fine views.

Bankfoot In the 19th-century this was a weaving community.

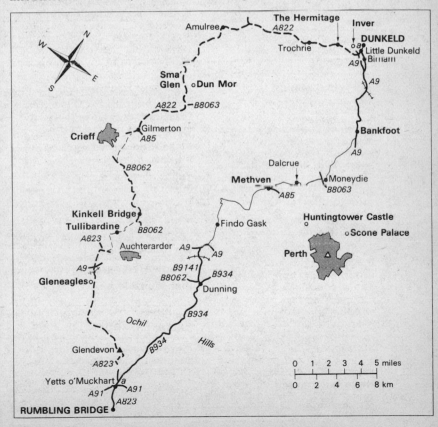

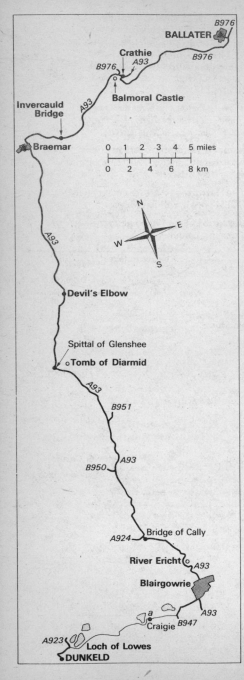

Methven The 17th-century castle is thought to have been built on the site of a battle in which Robert the Bruce was defeated by the English.

Huntingtower Castle A grand castellated house with interesting wooden ceilings (DoE, open), and the place where James IV was kept after being kidnapped by the Earl of Gowrie.

Scone Palace Mostly dating from 1803 (open) but incorporating parts of the old 16th-century palace. It was the coronation place of Scottish kings, and a religious centre.

Perth Known as the Fair City, it was the capital of Scotland until 1437. St John's Kirk has fine stained glass and ornaments, Charles I, Charles II, and Bonnie Prince Charlie all having worshipped here. The house of the *Fair Maid of Perth* has a craft museum; the Perth Museum and Art Gallery has displays of local history, ethnology and art.

Crieff Octagonal market cross, stocks, 17th-century tolbooth and 10th-century Crieff Cross. Views from 911-foot (278-m) Knock of Crieff to the north.

Kinkell Bridge Strathallan Aircraft Museum.

Tullibardine Ancient chapel (DoE, open).

Sma' Glen Fine scenery, and route of one of General Wade's military roads.

Dun Mor A large stone-built Iron Age fort commands the pass.

Gleneagles A popular golf-course.

Rumbling Bridge See Route 236.

Route 238   63 miles   101 km
BALLATER — DUNKELD

OS 1:250 000 nos 2, 4
Bartholomew's 1:100 000 nos 52, 49
OS 1:50 000 nos 53, 43, 44

Much of this route follows the A93, which in the holiday season is likely to carry heavy traffic.

Ballater The town grew up as a spa following a claim by an old woman that she had been cured of a skin disease by immersion in a local bog. In the days when the railway reached this far, the town was the scene of Royal arrivals and departures on their way to and from Balmoral Castle. On the bridge is a plaque telling of the destruction of previous bridges by floodwaters. Also links with Routes 239, 273, 274.

Crathie The parish church is attended by members of the Royal Family and has several interesting memorials; also one erected by Queen Victoria to her servant John Brown in the churchyard.

Balmoral Castle The Castle was bought by Prince Albert in 1852, and was substantially modified in the Scottish baronial style. The grounds are open in the summer months, when the Royal Family are not in residence.

Invercauld Bridge The older of the two bridges here was built in 1752 and is particularly graceful (DoE).

Braemar In 1715 the Earl of Mar raised the Jacobite standard here. The castle (open) was built in 1628, and was later used as a garrison for troops watching the unsettled Highlands. Each September the famous Braemar Gathering takes place, attracting up to 50,000 people, and usually attended by members of the Royal Family.

Devil's Elbow The name given to the tortuous series of bends that used to exist on this road. Built by the military in the mid-18th century, it rises to over 2000 feet (600 m). Much of the road has now been straightened for the benefit of modern traffic, although it is frequently blocked by snow in winter.

Tomb of Diarmid A stone circle and tumulus associated with Clan Campbell.

River Ericht Just to the east of the road, the River Ericht rushes through spectacular gorges.

Blairgowrie The centre for an area which specializes in growing soft fruits.

a If you next intend to follow Route 276 to Edzell, you can turn to it here.

Loch of Lowes There is a hide here from where ospreys can often be viewed. Ask locally for details of access.

Dunkeld See Route 237. Also links with Routes 276, 277.

Route 239   51 miles   82 km
AVIEMORE — BALLATER

OS 1:250 000 no. 2
Bartholomew's 1:100 000 nos 55, 52, 56 (just)
OS 1:50 000 nos 37, 36
1 inch:1 mile Cairngorms tourist map

Aviemore A tourist resort well known as a centre for winter sports, and which exudes an air of commercialism unique in the Highlands. The holiday and conference complex, the Aviemore Centre, was built in the 1960s. Links with Routes 240, 270, 271.

Lairig Ghru A rough track leading through the wild and remote scenery of the Cairngorm Mountains linking Aviemore to the Dee Valley, a distance of about 20 miles (32 km). The pass rises to 2750 feet (915 m) and is well known as an arduous walking route. It is possible to take a cycle over, but it is extremely strenuous and should only be attempted by the experienced and fit, with adequate equipment and 1:50 000 or 1:25 000 maps. In parts it is necessary to carry the cycle.

Chair Lift Reached by a narrow road from Coylumbridge, there are good views from the car park. For those unable or unwilling to walk, the chair lift provides transport to the highest restaurant in Britain.

The Cairngorms The main mountains are Cairn Gorm, Cairn Toul, Braeriach and Ben Macdui. This is the highest mountain massif in the British Isles, and the Cairngorms National Nature Reserve is also the largest.

Loch Garten The nesting place of the now rare osprey, a large fishing hawk. The Royal Society for the Protection of

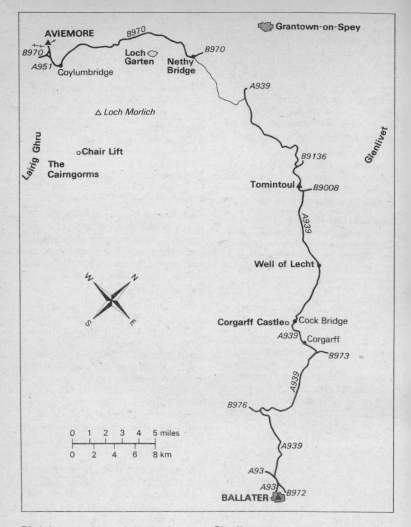

Birds have an observation point from where the birds can be watched.

Nethy Bridge Timber from here used to be floated down the river Spey to the coast.

Grantown-on-Spey The town was founded in 1776 by Sir James Grant, and grew as a centre for the Highland linen industry. There are sheep dog trials here in the summer.

Glenlivet The distilleries in this valley produce the world famous whisky of the same name.

Tomintoul At 1160 feet (354 m), this is the highest Highland village, built of local stone in the late 18th century. Museum of local history.

Well of Lecht An inscription on the well tells that the 33rd Regiment constructed this stretch of the road. Just up the valley to the north east are buildings of the 18th-century ironstone and manganese mines.

Corgarff Castle This castle (DoE, open) was burnt during 16th-century feuding, and later by the Jacobites. It was subsequently used as a garrison by soldiers employed to help suppress whisky smuggling.

Ballater See Route 238. Also links with Routes 273, 274.

Route 240　　45 miles　72 km
INVERNESS — AVIEMORE

OS 1:250 000 no. 2
Bartholomew's 1:100 000 no. 55
OS 1:50 000 nos 35, 26, 27, 36
1 inch:1 mile Cairngorms tourist map

This route through the mountains follows the A9 for part of the way. It can be a very busy road, so extra care should be taken.

Inverness The attractive 'capital' town of the Highlands, built on the banks of the river Ness. Of interest are the clock tower, 16th-century Abertarff House, and the Gothic Town House. The Museum and Art Gallery has a display about the Highland Region. Links with Routes 241, 263, 265.

a　The main route detours to the east to visit Culloden Moor, while the alternative route is more direct.

Culloden Moor It was here that Bonnie Prince Charlie was finally defeated in 1746, in a battle which resulted in the deaths of 1200 Highlanders and 76 from the army of the Duke of Cumberland. There is an information centre in the old Leanach Cottage (NTS).

Cumberland's Stone The Duke of Cumberland watched the progress of the battle from here.

Clava Cairns A group of three chambered tombs, with standing stones (DoE) dating from the Bronze Age.

Boar's Stone A Pictish relic (DoE).

Tomatin An angling centre, and once a

royal hunting ground associated with the King's castle at Inverness.

Slochd One mile to the north west of Slochd the road reaches its high point, at 1333 feet (406 metres).

b　If you next intend to follow Route 271 to Elgin, you can turn to it here.

Carrbridge During the winter months this is a busy ski resort.

Aviemore See Route 239. Also links with Routes 270, 271.

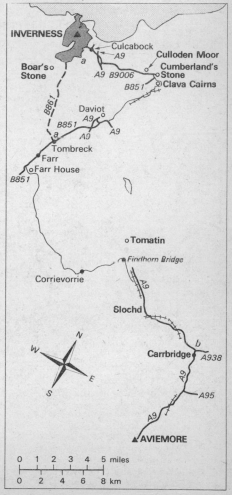

Route 241   42 miles   67 km
BONAR BRIDGE — INVERNESS

OS 1:250 000 no. 2
Bartholomew's 1:100 000 nos 55, 59
OS 1:50 000 nos 26, 21, 27 (just)

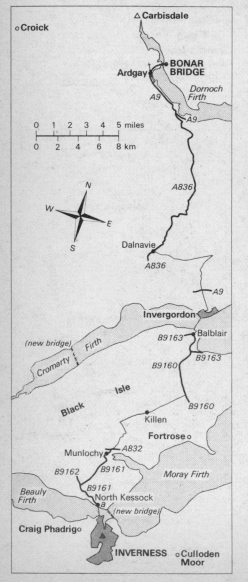

The two ferries used in this route, across the Cromarty Firth south of Invergordon, and between North Kessock and South Kessock (Inverness), may cease to operate with the completion of two new bridges (see map) and the route will have to be adapted accordingly.

Bonar Bridge Telford built the original bridge here at the beginning of the 19th century. The present spans were completed in 1973. Links with Routes 242, 260.

Carbisdale Castle Built of local stone in 1914, the castle stands on a dramatic site overlooking the Kyle of Sutherland, and is now a YH. It was here, during the Second World War, that King Haakon VII of Norway stayed while his government was in exile.

Croick Following the Highland Clearances, the people evicted from Glen Calvie sheltered in the churchyard here, and their messages scratched on the church windows can still be seen.

Ardgay There is a curious story attached to the quartz stone, set into the wall of the village inn. The stone used to move from place to place, and markets were held wherever it happened to be, until one day the people of Ardgay took possession of it permanently by fixing it into the inn wall where it remained.

Invergordon One of the deepest and safest harbours in Britain, and a naval dockyard since 1828. In 1931 this was the scene of a famous Royal Navy mutiny. It is now a busy industrial centre, having Europe's largest grain distillery, and the world's largest dry dock. British Aluminium have a smelting plant, and oil rigs were built here.

Fortrose Ruined cathedral (DoE).

Black Isle The name is derived either from a mistranslation of Duthac (a patron saint) for the Gaelic 'dubh', meaning black; or from the peninsula's lack of snow in winter, which makes it look dark. The fertile soil provides excellent farming land.

*a If you next intend to follow Route 263 to
Garve, you can turn to it here.*

Craig Phadrig The remains of a fort
where St Columba is believed to have
visited King Brude of the Picts in
AD 565.

Culloden Moor See Route 240.

Inverness See Route 240. Also links
with Routes 263, 265.

Route 242   36 miles   57 km
HELMSDALE — BONAR BRIDGE

OS 1:250 000 no. 2
Bartholomew's 1:100 000 no. 59
OS 1:50 000 nos 21, 17

Helmsdale The ruined 15th-century
castle was the location for a dramatic
feud in which Isobel Sinclair poisoned
the Earl and Countess of Sutherland so
that her son might succeed to the Earl-
dom of Caithness. But unfortunately for
the Sinclairs the son also drank the
poison. The town has a good natural
harbour. Links with Routes 243, 261.

Lothbeg A stone commemorating the
killing of the last known wolf in Sutherland. The land on the seaward side of
the village was drained in 1818 by
cutting a new channel for the river.

Kintradwell Broch This drystone
tower was used as a fortification by the
Picts.

Brora Scotland's oldest coal mine was
worked here, and it was from Brora that
the first settlers left for New Zealand.

Dunrobin Castle Dating partly from
the 14th century, this was once the
home of the Duke of Sutherland (open).
Inside there is an interesting museum.

Golspie A busy fishing town and
resort. There are good woodcarvings in
St Andrews Church, and the inscribed
Gaelic stone on the old bridge is the
rallying point for Clan Sutherland.
There is a statue of the 1st Duke of
Sutherland on the summit of Beinn a'
Bhragaidh, behind the town.

Dornoch The cathedral is a landmark
for miles around, and is the burial place
for sixteen Earls of Sutherland. Inside
there is a fine statue of the 1st Duke of
Sutherland, and an effigy of Sir Richard
of Moray. A stone marks the site of the
burning of the last woman to be
judicially executed for witchcraft in
Scotland, in 1722.

Spinningdale The ruined cotton mill
once employed one hundred people,

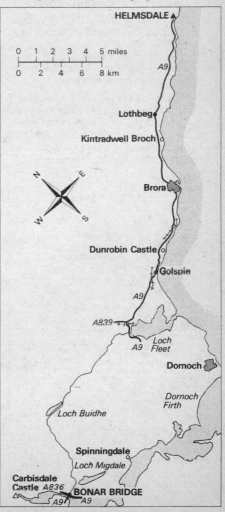

but its remoteness led to economic failure.

Carbisdale Castle See Route 241.

Bonar Bridge See Route 241. Also links with Route 260.

Route 243   23 miles   36 km
LYBSTER — HELMSDALE

OS 1:250 000 no. 2
Bartholomew's 1:100 000 no. 60
OS 1:50 000 nos 11, 17

Lybster The village was planned by Sir John Sinclair of Ulbster and was intended to survive on a fishing and farming economy. The harbour is delightful. Links with Route 244.

Latheron The bell tower for the church of this large parish was built on a ridge where the maximum number of people would be able to hear it. The Clan Gunn museum can be seen in the disused church. Such is the abundance of

antiquities that the locality has been declared a conservation area.

Janetstown The village has a charming natural harbour.

Braemore A memorial stands here to the Duke of Kent who was killed in an air crash in the Second World War.

Dunbeath Castle Situated spectacularly on the cliff edge, the castle dates from the 15th century and was once besieged for three days.

Berriedale The steep hills along this part of the A9 were a notorious challenge to early motor cars and drivers. Many of the sharpest hairpins have now been smoothed out.

Langwell Homestead A round stone walled house, locally called a 'wag'.

Broch A good example of this feature with a 14-foot (4-m) wall; it is by a burn in the valley below Ousdale.

Helmsdale See Route 242. Also links with Route 261.

Route 244   31 miles   50 km
JOHN O'GROATS — LYBSTER

OS 1:250 000 no. 2
Bartholomew's 1:100 000 no. 60
OS 1:50 000 nos 12, 11 (just)

John o'Groats Significant to many cyclists as the 'other end', being the final goal on the Lands End to John o' Groats ride. It is named after a Dutchman, John de Groot, who ran a ferry service to the Orkneys in the 15th century. A mound and flag pole mark the site of his octagonal house, which had eight doors; one for each of his eight descendants. Contrary to popular belief, this is not the most northerly point on mainland Britain; that distinction belongs to Dunnet Head. There are good views out to the Orkneys and Stroma. Links with Route 245.

a The A9 road, which the alternative route follows, has more traffic south of Wick than to the north; good coastal views. The main route is slightly longer, and cuts

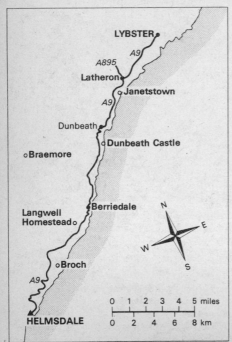

inland on quiet roads.

b If you next intend to follow Route 245 to Thurso, you can turn to it at this point.

Duncansby Head Most north-easterly point on the British mainland, with high cliffs providing dramatic views. The cliff scenery here includes huge chasms known as 'geos' and a natural rock bridge.

Stacks of Duncansby There are several sea stacks, caused by the collapse of natural rock arches, and the cliffs are the nesting grounds for many birds during May and June.

East Canisbay The slab on the south wall of the church is said to mark the grave of John de Groot. When the Queen Mother is staying at Castle of Mey she attends services in the church.

Ackergill Tower This is one of Scotland's oldest inhabited castles.

Noss Head There are spectacular views to the ruined castles of Sinclair and Girnigoe from the lighthouse. They both saw vicious clan feuds.

Wick The name is derived from the Norse word 'vik' meaning 'bay'. The town is now an important sea-fishing centre and supply port for the North Sea oil fields. The Carnegie Library and Museum has local history collections. Just to the south of the town is the castle of Old Wick (DoE, open).

Whaligoe The Cairn of Get (DoE) is a neolithic burial chamber in which skeletons and arrowheads have been discovered.

Grey Cairns There are three excellent cairns here (DoE).

Mid Clyth 'Hill o' many stones' (DoE).

Lybster See Route 243.

Route 245   19 miles   31 km
JOHN O'GROATS — THURSO

OS 1:250 000 no. 2
Bartholomew's 1:100 000 no. 60
OS 1:50 000 no. 12

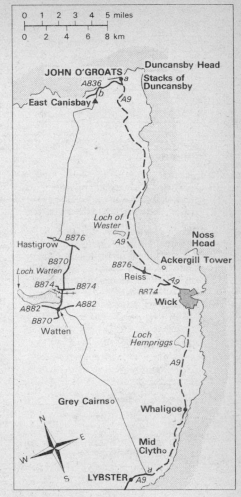

John o'Groats See Route 244.

Duncansby Head, Stacks of Duncansby and **East Canisbay** See Route 244.

a If you next intend to follow Route 244 to Lybster, you can turn to it here.

Castle of Mey Originally the seat of the 4th Earl of Caithness, the castle was bought by the Queen Mother in 1952 for use as a summer home. The gardens are sometimes open.

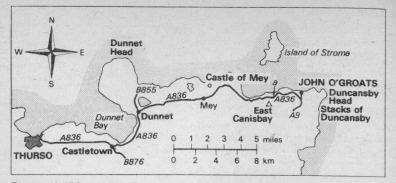

Dunnet A 17th-century minister at the small church was an early cartographer. A fine sandy beach is to the south-west.

Dunnet Head A worthwhile ride can be made to the Head, the most northerly point on mainland Britain. There are good views out to the Orkneys, and the famous stack, the Old Man of Hoy, can also be seen. The Head is well known for its sea fishing, and in 1975 a record halibut of 210 lbs was caught here.

Castletown The town grew with the development of local quarries where paving stone was extracted and sent by ship to the south.

Thurso See Route 246.

Route 246   44 miles   71 km
THURSO — TONGUE

OS 1:250 000 no. 2
Bartholomew's 1:100 000 no. 60
OS 1:50 000 nos 11, 10,12 (just)

Thurso A fishing town with some fine 17th-century houses and a museum containing plant and fossil collections. The remains of Thurso castle can be seen, and to the east of the town is Harold's Tower, the Sinclair burial place, built over the grave of Earl Harold, the ruler of Caithness, killed in a battle of 1196. In recent years the town has grown rapidly to provide accommodation for the people working at the

Dounreay atomic reactor. Links with Route 245.

a Ferries from Scrabster to Orkney.

Holborn Head There is an ancient fort site on the headland, and some dramatic cliff scenery.

Hill of Shebster On the summit of the hill is the chambered cairn of Cnoc Freiceadain (DoE).

St Mary's Chapel An ancient building maintained by the DoE.

Dounreay This is the site of Britain's first experimental atomic fast reactor, which is housed in an impressive steel sphere, 135 feet (41 m) in diameter. An exhibition set up in the control tower by the airfield describes the work carried out by the reactor.

Reay The present village replaces an earlier settlement which was buried by sand in the 18th century.

Strathy Point A lane leads out to the Point, where caves, natural arches, and Britain's newest lighthouse can be seen.

Bettyhill The village was founded by Elizabeth, Marchioness of Stafford, for crofters evicted during the Highland Clearances. There is a museum with carved stones in the church.

Invernaver The Nature Reserve here has a wide range of interesting wildlife and plants.

Tongue See Route 247. Also links with Route 261.

Route 247   50 miles 80 km
TONGUE — LAXFORD BRIDGE

OS 1:250 000 no. 2
Bartholomew's 1:100 000 nos 58, 60
OS 1:50 000 nos 9, 10

Tongue The ruined Caisteal Bharraich
was once the home of a Norse king, and
was later a stronghold of the Mackays.
Links with Routes 246, 261.

Moine House An inscription on the
east gable of the house commemorates
the building of the road.

Heilam This is a limestone area, and
kilns can be seen by the sea shore.

Loch Eriboll The deep waters of this
loch were used as a naval anchorage
during the Second World War. At the
end of the War, surrendered German
U-boats were brought here. Rare
Atlantic grey seals breed here.

Eriboll The track which zig-zags up the
hill to the south-east of the village offers
good views of Ben Hope from its
summit before it drops down to Loch
Hope.

Creag na Faoilinn This hill has a fine
echo.

Smoo Enormous Smoo Cave consists
of three chambers, the first being 200
feet (60 m) long and entered through a
50 foot (15-m) arch. The two inner
chambers are accessible only to experienced potholers. It is said to have been
used by smugglers in the past.

Balnakeil A craft village. The 17th-
century church has a monument to the
Gaelic poet Rob Donn Calder, sometimes known as the 'Burns of the
North'.

*a An exciting detour to Cape Wrath along
a single track road.*

*b The small ferry across the Kyle of
Durness operates during the summer season
only.*

Cape Wrath The extreme north-west
point of mainland Scotland, and the
goal of many a long distance cyclist. The

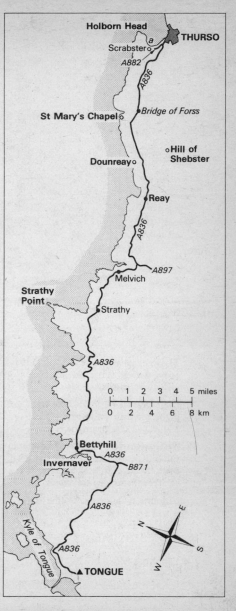

name is derived from the Viking word
'hvraf', meaning 'turning place', as this
was the landmark that told them to turn
south on their journeys to the Hebrides.

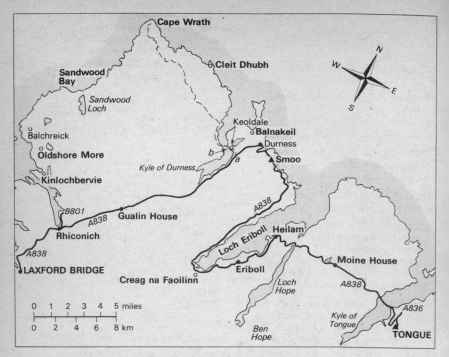

The lighthouse stands 400 feet (120 m) above the sea. It is a fine place for watching gannets.

Cleit Dhubh The cliffs here are the highest in mainland Britain, and rise 850 feet (260 m) from the sea.

Gualin House The house was built in the 19th century at the same time as the road, by the Marquess of Stafford as a shelter for stranded travellers.

Rhiconich Outcrops of some of the world's oldest rocks can be seen among the small lochs.

Kinlochbervie A busy fishing port.

Oldshore More In 1263 King Haakon of Norway anchored in the bay here, before continuing south in an attempt to invade Scotland.

Sandwood Bay This beautiful sandy bay is over a mile long, fringed with cliffs, and with a sea stack at its south-western end. A track to the bay, which

deteriorates into a footpath, leaves the road a quarter mile east of Balchreick.

Laxford Bridge See Route 248. Also links with Route 260.

Route 248   72 miles   115 km
LAXFORD BRIDGE — ULLAPOOL

OS 1:250 000 no. 2
Bartholomew's 1:100 000 no. 58
OS 1:50 000 nos 19, 15, 9

This route uses the Kylesku Ferry.

Laxford Bridge The name derives from the Norse 'lax' meaning salmon, and 'ford' meaning Fjord. Links with Routes 247, 260.

Scourie A crofting village and fishing resort.

Kylestrome Fine views of Quinag and Glas Bheinn mountains.

a The main route, which is fairly strenuous, turns west to explore the rugged

*and hilly coastline which is dotted with tiny
lochs and islands. The more direct alternative route passes through dramatic
mountain scenery.*

*b If you next intend to follow Route 260 to
Bonar Bridge, you can turn to it here.*

Eas Coul Aulin A spectacular waterfall
which plunges more than 600 feet
(180 m) down the lower slopes of Ben
More Assynt. It is situated near the
head of Loch Glencoul, and is reached
by foot, or boat from Kylesku Ferry.

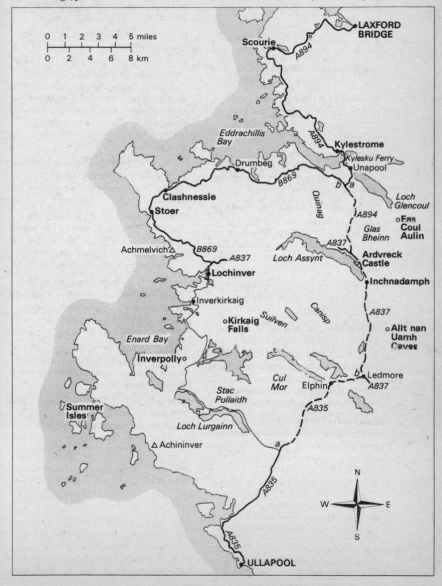

Ardvreck Castle This was the stronghold of the Macleods, and in 1650 the Marquis of Montrose was arrested here and sent to Edinburgh for execution following his attempted invasion on behalf of the exiled Charles II. The castle is now in ruins.

Inchnadamph The surrounding infertile landscape has many caves and underground streams.

Allt Nan Uamh Caves Human bones 8000 years old have been found here.

Clashnessie Once a strong crofting community. There are good views to the Hebrides.

Stoer Just to the south of the village is an interesting broch, with many of its stone blocks still in place. On the headland to the north-west are the remains of several crofting settlements.

Lochinver A fishing village popular among anglers and ornithologists. There are good views of Suilven, a ridge of Torridonian sandstone, which from this angle appears as a very steepsided cone.

Kirkaig Falls From Inverkirkaig, a pleasant path along a wooded valley leads to the Falls.

Inverpolly The location of the information centre for the Inverpolly National Nature Reserve. The Reserve covers a wild, remote and almost uninhabited area which is the haunt of deer, golden eagle, pine marten and wildcat, and includes the curiously shaped mountain, Stac Pollaidh.

Summer Isles Until the catches dropped early in the 19th century, these attractive islands were the homes of inshore herring fishermen.

Ullapool See Route 249.

Route 249   77 miles   124 km
ULLAPOOL — KINLOCHEWE

OS 1:250 000 no. 2
Bartholomew's 1:100 000 nos 54, 58
OS 1:50 000 nos 19, 20

Ullapool The town was founded in the late 18th century by the British Fisheries Society, as a fishing station. Today it is a popular centre for sea angling, and touring the Highlands. The Lochbroom Highland Museum has items of local interest. Links with Route 248.

a Ferries from Ullapool to the Hebrides and the Summer Isles (see Route 248).

b The alternative route involves crossing Loch Broom on a small ferry (although please note that the owners of the ferry have no obligation to carry cycles—it depends on goodwill) and negotiating a very steep track, whereas the main route threads its way inland across some wild and open moorland.

c The rough track links Allt na h'Airbhe hotel with the surfaced road at the top of the ridge. It is steep, and cycles have to be pushed.

Corrieshalloch Gorge A footpath leads to a precarious suspension bridge which crosses high over the precipitous Gorge and Falls of Measach (NTS) which plunge 150 feet (45 m).

Road of Destitution So called because it was constructed after the potato famine of 1846–7 by labourers whose payment was their food. It crosses wild and open moorland reaching a height of 1109 feet (338 m).

An Teallach The high ridges of this impressive mountain can be seen for miles around.

Scoraig This remote crofting village is reached by 4 miles (6.5 km) of rough track from Badrallach, most of which can be cycled. The people living there now are 'incomers', from different parts of the country.

Dundonnell Hotel Situated at the head of a lonely valley, the hotel is a useful place of shelter.

Gruinard Island The island was used as a testing ground for germ warfare in the Second World War. It is still contaminated and the public are prohibited access.

Cave This cave on the sea shore was once inhabited by a hermit.

Mellon Udrigle There are good views of the mountains of Coigach across a sea studded with islands.

Aultbea This was a naval base in both World Wars, and is now a NATO depot.

Tournaig By the loch-side is a cairn commemorating Alexander Cameron, a Tournaig bard.

Inverewe The unusual garden (NTS, open) was created out of a barren site and has rare and sub-tropical plants.

Gairloch A popular holiday resort, with fine views to Skye, the Hebrides, and Torridon Hills.

Loch Maree A beautiful inland loch set in fine mountain scenery, and dominated by the bulk of Slioch at its south-eastern end. The loch is known for its sea trout.

Isle Maree The chapel on the island is said to be a hermitage of St Maelrubha, founder of the Applecross monastery.

Nature Trails Several way-marked trails explore the natural habitats to be found on this edge of the Beinn Eighe National Nature Reserve.

Reserve Visitor Centre Information is provided on the huge variety of flora and fauna that can be seen.

Kinlochewe See Route 250. Also links with Route 262.

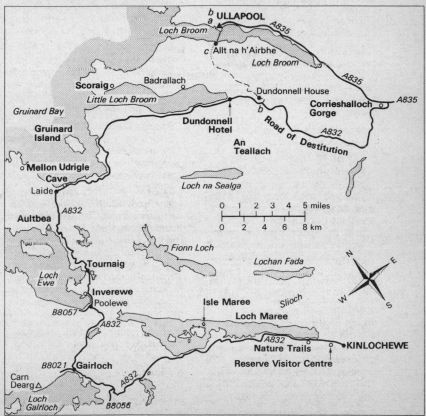

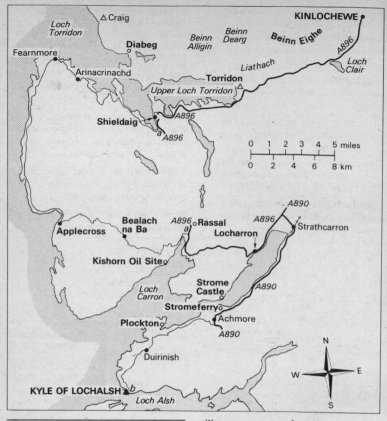

Route 250   74 miles   119 km
KINLOCHEWE —
KYLE OF LOCHALSH

OS 1:250 000 no. 2
Bartholomew's 1:100 000 no. 54
OS 1:50 000 nos 19 (just), 24, 33 (just)

Kinlochewe Set in the midst of some of Scotland's finest mountains. Links with Routes 249, 262.

Beinn Eighe The National Nature Reserve here, the first designated in Britain, covers 10,000 acres of mountain scenery. Parts of the ancient Caledonian pine forest are preserved, and the protected wildlife includes red deer, wild cats, eagles and pine martens.

Torridon On the small peninsula by the village are a group of standing stones known as the Church of Ploc. Just to the north are the magnificent mountains of Beinn Alligin, Beinn Dearg, Liathach and Beinn Eighe which provide some of the best climbing and walking in Scotland. The horizontal rock strata of red Torridonian sandstone has been eroded to produce a banded appearance, and some of the peaks are topped with white quartzite.

Diabeg A narrow road affording fine views leads to this remote village, and the start of the track to Craig YH.

Shieldaig Once dependant on crofting and fishing, this pretty village is now popular with summer tourists.

a The superlative ride to Applecross,

involving the dramatic but strenuous ascent of Bealach na Ba and scenic coast road, can however be omitted by continuing on the A896.

Applecross Before the new road from Shieldaig was built, this was one of the most inaccessible places on mainland Scotland. St Maelrubha, an Irish missionary, established a monastery here in AD 673, later to be destroyed by the Vikings. There is a Celtic cross in the old cemetery, and fine views across the sea to the islands of Raasay and Skye.

Bealach na Ba Otherwise known as 'Pass of the Cattle', and one of the highest roads in Britain. The narrow road climbs to a height of 2054 feet (626 m), with hairpins, steep drops and in places a gradient of 1:4. There are fine views from the top.

Kishorn Oil Site After a lengthy controversy, a site on the north side of the loch was transformed into a place for the construction of enormous oilfield production platforms.

Rassal One of the few semi-natural ash-woods in Britain, and a Nature Reserve.

Locharron A fishing village and dormitory for the nearby Kishorn oil site.

Strome Castle There are fine views of Skye from this ruined castle, which was blown up in 1602 by the MacKenzies during a clan feud (NTS, open).

Stromeferry This was a vital ferry link until the road up Loch Carron was built.

Plockton The village developed as a fishing and crofting community, set in a sheltered bay. A ferry can be taken to the island of Eilean na Creige Duibhe, a conservation area. The coast between here and Kyle of Lochalsh is protected by the NTS.

b There are ferries from the Kyle of Lochalsh to many of the Isles.

Kyle of Lochalsh See Route 264. Also links with Route 251.

Route 251   25 miles   40 km
**SLIGACHAN INN —
KYLE OF LOCHALSH**

OS 1:250 000 no. 1
Bartholomew's 1:100 000 no. 54
OS 1:50 000 nos 32, 33

This route involves the use of a ferry between Kyleakin and Kyle of Lochalsh. There are many opportunities for serious

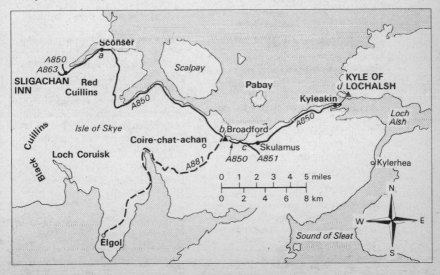

walking and climbing on Skye, particularly in the Red and Black Cuillins, although it should not be tried unless you are experienced and fully equipped.

Sligachan Inn Frequented by climbers and walkers. A path, to be attempted by experienced walkers only, leads through Glen Sligachan and over Drumhain Ridge to Loch Coruisk. Links with Routes 252, 253, 254.

Loch Coruisk This remote loch is set in the greatest mountain amphitheatre in Britain.

Black Cuillins These jagged mountains have fifteen peaks over 3000 feet (900 m) in height, and they form Britain's most precipitous range.

Sconser An 18th-century inn where Johnson and Boswell stayed.

a A ferry runs between Sconser and the island of Raasay.

Red Cuillins The gentler slopes of these rounded mountains contrast with their rugged neighbours.

b The detour leads to Elgol, where superb scenery may be enjoyed.

Coire-Chat-Achan The ruins of a farm where, according to Boswell, Dr Johnson was more warmed by Highland hospitality than anywhere else.

Pabay This island is renowned for its fossils.

Elgol Magnificent views of the Cuillins. Views south to the islands of Rhum, Canna, and Eigg. The Black Cuillins can be reached from here by experienced walkers. The view from Sgurr na Stri includes the Inaccessible Pinnacle near the summit of Sgurr Dearg. Boat trips from Elgol to Loch Coruisk.

c If you next intend to follow Route 254 to Mallaig, you can turn to it here.

Kyleakin The remains of a castle, thought to have been built by the daughter of a Norse king, can be seen.

d There are ferries from the Kyle of Lochalsh to many of the Isles.

Kyle of Lochalsh See Route 264. Also links with Route 250.

Route 252   48 miles   76 km
UIG — SLIGACHAN INN

OS 1:250 000 no. 1
Bartholomew's 1:100 000 no. 54
OS 1:100 000 nos 32, 23

This Route uses the same map as Route 253 below.

See comment on Skye, Route 251.

Uig It was here that Bonnie Prince Charlie first touched Skye having fled from the Outer Hebrides disguised as Flora Macdonald's maidservant. Links with Route 253.

a Ferries run from Uig to Tarbet and Lochmaddy on the Outer Hebrides.

Kingsburgh House Bonnie Prince Charlie was sheltered here by a kinsman of Flora Macdonald following his escape from the Outer Hebrides.

Fairy Bridge In the old days this bridge had an evil reputation among locals and it was said that no horse would cross it without shying.

Dunvegan Famous Dunvegan Castle dates from the 13th century, and has been inhabited continually by the Chiefs of Clan MacLeod for 700 years (open). The many treasures include relics of Bonnie Prince Charlie, Rory More's two-handed sword and four-pint drinking horn, letters from Dr Johnson and Sir Walter Scott, and the Fairy Flag said to have magical properties and used by the Clan in times of emergency. Dame Flora MacLeod of MacLeod, the last clan chief, died in 1976 at the age of 99.

Glendale This was in 1883 one scene of crofters' resistance to the Clearances by Highland Chiefs.

Boreraig There is a memorial cairn here to the MacCrimmons, who were the hereditary pipers to the MacCleod chiefs and founders and sustainers of the greatest school of Highland piping.

Dun Beag One of the best preserved brochs on the island.

b Fine mountain scenery can be seen on this detour to Glen Brittle.

Glen Brittle A popular centre for climbers; views of the Black Cuillins.

Black Cuillins, Red Cuillins and **Loch Coruisk** See Route 251.

Sligachan Inn See Route 251. Also links with Routes 253, 254.

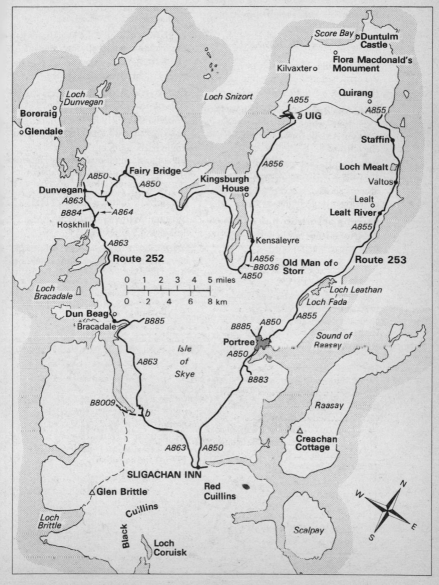

Route 253   36 miles   58 km
UIG — SLIGACHAN INN

OS 1:250 000 no. 1
Bartholomew's 1:100 000 no. 54
OS 1:50 000 nos 23, 32 (just)

This Route uses the same map as Route 252 above.

See comment on Skye, Route 251.

Uig See Route 252.

a Ferries run from Uig to Tarbet and Lochmaddy on the Outer Hebrides.

Flora Macdonald's Monument Her tombstone, which bears a tribute by Dr Johnson, can be found in Kilmuir churchyard.

Duntulm Castle Sited on a headland, but now in ruins. The adjacent bay has a greenish colour caused by the presence of fragments of olivine crystals.

Quirang The strange rock formations of this dramatic inland cliff include a

huge mass of rock with a field on top known as 'The Table, the 100-foot (30-m) Needle Rock and The Prison. The area was once used as a hiding place for stolen cattle.

Staffin The basaltic sea and inland cliffs in the area are of special interest to geologists.

Loch Mealt Where the loch drains to the sea there is a small waterfall.

Lealt River Close to the bridge over this river are three waterfalls.

Old Man of Storr The name given to the 160-foot (50-metre) strangely-shaped pinnacle of rock.

Portree The capital of Skye, and a small harbour. King James V stayed here while sailing through the Hebrides in an attempt to exert control over the outlying islands of his dominions.

Creachan Cottage Raasay YH.

Sligachan Inn See Route 251. Also links with Routes 252, 254.

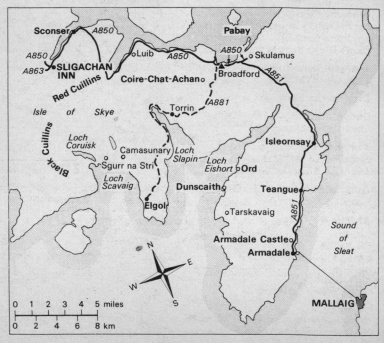

Route 254   35 miles   56 km
SLIGACHAN INN — MALLAIG

OS 1:250 000 no. 1 or 2
Bartholomew's 1:100 000 nos 50, 54
OS 1:50 000 nos 32, 33 (just), 40 (just)

This route uses a ferry between Armadale and Mallaig. The route passes the Black and Red Cuillins, Skye's two mountain ranges, some of the most popular climbing and serious walking country in Britain. They are also very hazardous, and should not be tried unless you are experienced and fully equipped.

Sligachan Inn See Route 251. Also links with Routes 252, 253.

Black Cuillins, Red Cuillins, Sconser, Coire-Chat-Achan, Pabay and **Elgol** See Route 251.

a The detour leads to Elgol, where superb scenery may be enjoyed.

b If you next intend to follow Route 251 to Kyle of Lochalsh, turn to it here.

Isleornsay Views east to the mainland and to Loch Horn, considered one of Scotland's finest lochs. Offshore is St Oran's Isle with chapel remains.

Teangue Remains of Knock Castle on a crag site by the shore.

Ord Superb views of the Cuillins.

Dunscaith The ruin of Dunscaith Castle on an isolated rock.

Armadale Castle Gothic Revival castle built in 1815. Armadale was the seat of Lord MacDonald of Sleat.

Armadale The Sabhel Mor Ostaig Gaelic College.

Mallaig See Route 255.

Route 255   41 miles   65 km
MALLAIG — SALEN

OS 1:250 000 no. 1
Bartholomew's 1:100 000 no. 50
OS 1:50 000 no. 40

Mallaig The main industry is fishing, and there are lobster ponds. Boat trips and ferries to the Hebrides. Links with Route 254.

Morar The eastern end of Loch Morar is, with the exception of one Scandinavian lake, western Europe's deepest inland water. The loch shore has some famous white sands which 'sing' in certain conditions.

Arisaig The tower clock in the church is a memorial to Alasdair MacMhaigstir Alasdair, a great Gaelic poet who took part in the Rising of 1745. It was in this vicinity that Bonnie Prince Charlie first landed for the Jacobite Rebellion. Views west to Eigg and north-west to the Cuillins on Skye.

Lochailort A sea-fish farming project was started in the loch in recent years.

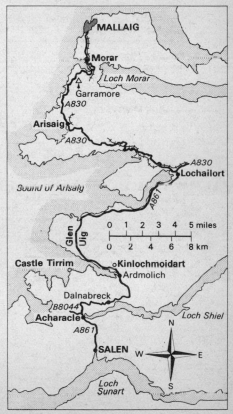

Glen Uig Long before the building of the motor road there was a 'coffin road' through this valley. The cairns and cross above the present road show where the old resting places used to be.

Kinlochmoidart A line of seven beeches in the grounds of Kinloch-moidart House commemorate the Seven Men of Moidart who landed with Bonnie Prince Charlie.

Castle Tirrim The ruins of a Mac-Donald castle on a dramatic site which is an island at high tide.

Acharacle An area where Gaelic is the first language.

Salen See Route 256. Also links with Route 268.

Route 256   50 miles   80 km
SALEN — GRULINE

OS 1:250 000 nos 1, 3
Bartholomew's 1:100 000 no. 47
OS 1:50 000 nos 40, 47

This route uses a ferry to cross the Sound of Mull between Tobermory and Mingary.

Salen The village grew up around a bobbin mill. Links with Routes 255, 268.

Mingary Castle An early 13th-century curtain-wall castle, which was once used as a prison for Covenanters.

Point of Ardnamurchan This is the most westerly place of the British mainland. It experiences sunrise and sunset about twenty-five minutes after Greenwich,

Tobermory The name is derived from the Gaelic 'Tobar Mhoire' meaning 'Well of Mary'. The well stands beside the ruins of an ancient chapel to the west of the town. An ancient settlement took advantage of the sheltered bay, but the present village was planned in 1788 by the British Fisheries Society. Boats to other islands and the mainland.

Bloody Bay The Spanish Galleon 'Florida' was sunk in the bay in 1588

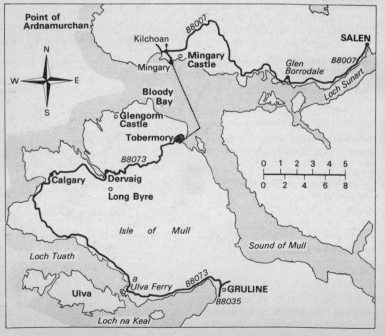

and dramatic stories attach to this event.

Glengorm Castle An impressively sited and still inhabited castle.

Dervaig The famed 'Little Theatre', which is in a converted barn, claims to be the world's smallest theatre.

Long Byre Folk museum.

Calgary Fine sand beach in the bay. The village gave its name to Calgary, Alberta, in Canada.

a Ferries run from Ulva Ferry to Ulva and Staffa, on which is Fingal's Cave.

Ulva The island once had about six hundred inhabitants who lived by farming and collecting kelp. It suffered severely under the highland clearances, and now there are very few inhabitants. A rough road along the north side of the island leads past deserted townships. The southern shore has black basalt cliffs and bays.

Gruline Links with Route 257.

Route 257 71 miles 113 km
GRULINE — CRAIGNURE

OS 1:250 000 no. 3
Bartholomew's 1:100 000 no. 47
OS 1:50 000 nos 48, 49

Without the dead-end ride to Iona, the route is 34 miles or 55 km long. The ferry from Mull to Iona does not run many times a day.

Gruline Links with Route 256.

Inch Kenneth This island was one of Iona's first dependencies. It has an ancient Celtic cross, church ruins and a chapel (DoE, open). Boswell and Johnson were impressed by Inch Kenneth during their Hebridean tour, and both wrote about it. A private ferry must be hired from Balnahard for the crossing.

Staffa Several miles off-shore but clearly visible is Staffa, whose basalt cliffs and cave inspired Mendelssohn's 'Fingal's Cave' overture.

Burgh An area of NTS land, including the unique MacCulloch's Tree fossil in the basalt columns. For directions inquire at Burg Cottage near Kilfinichen Bay.

Ben More Mull's highest mountain.

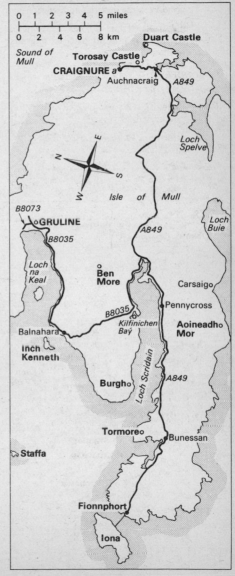

Aoineadh Mor Huge red basalt cliffs
with rock formations and arches. The
best views are to be had by walking
along the shore from Carsaig at low tide,
but be alert for the turning tide.

Tormore An area with old, once-
famed granite quarries and sandy bays.

Fionnphort The village has existed for
centuries as a resting place for pilgrims
to Iona.

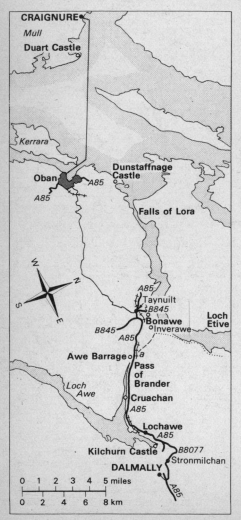

Iona St Columba landed here from
Ireland in 563 AD, after which Iona
became the cradle of Scotland's Christianity. Famous is the 13th-century
restored abbey, the 13th-century
nunnery ruins, and 9th-century Iona
Cross and McLean's Cross (DoE).

Duart Castle An open headland where
13th-century Duart Castle, dramatically
sited by the shore, has been opened to the
public by the 27th Chief, Lord Maclean
of Duart.

Torosay Castle Early Victorian house
in terraced, Italianate gardens (open).

*a Ferries run between Craignure and
Oban on the mainland.*

Craignure See Route 258.

Route 258   26 miles   41 km
CRAIGNURE — DALMALLY

OS 1:250 000 no. 3
Bartholomew's 1:100 000 no. 47
OS 1:50 000 nos 49, 50

*This route uses a ferry between Craignure
on Mull and Oban on the mainland,
increasing the total distance of the route.*

Craignure Before the tourist era this
was already a ferry point much used by
drovers, and their inn still exists. They
used to make the shorter crossing to
Kerrara, walk over the island, and then
make the cattle swim the remaining
distance to the mainland. Links with
Route 257.

Duart Castle See Route 257.

Oban Founded two centuries ago as a
fishing village, Oban is now the 'Gateway to the Isles' and a tourist resort
from which there are many boat trips.
McCaig's folly; two modern cathedrals;
and glass works (open).

Dunstaffnage Castle First built in the
13th century, Dunstaffnage was a royal
castle intended for use in war against the
Hebrides, which were then held by the
Norse (DoE, open).

Falls of Lora At Connel the powerful
tidal currents, called the Falls of Lora,

were a great hazard to ferries before the bridge was built.

Bonawe Bonawe Furnace is a complete early industrial lay-out of iron-smelting works (DoE).

a Detour to Loch Etive.

Loch Etive For the greater part of its length, Loch Etive enjoys its renowned beauty without the intrusion of a motor road, but the cyclist may explore the track alongside it. From the Inverawe lane, turn right through a gate onto a forestry road to Port na Mine. At a fork where the left track goes to Port na Mine, keep right.

Awe Barrage Salmon leap.

Pass of Brander The narrow pass was the scene of an unsuccessful attempt by the MacDougals to ambush Robert the Bruce in 1308.

Cruachan Water from Loch Awe is pumped up to a lake on Ben Cruachan as a means of storing electrical energy. The public may visit the station.

Lochawe The unique and fascinating 19th-century church of Conan.

Kilchurn Castle This 15th-century Campbell castle was on an island, but can now be reached on foot over a promontory as the loch level has lowered. Ruins (DoE, open).

Dalmally Links with Routes 259, 278.

Route 259   55 miles   88 km
DALMALLY — GOUROCK

OS 1:250 000 nos 3 or 4
Bartholomew's 1:100 000 nos 44, 47
OS 1:50 000 nos 50, 56, 63

Ferry between Dunoon and Gourock.

Dalmally Links with Route 258, 278.

Kilchurn Castle See Route 258.

Craig Nan Sassanach From the summit of this pass the dam and lake of the Ben Cruachan electricity storage scheme can be seen.

Trout Farm The public are sometimes allowed to look around.

Inveraray In the 18th century the old village was burnt to make way for the castle and the present village was planned. The castle is the seat of the Duke of Argyll, and houses collections including a superb arms display (open).

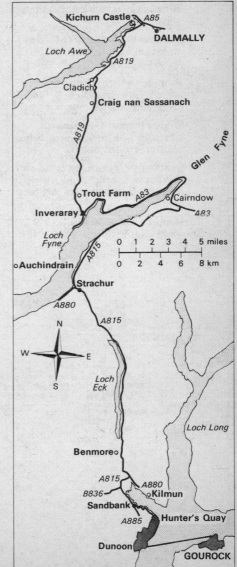

Auchindrain A complete village of an ancient community style, now preserved as a museum.

Glen Fyne A track up the valley passes close to falls on the river Fyne and its tributaries. The Allt na Lairige tributary has western Europe's first prestressed dam.

Strachur A saw-milling and woodworking village using timber from the Argyll Forest Park.

Benmore A large woodland garden with azaleas and reputedly the world's finest rhododendron collection (open).

Kilmun Forestry Commission arboretum with exotic trees including eucalyptus and redwoods.

Sandbank There are two famed yacht-building yards here, at which some America's Cup contenders have been built.

Hunter's Quay The first Scottish Yacht Club was founded here in 1856.

Dunoon A Clyde tourist resort from which ferries and boat-trips run. The Yachting Fortnight occurs in July, and the Cowal Highland Gathering in August, when the march of the 1000 pipers is performed. Statue of Burn's 'Highland Mary', who was born nearby. Dunoon is now a Campbell seat, and the fee, by degree of a charter of 1471, is 'one red rose when asked for', being payable to the monarch.

Gourock See Route 188.

Route 260   49 miles   79 km
LAXFORD BRIDGE —
BONAR BRIDGE

OS 1:250 000 no. 2
Bartholomew's 1:100 000 nos 58, 59
OS 1:50 000 nos 21, 16, 9, 15 (just); also 20 (just) for the alternative route.

The map for this Route is in two parts.

The alternative route uses the Kylesku ferry.

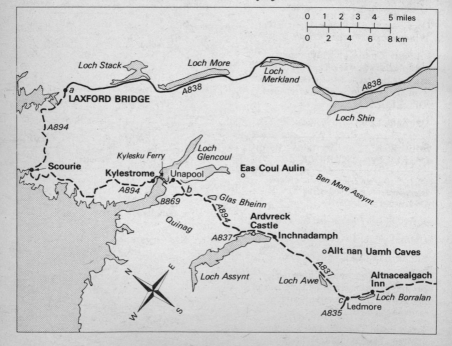

Laxford Bridge See Route 248. Also links with Route 247.

a The main route takes a fairly direct and level way along valley bottoms with fine loch side scenery, while the alternative route has a much greater variety of scenery including coastline, magnificent mountains, and delightful Strath Oykell. It also passes by several places of interest, and serves as a link with the southern part of Route 248.

Scourie, Kylestrome, Eas Coul Aulin, Ardvreck Castle, Inchnadamph and **Allt Nan Uamh Caves** See Route 248.

b or c If you next intend to follow Route 248 to Ullapool, turn to it at either.

Altnacealgach Inn One of the oldest fishing hotels in Scotland, in wild countryside and with fine mountain views.

Monument This commemorates the Great Plough, when the Duke of Sutherland reclaimed a large area with mechanical steam cultivators in the 1870s.

Lairg A market town and holiday resort.

Shin Waterfalls The B864 follows the west bank of the river Shin, giving access to spectacular waterfalls and a long salmon run.

Carbisdale Castle See Route 241.

Bonar Bridge See Route 241. Also links with Route 242.

Route 261	60 miles	96 km

TONGUE — HELMSDALE

OS 1:250 000 no. 2
Bartholomew's 1:100 000 no. 60
OS 1:50 000 nos 17, 10, 16

Tongue See Route 247. Also links with Route 246.

Altnaharra A popular angling resort.

Chambered Cairn Located by Kinbrace Burn, this is one of many cairns in

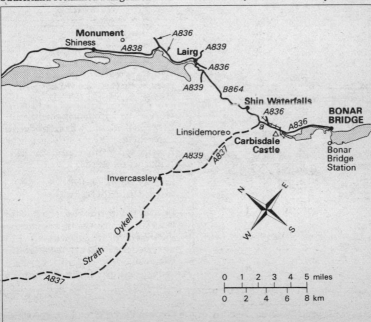

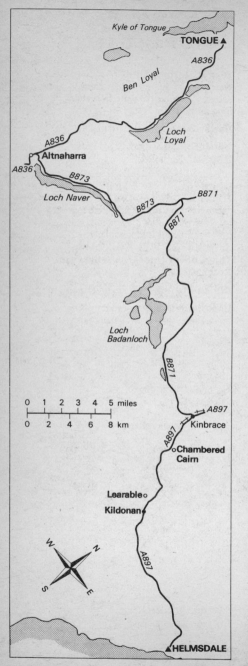

the vicinity. It has three chambers reached by a 25-foot (8-m) passage.

Learable On the hillside to the north-west of this house are many stone rows, cairns and hut circles.

Kildonan Gold found in Kildonan Burn led to a minor 'Sutherland Gold Rush' in 1868–9, but only £6000 worth of dust was extracted.

Helmsdale See Route 242. Also links with Route 243.

Route 262   26 miles   42 km
KINLOCHEWE — GARVE

OS 1:250 000 no. 2
Bartholomew's 1:100 000 nos 55, 54
OS 1:50 000 nos 19, 20, 25

Kinlochewe See Route 250. Also links with Route 249.

Garve See Route 263.

Route 263   24 miles   38 km
GARVE — INVERNESS

OS 1:250 000 no. 2
Bartholomew's 1:100 000 no. 55
OS 1:50 000 nos 20, 26

This route requires the use of a ferry between North Kessock and South Kessock (Inverness).

Garve The surrounding countryside has been made much more productive in recent years by the introduction of forestry and hydro-electric schemes. Links with Route 262.

Falls of Rogie The falls are in the wooded valley of Black Water.

Contin Before roads were built in the late 18th century, Contin was situated at the start of the rough tracks that traversed the Highlands to Poolewe and Ullapool, on the west coast. Buyers from the north of England came to purchase sturdy ponies for use in the coal mines at the horse fair held here.

Muir of Ord The 'muir', which is now the golf course, used to be the site of

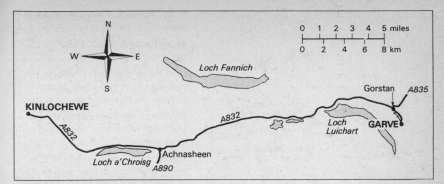

huge cattle, sheep and horse markets. In recent years industry has been attracted to the town.

Gilchrist The church here was the scene of a ghastly incident in the 17th century. It is said that the Macdonalds set fire to the church filled with local people, and the cries of the dying were drowned by the skirl of a piper.

Beauly Priory ruins (DoE, open).

Black Isle See Route 241.

a If you next intend to follow Route 241 to Bonar Bridge, you can turn to it here.

Inverness See Route 240. Also links with Routes 241, 265.

Route 264   50 miles   80 km
KYLE OF LOCHALSH—INVERGARRY

OS 1:250 000 no. 2
Bartholomew's 1:100 000 nos 50, 54
OS 1:50 000 nos 33, 34

Kyle of Lochalsh Terminus of the road and railway to the Isles, recently involved in oilfield activities. There are views of the Cuillin mountains on the Isle of Skye. On the Plock, to the west of Kyle, is an indicator identifying the mountains. Links with Routes 250, 251.

a There are ferries from the Kyle of Lochalsh to many of the Isles.

Ardelve The Falls of Glomach can be reached from here, at a distance of 11 miles (18 km).

Eilean Donan Castle One of the most photographed castles in Scotland, and for a long time the stronghold of the Mackenzies of Kintail. In 1719 it was largely destroyed by a bombardment from English ships attacking the Spanish defenders, sympathizers of the Jacobites. It was extensively restored in 1932 (open).

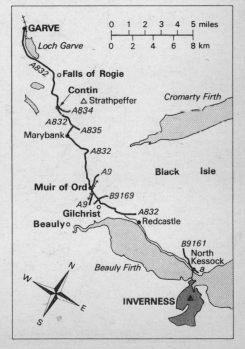

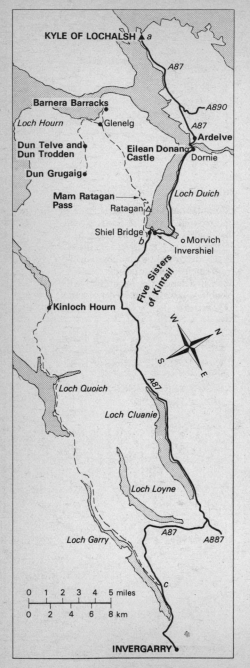

b A delightful detour of scenic and historic interest.

Mam Ratagan Pass There is a viewpoint at the summit.

Dun Telve and Dun Trodden The remains of two of the best preserved brochs in Scotland (DoE).

Dun Grugaig The remains of an enclosure standing on the edge of a steep gorge.

Bernera Barracks Built in 1722 by General Wade, and later used to shelter victims of the Highland Clearances.

Five Sisters of Kintail These mountains have some of the steepest grass slopes in Scotland.

c A detour through wild country by means of a single track road.

Kinloch Hourn Set in some of the finest mountain scenery in Britain.

Invergarry See Route 266. Also links with Route 265.

Route 265   40 miles 65 km
INVERNESS — INVERGARRY

OS 1:250 000 no. 2
Bartholomew's 1:100 000 nos 52 (just), 55
OS 1:50 000 nos 26, 34

Inverness See Route 240. Also links with Routes 241, 263.

Culloden Manor and **Boar's Stone** See Route 240.

Craig Phadrig The remains of a fort where St Columba is believed to have visited King Brude of the Picts in AD 565.

Loch Ness World famous because of its legendary monster, subject of much fascination.

Foyers South of the village are the famous Falls of Foyers. In 1896 Britain's first hydro-electric power scheme was installed here, greatly reducing the volume of water passing over the Falls. It has since been replaced by a more modern power station.

Fort Augustus Named after the fort constructed here by Augustus, Duke of Cumberland, following the Jacobite rising of 1715. The site is now occupied by a school and an abbey, part of which was designed by Joseph Hansom, inventor of the hansom cab.

a The lane leaving the A82 here leads to the start of the track over the Corrieyairack Pass, a difficult rough stuff route which links Fort Augustus with Laggan, on Routes 269 and 270.

Corrieyairack Pass A popular but very arduous rough stuff route reaching an altitude of 2507 feet (765 m). It should only be attempted by the experienced and fit, with adequate equipment, preparation and 1:50 000 or 1:25 000 maps. It is wild and affords glorious views but involves 19 miles (30 km) of rough track without shelter, and a ford to cross. The track over the Pass was built by General Wade in the 18th century, and was used by Bonnie Prince Charlie in his march south.

Invergarry See Route 266. Also links with Route 264.

Route 266   16 miles   25 km
INVERGARRY — SPEAN BRIDGE

OS 1:250 000 no. 2
Bartholomew's 1:100 000 no. 51
OS 1:50 000 no. 34

Invergarry An area of fine scenery. Invergarry castle, now a ruin, was for centuries the ancestral home and fortress of the MacDonnells of Glengarry. Just north of Invergarry is the Well of the Heads and a monument commemorating the gruesome deeds that took place there. Home of the Highland bonnet known as the Glengarry. Forestry Commission walks in Garry Gorge. Links with Routes 264, 265.

Caledonian Canal Finished in 1847, and built so that boats could avoid the hazardous journey around northern Scotland, the Canal cuts right across from Beauly Firth near Inverness to Loch Linnhe, near Fort William.

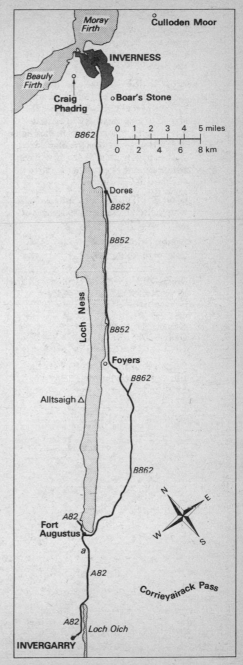

South Laggan Loch Lochy YH.

Commando Memorial Commemorates the commando soldiers who trained in the surrounding hills during the Second World War.

High Bridge Only the remains can be seen. It was built by General Wade in 1736 as part of his road network designed to give the troops of central government greater access to the Highlands. It was here that the first skirmishes took place in 1745, three days before Bonnie Prince Charlie raised his standard at Glenfinnan.

Glen Roy The famous 'parallel roads' were caused by successive changes of water level during an ice age.

Spean Bridge See Route 267. Also links with Route 269.

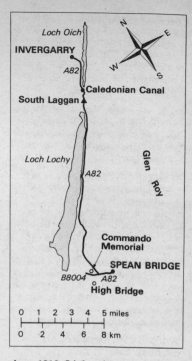

Route 267   40 miles   64 km
SPEAN BRIDGE — CORRAN

OS 1:250 000 nos 2, 4
Bartholomew's 1:100 000 no. 50
OS 1:50 000 nos 41, 40
1 inch:1 mile Ben Nevis/Glen Coe tourist map

Spean Bridge The bridge over the river Spean was built by Telford in 1819, and the parish church was built in about 1812. Links with Routes 266, 269.

Glen Roy, High Bridge and

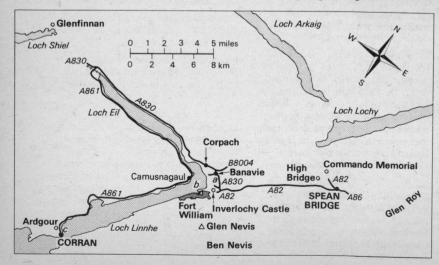

Commando Memorial See Route 266.

a The long but pleasant ride around Loch Eil can be omitted by using the busy A82 down the east side of Loch Linnhe. If you use the A82 and wish to join Route 268 you will have to take the ferry to Corran. If you take the main route around Loch Eil, and wish to join Route 279 you take the ferry from Corran. An alternative to both is to use the ferry between Fort William and Camusnagaul (b) and cycle along the west side of Loch Linnhe.

b A ferry runs between Fort William and Camusnagaul.

Inverlochy Castle A 13th-century castle, with walls and towers with longbow slits still visible.

Fort William The town is now a tourist centre, although for two centuries, up until 1855, it was also the site of an important military fort. The West Highland Museum has natural and folk history exhibits, and a section on the Jacobite Rising of '45 which includes the secret portrait of Bonnie Prince Charlie (it can only be seen when reflected onto a curved, polished surface).

Ben Nevis At 4406 feet (1343 m), this is the highest mountain in Britain, the north face of which provides climbers with very severe conditions in winter. A 5-mile (8-km) footpath leads to the summit from Achintee Farm, in Glen Nevis. Extreme care should be taken while ascending and descending this mountain.

Glen Nevis A lane leads for 5 miles to the head of this delightful glen, passing Polldubh waterfall. A rough track continues to the 450-foot (140-metre) Steall waterfall.

Banavie Here the Caledonian Canal reaches a sea loch, and the locks raise the water level of the canal by 64 feet (20 m) in one mile, in a stretch known as Neptune's Staircase. The canal was surveyed by Thomas Telford and was completed in 1847.

Corpach There is a large pulp and paper mill here providing employment for local people. There are good views of the north east face of Ben Nevis.

Glenfinnan The tower surmounted by a statue of a kilted Highlander commemorates the raising of Bonnie Prince Charlie's standard in 1745 as a rallying point for the clans. NTS visitor centre.

Ardgour The church is one such designed by Thomas Telford built by the government in the early 19th century in an effort to halt the population drift from Scotland.

c The long but pleasant ride around Loch Eil can be cut out of this route by using the Corran ferry, and the busy A82 down the east side of Loch Linnhe. An alternative to both is to cycle along the west side of Loch Linnhe and use the ferry between Fort William and Camusnagaul (b) to Routes 268, 279.

Corran Links with Routes 268, 279.

Route 268   24 miles   38 km
SALEN — CORRAN

OS 1:250 000 nos 1, 4
Bartholomew's 1:100 000 nos 47 or 50
OS 1:50 000 nos 40, 41 (just) and 49 (just)

Salen The village grew up around the bobbin mill, since destroyed. Links with Routes 255, 256.

Strontian During the 19th-century church troubles the landlord would not build a church, and so the inhabitants anchored a 'floating church' on the loch.

Lead Mines The lead mined around Strontian was long known to contain a mineral called 'strontianite', and the element strontium was discovered in it in 1787. The shafts of the old lead mines can be reached on foot by following the Nature Conservancy trail through Arriundle Oakwood, and then crossing wild country beyond.

Glen Tarbert 'Tarbert' means a neck of land which does not rise to any great

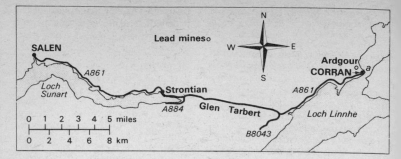

height. Over this boats used to be carried in order to avoid a long journey by water.

Ardgour See Route 267.

a There is a frequent ferry from Corran to the east side of Loch Linnhe.

Corran Links with Routes 267, 279.

Route 269   29 miles   47 km
LAGGAN — SPEAN BRIDGE

OS 1:250 000 no. 2
Bartholomew's 1:100 000 no. 51
OS 1:50 000 nos 35, 34, 42 (just)

Laggan Links with Route 270.

a The Corrieyairack pass, a difficult rough stuff route (see below) links Laggan

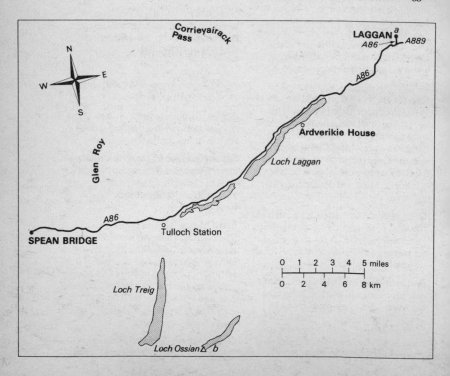

on this route, with Fort Augustus on Route 265. A lane west from Laggan leads to the start of the Pass.

Corrieyairack Pass A lane west from Laggan leads to the start of the Pass. See also Route 265.

Ardverikie House Queen Victoria considered buying this house for her Highland home but was dissuaded by persistent rain and chose Balmoral.

b This YH can only be reached by railway, or on foot.

Glen Roy See Route 266.

Spean Bridge See Route 267. Also links with Route 266.

Route 270   28 miles   44 km
AVIEMORE — LAGGAN

OS 1:250 000 no. 2
Bartholomew's 1:100 000 no. 51
OS 1:50 000 no. 35

Aviemore See Route 239. Also links with Routes 240, 271.

Lairig Ghru, Chair Lift and **The Cairngorms** See Route 239.

Loch an Eilein On the island can be seen the ruins of a medieval tower stronghold once used by the notorious Alexander, Earl of Buchan, better known as the 'Wolf of Badenoch'. In earlier times he terrorized the lowlands of Moray. Rothiemurchus Forest, to the east, is one of the few remaining tracts of Scots Pine forest, and is the home of reindeer.

Insh Church Inside the small church is an ancient 'magic' square bell.

Glen Feshie There is a 22-mile (35-km) walk from Glen Feshie to Braemar, which should only be attempted with proper equipment and preparation.

Ruthven Barracks The barracks were captured by the Highlanders during the uprising of '45, and it was here, after their defeat at Culloden, that Bonnie Prince Charlie informed his remaining men that he did not intend to raise his standard again. The Highlanders then burnt the barracks to prevent them from falling into Government hands (DoE, open).

Kingussie The village was planned in the 18th century as a woollen manufacturing centre and is the home of the Highland Folk Museum.

Newtonmore Pony-trekking originated here, and the Clan Macpherson house and museum has clan relics.

Laggan Links with Route 269.

Route 271   46 miles   74 km
ELGIN — AVIEMORE

OS 1:250 000 no. 2
Bartholomew's 1:100 000 nos 55, 56
OS 1:50 000 nos 27, 28, 36

Elgin This market town has the ruins of a fine 13th-century cathedral (DoE)

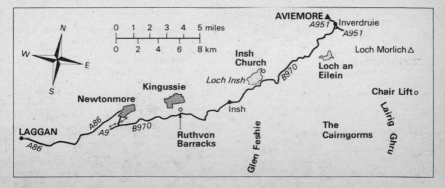

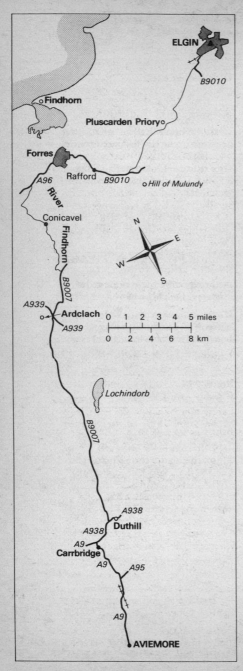

which was burned in 1390, along with part of the town, by the notorious Wolf of Badenoch. Close to the cathedral is the Bishop's Palace (DoE). In 1746, prior to the Battle of Culloden, Bonnie Prince Charlie stayed at Thunderton House, now a hotel. The Elgin Museum contains a local history collection which includes Pictish stones and fossils. Links with Route 272.

Pluscarden Priory Damaged by the Wolf of Badenoch in 1390, the priory has been rebuilt by Benedictine monks.

Forres The three witches burnt here in AD 965, accused of causing the death of King Duffus, were made famous by Shakespeare in *Macbeth*. Superb views from the 70-foot (21-m) monument to Lord Nelson which is sited on top of wooded Cluny Hill to the south-east. The Falconer Museum has a famous collection of fossils and other items of local interest. Curious Sueno's Stone (DoE) can be seen one mile east of the town.

Findhorn Once a busy port, this is now a resort and home of the Findhorn Foundation, a community who arrived in 1962 and through 'inner guidance' succeeded in making fertile the barren coastal sand dunes.

River Findhorn There are fine walks to be enjoyed along the banks.

Ardclach Bell tower (DoE, open).

Duthill The church and mausoleum have been the burial place of the Clan Grant chiefs since 1585.

Carrbridge During the winter months this is a busy ski resort.

Aviemore See Route 239. Also links with Routes 240, 270.

Route 272   26 miles   41 km
ELGIN — DUFFTOWN

OS 1:250 000 no. 2
Bartholomew's 1:100 000 no. 56
OS 1:50 000 no. 28

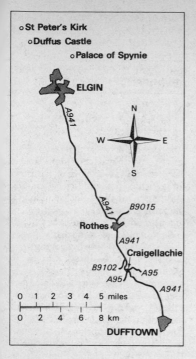

o St Peter's Kirk
o Duffus Castle
o Palace of Spynie

ELGIN

A941

N
W   E
S

A941   B9015
Rothes
A941
Craigellachie
B9102   A95
A95   A941

0 1 2 3 4 5 miles
0 2 4 6 8 km
DUFFTOWN

Route 273   46 miles   74 km
DUFFTOWN — BALLATER

OS 1:250 000 no. 2
Bartholomew's 1:100 000 nos 52, 56.
OS 1:50 000 nos 28, 37.

Dufftown With good barley, peat and
water close at hand, the town has grown
to be an important centre of malt distilling. To the north is Balvenie Castle,
one of the largest and best preserved in
Scotland (DoE, open). It dates from the
14th century and was visited by Edward I
and Mary Queen of Scots. Links with
Route 272.

Auchindown Castle The fine old
ruins (DoE), lie within prehistoric
earthworks.

Glen Fiddich This glen gave its name
to the famous malt whisky.

Glacks of Balloch There are good
views from the 1197-foot (400-metre)
col.

Cabrach The high plateau here is
known as The Cabrach and is an area of
desolate moors and deer forests.

Craig Castle A huge 16th-century
tower house.

St Mary's Church An attractive stone
church, now in ruins, with a fine door in
the south wall (DoE). On a mound near
the church once stood the earth and
timber fortress of the Comyns.

Lumsden The village was built in
1825, in what was previously a barren
area.

Kildrummy Castle This 14th-century
castle (DoE, open) was besieged in the
15th century by the son of the Wolf of
Badenoch, and later dismantled after
the Jacobite Rising. It has a fine 10-
acre garden.

Glenbuchat Castle Now in ruins
(DoE), this is an excellent example of a
Z-plan tower house.

Kirkton of Glenbuchat The old kirk is
a fine example of a traditional kirk, with
its cobbled and stone floor, and laird's

Elgin See Route 271.

St Peter's Kirk A delightful old
church, with a tall 14th-century cross in
the churchyard (DoE).

Duffus Castle The ruined stone castle
was built on an earlier Norman mound
(DoE, open).

Palace of Spynie The ruins of the
massive 15th-century castle (DoE,
open) built by the Bishops of Moray,
and once visited by Mary Queen of
Scots. It originally stood on an island.

Rothes A distilling centre on an
attractive site by the River Spey.

Craigellachie Delightfully situated on
the River Spey, the village also marks
the boundary of Clan Grant land, whose
battle-cry is 'Stand fast, Craigellachie!'
The famous bridge was built by
Thomas Telford.

Dufftown See Route 273.

loft. The pretty valley of Glenbuchat has been seriously depopulated over the last century, leaving many of the dwellings uninhabited.

a If you next intend to follow Route 274 to Aberdeen, you can turn to it here.

Loch Kinord Crannog Island was constructed by man in the Bronze Age.

Cambus O'May Byron, the poet and satirist, spent part of his childhood here.

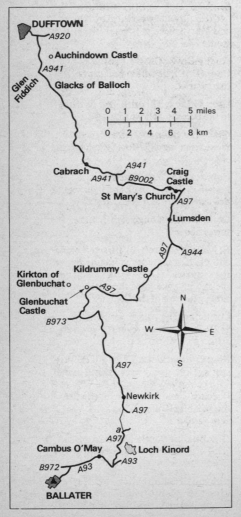

Ballater See Route 238. Also links with Routes 239, 274.

Route 274   49 miles   78 km
ABERDEEN — BALLATER

OS 1:250 000 no. 2
Bartholomew's 1:100 000 no. 52
OS 1:50 000 nos 37, 38

Aberdeen This is Scotland's third largest city, known for its importance as a centre for the North Sea oil industry, for its fishing port and fine old granite buildings. One of the oldest buildings in the town is Provost Ross's House (open), built in 1530. Both the Church of St Nicholas and St Machar's Cathedral (DoE) have interesting features, and 17th-century Provost Skene's House (open) contains a museum of local history and domestic life. The University has two medieval colleges, and the Old Tolbooth was the scene of public executions until 1857. There is an Anthropological Museum and Natural History Museum at the University, and in James Dun's House there is a museum for children. Links with Route 275.

a Ferries to the Shetland Islands.

Cullerlie Stone Circle Excavations here have revealed the existence of seven cremation burials (DoE).

Loch of Skene Local legend has it that the warlock Laird of Skene once drove his carriage across the loch after only one night of frost.

Echt Georgian church.

Castle Fraser A spectacular castle (NTS, open) built to a Z-plan, and completed in 1636.

Barmekin Hill On the summit are five concentric lines of fortification built by the Picts. On the eve of the Civil War the hill-fort was used as an assembly ground for troops.

Midmar Castle A turreted 17th-century baronial castle.

b *The main route continues along the ridge of hills whereas the alternative route drops to the valley to visit three points of interest.*

Peel Ring A moated earth mound (DoE), on which a building once stood.

Auchlossan The area of flat land here was a loch until drained in 1860.

Macbeth's Cairn Traditionally the site where Macbeth, King of the Scots, was slain by Malcolm, who later became King.

Craigievar Castle This spectacular castle has remained virtually unaltered since it was built in 1626 (NTS, open). It is crowned by a wealth of turrets, and inside over the main stair is the family motto *Do not vaiken sleiping dogs.*

Culsh Farm There is an Iron Age earth house here (DoE).

Tomnaverie Stone Circle This monument dates from around 1800 BC (DoE).

c *If you next intend to follow Route 273 to Dufftown, you can turn to it here.*

Loch Kinord and **Cambus o'May** See Route 273.

Ballater See Route 238. Also links with Routes 239, 273.

Route 275   50 miles   80 km
ABERDEEN — EDZELL

OS 1:250 000 nos 2, 4 (just)
Bartholomew's 1:100 000 no. 52
OS 1:50 000 nos 45, 38

Aberdeen See Route 274.

a *Ferries to the Shetland Islands.*

Findon The small village gave its name to the Finnannhaddock, which was specially prepared by splitting, drying and then colouring in the smoke of peat.

b *The main route turns inland here to link a succession of interesting places, and includes a climb through the hills to a height of 1488 feet (454 m). The alter-*

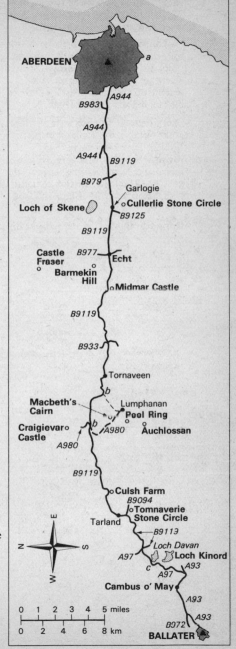

native route involves a section on the busy A92 along a scenic coastline and some quiet lanes along the edge of the hills.

Muchalls The early 17th-century castle has elaborate plasterwork ceilings and fireplaces and a secret staircase (open). There are many dramatic rock formations on the jagged coastline between Newtonhill and Doonie Point.

Stonehaven Of significance to cyclists as the birthplace of inventor Robert William Thomson who in 1845 patented the pneumatic tyre. He also invented the dry dock and the fountain pen. The Tolbooth Museum contains items associated with fishing and local history.

Dunnotar Castle The impressive ruins

of this 14th-century castle (open) are perched 160 feet (49 m) above the sea affording spectacular views.

St Mary's Chapel Now in ruins, the chapel was built by the Knights Templars in 1287.

Peterculter This village, which grew around a paper mill, has a particularly pleasant parish church.

Normandykes An extensive Roman marching camp.

Drum Castle The castle has a 13th-century square tower which is one of the three oldest tower houses in Scotland (NTS, open). A delightful mansion was added later.

Crathes Castle A fine 16th-century

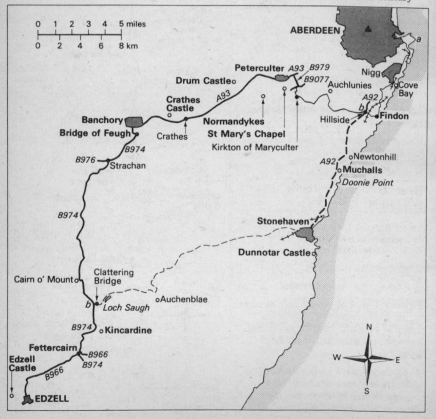

baronial castle with painted ceilings and beautiful gardens (NTS, open).

Banchory The factory where Dee lavender water is distilled (open).

Bridge of Feugh Near the 18th-century bridge is a pretty gorge, and a salmon leap which can be viewed from an observatory platform.

Kincardine This was once a market town and the site of a great fortress, though little remains today.

Fettercairn The great royal arch commemorates a visit by Queen Victoria. In the square is the shaft of the Kincardine town cross, which has been notched to show the length of the Scottish measurement known as an 'ell'.

Edzell Castle The castle (DoE, open) was built in the 16th century and has a unique Renaissance garden, the walls of which have a wealth of heraldic and symbolic decoration.

Edzell Links with Route 276.

Route 276   55 miles   88 km
EDZELL — DUNKELD

OS 1:250 000 no. 4
Bartholomew's 1:100 00 nos 52, 49
OS 1:50 000 nos 53, 54, 44

Edzell Links with Route 275.

Edzell Castle See Route 275.

Brechin By the cathedral is an 87-foot (27-metre) high round tower dating from the 10th or 11th century, once used as a watch-tower and refuge (DoE). The Maison Dieu Chapel is open (DoE). The castle, which is now rebuilt, was besieged by Edward I for three weeks in 1303 before falling. Most of the town is built of red sandstone.

Brown Caterthun A large hill-fort with six lines of defence.

White Caterthun This fort has two enormous walls, one of which could have been 40 feet (12 m) thick, and ramparts and ditches (DoE).

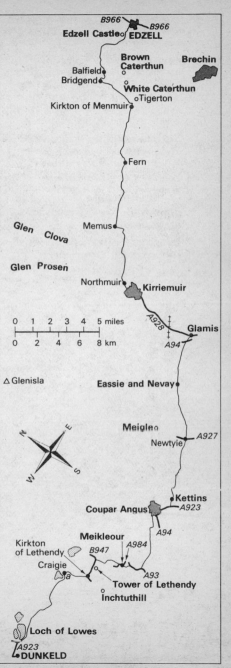

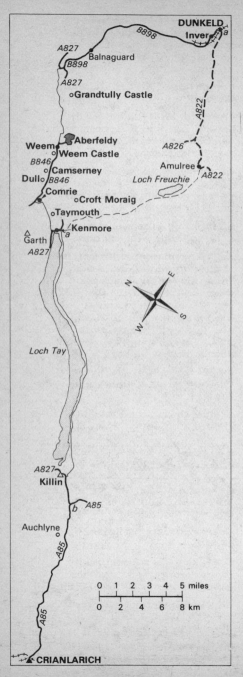

Glen Clova and **Glen Prosen**
Delightful detours can be made up these two scenic glens.

Kirriemuir This picturesque town was once based on the local weaving industry, and is better known as the birthplace of J. M. Barrie, creator of Peter Pan. The house where he was born is now a museum containing mementos and manuscripts (NTS, open).

Glamis The imposing 14th-century castle was rebuilt in the 17th century in the style of a French château (open) and has a celebrated secret chamber and grounds laid out by Capability Brown. The castle has associations with Macbeth, and various members of the Royal Family. In the pretty village is the Angus Folk Museum, illustrating past domestic and farm life (NTS).

Eassie and Nevay There is a fine example of an inscribed Pictish stone in the churchyard (DoE).

Meigle The museum contains twenty-five sculptured Celtic monuments and an excellent early sculpture.

Kettins There is a 16th-century bell and belfry preserved in the churchyard, and a sculptured stone that was once used to bridge a stream.

Coupar Angus Only a part of the gatehouse survives of what was once a Cistercian abbey.

Meikleour The village still has some jougs (iron neck rings) to which offenders would be attached for punishment. Along the roadside to the south of the village, bordering the grounds of Meikleour House, is a long beech hedge, planted in 1746, and now standing at a height of 90 feet (30 m).

Tower of Lethendy This 16th-century building was altered in Victorian times and may once have been surrounded by a moat.

Inchtuthill The site of a Roman legionary fortress which was abandoned before completion. A cache of 12 tons of Roman nails has been found.

a If you next intend to follow Route 238 to Ballater, you can turn to it here.

Loch of Lowes See Route 238.

Dunkeld See Route 237. Also links with Routes 238, 277.

Route 277   64 miles   103 km
DUNKELD — CRIANLARICH

OS 1:250 000 no. 4
Bartholomew's 1:100 000 no. 48
OS 1:50 000 nos 51, 52; 50 (just)

Dunkeld See Route 237. Also links with Routes 276, 238.

a The alternative route between Dunkeld and Kenmore involves a steep climb over a high pass, but affords fine views.

Inver See Route 237.

Grandtully Castle The seat has been Stuart since the 14th century, but the present castle dates principally from the 16th century. A signpost near the castle directs to St Mary's church which has a fine ornamental ceiling (DoE, open).

Weem General Wade stayed at the hotel in Weem during the building of Aberfeldy Bridge. During his campaign to overcome the rebellious Scots clans in the 18th century, General Wade and his troops built over 250 miles (400 km) of roads and bridges, some of which are still main lines of communication. Weem church has been a Menzies mausoleum since 1839. On Weem Rock are St David's well and chapel cave, to which local legends attach.

Aberfeldy A tourist resort containing General Wade's picturesque five-arch bridge and Black Watch monument. Various nature and archaeological trails are laid out in the area.

Weem Castle The 16th-century Castle Menzies, which the Clan Menzies hope to use as a clan centre.

Camserney Preserved cruck cottage and old mill.

Dull Traditionally this is the site of a monastery founded by Adamnan, the biographer of St Columba. A stone cross is one of several which used to mark an area of sanctuary. There are many prehistoric remains in the vicinity.

Comrie Ruin of 14th-century Comrie Castle.

Taymouth In 1847 the Earl of Breadalbane, then owner of Taymouth Castle, reintroduced the capercailzie game bird to Scotland.

Kenmore Robert Burns visited here. The lines he wrote over the inn fireplace in praise of the beauty of the area can yet be seen.

Croft Moraig A fine group of standing stones and a large prehistoric circle.

Killin A tourist resort, with ruins of the 17th-century Finlarig Castle which was once a Campbell seat. Traditionally there is a pit near the castle where the gentry were executed, whereas the common people were hanged from a nearby oak tree. The eight healing stones of St Fillion are at the tweed mill near the Bridge of Dochart.

b If you next intend to follow Route 280 to Callander, via Lochearnhead, you can turn to it at this point.

Crianlarich Links with Routes 278, 279, 280.

Route 278   23 miles   37 km
CRIANLARICH — DALMALLY

OS 1:250 000 nos 3 or 4
Bartholomew's 1:100 000 no. 48
OS 1:50 000 no. 50

Crianlarich Links with Routes 277, 279, 280.

Ben Dorain This mountain, much praised in poetry, is said to have the longest unbroken grass slope in Britain.

Bridge of Orchy Until the construction of the A82 roads over Rannoch Moor all used this bridge.

a If you next intend to follow Route 279 to Corran, you can turn to it here.

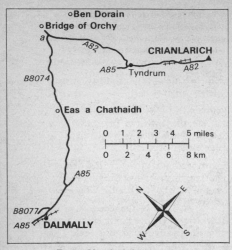

Ben Dorain
Bridge of Orchy
a
A82
CRIANLARICH
A85
Tyndrum   A82
B8074
Eas a Chathaidh

0 1 2 3 4 5 miles
0 2 4 6 8 km

A85

B8077
A85 DALMALLY

Eas a Chathaidh By the Forestry Commission bridge over the river are waterfalls where strangely eroded rocks may be seen if the water is low. Glen Orchy is famed for fishing. In the 1820s speculators cleared the valley of its Scots pines for sixpence (6d.) a tree.

Dalmally Links with Routes 258, 259.

Route 279   43 miles 69 km
CORRAN — CRIANLARICH

OS 1:250 000 no. 4
Bartholomew's 1:100 000 nos 48; 47 or 50
OS 1:50 000 nos 41, 50

Corran Links with Routes 267, 268.

Ardgour See Route 267.

a If the next route you intend to follow is the alternative version of Route 267 to Spean Bridge, you can turn to it here.

Onich To the south of the village is Clach a'Charra, a perforated monolith.

North Ballachulish The bridge was opened only in 1975. The alternative to the ferry was a long detour around the head of Loch Leven.

South Ballachulish The area is one of much devastation from slate-quarrying. The first quarry opened in 1761. South of the main road is an inclined ramp and

arch. The Scottish Episcopal church has one of the few Gaelic prayer books

Glencoe Village A thatched cruck cottage houses a folk museum which includes relics of the Jacobite Rebellion and Bonnie Prince Charlie.

Leacantuim Glencoe YH.

Clachaig Hotel Nearby is the Signal Rock, from which, early on 13 February 1692, the Campbells were signalled to attack their hosts, the MacDonalds, resulting in the Massacre of Glen Coe.

Glen Coe Probably deriving its name from the Gaelic for 'narrow glen', this spectacular valley hemmed in by towering mountains is a favourite amongst walkers and rock-climbers.

b If you are following this route towards Crianlarich, you can follow a rough-stuff route over Rannoch Moor which involves about 2 miles (3 km) of walking and about 5 miles (8 km) of careful cycling over bumpy terrain, but which allows you to experience the grandeur of the moor away from the noise of traffic. From the A82 take the lane for White Corries. At Blackrock Cottage, fork left from the road onto a track. Do not go left to the other cottage. Soon, where the track forks in two, go left. Pass to the left of a cairn by the summit, then descend to pass to the left of Ba Cottage ruin. Cross the lovely arch of Ba Bridge then, after a further 3 miles (5 km) do not fork left by the trees but continue on the more gentle slope obliquely downhill. You should allow at the very least two and a half hours for this track, and you should be equipped with a 1:50 000 map, compass and spare food.

White Corries A championship ski-centre.

Rannoch Moor This large area of heather and peat bog with myriads of tiny lochs is one of Scotland's bleakest places. Part of it is now a nature reserve.

Ba Bridge Before improved road engineering enabled the present A82 to be built higher up the moor to the east, several roads had crossed Rannoch Moor roughly along the lines of this old road, and Ba Bridge testifies to the elegance and endurance of the building. Ba Corrie to the west, said to be Scotland's largest corrie, was used in medieval times for hunting, the deer being driven into the corrie for the kill.

Victoria Bridge Some of the Scots pines around Loch Tulla and in the area generally are remnants of the ancient Caledonian Forest.

c If you are following this route towards Corran, you can follow a rough-stuff route over Rannoch Moor which involves about 5 miles (8 km) of careful cycling over bumpy terrain and about 2 miles (3 km) of walking over an unrideable descent, and which allows you to experience the grandeur of the moor away from the noise of traffic. At Victoria Bridge continue through the gate with the 'Road Closed' order on it. Follow the track obliquely up the hill, then levelling out to proceed to Ba Bridge. Continue to pass to the right of Ba Cottage ruin, and further uphill to pass to the right of a cairn at the summit, after which descend to the lane. You should allow at the very least two and a half hours for this track, and you should be equipped with a 1:50 000 map, compass and spare food.

Bridge of Orchy and **Ben Dorain** See Route 278.

d If you next intend to follow Route 278 to Dalmally, turn to it here.

Crianlarich Links with Routes 277, 278, 280.

Route 280   44 miles   71 km
CRIANLARICH — CALLANDER

OS 1:250 000 nos 3 or 4
Bartholomew's 1:100 000 no. 48
1 inch:1 mile Loch Lomond/Trossachs tourist map
OS 1:50 000 nos 50 (just), 56, 57 (excluding 56 and including 51 for the alternative route)

Total distance using the alternative route is 30 miles or 48 km.

Both routes shown are scenic, but the main route explores the Trossachs which has long

been an area of acclaimed beauty, and which, together with Loch Lomond, is favoured by Glaswegians for weekend trips. The main route involves a ferry which is seasonal only, whereas the shorter alternative is independent of ferries.

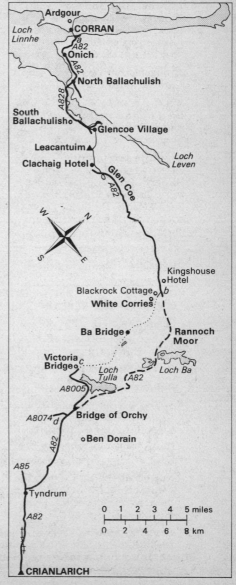

Crianlarich Links with Routes 277, 278, 279.

Rob Roy's Cave A cave on a steep hillside which was a refuge for Rob Roy MacGregor.

Inversnaid Garrison After the 1715 Rising a garrison was built here. It was burnt in the Rising of '45, after which it was incorporated into the farm that today bears its name.

Stronachlachar Views over Loch Katrine at its less frequented end.

a   A forestry track goes around the north side of Loch Katrine. Permission to cycle it must be obtained from the Forestry Commission (see Appendix 7).

Aberfoyle A centre for the Queen Elizabeth Forest Park, in which the Forestry Commission have laid out walks. Sir Walter Scott often stayed at the Old Manse. The ruined church has graves with cast iron mort safes to thwart body snatchers.

b   If you next intend to follow Route 281 to Glasgow, you can turn to it here.

Inchmahome A priory on a loch island, which can be reached by seasonal ferry from Port of Menteith (DoE, open).

Quarry The now disused Aberfoyle quarries at one time produced nearly 1.5 million slates yearly.

Loch Katrine This is the lake of Walter Scott's *The Lady of the Lake.* Its water is sent to Glasgow through a 34-mile (55-km) underground aqueduct. There are steamer trips on the lake.

The Trossachs The beauty of this area has long been acclaimed, especially since it has featured in the writings of Sir Walter Scott and William Wordsworth.

c   If you next intend to follow Route 277 to Dunkeld, you can turn to it here.

Lochearnhead This village came into

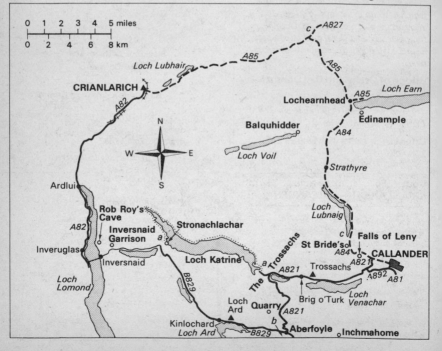

being as the important meeting place of roads and the railway, the latter no longer there.

Edinample A 17th-century castellated lochside castle.

Balquhidder The scenic Braes of Balquhidder. The valley was a haunt of Rob Roy, and he was buried in one of the two churches c.1740.

St Bride's The chapel features in Walter Scott's *The Legend of Montrose*.

Falls of Leny Both the Pass and the Falls of Leny are tourist beauty spots.

Callander See Route 281. Also links with Route 282.

Route 281   33 miles   53 km
CALLANDER — GLASGOW

OS 1:250 000 nos 3 or 4
Bartholomew's 1:100 000 no. 45
OS 1:50 000 nos 64, 57
1 inch:1 mile Loch Lomond/Trossachs tourist map

This route serves to link Glasgow with the Highlands, and in so doing necessitates the use of some busy roads between Lennox-town and Glasgow.

Callander A resort for visiting the Trossachs, and near tourist beauty spots including the Falls of Bracklinn, Pass of Leny and Falls of Leny. It has some Regency buildings. Links with Routes 280, 282.

a The alternative route explores the Trossachs, for long an area of acclaimed beauty, and favoured among Glaswegians for weekend trips. The main route is more direct and less hilly.

Falls of Leny, The Trossachs, Loch Katrine, Quarry, Aberfoyle and **Inchmahome** See Route 280.

b If you wish to take the main route of Route 280 to Crianlarich, join it here.

Culcreuch Tower A 16th-century keep.

Loup of Fintry A fine waterfall on Endrick Water.

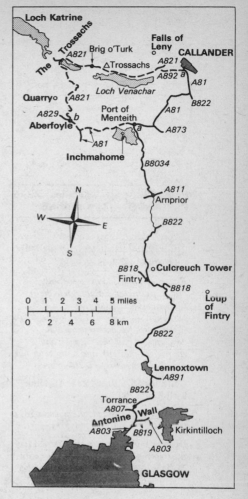

Lennoxtown The town grew with the introduction of calico printing at the end of the 18th century.

Antonine Wall Little remains now of the wall of turf and clay constructed to keep out the Picts when Antonius Pius was Emperor of Rome. It ran for 37 miles (59 km), between Bo'ness in the east and Bowling in the west.

Glasgow See Route 194. Also links with Route 193.

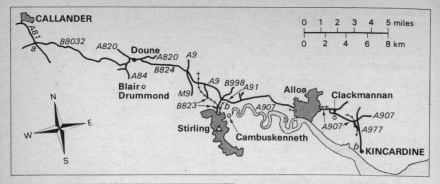

Route 282   30 miles   48 km
CALLANDER — KINCARDINE

OS 1:250 000 nos 3 or 4
Bartholomew's 1:100 000 no. 45
OS 1:50 000 nos 57, 58, 65 (just)

*Routes 282 and 283 are essentially
practical, linking Edinburgh to the
Western Highlands, rather than of
particular scenic merit. The closeness of the
River Forth has both restricted the
development of a lane network and
encouraged industry, and so the route has
significant stretches of built-up areas.*

Callander See Route 281. Also links
with Route 280.

*a If you next intend to follow Route 281 to
Glasgow, you can turn to it here.*

Doune The town was once famed for
the making of pistols. The 14th-century
castle is in good repair; it used to be a
Royal Palace (open). Doune Park
Gardens, including walled and rose
gardens and woodland walks date from
the 19th century (open).

Blair Drummond Safari Park.

Stirling Royal Stirling Castle, dramatically sited above a basalt cliff,
contains the headquarters and museum
of the Argyll and Sutherland Highlanders (DoE, open). Old buildings in
the city include the Guildhall, Argyll's
Lodging (DoE), Mar's Wark (DoE,
open), King's Knot (DoE, open) and
the 15th-century church of Holy Rood.
A mercat cross; Stirling Old Bridge
(DoE, open).

Cambuskenneth Abbey ruins (DoE,
open).

*b A quieter way between Stirling and
Kincardine is via the A876 and A905
south of the River Forth, and missing both
Alloa and Clackmannan.*

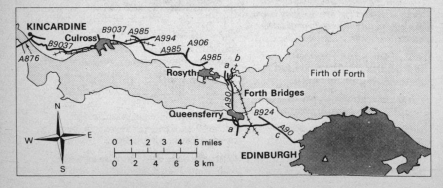

Alloa A busy industrial centre. Interesting buildings are a 15th-century tower, a 17th-century ruined kirk and its yard, and 19th-century Alloa House.

Clackmannan The town has some good examples of restored domestic architecture, clock tower (DoE, open), and 17th-century tolbooth bell tower. The Kings Stone or 'Clack Mannan' is in the main street. Burgh cross.

Kincardine See Route 283.

Route 283　　　27 miles　43 km
KINCARDINE — EDINBURGH

OS 1:250 000 nos 3 or 4
Bartholomew's 1:100 000 no. 45
OS 1:50 000 nos 65, 66

See comments Route 282.

Kincardine Birthplace of Sir James Dewar, inventor of the vacuum flask. Links with Route 282.

Culross The NTS, the DoE, local bodies and individuals have worked for forty five years to restore and preserve this village as a living survival of early Scottish domestic architecture. Interesting buildings include Bishop Leighton's House, and The Study and Town House (both NTS, open). Culross Palace has fine wall ceiling paintings (DoE, open). The Abbey is the remains of a Cistercian monastery (DoE, open). Dunimarle museum.

Rosyth Rosyth Castle (DoE).

a When approaching the Forth Road Bridge, look out for signs directing you to the cycle-path which runs alongside the motor road on the bridge, and which you must use.

b If you next intend to follow Route 236 to Rumbling Bridge, turn to it here.

Forth Bridges and **Queensferry** See Route 236.

c If you next intend to follow Route 193 to Glasgow, you can turn to it here.

Edinburgh See Route 122. Also links with Routes 123, 192, 193, 236.

Route 284　　　79 miles　126 km
STORNOWAY — STORNOWAY

OS 1:250 000 no. 1
Bartholomew's 1:100 000 no. 57
OS 1:50 000 no. 8

Stornoway An important fishing port, centre of the Harris Tweed industry and largest town in the Outer Hebrides. The herring fishing fleet is much reduced in size nowadays, and the town is looking to the oil industry. Lewis Castle was built in 1840 and given to the town by Lord Leverhulme. He bought the island after the First World War, but his efforts to modify the crofting way of life and modernize the industries were not successful. A monument at the harbour entrance commemorates an attempt by Bonnie Prince Charlie to buy a boat here. Links with Route 285.

a Ferries run from Stornoway to Ullapool on the Scottish mainland.

St Columba's Church Some 14th-century ruins with monuments including tombs of the Macleods.

Tiumpan Head Rocky coast scenery and a lighthouse. Extensive views of the mainland.

b The detour to the Butt of Lewis and back to this road junction covers 35 miles (56 km) altogether.

Barvas During the Napoleonic Wars the minister encouraged locals to reclaim the barren soils by applications of powdered sea shells and seaweed. More recently chemicals have been used, and much barren moorland throughout the Hebrides has been reseeded with grass.

Ballantrushal Just south west of the lane running through Ballantrushal towards the coast is the notable 18 foot (5·5 m) Thrushel Stone.

Steinacleit This neolithic cairn and stone circle (DoE) can be found to the south-east of Loch an Duin.

Butt of Lewis Rocky cliff scenery, fine views and a lighthouse.

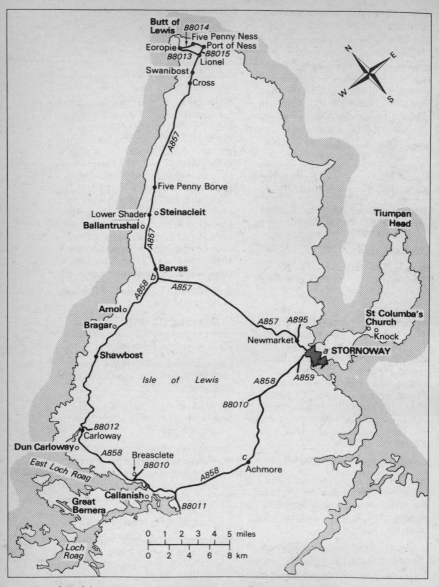

Arnol A traditional 'black house' is preserved as a museum here (DoE, open). In order to stand up to the severe weather these houses were built with thick drystone walls, no chimney, a small door, and often no windows.

Bragar A whalebone arch about 20 feet (6 m) high stands here, with the harpoon which killed the whale.

Shawbost Harris tweed is produced here. In a disused church is a museum created by children illustrating the traditional life of Lewis.

Dun Carloway An exceptionally well preserved Iron Age broch (DoE). It was built by Picts or Celts, some of the earliest inhabitants of the islands, as a defensive site against Roman slave traders or Norsemen.

Callanish This famous group of standing stones (DoE) is regarded as the most remarkable antiquity in the Western Isles, and of its kind second only to Stonehenge. It was probably erected by a pre-Celtic race of Iberian stock 2000–1500 BC and used for sun-worship.

Great Bernera A bridge to the island was built in 1953 after locals threatened to blow up the cliffs to create a causeway. The island is known for its lobster fishing.

c If you next intend to follow Route 285 to Tarbert, you can take the lane south east and join it when you reach the A859.

Stornoway See above.

Route 285   34 miles   54 km
STORNOWAY — TARBERT

OS 1:250 000 no. 1
Bartholomew's 1:100 000 no. 57
OS 1:50 000 nos 8, 14

Stornoway See Route 284.

a Ferries run from Stornoway to Ullapool on the Scottish mainland.

Clisham At 2622 feet (874 m) this is the highest peak in the Outer Hebrides.

Ardhasig Remains of a whaling station set up by Lord Leverhulme.

b If you next intend to follow Route 284 in a clockwise direction to Stornoway, you can take the lane north west from here and join it at Achmore.

c A scenic ride can be made along the coast to Kyles Scalpay.

d Ferries run from Tarbert to Uig on the Isle of Skye, and to Lochmaddy on North

Uist where Route 287 can be joined. Taking the latter ferry is an alternative to following Route 286.

Tarbert Links with Route 286.

Route 286   29 miles   46 km
TARBERT — LOCHMADDY

OS 1:250 000 no. 1
Bartholomew's 1:100 000 nos 53, 57
OS 1:50 000 nos 18, 14

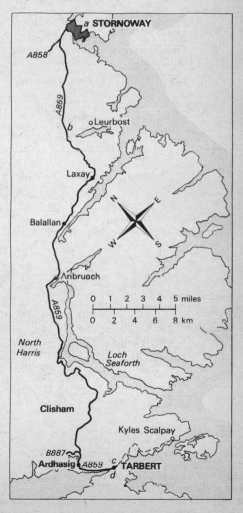

This route requires the use of a seasonal ferry between Leverburgh and Newton-ferry. You have the option of bypassing this route by taking the ferry which runs between Tarbert and Lochmaddy.

Tarbert Links with Route 285.

a Ferries run from Tarbert to Uig on the Isle of Skye, and to Lochmaddy on North Uist where Route 287 can be joined.

b A scenic ride can be made along the coast to Kyles Scalpay.

Borve Lodge Once the home of Lord Leverhulme.

Chaipaval Good views from the top of this hill.

Leverburgh Lord Leverburgh attemp-

ted to turn this village into a major port, building a pier, houses, kippering sheds, lighthouses and roads, and changing its name from Obba to Leverburgh. However, he died in 1925 soon after building was completed, and the scheme came to nothing.

c A ferry plies between Leverburgh, the island of Bernera and Newtonferry.

Rodel Notable for St Clement's Church with its richly carved interior (DoE), built in 1500 by the 8th Chief of the MacLeods whose tomb is inside. It has associations with Iona Cathedral. The key is obtainable from the hotel.

Berneray It is said that this island was once linked to Pabay, before a great

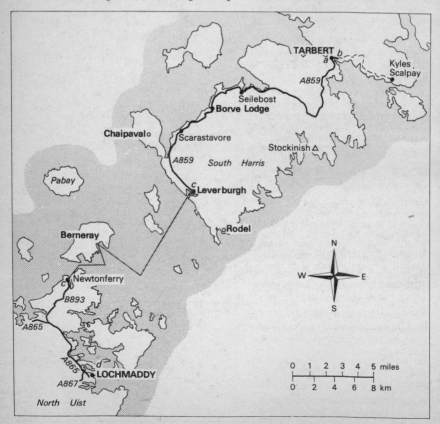

storm in the 16th century swept away some lowland, so separating the islands.

d Ferries run from Lochmaddy to Uig on the Isle of Skye, and Tarbert on Harris where Routes 285 and 286 can be joined.

Lochmaddy See Route 287.

Route 287   41 miles   65 km
LOCHMADDY — LOCHBOISDALE

OS 1:250 000 no. 1
Bartholomew's 1:100 000 no. 53
OS 1:50 000 nos 18, 22, 31

This route does not require the use of ferries—all the islands are linked by bridges.

Lochmaddy The main town and port of North Uist, once an important fishing and curing station. Links with Route 286.

a Ferries run from Lochmaddy to Uig on the Isle of Skye, and Tarbert on Harris where Routes 285 and 286 can be joined.

North Lee, South Lee There are fine views from the tops of these hills over the lochans and islands of North Uist, and across the Little Minch to Skye. Only venture onto the hills in good weather, and with suitable equipment.

Langass Barp A chambered cairn on the north-west slope of Ben Langass.

Carinish The ruined temple of Carinish dates from the 14th to 16th century.

Eaval Excellent panoramic views from the hill. Only attempt an ascent in good weather and with suitable equipment.

Bailivanish The principal community on Benbecula, which has largely grown because of the nearby airfield and rocket range.

Rueval Superb views from the top of this hill.

Borve Castle Now in ruins, but once the stronghold of the chiefs of Benbecula.

Eochar A 'Black House' Museum with relics of Bonnie Prince Charlie.

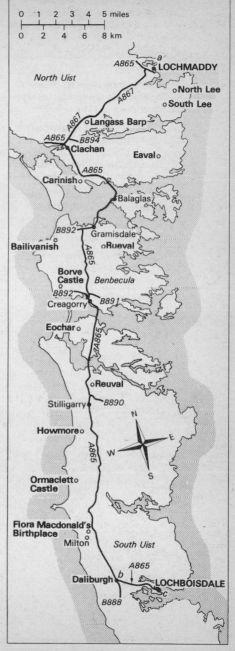

Reuval The 30-foot (9-m) marble statue of 'Our Lady of the Isles' stands on this rocky hill, and is a landmark for seafarers.

Howmore Burial ground of the chiefs of Clanranald.

Ormaclett Castle This castle was occupied for only seven years before it was burnt down in 1715.

Flora Macdonald's Birthplace A memorial cairn marks the site. It was from South Uist that Bonnie Prince Charlie, disguised as Flora Macdonald's maid, took a small boat for Skye.

Daliburgh About one mile (1½ km) to the south-west is a Pictish Wheel.

b If you next intend to follow Route 288 to Castlebay, you can turn to it here.

c Ferries run from Lochboisdale to Oban on the Scottish mainland, and to Castlebay on Barra to join Route 288.

Lochboisdale See Route 288.

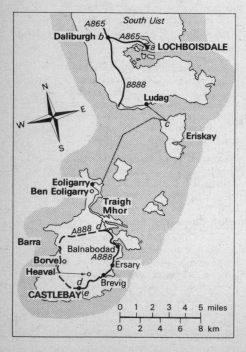

Route 288   17 miles   27 km
LOCHBOISDALE — CASTLEBAY

OS 1:250 000 no. 1
Bartholomew's 1:100 000 no. 53
OS 1:50 000 no. 31

This route uses a privately owned ferry between Ludag and Eoligarry. If cycling north to south, an alternative route is to take the ferry from Lochboisdale to Castlebay and then to cycle around Barra on the A888. If cycling south to north, the alternative is to cycle around Barra, return to Castlebay, and then take the ferry to Lochboisdale.

Lochboisdale A small port, 'capital' of South Uist. Links with Route 287.

a Ferries run from Lochboisdale to Oban on the Scottish mainland, and to Castlebay on Barra.

Daliburgh See Route 287.

b If you next intend to follow Route 287 to Lochmaddy, you can turn to it here.

Ludag Good views to Barra and Eriskay.

Eriskay Bonnie Prince Charlie first set foot on Scottish soil here in 1744, having arrived from France to precipitate the '45 Rising. The small, pink sea-bindweed found on Prince's Strand is said to have grown from seeds which fell from the Prince's pockets after landing. In 1941 the ship 'Politicia' ran aground off the island with a cargo of whisky, the subsequent events which took place being the basis of Compton Mackenzie's comic novel *Whisky Galore*. The island is known for its Gaelic melodies. In St Michael's Church is a ship's bell recovered from the German battleship 'Derflinger', sunk at Scapa Flow in the Orkney Isles.

c Ferries link Eriskay with South Uist and Barra.

Eoligarry Several carved slabs can be seen at ruined Cille-Bharra, once the church of St Barr.

Ben Eoligarry A fine viewpoint.

Traigh Mhor This broad stretch of sand is the island's airfield when the tide is out.

d The main route follows the eastern coast of Barra, while the slightly longer alternative route visits the west coast with its fine sandy beaches.

Borve The bays of this coastline have fine sandy beaches.

Heaval Panoramic views from the top of this 1260-foot (380-m) hill.

Barra The island is thought to have been named after St Finbarr of Cork, who came from Ireland to convert the islanders to Christianity in the 6th–7th century.

e Ferries run from Castlebay to Oban on the Scottish mainland, and to Lochbois-dale on South Uist.

Castlebay The main town of Barra. On a rocky island just offshore stands romantic Kisimul castle, the ancient seat of the MacNeil's who once owned Barra and the surrounding islands. It has many legends, and dates from the 11th century. Links to Oban by ferry with Routes 257 and 258.

Route 289   107 miles   171 km
STROMNESS — STROMNESS

OS 1:250 000 no. 1
Bartholomew's 1:100 000 no. 61
OS 1:50 000 nos 6, 7

This route of two circuits, one to the east and one to the west of Kirkwall, could be started and finished at Burwick on the island of South Ronaldsay just as reasonably as at Stromness. Both are ferry ports for the Scottish mainland.

The Island of Mainland is explored on this route but many of the other, smaller islands have their attractions. Some are large enough to merit cycling, others not. Enquire locally about inter-island ferries.

Stromness A port for ships to Scotland and the Baltic which gained in importance in the mid-17th century.

Parts of it are laid out in the Norse fashion, several houses having private jetties. The Orkney Natural History Museum includes exhibits of Orkney bygones and shipping.

a Ferries run between Stromness and Thurso on the north coast of the Scottish mainland.

Hoy The heather-clad island of Hoy is much hillier than any of the other islands of Orkney, and its name means 'The High Island'. It is rich in rare wild plants.

Dwarfie Stane The impressive neolithic tomb (DoE) has been hollowed out of a single great rock. It is unique in Britain.

St John's Head Rising to 1140 feet (350 m), these are the highest perpendicular cliffs in Britain.

Old Man of Hoy A gaunt 450-foot (140-m) tall sandstone pillar stands isolated from the nearby cliffs. It is renowned for its spectacular appearance and as a challenge to the most expert of rock climbers.

Murra Hoy YH.

Skara Brae The hut foundations of a Stone Age village, built between 2500 and 2000 BC, have been excavated to reveal many domestic details such as beds, cupboards and cooking utensils. The site (DoE) contains much to interest the public.

Marwick Head The cliffs here form an important sea-bird colony. The tower is a memorial to the War Minister, Lord Kitchener, who died on a sinking ship in 1916.

Brough of Birsay The Brough is a tidal island (DoE). On it and the opposite shore of Mainland are a wealth of interesting buildings; remains from the 8th and 9th century Christian times and the following Norse era. This was the seat of Thorfinn the Mighty, who ruled all the northern and western isles and a large part of mainland Scotland, and there are remains of his hall (DoE, open) and cathedral church. Viking longhouses. An impressive 16th-century palace has been renovated.

Gurness Iron Age broch (DoE).

Eynhallow Sound At times there is a tidal race through the sound.

Rousay Hillier than all the other Orkney islands except Hoy, Rousay has some good cliff walks in the north and west, and some fine remains from the

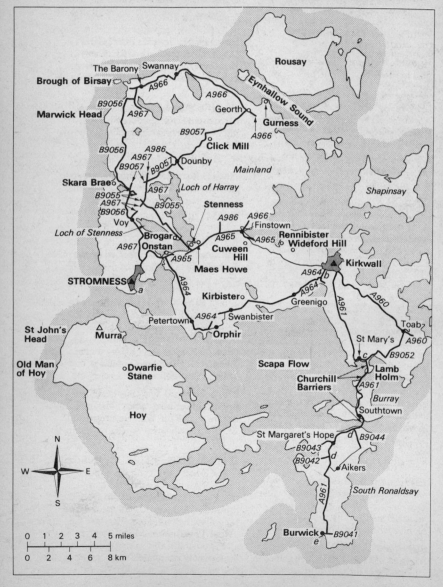

Stone and Iron Ages.

Click Mill In the care of the DoE and open to visitors.

Brogar The tallest stone in this Bronze Age ring (DoE) stands at 15 feet (5·5 m), and is considered by some as Britain's most impressive megalithic monument after Stonehenge.

Stenness Bronze Age stone circle (DoE).

Maes Howe One of Britain's most awesome prehistoric remains, this great burial chamber was built around 2000 BC with superbly worked stone blocks (DoE). Nearly three millennia later some Norsemen sheltering from the weather engraved a wealth of runic inscriptions on its walls.

Cuween Hill Chambered cairn (DoE).

Rennibister Prehistoric earth house (DoE, open).

Wideford Hill Chambered cairn (DoE).

Kirkwall This was the chief seat of the Norse rulers of Orkney from the 9th to the 15th centuries, and the town has many buildings in the Scandinavian style. The 12th-century Romanesque cathedral is named after St Magnus, the Earl of Orkney who was martyred on the island of Egilsay. Ruins of the 12th-century Bishop's Palace (DoE, open). Earl Patrick's Palace (DoE, open) is a fine example of Renaissance architecture. Northwest of the town is the prehistoric Grain Earth House (DoE, open).

b The east and west circuits of this route can be done independently. The western

circuit is 63 miles (101 km) long, and the eastern one 44 miles (71 km) long.

c The route can be cycled without the dead-end detour between Lamb Holm and Burwick, in which case the distance is shortened by 27 miles (43 km).

Scapa Flow This large expanse of virtually land-locked water was the main anchorage for Britain's fleet in both World Wars, although German submarines managed to penetrate it once in each war. Now it enjoys renewed importance as an oil terminal.

Churchill Barriers Constructed from thousands of concrete blocks at the orders of Sir Winston Churchill, the barriers were intended to improve the safety of the Scapa Flow anchorage.

Lamb Holm Some of the Italian prisoners of war who were employed on the Churchill Barrier constructed themselves a chapel from Nissen hut scraps. The chapel has a beautiful interior with freehand painting.

d You can follow one side of the small St Margaret's Hope and Aikers road loop when proceeding south, and the other side when proceeding north.

e Seasonal ferries run between Burwick and John O'Groats on the north-east coast of the Scottish mainland.

Kirbister This ancient name meaning 'church farm' testifies to the Christianity of Orkney before the Norse invasion.

Orphir St Nicholas' ancient Church and the Earl's Bu (both DoE, open).

Onstan Chambered cairn (DoE).

Stromness See above.

EIRE AND NORTHERN IRELAND

Ireland's nickname, Emerald Isle, is most truly earnt by its central lowlands. Here a gentle scenery of green fields is interrupted by an occasional lone hill or small mountain ridge. Set around the lowlands is a broken coastal ring of more barren landscape, where mountains alternate with bog, rocky wastes and pockets of poor farmland. A striking feature of Ireland's mountains is that they often rise quite abruptly from the surrounding lowland as isolated peaks or small groups. Their gaunt or rounded shapes can be admired from afar, and cyclists will appreciate the way in which roads skirt round their sides to give mountain inspiration without the perspiration. (A few stiff passes do break this rule.) Virtually only in Wicklow, Mourne and Kerry do the Irish highlands take the form of a great block divided by deep valleys. Here there will be ups and downs, but by and large cycling in Ireland is fairly on the level.

The coast offers plenty of variety: sand-dunes, rocky inlets and Europe's highest cliffs where the mountains of Donegal and Mayo meet the sea. In fact the mountainous coastal areas of Wicklow, Kerry, Clare, Connemara, Mayo, Donegal and also Antrim have long been favourite cycle-touring areas. Inland, many hollows in the undulating lowlands have loughs: Lough Neagh is the largest lake in the British Isles. The bogs, very much a part of the Irish scene, cover both mountain and lowland expanses. Turfs cut from trenches in the peat are stacked near the roadside, ready to be transported home for fuel.

Although the sun can shine with clear brightness in Ireland it has to be admitted that it is not renowned for doing so. The Irish will greet you with a friendly 'Soft Day', when dampness in the air blurs the view. Remember that the east side is sunnier and that the downpours which drive you to shelter also give Ireland its lush fields and hedgerows. The rainclouds are blown inland by frequent strong west or south-west winds.

Dublin, Belfast, Cork and Limerick are the only cities of substantial size. Towns are neither numerous nor large, serving just as necessary market centres, functional but often drab. The clustering village is rare, a much commoner sight being that of houses and cottages sprinkled generously over a wide area. The search for shops, pubs and post offices in these scattered settlements can become something of a treasure hunt. As they are often in the rooms of private houses it is easy to miss them, and asking their whereabouts is a good excuse to get chatting to the locals. On one such occasion, the cyclists stopped before a small cluster of houses to ask directions for the village of Skibereen. The answer came 'It's all full o' Skibereen round here', rendered in the delightful local accent.

Map reading can be made tricky by the loose-knit villages as they are not easy to mark accurately. Precisely where within a settlement the place name is put on the map is a matter of choice, and in many cases the OS and Bartholomew's series differ. Moreover, the two series have quite often chosen the names of different parts of a settlement, and so a village on the Bartholomew's map may have both a different location and a different name on the OS map. Thus the route maps will sometimes show places which are not found on one or other of the commercial map series, but with care the route can still be followed. Even if you do get confused, the locals will set you on the right road with a smile. More unfortunately, the two series also differ with regard to certain road numbers and the shape of lanes. These discrepancies are noted in the route texts wherever they might cause a problem.

Ireland is full of relics from its unique history, the earliest being the varied and sometimes very impressive stone tomb-chambers and man-made islands or 'crannogs'. The Hill of Tara, ancient capital of Ireland, is particularly rich in remains. The Celts in Ireland were left unmolested in the earlier centuries AD and Celtic Christianity flourished, producing distinctive styles. The monastery, rather than the bishop's see and its cathedral, was the most important religious power. In exploring monastic ruins you will find vivid clues to the early Celtic Christians in the finely carved high crosses and the detached, fortified belfries called round towers. The small size of many Irish cathedrals will remind you that the bishoprics were weak compared to their European counterparts.

Of the large number of dots on Irish maps marked 'castle' some indeed represent grand or defensive structures, but many are simply country mansions. Several times in the past British monarchs tried to enhance their power in Ireland by encouraging English and Scottish settlement of land taken from the Irish. This tactic was called 'the Plantation'.

You will be able to explore many interesting buildings and ruins without let or hindrance. Those marked 'NM' usually have unrestricted visiting.

Border

N
W   E
S

BALLYCASTLE
351
352
DUNFANAGHY
348   349
DUNGIVEN
CARRICKFERGUS
DOOCHARRY   RAPHOE
362
350
353
347   DONEGAL
Political
boundary
363
354   DUNDRUM
346   ENNISKILLEN
SLIGO
NEWRY
364
328   345
BARNATRA   365   DUNDALK
BALLINA   357   CAVAN
326   329   BOYLE   356   358
327   MALLARANNY   361   KELLS   DROGHEDA
326   360
WESTPORT   359
325   DUBLIN
330   KILLUCAN   335
ATHLONE   334   340
CLIFDEN   KILCONNELL   LARAGH
324   SCREEB   332   333   336   337
323   GALWAY   344   ARKLOW
322   MOUNTRATH   341
KINVARRA   343   CARLOW
321   331   312   342   339
ENNISTIMON   313   KILKENNY   338
CLARECASTLE   316   HOLYCROSS   311   ENNISCORTHY
320   317   DONOHILL   314   310
KILKEE   318   LIMERICK   315   307   ROSSLARE
319   304   301   CLONMEL   308   HARBOUR
ARDAGH   WATERFORD   309   DUNCORMICK
303   306
TRALEE   BALLYHOOLY   305
302   KILLORGLIN   MILLSTREET   300
294   296   299   CORK
295   DINGLE   KILLARNEY   298
297   KENMARE   290
293   292
BANTRY
291   ROSS CARBERY

0   10   20   30   40   50 miles
0   20   40   60   80 km

Those marked 'open' are so in a more organized and fee-exacting fashion. But in Ireland if you wish to see something then just go ahead, asking permission and guidance locally.

The friendliness of the Irish is a legend based on truth as you will discover whatever your type of accommodation. There are large distances between official campsites, so if you do opt to camp you will have to ask permission to do so on people's land. You are sure to meet with much helpfulness. Most youth hostels are open all year round and they tend to be simpler and more informal than those in England. Bed and breakfast accommodation is plentiful in the tourist and scenic mountain areas. Do tap the local grapevine for news of folk-singing evenings. In some areas called the Gaeltacht the exclusive use of the Irish language is being encouraged, although you will always be able to find people who speak English. But in these areas the roads signs are in Gaelic only, and although their meanings are usually obvious from their positions and symbols, take extra care.

The Irish island is divided between the independent country of Eire and Northern Ireland, the latter being part of the United Kingdom. Because of the troubles in Northern Ireland (sometimes called Ulster) there are restrictions with regard to crossing the border between the two countries. Minor roads at the border are spiked and you are strongly recommended to stick to using the official crossings. All the relevant routes in this book use such border posts (though the situation could change). Information about others is available from the Irish Tourist Boards.

Donegal in the north west shows Ireland at its most rugged. Hills and mountains rise with impressive abruptness from the narrow coastal plain which meets the sea in a rocky and broken coastline. The plain is lively, dotted with the homes of cottage farmers, some of them the traditional whitewashed cottages. Despite its green pastures Donegal gives an impression of barrenness: there are few sheltering trees and the white rock breaks through the ground.

Travelling east from Donegal you first come to the border between Eire and Northern Ireland and so to the fertile valley of the river Foyle; then to the rounded, thinly populated Sperrin Mountains before dropping to prosperous farmlands around the river Bann and Lough Neagh. In the heyday of the Irish linen industry this was the chief flax-growing area.

In the Antrim Plateau in the north east is scenery unique to Ireland. Most famed is the Giant's Causeway where the sea breaks over dark columns of basalt rock. Inland, the plateau is an open, gently rising and falling moorland, broken in places by the Glens of Antrim which are renowned for their beauty, their upper slopes topped by sheer cliffs of dark basalt.

Stretching over most of Ireland's width, roughly from Sligo and the Northern Ireland border down to Galway, Slieve Bloom and Dublin, the central lowlands spread out—a flat patchwork of fields relieved now and then by bog, woodland, low hills or winding ridges. West of the river Shannon the area becomes gradually less fertile, the hedges give way to stone walls and small patches of bare limestone break the ground, until low but impressive jagged ridges of hills appear.

Although too small an area for extensive touring, the rounded Mountains of Mourne are attractive, their tops covered in heather moorland and grazed by hardy sheep, and below deep valleys farmed or planted with conifers.

Just south of Dublin lie the Wicklow Mountains. They are the biggest compact group of highland in Ireland, though in many respects they are similar to the Mountains of Mourne. They do have long and steep gradients, and some of the country's most luxuriant woodland. Easily accessible, both to the Irish via trains to Dublin and to the British via the port of Dun Laoghaire, the Wicklow Mountains are large enough to provide a week's tour.

To the west of the central lowlands lie the barren peninsulas of Connemara and Mayo. Both follow the pattern of a core of mountains rising from great expanses of flat land so that their shapes haunt the landscape from afar. Riding towards Connemara's Twelve Bens over the plains you pass many small loughs. In Mayo you will find the impressive monotony of Ireland's biggest bog below the Nephin Mountains. There are vast uninhabited areas though where conditions are right houses and old-style cottages are thickly scattered.

County Clare is mostly lowland but it has a strong atmosphere of the untamed. There are the superb sheer Cliffs of Moher and, especially in the west, large wild expanses of land where moorland is broken by limestone rocks and abrupt, flat-topped hills. This sparsely inhabited area culminates in the eroded and almost lunar landscape of the Burren near Ennistimmon; its harsh beauty has won admiration from George Bernard Shaw down to many a humble cycle-tourist.

South of the central lowland, much of Ireland is a pattern of rough land atop broad hill ridges alternating with wide tongues of fertile lowland, the 'grain' running roughly east–west. The south coast has some pleasant winding estuaries, and west of Cork are some attractive headlands and inlets. Caught between the Wicklow Mountains and the coast is the 'Garden of Ireland'.

In the south west, Kerry combines the fertile and the rugged, and in the west there is the extra pleasure of the sea near at hand and frequently in view. Projecting into the sea are rocky peninsulas with sandy bays. The coastal lanes are most scenic, as are some of the narrow roads across the peninsulas and through the mountains of Macgillycuddys Reeks with their secluded grassy valleys. But beware the main road from Bantry and the coast to Kenmare which is busy with motorists touring the 'Ring of Kerry'.

Route 290   45 miles   72 km
CORK — ROSS CARBERY

Bartholomew's ¼ inch:1 mile no. 4
OS ½ inch:1 mile nos 25, 24 (just)

Cork The city was founded in the 6th-

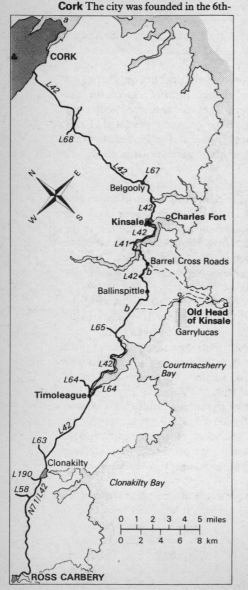

7th centuries on two islands, the name
being derived from the word for marsh.
Much of the town was destroyed by the
British in 1920. It has one of the best
natural harbours in Europe and has
grown to be a busy industrial centre and
the third largest city in Ireland. Of
particular interest are 19th-century St
Finbarr's Cathedral, St Anne's Church,
the University College, the Butter
Market and Skiddy's almshouses.
There are many pleasant Georgian
houses and walks by the river. Blackrock Castle ruins have good views.
Links with Routes 299, 300.

*a Ferries link Cork with the Welsh ports
of Fishguard and Pembroke.*

Kinsale The well-protected harbour
was once an important naval base.
Desmond Castle (NM) housed French
prisoners of war in Napoleonic times,
and there is a small museum in the 17th-
century market house. St Multose
Church dates from the 13th century.

Charles Fort Now an impressive ruin,
this fort was built around 1677.

*b The alternative route follows attractive
lanes down to the Old Head of Kinsale.*

Old Head of Kinsale On the highest
point of this spectacular headland are
the remains of a signal station dating
from the Napoleonic Wars. There are
magnificent views. At the neck of the
peninsula are the remains of a 15th-
century castle.

Timoleague Ruins of a large 14th-
century Franciscan friary (NM).

Ross Carbery The 17th-century cathedral has an interesting choir screen.
Links with Route 291.

Route 291   74 miles   119 km
BANTRY — ROSS CARBERY

Bartholomew's ¼ inch:1 mile no. 4
OS ½ inch:1 mile no. 24

Bantry A market town at the head of a
deep, safe harbour. This was once a
fishing station for the British Atlantic
fleets, but is now a huge oil terminal.

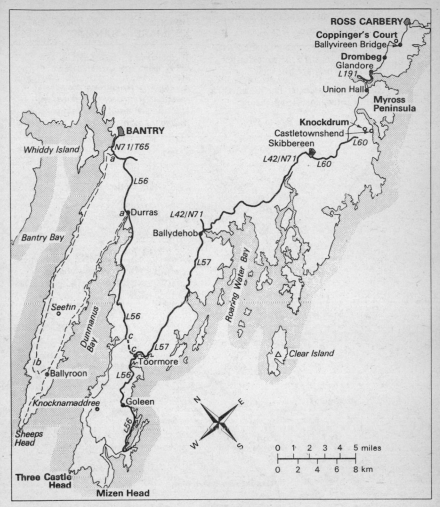

Partly Georgian Bantry House (open) has views, Italianate gardens and a unique collection of tapestries and furniture. Links with Route 292.

a The alternative route follows delightfully quiet lanes out to the end of Sheeps Head peninsula, affording fine views.

b A section of lane is not shown on the 1977 Bartholomew's map.

Three Castles Head By the small lake stands Dun Locha promontory fort.

Mizen Head The most south-westerly point in Ireland, offering superb views from the top of its towering cliffs. The lighthouse stands on a dramatic site.

c The main route continues down the peninsula, following scenic coast roads, while the alternative route cuts this out by using the L56.

Knockdrum 'The Fort' is a good example of a stone ringfort.

Myross Peninsula Daniel Corkery

called this 'one of the most secret places in Ireland'.

Drombeg A recumbent stone circle with markings. To the west is an ancient hut site. There are fine views.

Coppinger's Court The remains of a 17th-century fortified mansion.

Ross Carbery See Route 290.

Route 292   87 miles   140 km
KENMARE — BANTRY

Bartholomew's ¼ inch:1 mile no. 4
OS ½ inch:1 mile nos 24, 20 (just)

To enjoy the magnificent coastal and mountain scenery of this particularly splendid peninsula to the full, you should follow the main route all the way. How-

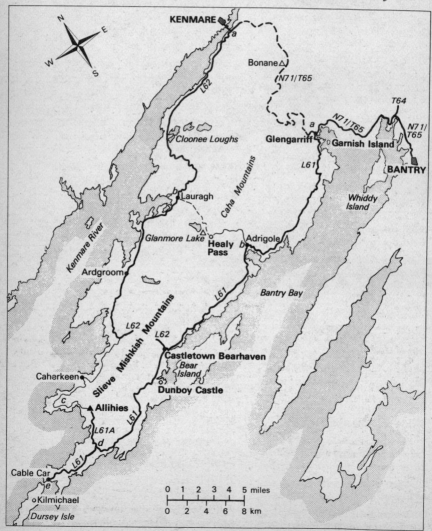

ever, of the three passes crossing the peninsula, the Healy Pass is particularly rewarding to include as a detour.

Kenmare Situated at the head of a delightful sea-lough, with good bathing nearby. The town is known for tweed and lace-making. Links with Routes 293, 297.

a The alternative route follows a tortuous mountain road involving tunnels and a profusion of wildly beautiful views. It is fair compensation should you be unable to explore the peninsula, but there will be summer holiday traffic.

b This alternative route is a worthwhile addition to the main route and useful for cutting short a tour of the peninsula.

Healy Pass There are some superb views from the crest of this 1084-foot (330-m) mountain pass.

Slieve Mishkish Mountains A popular haunt of botanists and walkers.

c The lane between Caherkeen and Allihies is shown on the Ordnance Survey map of 1977 to follow a different course.

Allihies A useful centre for exploring the end of the peninsula.

d The main route detours out to the tip of the peninsula here, from where a cable-car to Dursey Isle can be taken.

e An exhilarating ride in a cable-car suspended high over the sea takes passengers between the mainland and Dursey Isle. Before it was built, islanders had to rely on using small boats.

Dunboy Castle No roof remains on this impressive castle—the last in the south-west to fall to the Elizabethan forces during the Nine Years' War.

Castletown Bearhaven A busy fishing port.

Glengarriff A delightful place with a mild climate and luxuriant flora.

Garnish Island Exquisite gardens (open); here George Bernard Shaw wrote *St Joan*. Boats from Glengarriff.

Bantry See Route 291.

Route 293   84 miles   135 km
KILLORGLIN — KENMARE

Bartholomew's ¼ inch:1 mile no. 4
OS ½ inch:1 mile nos 20, 24

This route involves the use of a ferry between Knight's Town on Valencia Island, and the mainland.

Killorglin A market town known for its curious August Poc Fair. The central character is a large white male goat (the Poc) who presides from a high platform. Links with Routes 294, 296.

a The alternative route follows lanes south, past lakes and mountains to the delightful valley of the River Caragh.

Lough Acoose Good place for start of walks in Macgillycuddy's Reeks.

Carrauntoohill Ireland's highest mountain at 3414 feet (1040 m).

Glenbeigh A small tourist and angling resort.

Knocknadobar An ancient pilgrims' path, which passes stations of the cross, leads to the 2267-foot (691-m) summit.

Leacanabuaile A 9th- or 10th-century stone ring-fort with the remains of four dry-stone huts (NM).

Ballycarbery Castle Built in the 15th century; interesting carvings.

Cahersiveen There are a great many ancient monuments in the locality.

b The main route continues west on tiny lanes to explore the fine coast and hill scenery found at the tip of the 'Ring of Kerry'. It involves the use of a ferry. The alternative route is more direct, and uses the main road.

Knight's Town The main town on the island. This was the eastern station of the first transatlantic cable to be laid.

Bray Head Fine cliffs, rising to 800 feet (250 m).

Skellig Rocks On Great Skellig is the best preserved monastic site in Ireland. Large bird sanctuary. Boats from Waterville, Ballinskelligs or Valencia Island.

Darrynane Abbey The ancestral home of Daniel O'Connell (NM). Known as the 'Great Liberator', he was the first of the great 19th-century Irish leaders in the British House of Commons.

Caherdaniel Just to the west is a fine small stone ring-fort. A track to the north leads to the col between the mountains of Cahernageeha and Mullaghbeg; fine views.

Staigue Fort The finest preserved historic fortress in Ireland outside the Aran Isles, with elaborate stairways and 13-foot thick ramparts.

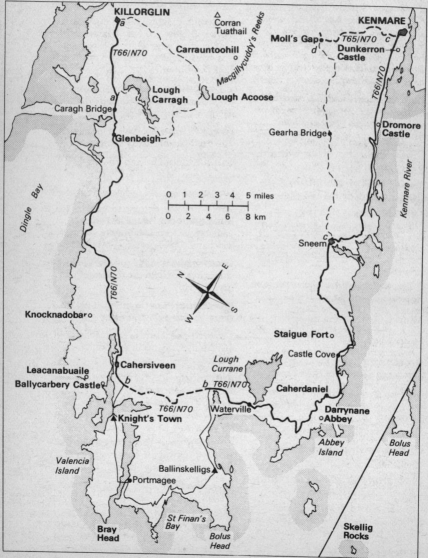

c The alternative route takes you through superb mountain scenery, while the main route follows the coast.

Moll's Gap The wonderful mountain panorama from here includes the peaks of Macgillycuddy's Reeks, and the Gap of Dunloe.

d If you next intend to follow Route 296 to Killarney, you can turn to it here.

Dromore Castle The ruins of the O'Mahony stronghold.

Dunkerron Castle The chief fortress of O'Sullivan Mor, and now in ruins.

Kenmare See Route 292. Also links with Route 297.

**Route 294   33 miles   53 km
DINGLE — KILLORGLIN**

Bartholomew's ¼ inch:1 mile no. 4
OS ½ inch:1 mile no. 20

Dingle See Route 295. Also links with Route 302.

a Boats from Dingle to the Blasket Isles.

Ballintaggert There are nine ogham stones in the ancient oval graveyard here (NM).

Aglish West of here is the 12-foot (4-metre) Aglish Boulder and dolmen.

Minard Castle This former fortress of the Knights of Kerry was ruined by the Cromwellians.

Ardcanaght At the burial ground here are two ogham stones and a Bronze Age cup and ring stone (NMs).

Castlemaine This market town is named after a castle destroyed by Cromwellians. Much trade was lost when the river Maine silted up.

Kilcolman Abbey In the corner of the grounds are the remains of Killagha priory, which was founded in 1215.

Killorglin See Route 293. Also links with Route 296.

**Route 295   37 miles   59 km
DINGLE — DINGLE**

Bartholomew's ¼ inch:1 mile no. 4
OS ½ inch:1 mile no. 20

Dingle The name of this small market town and fishing port is derived from the word for 'fortress'. This is the most westerly town in Europe. Links with Routes 294, 302.

Dunbeg A spectacular and complex promontory fort protected by cliffs and a huge drystone wall. The area has many stone forts, souterrains and clochans.

Slea Head Dramatic cliff scenery and views out to the Blasket Isles.

Great Blasket Island The largest of the group of islands and inhabited until 1953. A book called *Twenty Years Agrowing* by Maurice O'Sullivan describes life in this remote place.

Ballyferriter At nearby Reask is a beautiful late Celtic stone.

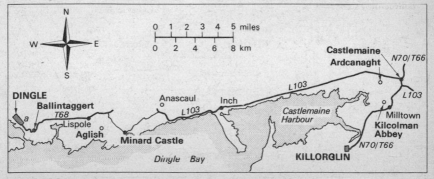

Mountain from the village.

Brandon Mountain The second highest mountain in Ireland. Just below the summit are St Brendan's Well, some ruined clochans, and the remains of St Brendan's Oratory (NMs), all associated with Brendan the Navigator (a Celtic saint and hero of legendary voyages in the Atlantic). The cross on the Oratory is made from parts of a German bomber which crashed on the mountain during the Second World War. Good walks along the ridges to Brandon Peak and Masatiompan.

Masatiompan In the col to the south of the summit of this mountain is the Brandon Monument, with incised crosses and an inscription reading 'The priest Ronann son of Comogann'.

Brandon Head Great cliffs.

Dingle See above.

Route 296   15 miles   24 km
KILLORGLIN — KILLARNEY

Bartholomew's ¼ inch:1 mile no. 4
OS ½ inch:1 mile no. 20 or 21

Killorglin See Route 293. Also links with Route 294.

Kilgobnet There is a cross slab here, on an ancient church site.

Macgillycuddy's Reeks This mountain range was the stronghold of the Macgillycuddy clan, the word 'Reeks' derived from 'rocks'.

Smerwick To the south-east of the village are the remains of a fort where, in 1580, English forces massacred more than six hundred Italian and Spanish soldiers and seventeen Irish people (NM). There are fine views.

Gallarus Oratory This famous dry masonry early Christian church has walls three feet thick (NM).

Kilmalkedar A 12th-century Romanesque church and an ogham alphabet stone are two of the many antiquities to be found in the area.

Ballybrack The Saint's Road, a pilgrims' track marked with Stations of the Cross, leads to the summit of Brandon

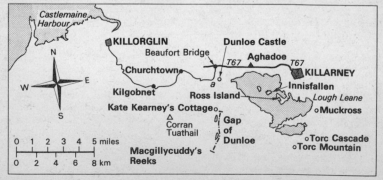

Churchtown The burial place of the Macgillycuddy clan.

a If you next intend to follow Route 297 to Kenmare, you can turn to it here.

Dunloe Castle Now modernized, and standing in fine grounds.

Kate Kearney's Cottage Very commercialized; named after a 19th-century local beauty who sold poteen to tourists.

Gap of Dunloe This impressive and dark defile through the mountains has a rough track free of motor traffic.

Aghadoe Killarney YH.

Innisfallen On this small island are the remains of a monastery (NM) which was founded in the 6th–7th century. Boats from Ross Castle pier.

Ross Island The fine remains of a grand castle which was once besieged by a Cromwellian force of over 2000.

Muckross The well preserved ruins (NM) of a friary founded in 1448.

Torc Cascade This waterfall is one of the best known Killarney beauty spots. Much of the surrounding land is in the Bourne Vincent Memorial Park, an extensive area of fine scenery that was presented to the nation in 1932 by two Californians, Mr and Mrs Bowers Bourne.

Torc Mountain The superb view from the top is one of the best in the area.

Killarney See Route 297. Also links with Route 298.

**Route 297   21 miles   34 km
KILLARNEY — KENMARE**

Bartholomew's ¼ inch:1 mile no. 4
OS ½ inch:1 mile no. 20 or 21

Killarney The celebrated and commercialized tourist resort renowned for its romantic mountain and lake scenery, and for its luxuriant flora. St Mary's Cathedral is a good example of a Gothic Revival church and was completed in 1912. Art gallery in the Town Hall. Links with Routes 296, 298.

a The alternative route ventures into the midst of Macgillycuddy's Reeks by way of a rough track through the Gap of Dunloe, and a tiny lane through the empty valley of the Owenreagh river. The main route follows the busier T65/N71 road past the popular sights found around the lakes of Killarney.

Innisfallen, Ross Island, Muckross, Torc Cascade, Torc Mountain, Kate Kearney's Cottage, Gap of Dunloe and **Macgillycuddy's Reeks** See Route 296.

b If you next intend to follow Route 298 to Millstreet, you can turn to it here.

Looscaunagh Hill High on this hill is famous 'Ladies View', a name given following pleasure expressed by the Ladies in Waiting to Queen Victoria when they visited here.

c If you next intend to follow Route 296 to Killorglin, you can turn to it here.

d The surface of the track through the Gap of Dunloe is mostly reasonable, although the approach from the south cannot be cycled.

Moll's Gap See Route 293.

Kenmare See Route 292. Also links with Route 293.

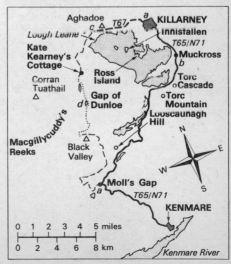

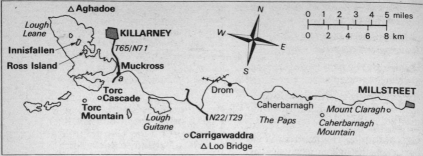

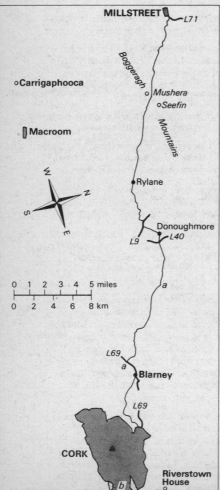

Route 298   26 miles   42 km
KILLARNEY — MILLSTREET

Bartholomew's ¼ inch:1 mile no. 4
OS ½ inch:1 mile no. 21

Killarney See Route 297. Also links
with Route 296.

Aghadoe Killarney YH.

**Innisfallen, Ross Island, Muckross,
Torc Cascade** and **Torc Mountain**
See Route 296.

*a If you next intend to follow Route 297 to
Kenmare, you can turn to it here.*

Carrigawaddra On the northern
slopes of this mountain is Robbers
Cave, the hideout and training ground
of Owen MacCarthy, the famous 16th-
century robber.

Millstreet Links with Routes 299,
305.

Route 299   33 miles   52 km
MILLSTREET — CORK

Bartholomew's ¼ inch:1 mile no. 4
OS ½ inch:1 mile nos 21, 22 (just)

Millstreet Links with Routes 298, 305.

Macroom The castle was once owned
by Admiral Sir William Penn, the father
of William Penn of Pennsylvania.

Carrigaphooca The remaining tower
of this castle (NM) stands on rock which
was, according to local superstition, the
haunt of a 'puca', or malicious being;
hence its name.

a Between the points 'a', the route follows the east bank of the Shournagh River.

Riverstown House Some of the rooms have superb plasterwork (open).

Blarney The 15th-century castle (open) with its huge keep, is best known for the curious custom attached to the stone up in the battlements. 'Kissing the Blarney Stone' is a favourite among tourists, and is reputed to endow eloquence upon those who do so. Rock Close is a delightful little dell, with huge rocks, yew trees and ilexes (open).

b Ferries link Cork with the Welsh ports of Fishguard and Pembroke.

Cork See Route 290. Also links with Route 300.

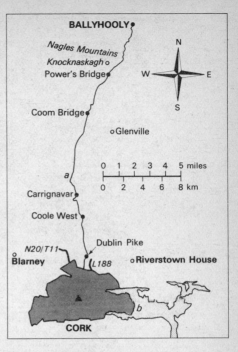

Route 300   19 miles   31 km
BALLYHOOLY — CORK

Bartholomew's ¼ inch:1 mile no. 4
OS ½ inch:1 mile no. 22

Ballyhooly The castle was wrecked in the war of 1641–52 but was restored in 1862. Links with Routes 301, 305, 306.

Riverstown House and **Blarney** See Route 299.

a A short section of road here is not marked on the Bartholomew's map of 1977.

b Ferries link Cork with the Welsh ports of Fishguard and Pembroke.

Cork See Route 290. Also links with Route 299.

Route 301   49 miles   79 km
LIMERICK — BALLYHOOLY

Bartholomew's ¼ inch:1 mile nos 3 or 4, 5
OS ½ inch:1 mile nos 22, 18, 17

Limerick Founded by the Vikings, Limerick is now Eire's third city, of which a good view can be had from the north Shannon bank. Norman King John's castle; 12th-century St Mary's Cathedral; the Treaty stone, where Catholics were given better rights in

1691; Custom House. The Newtown Pery area has a Georgian aspect. Links with Routes 304, 313, 316, 317, 331.

Monasternenagh The impressive ruins of a Cistercian Abbey founded in the 12th century by the King of Thomond in thanksgiving for his victory over the Danes.

Lough Gur This area abounds in remains dating from neolithic to medieval times, including Ireland's largest stone circle, forts, cairns, cultivation terraces and a 15th-century tower house. There are two man-made islands in the lake (crannogs), and a legend associated with the Earl of Desmond's curse.

Hospital The village took its name from the Preceptory of the Knights Hospitallers of St John of Jerusalem, which was founded here in the 13th century. There are some interesting tombs in the remains of the 'Hospital Church' (NM).

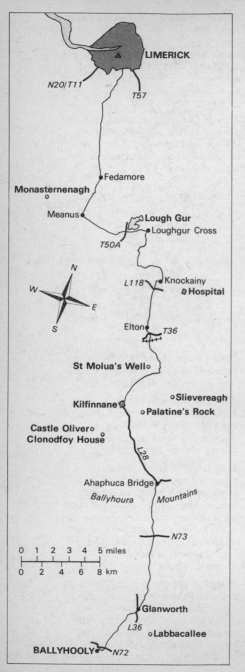

St Molua's Well A holy well at which ceremonies take place at the beginning of August each year.

Slievereagh On the top of this hill are the remains of prehistoric settlements. There are a ring-fort, souterrains and tumuli; also fine views.

Kilfinnane The huge mound surrounded with banks and ditches was originally a ring-fort, and had a medieval fortress built on top.

Palatine's Rock The meeting place of the many Palatinate Germans who came to settle in the area in the mid 18th century.

Castle Oliver Lola Montez, mistress of Ludwig I, 'the Mad King' of Bavaria, was born here.

Clonodfoy House The folly on the hill was built during a famine to provide employment.

Glanworth A pretty village with an ancient river bridge.

Labbacallee The largest and finest of the Irish wedge-shaped gallery graves (NM).

Ballyhooly See Route 300. Also links with Routes 305, 306.

Route 302   29 miles   46 km
TRALEE — DINGLE

Bartholomew's ¼ inch:1 mile no. 4
OS ½ inch:1 mile no. 20

Tralee This county town has a small sea port and a market. St John's Church is Gothic Revival; the Court House has an Ionic portico. Links with Route 303.

Ardfert The lovely ruins of 13th-century St Brendan's Cathedral (NM) and 13th-century friary (NM) can be visited.

Slieve Mish Mountains This means 'Mountains of the Phantoms'.

Castlegregory There are fine sands.

Connor Pass There are good views

across Dingle Bay and Brandon Bay from the top of the Pass.

a Boat from Dingle to the Blasket Isles.

Dingle See Route 295. Also links with Route 294.

Route 303   42 miles   68 km
ARDAGH — TRALEE

Bartholomew's ¼ inch:1 mile no. 4
OS ½ inch:1 mile nos 17, 21

Ardagh Just to the west of the village is a large ring-fort (NM) where, in 1868, the famous Ardagh chalices and brooches were discovered under a bush. Links with Route 304.

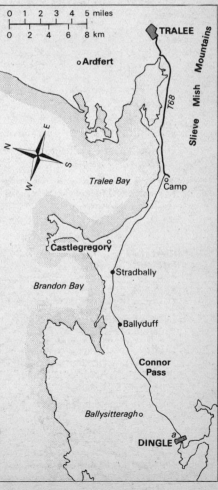

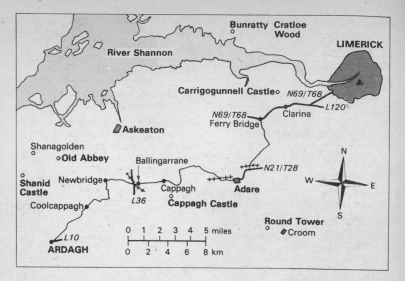

Glenaster Waterfall A delightful fall approached by footpath up a gorge.

Glenquin Castle A tall, fortified tower which has been restored.

a A ferry across the Shannon from Tarbert (north of Kilkinlea) allows a short cut to Route 318 in County Clare.

Tralee See Route 302.

Route 304   28 miles   46 km
LIMERICK — ARDAGH

Bartholomew's ¼ inch:1 mile nos 4, 3
OS ½ inch:1 mile no. 17

Limerick See Route 301. Also links with Routes 313, 316, 317, 331.

Cratloe Wood Ancient oakwood which has provided timber for such buildings as Westminster Hall and Amsterdam City Hall.

Bunratty Fine 15th-century castle in complete condition.

River Shannon The longest river in Ireland.

Carrigogunnell Castle The ruins of a great O'Brien stronghold sited on crags

overlooking the flat estuary of the Shannon.

Adare A pretty village with thatched cottages. The impressive Tudor revival manor was built in the 19th century, and has odd carved messages in the stone walls. The garden is open. By the ruins of the Franciscan friary is a tablet marking the spot where John Wesley, one of the founders of the Methodist movement, preached. Ruined Desmond's Castle, by the river, has two great halls and was dismantled by the Cromwellians.

Round Tower Incomplete, with a Romanesque doorway.

Cappagh Castle This ruined 15th-century stronghold of the Knights of Glin had a double bawn and a five-storey tower.

Askeaton The remains of a great castle built by the Earls of Desmond in the 14th century (NM) stand on a small island in the River Deel. The remnants of a grand 15th-century great hall can also be seen. The 13th-century Franciscan friary has fine cloisters.

Old Abbey The ruins of an Augustinian nunnery with cloister court, dovecot and fish-pond surviving.

Shanid Castle The motte-and-bailey, and parts of the polygonal keep remain.

Ardagh See Route 303.

Route 305   34 miles   54 km
BALLYHOOLY — MILLSTREET

Bartholomew's ¼ inch:1 mile no. 4
OS ½ inch:1 mile nos 21, 22

Ballyhooly See Route 300. Also links with Routes 301, 306.

Kilcolman Castle The 16th-century English poet Edmund Spenser wrote the 'Faerie Queene' in this castle. Set over a lovely lough, it is now in ruins.

Buttevant The ruined friary (NM) has an unusual two-storey crypt.

Ballybeg Abbey The cloister walls, dovecot and belfry remain of this 13th-century Augustinian priory.

Mallow A market town with some elegant houses dating from its days as a spa. The castle is now in ruins (NM); close by is the Tudor revival Jephson manor.

a The alternative route detours north into the hills to link three interesting castles, while the main route continues in the valley.

Lohort Castle This 15th-century tower house was severely damaged by Cromwellian artillery in 1650, but was subsequently repaired, and has been lived in since.

Liscarroll One of the largest 13th-century castles in Ireland (NM), with a huge bawn.

Kanturk The large fortified house (Kanturk Castle) was never completed, because jealous English settlers complained to the Privy Council that it was much too large for an Irish subject (NM).

Millstreet Links with Routes 298, 299.

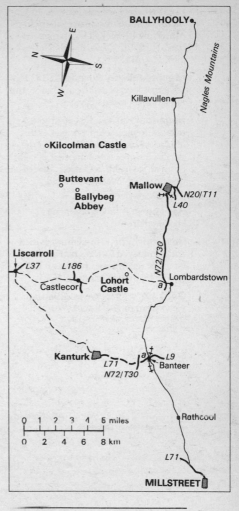

Route 306   43 miles   69 km
CLONMEL — BALLYHOOLY

Bartholomew's ¼ inch:1 mile no. 4 or 3
OS ½ inch:1 mile no. 22

Clonmel Evidence of the town's past dependence on water trade can be seen in the many old riverside warehouses. The Franciscan church and Methodist church are interesting, and the Protestant church has good glass. The

Court House was built in 1800, and there is a museum and art gallery in the Municipal Library. The Mainguard dates from 1674. Links with Routes 307, 314, 315.

Mount Melleray Founded in 1832 by Irish monks expelled from France, this is a Trappist monastery.

Sugarloaf Hill The L34 road south-east of Clogheen climbs much of this hill, providing superb views. On the northern slopes is the unusual upright tomb of S. Grubb, a Quaker, placed so that he could 'overlook' his old property, Castlegrace.

Bay Lough A tiny lake among rhododendrons.

Burncourt The 17th-century gabled and chimneyed fortress house was burnt by its owner to prevent it falling into Cromwellian hands (NM).

Galtymore There are magnificent views from the 3018-foot (920-m)

summit of this mountain, which can be ascended on foot from the pretty village of Glengarra 1.5 miles (2·5 km) north-west of Burncourt.

Mitchelstown Caves In the group of caverns known as Desmond's Cave the Earl of Desmond unsuccessfully sought shelter from the British in 1601. One of the chambers is the largest in the British Isles, and the group known as New Cave has excellent stalagmite and stalactite formations. A local guide is necessary if you wish to visit the caves.

Araglin Valley A wild and lovely valley which can be explored by delightful little lanes.

Fermoy The town grew up around the 18th-century military barracks, and was until 1922 one of the most important British military bases in Ireland.

Labbacallee See Route 301.

Ballyhooly See Route 300. Also links with Routes 301, 305.

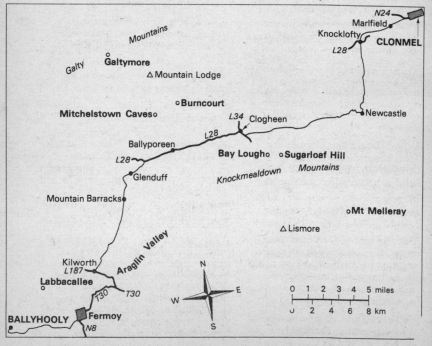

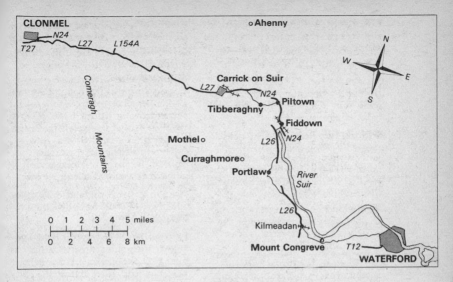

Route 307 33 miles 53 km
CLONMEL — WATERFORD

Bartholomew's ¼ inch:1 mile no. 3
OS ½ inch:1 mile nos 22, 23

Clonmel See Route 306. Links with Routes 314, 315.

Carrick on Suir It is claimed that Anne Boleyn, mother of Queen Elizabeth I of England, was born in the grand manor house and castle (NM).

Ahenny The two 18th-century high crosses here are particularly fine and were part of an old monastic site.

Mothel Remains of a priory (NM).

Tibberaghny The site of an early monastery, with remains of a church and carved cross shaft, and a 15th-century castle.

Piltown In 1642 a battle took place here in which a member of the Butler family was captured. The ransom demanded by the Earl of Desmond was two important Irish manuscripts, which are now in English museums.

Fiddown There are some medieval tomb fragments in the church.

Portlaw A leather tanning village which was founded originally by a Quaker family for the workers of their cotton-spinning mills.

Curraghmore Beautiful grounds (open) surround a grand 18th-century house which incorporates an older castle.

Mount Congreve The gardens and woodlands surrounding the house are open.

Waterford See Route 308.

Route 308 27 miles 44 km
WATERFORD — DUNCORMICK

Bartholomew's ¼ inch:1 mile no. 3
OS ½ inch:1 mile no. 23

This route requires the use of a ferry between Arthurstown and Passage East.

Waterford A busy port and famous glass-making centre. There are some very fine medieval streets and buildings, and a museum in Reginald's Tower. The long shipping quay and remains of Grey Friars priory (NM) are interesting. Links with Route 307.

Faithlegg Castle The remains of a

castle whose garrison was butchered by Cromwell in 1649.

Cheekpoint Hill Fine views over the water approaches to Waterford.

Geneva Barracks The site of an unsuccessful 18th-century attempt to found a city of intellectuals and watchmakers from Geneva.

Arthurstown Ballyhack Castle was wrecked by Cromwell.

Dunbrody Abbey A fine example of medieval architecture dating from the 13th century (NM).

Greatisland The large earthworks of Kilmokea are of uncertain origin, but possibly comprise the remains of an Anglo-Norman village.

J. F. Kennedy Memorial Park An arboretum has been laid out surrounding the 888-foot (270-m) Slievecoilta hill in memory of President Kennedy.

Dunganstown The remains of the family home of Patrick Kennedy, great-grandfather of President Kennedy, who visited here twice.

Clonmines The site of a medieval town with the remains of four castles and three churches.

Wellingtonbridge Named after the 'Iron Duke' of Wellington.

Bannow Only the church and a chapel remain of the town that was destroyed by drifting sands.

Duncormick Links with Route 309.

Route 309   16 miles   26 km
ROSSLARE HARBOUR — DUNCORMICK

Bartholomew's ¼ inch:1 mile no. 3
OS ½ inch:1 mile no. 23

Rosslare Harbour A seaside resort. Links with Route 310.

a Ferries run from Rosslare to Wales and France.

Carnshore Point Just to the north of this sandy point are the remains of an ancient monastery, with cashel, small church, inscribed boulder, and Holy Well of St Vogue.

Lady's Island There is a ruined abbey here, remains of a 13th-century granite castle, and a leaning tower.

Tacumshane One of the last Irish windmills survives here, in good condition (NM). Tacumshane Lake, to the

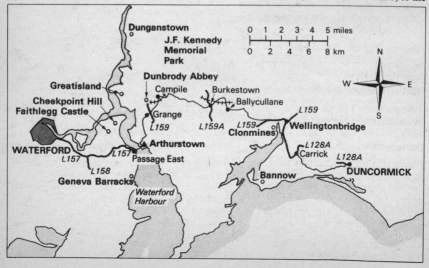

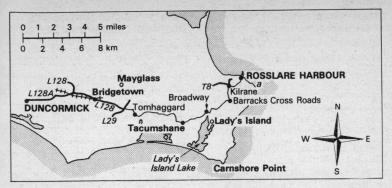

south-west, has been cut off from the sea by current-borne deposits and is now a salty lagoon.

Mayglass The church was burnt down in the insurrection of 1798, and a tablet commemorates the unfortunate leader of the Catholic peasants who was beheaded and buried here following the collapse of the rising.

Bridgetown The surrounding area was one of the first to be colonized in Ireland by the Anglo-Normans. Their many castles and isolated existence hindered assimilation by gaelic Ireland in the 14th and 15th centuries and their strange dialect survived until relatively recently.

Duncormick Links with Route 308.

Route 310   29 miles   47 km
**ENNISCORTHY —
ROSSLARE HARBOUR**

Bartholomew's ¼ inch:1 mile no. 3
OS ½ inch:1 mile no. 23

Enniscorthy A market town with a fine 19th-century cathedral and a castle housing a museum of local history. Vinegar Hill, to the east of the town, was the site of the insurgents' camp following their storming of the town in reaction to the burning by the British of local farmhouses. They were later driven from the hill. The windmill (remains NM), was their command

post. Links with Routes 311, 338, 339.

Ferrycarrig The scene of a skirmish between British troops and insurgents in 1798. On the north bank of the River Slaney is the tall tower of a 15th-century castle, and on the south bank a tower commemorating men of Wexford who fell in the Crimean War.

Beggerin Island This was a refuge for

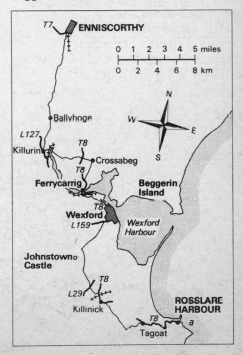

the people of Wexford in 1171 when under siege. It is now reclaimed from the sea.

Wexford Once a busy seaport and a walled town, now a manufacturing centre and tourist resort. The remains of Selskar Abbey can be seen (NM) and there used to be a bull ring. There is a statue of John Barry, the 'father' of the US Navy, and an 18th-century theatre.

Johnstown Castle A 19th-century

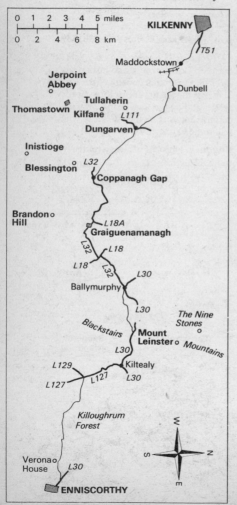

mansion incorporating an old castle. The grounds (open) are well laid out.

a Ferries run from Rosslare to Wales and France.

Rosslare Harbour See Route 309.

Route 311   39 miles   62 km
KILKENNY — ENNISCORTHY

Bartholomew's ¼ inch:1 mile no. 3
OS ½ inch:1 mile no. 19

Kilkenny A particularly interesting town with an Anglo-Norman castle and an 18th-century bridge. Also of interest are the Bishop's Palace, the arcaded Tholsel which was built in 1761 as the Exchange and Town Hall, and Rothe House (NM) which houses a museum. The 13th-century Gothic cathedral has many tombs and monuments. In 1324 Dame Alice, of Kyteler's Inn, was charged with witchcraft; she escaped but her maid was burnt at the stake. Links with Routes 312, 314, 342, 343.

Dungarven A fragment of a tomb in the old churchyard has a very rare miniature effigy of a knight and his lady.

Tullaherin There was an early monastic site here, today marked by a 73-foot (20-m) round tower (NM).

Kilfane Ruined church (NM), with an excellent effigy dating from the 14th century.

Thomastown A small market town with the remains of two castles and a ruined 13th-century church (NM).

Jerpoint Abbey The ruins of this fine Cistercian abbey (NM) date from the 12th century. There are some particularly good carvings, effigies and monuments, and a cloister arcade.

Blessington A trivallate ring-fort stands on the west of Saddle Hill.

Inistioge Set in delightful surroundings, with a fine 18th-century bridge.

Coppanagh Gap Fine views from the road hereabouts.

Brandon Hill Stone circle and cairn on the summit, and fine views.

Graiguenamanagh The place takes its name from 'Granary of the Monks'. The 12th-century abbey is a copy of Strata Florida Abbey in Wales and contains the effigy of a knight and two High Crosses.

Mount Leinster The highest of the Blackstairs Mountains at 2610 feet (795 m). It can be ascended by road then track via The Nine Stones.

Enniscorthy See Route 310. Also links with Routes 338, 339.

Route 312   29 miles   47 km
KILKENNY — HOLYCROSS

Bartholomew's ¼ inch:1 mile no. 3
OS ½ inch:1 mile nos 18, 19 (just)

Kilkenny See Route 311. Links with Routes 314, 342, 343.

Dunmore Cave A local guide is necessary if you wish to explore these limestone caves. Legend has it that one thousand Irish people were massacred by the Vikings here.

Tullaroan Remains of a small medieval church. The surrounding area is rich in ring-forts and earthworks.

Kilcooly Abbey Interesting remains of a small Cistercian abbey; dovecot.

Church The ruins of this 13th-century church stand on a 459-foot (140-m) mound, surrounded by peat bog. It can be reached by a peat cutters track.

Grallagh Castle Parts of the bawn are still visible around this 16th-century tower (NM).

Moycarkey Castle A 16th-century tower at the centre of a large bawn.

Thurles A market town with a 15th-century tower by the bridge over the River Suir, and a cathedral.

Brittas Castle The building of this 19th-century copy of Warwick Castle came to a halt when the proprietor was killed by falling masonry.

Holycross The abbey was founded in the 12th century, taking its name from a relic of the True Cross. The interesting ruins include a 15th-century shrine, a sedilia and good carvings in the remains of the cloister. Links with Route 313.

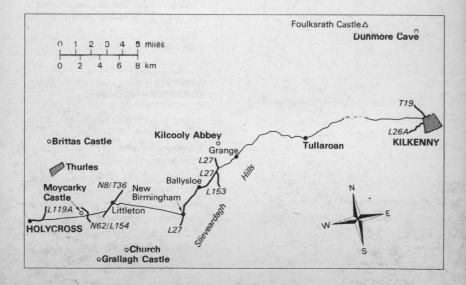

Route 313   40 miles   64 km
LIMERICK — HOLYCROSS

Bartholomew's ¼ inch:1 mile no. 3
OS ½ inch:1 mile nos 18, 17 (just)

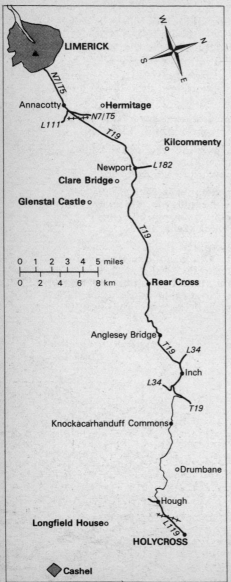

Limerick See Route 301. Also links with Routes 304, 316, 317, 331.

Hermitage A picturesque 18th-century ruin set in the wooded Shannon valley.

Clare Bridge To the west is pretty Clare Glen, with waterfalls.

Glenstal Castle A mock Norman castle forming the nucleus of St Columba's Abbey and a school.

Kilcommenty An ancient church site with a well which still attracts pilgrims, and 'St Cominad's Bed', a boulder with the 'prints of the saint's ribs and hands'.

Rear Cross Half a mile north-east there is a good megalithic tomb. On the mountain top above here is Terrot, a stone pile over a boy who went hunting instead of attending mass, and died in summer snow. Many megalithic monuments in the surrounding hills.

Longfield House A typical small residence of an Irish gentleman (open).

Cashel The town is popular among tourists, and has much historical interest. Sited on top of the Rock of Cashel is a group of ruins that include remains of the town's defences, St Patrick's Cathedral (and round tower and chapel), the bishop's castle, and an ancient cross.

Holycross See Route 312.

Route 314   36 miles   58 km
KILKENNY — CLONMEL

Bartholomew's ¼ inch:1 mile no. 3
OS ½ inch:1 mile nos 22, 18, 19

Kilkenny See Route 311. Also links with Routes 312, 342, 343.

Burnchurch The ruined tower house (NM) has an unusual number of passages and chambers in the walls and was the site of one of Cromwell's camps in 1650.

Kells (Ceanannas) Just to the east of the village are the ruins of Ireland's largest monastic enclosure (NM), a fortified Augustinian Priory.

Kilree The site of an early monastery, the remains including an ancient church, round tower belfry and high cross (NM).

Jerpoint Abbey See Route 311.

Dunnamaggan There is an ancient church here, and a high cross with unusual carvings.

Lamoge There are two ogham stones.

Ahenny and **Carrick on Suir** See Route 307.

Killamery The only relic of a monastery that was founded here in the 6th century is a beautifully carved 8th-century high cross (NM).

Kilcash There is a typical tower house here, and an ancient church.

Slievenamon Mountain A feature in Irish mythology, it has good views from the summit and slopes.

Kiltinan The remains of the once great rock fortress can be seen, and also the fortified well.

Clonmel See Route 306. Also links with Routes 307, 315.

Route 315   27 miles   43 km
DONOHILL — CLONMEL

Bartholomew's ¼ inch:1 mile no. 3
OS ½ inch:1 mile nos 18, 22 (just)

Donohill There is a motte and bailey, and the remains of a manorial church. Links with Route 316.

Golden Hills The remains of a castellated house of eccentric design.

Longfield House and **Cashel** See Route 313.

Thomastown Castle A ruined 18th-century house with a formal garden.

Athassel In four acres are the magnificent ruins of St Edmund's Priory,

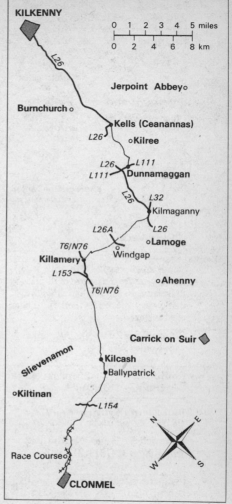

once one of the most important Norman monasteries in Ireland (NM).

Knockgraffon Mote An excellent motte and bailey marks the site of a 12th-century Anglo-Norman castle that once guarded a crossing over the River Suir. Nearby are the remains of a medieval church and the ruins of a 16th-century castle.

Cahir On a rock island in the River Suir

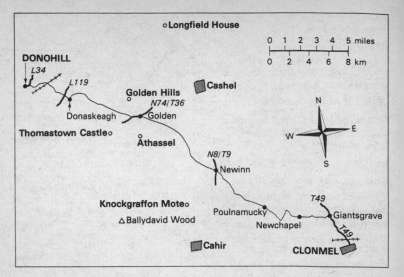

stands an impressive 15th–16th
century castle, the largest of its period
in Ireland. In Elizabethan times the
castle was a safe retreat for the Catholics
of Munster.

Clonmel See Route 306. Also links
with Routes 307, 314.

Route 316   26 miles   43 km
LIMERICK — DONOHILL

Bartholomew's ¼ inch:1 mile no. 3
OS ½ inch:1 mile nos 18, 17 (just)

Limerick See Route 301. Also links
with Routes 304, 313, 317, 331.

Glenstal Castle and **Clare Bridge** See
Route 313.

Donohill See Route 315.

Route 317   24 miles   39 km
CLARECASTLE — LIMERICK

Bartholomew's ¼ inch:1 mile no. 5
OS ½ inch:1 mile no. 17

Clarecastle The name derives from the
castle which guarded the river crossing.
Links with Route 318.

Clare Abbey Ruins dating from the
12th century (NM).

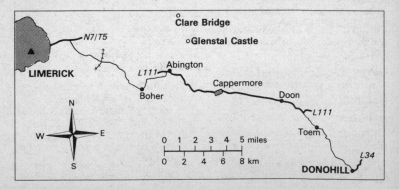

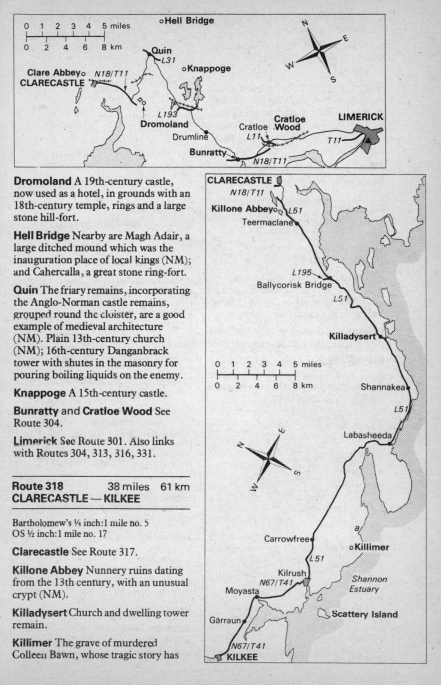

Dromoland A 19th-century castle, now used as a hotel, in grounds with an 18th-century temple, rings and a large stone hill-fort.

Hell Bridge Nearby are Magh Adair, a large ditched mound which was the inauguration place of local kings (NM); and Cahercalla, a great stone ring-fort.

Quin The friary remains, incorporating the Anglo-Norman castle remains, grouped round the cloister, are a good example of medieval architecture (NM). Plain 13th-century church (NM); 16th-century Danganbrack tower with shutes in the masonry for pouring boiling liquids on the enemy.

Knappoge A 15th-century castle.

Bunratty and **Cratloe Wood** See Route 304.

Limerick See Route 301. Also links with Routes 304, 313, 316, 331.

Route 318   38 miles   61 km
CLARECASTLE — KILKEE

Bartholomew's ¼ inch:1 mile no. 5
OS ½ inch:1 mile no. 17

Clarecastle See Route 317.

Killone Abbey Nunnery ruins dating from the 13th century, with an unusual crypt (NM).

Killadysert Church and dwelling tower remain.

Killimer The grave of murdered Colleen Bawn, whose tragic story has inspired a novel, a play and the opera *The Lily of Killarney*.

a Ferries to County Kerry. Short-cut to Route 303 at Kilkinlea, south of Abbeyfeale.

Scattery Island The remains of the monastery founded in the 6th century include cashel, round tower and well ruins (NM). Pebbles from the island are considered to be a charm against ship-wreck.

Kilkee See Route 319. Also links with Route 320.

Route 319   35 miles   56 km
KILKEE — KILKEE

Bartholomew's ¼ inch:1 mile no. 5
OS ½ inch:1 mile no. 17

This peninsula circuit, which includes good views over coastal features and the Shannon estuary, can be short-cut by roads linking the two sides of the peninsula.

Kilkee Good bathing in pollock holes in the rocks. Links with Routes 318, 320.

Bishop's Island A legendary bishop fled his parishoners in a time of famine. The widening of the gulf between his

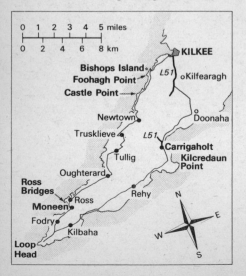

refuge island and the mainland pre-vented his return, and so he starved to death.

Foohagh Point Traces of a promon-tory point. An impressive sea cave and a sea tunnel.

Castle Point Remains of both a pro-montory fort and a castle.

Ross Bridges Sea arches.

Moneen The church has good glass and the 'Little Ark', which was wheeled to the beach for celebration of Mass during penal times, when the landlord prohibited Mass on the land.

Loop Head Otherwise this is called Leap Head after the legend of the knight who leapt to the off-shore Dermot and Grania's Rock to escape a hag. His 'footprint' is on the landward side of the chasm. There is a lighthouse.

Kilcredaun Point Nearby are the ruins of two churches, one with Romanesque features. There is a 19th-century coastal battery.

Carrigaholt Turreted bawn and tower (NM).

Kilkee As above.

Route 320   30 miles   48 km
ENNISTIMON — KILKEE

Bartholomew's ¼ inch:1 mile no. 5
OS ½ inch:1 mile nos 14, 17

Ennistimon Market town by pretty river falls. Links with Route 321.

a Most of the route between Ennistimon and Doonbeg follows quiet inland lanes. The busier main road to the west gives more coastal views.

Kilfarboy Gaelic poets, writers and scholars are buried in the graveyard of the ruined 15th-century church.

Miltown Malbay Market town.

Doonbeg An Armada ship was grounded near the river mouth. There are 15th–16th century castle remains and beaches with lovely shells.

George's Head A sea tunnel. The remains of a promontory fort and ring barrow.

Kilkee See Route 319. Also links with Route 318.

Route 321   46 miles   74 km
KINVARRA — ENNISTIMON

Bartholomew's ¼ inch:1 mile no. 5
OS ½ inch:1 mile no. 14

Kinvarra A market and fishing village.

The recently restored 16th-century Dungory Castle is sited on a rock, with a ring-fort nearby. Links with Routes 322, 331.

Doorus Kinvarra YH.

Oughtmama Ruins of three 12th-century churches with early gravestones (NMs).

Corcomroe Abbey Ruins of a Cistercian house.

Newtown Castle A circular tower on a pyramidal base.

Ballyallaban Cahermore stone ring-fort with remains of houses and a medieval gateway. The area has a wealth of prehistoric sites.

Noughaval Remains of a church, crosses and a hermit's tiny oratory. Prehistoric remains on the ridge to the south-east.

Kilfenora Display centre of the bare limestone Burren country through which parts of this route pass. The limestone is of great interest to geologists, botanists and local historians, and the unusual scenery has inspired men of letters including Shaw and Yeats. There are ruins of a cathedral with grotesque effigies and carved 12th-century crosses (NM).

Lisdoonvarna Spa-town and resort.

Ballynalacken Castle A 15th-century tower and bawn in good condition.

Fisherstreet Also called 'Doolin', this is the nearest port to the Aran Isles. It has a cave system.

O'Brien's Tower Superb views of the 600-foot (180-m) Cliffs of Moher from this disused 19th-century tea-house.

Birchfield House A 19th-century castellated house in ruins.

Liscannor The bay, being easy for invading forces, has often been under threat, for example during Armada times and the Second World War.

Ennistimon See Route 320.

Route 322   21 miles   34 km
GALWAY — KINVARRA

Bartholomew's ¼ inch:1 mile no. 5
OS ½ inch:1 mile no. 14

Galway The town grew around an Anglo-Norman castle. It endured a nine-month blockade by the Cromwellians. Lynch's Castle, a 16th-century tower house with the arms of Henry VII, is now a bank. Once famous for limestone houses, there are still fragments. Remains of town walls; Old Fish Market. The university, founded 1845, gives some courses in Irish. The parish church has gravestones carved with craft symbols set in the floor. Links with Routes 323, 330, 332.

a Ferries run from Galway to the Aran Isles.

Roscam An early monastic site with remains of a round tower, medieval church, cashel and bullaun stones (NM).

Oranmore A large 16th-century castle tower. There are several ring-forts with souterrains in the area.

Kilcornan The house incorporates a 15th–16th century castle tower.

b A lane used in the route is not shown on the Bartholomew's map.

Kiltiernan An early monastic site of around 4 acres, with remains of a cashel, church with a good door, souterrain and houses (NM).

Doorus Kinvarra YH.

Kinvarra See Route 321. Also links with Route 331.

Route 323   32 miles   52 km
SCREEB — GALWAY

Bartholomew's ¼ inch:1 mile no. 5
OS ½ inch:1 mile no. 10

Some development has taken place along the L100 between Galway and Spiddle which impairs the scenery; it cannot, however, be avoided.

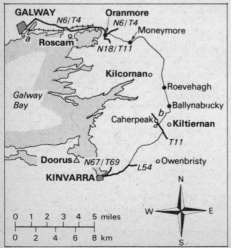

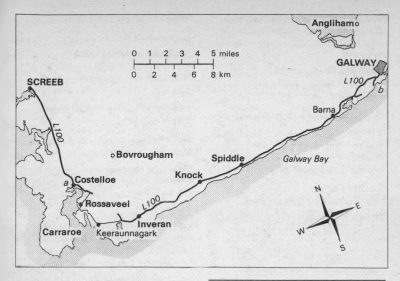

Screeb Links with Route 324.

Costelloe Headquarters of Radio Gaeltachta.

Carraroe A lonely peninsula with beaches and a coral strand, the home of Charles Lamb, the artist.

a The islands of Gorumna and Lettermore (see Route 324) can be reached by road from here.

Bovrougham The hill summit affords wide views, although it is low.

Rossaveel An area of traditional cottages. Peat boats to the Aran Isles.

Inveran Castle ruin by the shore. The 20th-century church of St Colmcille at Tully has good copper and enamel work.

Knock Connemara marble processing factory.

Spiddle A 20th-century Celtic Roman-esque church.

Angliham Black marble quarries.

b Ferries run from Galway to the Aran Isles.

Galway See Route 322. Also links with Routes 330, 332.

Route 324　　45 miles　72 km
CLIFDEN — SCREEB

Bartholomew's ¼ inch:1 mile no. 5
OS ½ inch:1 mile no. 10

Clifden The town was founded in 1812 by John Darcy. The Protestant church has a copy of the Cross of Cong. Connemara Pony Show is held here in August. Links with Route 325.

Clifden Castle The ruin of John Darcy's castle on scenic Belleek peninsula.

Monument A monument to Alcock and Brown who made the first trans-atlantic flight, west to east, in June 1919.

a The main route follows the lovely coast road, but the alternative is also beautiful, being a very quiet and open road with views over low land with rocks and lochans to distant mountains on either side.

Alcock and Brown Cairn In the bog-land the cairn marks the place where the pilots crash-landed after their trans-atlantic flight. Nearby are the remains of Marconi's first transatlantic wireless telegraph station on the European side, destroyed in Anglo-Irish troubles. Ask the precise directions in Ballinaboy.

Roundstone Built in the 1820s and settled with Scots fishermen, Roundstone is now popular among artists and botanists.

Inishnee On the island are St Brendan's monument and curative well.

Benlettery Green marble quarries.

Benlettery Castle Now a hotel, this was the home of 18th-century 'Humanity Dick' Martin, RSPCA promoter and noted duellist.

Cashel The name is taken from the ring-fort on the hill by the hotel.

Glinsk A fine 17th-century castle with chimneys and shutes in the masonry for

pouring boiling liquid on the enemy (N

Mweenish Fine beaches.

St Macdara's Isle A venerable isle with early ecclesiastical ruins (NMs). Boats dip their sails three times in passing. Accessible by boat from Mace.

Lough Skannive Walled crannog, or man-made island.

Kilkieran Summer currach racing and a seaweed processing factory.

Pearce's Cottage At Turlough is the cottage of Patrick Pearce, an inspirer of the early 20th-century National Movement (NM).

Gorumna and **Lettermore** Two quiet, lovely islands with ancient churches. Accessible by road from Costelloe (see Route 323).

Screeb Links with Route 323.

Route 325   71 miles   115 km
WESTPORT — CLIFDEN

Bartholomew's ¼ inch:1 mile no. 5
OS ½ inch:1 mile no. 10

Westport Planned in the 18th century by James Wyatt, Westport has old quays and warehouses. The Protestant church has art nouveau decoration. Westport House has good plasterwork and silver, a zoo park and ornamental waters using the tides. Links with Routes 326, 329, 330.

Knappagh The circular shape of the churchyard suggests antiquity.

Murrisk Abbey There are 15th-century friary ruins by Clew Bay shore.

Croagh Patrick Ireland's Holy Mountain, on the summit of which St Patrick fasted for forty days and nights. The clear track starting near Murrisk Abbey is walked by thousands, some in bare feet, on the night of July's last Saturday, followed by Mass at dawn by the chapel on the summit. There are views over the unique seascape of Clew Bay, which is said to have an island for every day of the year.

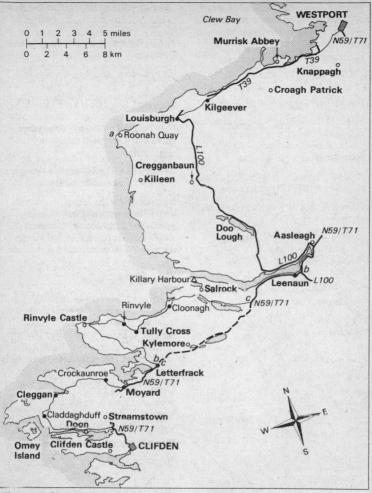

Kilgeever Church ruins at which some pilgrimages to Croagh Patrick end.

Louisburgh Founded in 1802, Louisburgh was probably named after the one in Canada.

a Boats run from Roonah Quay to the islands of Caher, Clare and Inishturk.

Cregganbaun The nearby gallery grave was used as a Mass Rock in Penal times.

Killeen Great cross-pillar. Nearby is a

37-arch clapper footbridge.

Doo Lough 'Doo' comes from the Irish for 'black'.

Aasleagh Salmon falls.

b At this point the L100 can be followed south-east through the beautiful Maum Valley, to join Route 330 at Maum.

Leenaun The 9-mile (15-kilometre) long Killary Harbour was the fleet anchorage for the British Atlantic Fleet in the First World War.

c The main route follows lanes near the coast, in parts lovely though in other parts fairly built up. The alternative follows a busier road through more open country closer to mountains.

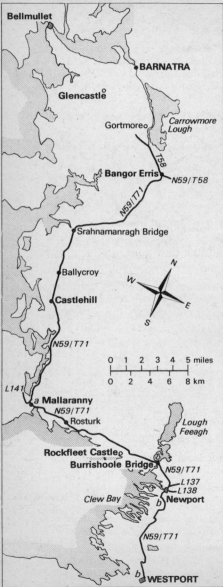

Salrock At this hamlet, supposedly the burial place of St Roc, the custom of throwing tobacco pipes used at the Wakes onto the grave of the deceased is followed.

Tully Cross Modern cottages in the traditional style.

Rinvyle Castle There are 14th-century castle ruins. The area has good beaches. Nearby are Tonadooravaun gallery grave and Deryinver pillarstone alignment.

Letterfrack The village is a 19th-century Quaker foundation.

Kylemore By the lough, in grounds with rhododendrons and fuchsias, stands the 19th-century Gothic castle which houses Kylemore Abbey and nunnery. The pottery and grounds are open.

Moyard Pillar stone.

Cleggan Mailboats go to the island of Inishbofin, which has been used as a 'concentration camp' for priests and monks. It has a Cromwellian star-fort, fishermen's graves with broken oars upon them, and cliffs from where seals can be seen.

Omey Island From Claddaghduff, poles mark a low-water 'path' over the sands to this island, which has rocky outcrops and church ruins.

Doon The ruined castle was a seat of the O'Flaherty family, the most important in the area before the Anglo-Norman conquest.

Streamstown White marble quarry.

Clifden Castle See Route 324.

Clifden See Route 324.

Route 326   46 miles   74 km
BARNATRA — WESTPORT

Bartholomew's ¼ inch:1 mile no. 5
OS ½ inch:1 mile nos 6, 10 (just) or 11 (just)

Barnatra Links with Route 328.

Belmullet A decayed seaport at the

entry to the lonely, moorland Mullet and Erris peninsula, with a remote, beautiful coast of cliffs, dunes and beaches in the north and a wealth of prehistoric and ecclesiastical ruins.

Glencastle Hill with wide views and a rock-fort nearby.

Bangor Erris Tunes can be played on the north parapet stones of Bellacorick 'musical' Bridge.

Castlehill Carved pillarstone.

Mallaranny See Route 327.

a Route 327 starts and ends at Mallaranny, exploring the peninsula and Achill Island to the west.

Rockfleet Castle The tower is of a castle which was once the home of Grainne Ni Mhaille, the Irish heroine who made a stand against the English in the 16th century (NM).

Burrishoole Bridge The 15th-century Dominican friary remains (NM).

Newport A 20th-century Irish Romanesque church.

b Between Newport and Westport, where the route passes through an unusual landscape of miniature valleys and ridges, there are several side-roads to Clew Bay.

Westport See Route 325. Also links with Routes 329, 330.

**Route 327   70 miles   112 km
MALLARANNY — MALLARANNY**

Bartholomew's ¼ inch:1 mile no. 5
OS ½ inch:1 mile no. 6

This peninsula and island route can be adapted by the omission of road loops, or the dead-end ride in the west. The order of the points of interest shows the recommended sequence.

a This route is a branch from Route 326 at Mallaranny.

Mallaranny Beaches; giant and rare plants grow in the mild climate.

Corraun Church with a 20th-century window to St Brendan.

Currane Hill Wide, varied summit views.

Achill Sound Boat hire.

Cloghmore A well-preserved castle tower (NM).

Achillbeg Island Several promontory forts with remains of huts and graves.

Menawn A surfaced drive leads to the mast at the summit.

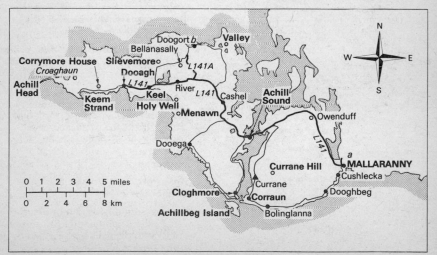

Holy Well Views of the 800-foot
(250-m) sheer cliffs of Minaun, and the
Cathedral Rocks at low tide.

Keel Trawmore Strand.

Dooagh Salmon-netting is carried out.

The cairn by the coast guard station was
a mass altar in Penal times.

Corrymore House This was the home
of the 19th-century Captain Boycott,
whose ostracism gave the verb 'boycott'
to the English language.

Keem Strand Haunt of the harmless
basking-shark.

Achill Head Reached by a fairly strenuous walk from Keem Strand, Achill
Head has great sheer cliffs to the south-
west, and to the north-east Mount
Croaghaun drops 2000 feet (600 m) to
the sea. Although not sheer, the cliffs
are one of two contenders for the title of
highest in the British Isles.

Slievemore A good example of an
18th-century Irish village, now used as a
buaile, inhabited during summer
pasturing only. The 8-mile walk round
Slievemore Mountain passes many prehistoric remains.

*b Boats for hire to see the Seal Caves
below Slievemore.*

Valley Pretty village.

Mallaranny See above.

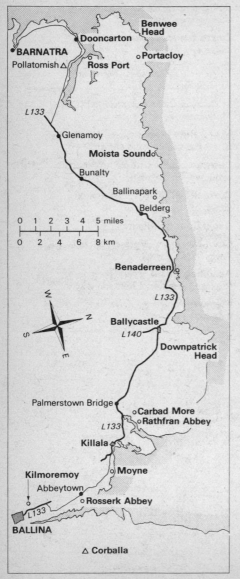

Route 328   47 miles   75 km
BARNATRA — BALLINA

Bartholomew's ¼ inch:1 mile no. 5
OS ½ inch:1 mile no. 6

Barnatra Links with Route 326.

Dooncarton Cliff fort commanding
good views.

Portacloy Cliff-girt cove and beach.

Benwee Head A head with sheer cliffs,
arches, stacks and panoramic views
including the off-shore sheer Stags of
Broadhaven. Doonvilla is a great
promontory fort.

Ross Port Stone Druids circles and a
chamber tomb (NMs).

Moista Sound Accessible by a long,
rough route, continuing the Ballinapark
road, is this dramatic steep sea chasm
with a tiny mouth.

Benaderreen A cove of sheer, striped cliffs.

Ballycastle Some traditional cottages. Digs have discovered settlements from c. 3000 BC.

Downpatrick Head Pilgrimages are made to the ecclesiastical ruins on the last Sunday in July. Poulnachantinny puffing hole is a blow hole from which sea-water spouts under certain conditions. On the off-shore stack of Doonbristy is an impressive promontory fort.

Carbad More A complex cairn with gallery graves and ring-forts.

Rathfran Abbey Ruins of a 13th-century friary and a stone circle (NMs).

Killala A round tower and souterrain (NM).

Moyne Substantial remains of a 15th-century abbey, with 16th-century graffiti and good views from the tower.

Rosserk Abbey The ruins of the 15th-century abbey, burnt by the English governor in 1590, are the best preserved of their type.

Kilmoremoy Fragments of the 'great church of Moy' founded by Olean, disciple of St Patrick.

Corballa Erriscrone YH.

Ballina See Route 329. Also links with Routes 345, 357.

Route 329   38 miles   61 km
BALLINA — WESTPORT

Bartholomew's ¼ inch:1 mile no. 5
OS ½ inch:1 mile nos 6, 11

Ballina Market and Roman Catholic cathedral town. A salmon festival is held in July. Cloghogle is the remains of a chambered tomb (NM). Links with Routes 328, 345, 357.

Kilmoremoy See Route 328.

Corballa Enniscrone YH.

Castle Gore The 18th-century Castle

Gore with ruins of 16th-century Deel Castle in the grounds.

Crossmolina Remains of a 10th-century 'abbey'. Several ring-forts are in the area.

Ballybrannagh A long cairn and three court graves.

Castle Island Ruins of an O'Conor castle.

Errew Abbey At the head of the lonely

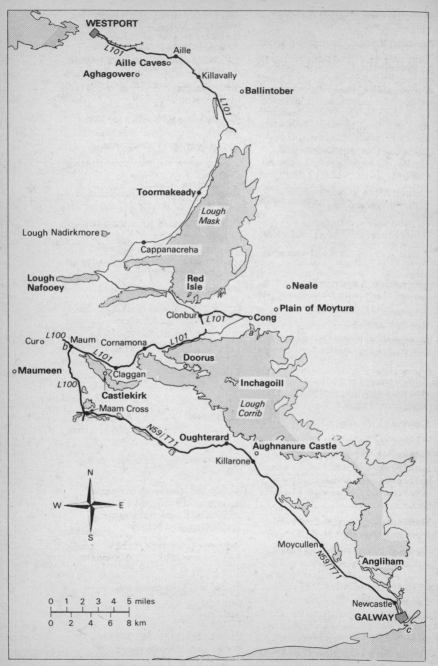

peninsula stand the ruins of a simple 13th-century abbey (NM).

Pontoon Bridge The river joining the two loughs flows north, except after heavy rain when Lough Conn rises quicker, making it flow south. An area of large rocking stones.

a The alternative route uses a hill pass to visit Castlebar, whereas the main route stays below the hills.

Castlebar Founded in the 17th-century, the town was the scene of the 'Castlebar Races' battle in 1798. The town hall was a linen hall. John Wesley laid a stone in the chapel, which is now an art centre.

Westport See Route 325. Also links with Routes 326, 330.

Route 330 84 miles 136 km
WESTPORT — GALWAY

Bartholomew's ¼ inch:1 mile no. 5
OS ½ inch:1 mile nos 11, 14

Westport See Route 325. Also links with Routes 326, 329.

Aghagower Ruins of a round tower, and the 'Church of the Teeth', said to have been founded by St Patrick (NMs).

Aille Caves A sink hole and complex of caves, used for mass in Penal times.

Ballintober The 13th-century restored Royal Abbey is Ireland's only one which has been in continuous use till today, despite damage from Henry VIII and the Cromwellians.

Toormakeady An early Irish college and a knitwear centre are based here.

Lough Nafooey Famed for its beauty and a legendary monster.

Red Isle A one-time O'Flaherty seat.

Cong The 12th-century Royal Abbey, on a 6th-century monastery site, has a good carved doorway. There are fragments of a 13th-century abbey (NM); and a Monks' Fishing House on a river

island (NM). Rivers connecting and feeding the loughs have worn caves in the limestone, including Kelly's Cave (NM) and Pigeon Hole. The Mask–Corrib canal, made to provide work in the great famine, will not hold water as it is in porous limestone. Every funeral procession into Cong adds another Crusheen (wooden cross) to those already by the roadside. The 19th-century Ashford Castle is a mock fortress built by the Guinness family.

a Boats run from Cong to the island of Inchagoill.

Neale A nine-tiered pyramidal cairn, a classical temple and a great gallery grave.

Plain of Moytura An area of many antiquities, including a 60-foot (20-metre) cairn, falsely associated with the mythical battle between the Tuatha De Danann and the Firbolgs.

Doorus Good views from here.

Castlekirk The massive remains of a 13th-century island castle are associated with a legend of a hen, given by a witch, which could lay enough eggs for food in seige (NM).

b At this point the L100 can be followed north-west through the beautiful Maum Valley, to join Route 325 near Leenaun.

Maumeen St Patrick's Bed and curative well is the goal of pilgrimages from Cur on the last Sunday of July.

Oughterard Boats and boatmen for fishing for hire.

Inchagoill Island with the ruins of ancient St Patrick's church, and a stone with Ireland's oldest inscription in Latin characters (NMs).

Aughnanure Castle Ruins of a fine 16th-century castle, much ruined by river erosion.

Angliham Black marble quarries.

c Ferries run from Galway to the Aran Isles.

Galway See Route 322. Also links with Routes 323, 332.

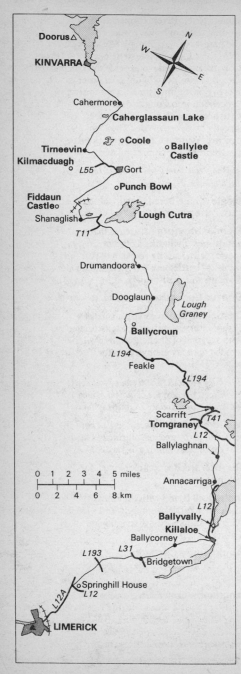

Route 331   60 miles   97 km
KINVARRA — LIMERICK

Bartholomew's ¼ inch:1 mile no. 5
OS ½ inch:1 mile nos 14, 15 (just), 17, 18

Kinvarra See Route 321. Also links with Route 322.

Doorus Kinvarra YH.

Caherglassaun Lake Linked underground to the sea, this lake rises and falls with the tides.

Tirneevin Church with fine glass.

Kilmacduagh Remains of an eminent early monastery, including a round tower, cathedral and 14th–15th century Abbot's House (NMs).

Coole In this estate which played an important role in the 19th–20th century arts revival, there is a tree carved with the initials of Shaw, Yeats, O'Casey and others.

Ballylee Castle Yeats lived beside the tower and wrote of it in his poems.

Punch Bowl A deep swallowhole and gorge.

Fiddaun Castle A fine 16th-century castle sited between two loughs.

Lough Cutra The church and castle ruins stand on islands in the lough.

Ballycroun Three gallery graves.

Tomgraney The church incorporates a pre-Romanesque church.

Ballyvally A massive, tree-planted ring-fort.

Killaloe A fishing centre. The 12th-century Transitional cathedral has St Flannan's Church (NM) in its yard. Also St Mo-Lua's Oratory (NM).

Limerick See Route 301. Also links with Routes 304, 313, 316, 317.

Route 332   32 miles   51 km
KILCONNELL — GALWAY

Bartholomew's ¼ inch:1 mile no. 5
OS ½ inch:1 mile nos 14, 15

Kilconnell Fine ruins of a 15th-century Franciscan friary (NM). This is the traditional burial place of St Ruth following his death at the Battle of Aughrim. Links with Route 333.

Athenry The grand castle (NM) has a 13th-century keep, and much of the old town wall survives, including five of its towers. The friary, now in ruins, was founded in 1241.

Galway See Route 322. Also links with Routes 323, 330.

Route 333   35 miles   56 km
ATHLONE — KILCONNELL

Bartholomew's ¼ inch:1 mile no. 2
OS ½ inch:1 mile no. 15

Athlone The town has a long and turbulent past, because of its strategic position at a crossing of the River Shannon. The riverside castle of 1210 suffered the heaviest bombardment in Irish history in 1691. The 19th-century riverside fortifications were built against the threat of French invasion. There is a notable early railway station. It is a centre for boat trips to Lough Ree and Clonmacnoise. Links with Routes 334, 344.

a If you next intend to follow Route 344 to Mountrath, you can turn to it here.

Clonfinlough The Clonfinlough Stone is an unimpressive but very ancient monument (NM) said to mark the site of a prehistoric battle.

Clonmacnoise A 6th-century monastic city once famed for its learning and culture. There are many fine remains, including more than four hundred early gravestones, two round towers, three high crosses, two holy wells, and eight churches (NMs).

Shannonbridge The power station uses milled peat. There is a well-preserved small 19th-century fort.

Clonfert A monastery was founded here by St Brendan, and in the 12th century a cathedral built. The fine

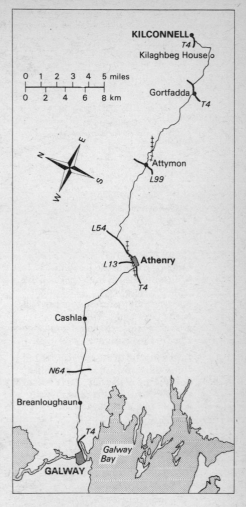

Romanesque west doorway has survived.

Ballinasloe A market town, its October Fair being the largest livestock fair in Ireland. When horses were used more this was the largest horse fair in Europe. Local limestone quarries supplied masonry for shop fronts in New York. The castle used to guard the crossing over the River Suck.

Aughrim This was the scene of the

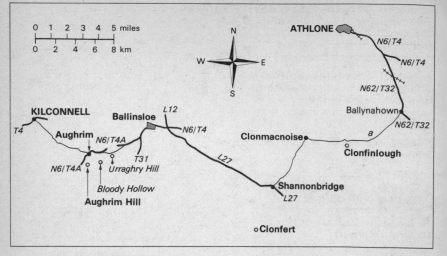

deciding battle of the Jacobite–Williamite war, in 1691, in which the Jacobites were beaten. The Jacobite lines were drawn up on Aughrim Hill, facing those of the Williamites on Urraghry Hill. Ferocious fighting took place in Bloody Hollow.

Aughrim Hill In the battle of 1691 St Ruth, the Jacobite leader, was killed near the top of this hill. There is a small ring-fort (NM) on the summit, and another to the south-east (NM).

Kilconnell See Route 332.

Route 334   38 miles   61 km
KILLUCAN — ATHLONE

Bartholomew's ¼ inch:1 mile no. 2
OS ½ inch:1 mile nos 12, 13, 15 (just)

Killucan The church has a medieval font. In nearby Rathwire is a motte and bailey, with the foundations of a stone castle. Links with Route 335.

Mullingar The market centre for the surrounding rich cattle lands, with a 20th-century cathedral.

Belvedere Near the 18th-century house is Jealous Wall, a Gothic ruin supposedly built to prevent Lady Belvedere from seeing the house of the

Lordship's brother, as she was suspected of being his paramour.

Slanemore Hill There are three tumuli on the top, and a splendid view.

Uisneach Hill For long regarded as the centre of Ireland. The view from the 603-foot (184-m) summit embraces twenty of Ireland's thirty-two counties on a clear day. There are numerous prehistoric remains on the hill which was used by pagans as a seat of fire cult.

Killare The remains of the church mark the site of a monastery.

Hallstown House The triangular mound to the north-west of the house is said to contain the heads of those slain in the Battle of Washford.

Clare Hill The remains of a sturdy castle on the 433-foot (132-m) summit.

Athlone See Route 333. Also links with Route 344.

Route 335   45 miles   73 km
KILLUCAN — DUBLIN

Bartholomew's ¼ inch:1 mile no. 2
OS ½ inch:1 mile nos 13, 16

Killucan See Route 334.

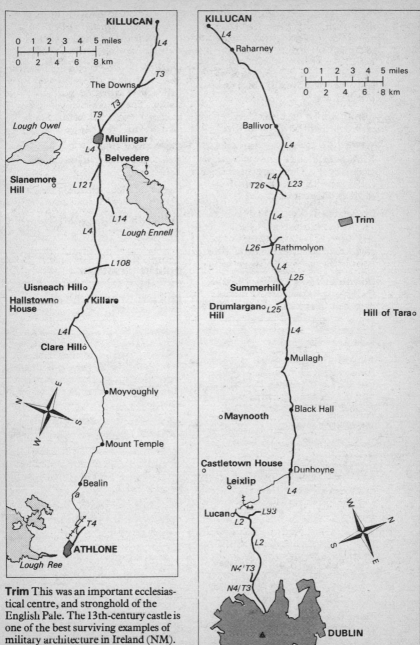

Trim This was an important ecclesiastical centre, and stronghold of the English Pale. The 13th-century castle is one of the best surviving examples of military architecture in Ireland (NM). Remnants of St Mary's Priory include the Yellow Steeple (NM), a 125-foot (38-m) bell tower. Sheep Gate (NM) is one of the town's old gates; monument to the Duke of Wellington who grew up here; 19th-century cathedral. One mile east are the ruins (NM) of the cathedral and priory destroyed by fire in the Middle Ages.

Summerhill A planned village, with a carved memorial cross on the green.

Hill of Tara The famous seat of the Kings of Tara, and a centre of paganism since 2000 BC. There are many remains (NM) including forts and burial mounds. Pleasant views.

Drumlargan Hill In 1647 this was the site of a battle between the Parliamentarian army of Dublin and the Confederate Catholics, three thousand of the latter being massacred after the battle.

Maynooth Massive ruins of a castle (NM), with a gatehouse, keep, and great hall. St Patrick's College is the main Catholic seminary in the British Isles, and has a small museum (open) containing ecclesiastical exhibits and early electrical apparatus.

Leixlip The name comes from 'Salmon Leap' referring to the falls on the River Liffey, now harnessed by a power station. The church incorporates a medieval tower, and there are two medieval towers in the castle.

Castletown House The finest Georgian country house in Ireland, built in 1722 (open).

Lucan A fashionable spa in the 18th century, with a Palladian house.

Dublin See Route 336. Also links with Routes 340, 359, 360.

Route 336   44 miles   71 km
DUBLIN — LARAGH

Bartholomew's ¼ inch:1 mile nos 2, 3
OS ½ inch:1 mile no. 16

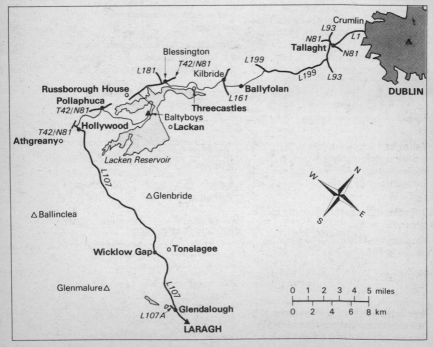

Routes 336 and 340 both link Dublin and Laragh. Route 340 follows the course of the old military road through the heart of the Wicklow Mountains, while Route 336 follows gentler terrain to the west, and passes more points of interest.

Dublin The Norsemen are regarded as the real founders of Dublin; Olaf the White captured it in 852. Now the city is Eire's capital and a busy port. It was the English base in Eire between 1172 and 1922. There is much Georgian architecture. There are two Church of Ireland cathedrals, Christchurch Cathedral built by the Normans on a Danish foundation, and a slightly later Norman cathedral, St Patrick's. Famous buildings include the old Parliament House (c. 1730), the Custom House (1791); the Roman Catholic Pro-Cathedral in Graeco-Roman style (completed 1825); the Four Courts. There are two universities: Trinity College (Dublin University) and the National University of Ireland. Many galleries and museums include the National Gallery, the National Museum (containing the Tara Brooch, the Ardagh Chalice and the Cross of Cong); Trinity College Library (the *Book of Kells*); also the Botanical Gardens. Many literary and theatrical connections; birthplace of R. B. Sheridan, Oscar Wilde, Thomas Moore and G. B. Shaw; home of the Abbey Theatre. Links with Routes 335, 340, 359, 360.

Tallaght There was an important monastery here in the 6th century, and at a later date a castle was built which formed the main outpost of the English Pale.

Ballyfolan Small tumulus with remains of a stone circle.

Threecastles Keep of a 14th-century castle (NM).

Lackan Just east of this early monastic site is St Boodin's Well, once famed for its cures.

Russborough House One of Ireland's best Palladian country houses, designed for a wealthy Dublin brewer (open).

Pollaphuca The River Liffey plunges through a gorge, and then down a series of waterfalls for 150 feet (45 m). At the foot of the middle fall is Puca's pool, named after a malicious sprite. The volume of water was much greater before the Liffey power station diverted the river underground.

Hollywood The name refers to a holy wood associated with St Kevin of Glendalough, whose first hermitage was hereabouts.

Athgreany The Piper's Stones are a circle of granite boulders, with a single outlier, said to represent a piper and dancers who were petrified for violating the Sabbath.

Wicklow Gap The road summit (1469 feet/448 m) as it rises between Hollywood and Laragh. Between here and Glendalough are parts of St Kevin's road, a pilgrim route.

Tonelagee An easy walk to the summit provides tremendous views over the wild scenery of the Wicklow mountains.

Glendalough Set deep in the heart of the Wicklow Mountains, the 'Valley of the Two Lakes' is famous for its fine scenery and monastic remains: the monastery was founded in the 6th century by St Kevin and survived as an 'ecclesiastical city' until the 17th century. The remains include a gatehouse, churches, ring-fort, round tower (103 feet/31 m high), and cathedral (NMs).

Laragh See Route 337. Also links with Routes 339, 340, 341.

Route 337　　　　20 miles　　33 km
LARAGH — ARKLOW

Bartholomew's ¼ inch:1 mile no. 3
OS ½ inch:1 mile nos 16, 19

Routes 337 and 338 link Laragh with Enniscorthy, as does Route 339. The first two routes cover gentler terrain and visit the coast.

Laragh The barracks were built to

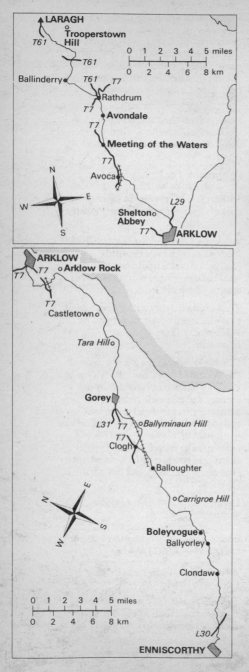

guard the Old Military Road which ran south from Dublin through the Wicklow Mountains. Glendalach YH. Links with Routes 336, 339, 340, 341.

Trooperstown Hill There are fine views from the top of the hill. In the valley just to the south-west is pretty, wooded Clara Valley.

Avondale The birthplace and home of Charles Stewart Parnell, the nationalist leader of the struggle for Irish Home Rule in the late 19th century. There is a museum and arboretum here.

Meeting of the Waters The confluence of the Avonmore and Avonbeg rivers, made famous by the 19th-century poet, satirist and musician, Thomas Moore.

Shelton Abbey Formerly the seat of the Earls of Wicklow.

Arklow See Route 338.

Route 338   34 miles   55 km
ARKLOW — ENNISCORTHY

Bartholomew's ¼ inch:1 mile no. 3
OS ½ inch:1 mile no. 19

Arklow A fishing port and small resort. The town has for long built small wooden boats, and now produces pottery. There is a maritime museum, and a statue commemorating the defeat of the Wexford Insurgents in 1789. Links with Route 337.

Arklow Rock Good views of mountains and coast from the top.

Gorey This market town was attacked by the insurgents in 1789, while on their way to the coast road to Dublin.

Boleyvogue It was the burning of the Catholic chapel and several local farmhouses by the British that caused the Wexford Insurrection of 1798. The initial successes of the insurgents led to a country-wide revolt.

Enniscorthy See Route 310. Also links with Routes 311, 339.

Route 339
50 miles   80 km
LARAGH — ENNISCORTHY

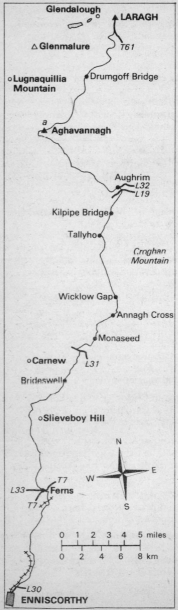

Bartholomew's ¼ inch:1 mile no. 3
OS ½ inch:1 mile nos 16, 19

Route 339 links Laragh to Enniscorthy, as do Routes 337 and 338. This route goes via the old military road through the Wicklow Mountains and southern foothills.

Laragh See Route 337. Also links with Routes 336, 340, 341.

Glendalough See Route 336.

Glenmalure The ride up the valley from Drumgoff Bridge is dramatic.

Aghavannagh The YH is in one of the posts that used to guard the Military Road, constructed at the turn of the century to aid control of the remoter areas and running through the Wicklow Mountains. At a later date it was a shooting lodge, and then a country house.

Lugnaquillia Mountain At 3039 feet (926 m) this is the highest mountain in Leinster. It can be ascended from Aghavannagh if you have sufficient equipment and experience of navigating in mists, which can suddenly envelop the mountain.

a If you next intend to follow Route 341 to Carlow, you can turn to it at this point.

Carnew In the rising of 1798 insurgents captured the 17th-century castle from the British. Thirty-six of them were later executed in the castle, and there is now a monument to them.

Slieveboy Hill Good views from the summit (1387 feet/423 m).

Ferns This was once the principal diocese in the ancient kingdom of Leinster. St Mary's Abbey (NM) has an interesting square belfry which turns into a round tower higher up, and the remains of the cathedral, burnt down in 1577, can be seen incorporated in St Edan's cathedral. The castle (NM) was dismantled in 1641 by the Parliamentarians who also slaughtered the townspeople.

Enniscorthy See Route 310. Also links with Routes 311, 338.

Route 340   27 miles   43 km
DUBLIN — LARAGH

Bartholomew's ¼ inch:1 mile nos 2, 3
OS ½ inch:1 mile no. 16

*Routes 336 and 340 both link Dublin and
Laragh. Route 340 follows the course of
the old military road through the heart of
the Wicklow Mountains, while Route 336
follows gentler terrain to the west, and
passes more points of interest.*

Dublin See Route 336. Also links with
Routes 335, 359, 360.

Mount Venus Ruined chamber tomb
with an enormous granite capstone.

Montpelier On the summit of this
1271-foot (387 m) mountain stand ruins
of a massive 18th-century lodge known
as the Hell Fire Club, where Dublin's
more daring young men indulged in
revelry.

Kippure A road leads to the top of this
mountain (2475 feet/755 m), from
where there are superb views.

Sally Gap A 1631-foot (497-m) col on
the old Military Road.

Glendalough See Route 336.

Laragh See Route 337. Also links with
Routes 336, 339, 341.

Route 341   37 miles   58 km.
LARAGH — CARLOW

Bartholomew's ¼ inch:1 mile no. 3
OS ½ inch:1 mile nos 16, 19

Laragh See Route 337. Also links with
Routes 336, 339, 340.

Glendalough See Route 336.

Glenmalure, Aghavannagh and
Lugnaquillia Mountain See Route
339.

*If you next intend to follow Route 339 to
Enniscorthy, you can turn to it here.*

Clonmore The site of a 6th-century
monastery; there are high crosses in the
two churchyards, and St Mogue's
Cross. Remains of a 13th-century
English royal castle.

Acaun Bridge On the east bank of the
river is Haroldstown portal dolmen
(NM), used in the past as a house.

Rathgall An impressive stone ring-fort
(NM) on the hill top, covering 18 acres.
Close by is another ring-fort and a stone
circle.

Mount Brown Dolmen A good
example of a portal dolmen, with a
capstone weighing over 100 tonnes.

Carlow See Route 342.

Route 342   23 miles   37 km
CARLOW — KILKENNY

Bartholomew's ¼ inch:1 mile no. 3
OS ½ inch:1 mile no. 19

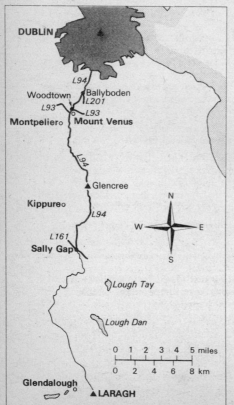

Carlow A market town with various small industries. Little remains of the once grand castle (NM). There is a 19th-century Court House, and a cathedral. Links with Route 341.

Killeshin A fine Romanesque doorway, ancient font and parts of the walls survive from the 11th-century church (NM).

Black Bridge These hills lie over Ireland's important Leinster coalfield.

Oldleighlin Small, medieval St Laserian's Cathedral has a 12th-century font and a tomb chest.

Clara Castle A well-preserved 16th-century tower house (NM).

Kilkenny See Route 311. Also links with Routes 312, 314, 343.

Route 343	29 miles	47 km
MOUNTRATH — KILKENNY		

Bartholomew's ¼ inch:1 mile no. 3
OS ½ inch:1 mile nos 15, 18, 19 (just)

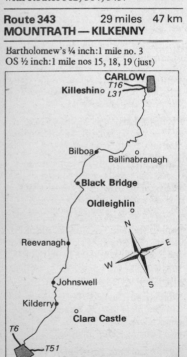

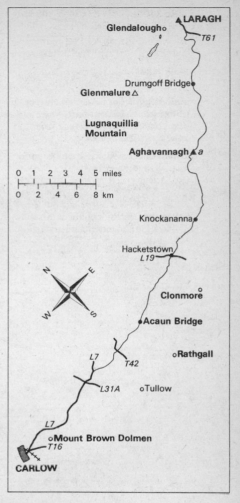

Mountrath In earlier times the town thrived on the linen industry. Links with Route 344.

Abbeyleix The village was laid out in the middle of the 18th century by an 'improving' landlord, Viscount de Vesci, and has a market house.

Timahoe An excellent 12th-century round tower (NM) with a Romanesque doorway is all that remains from the monastery that once stood here. The nearby church was converted into a castle in the 17th century.

Haywood House An 18th-century house with a folly and Italianate garden.

Ballinakill Little remains of a castle destroyed by the Cromwellians.

Ballyragget The castle was built in the 15th-century and is still in good condition, having served as a British military post in 1798.

Castlecomer Named after the castle that was built here following the Anglo-Norman invasion. In the 17th-century English colonists settled here and Sir Christopher Wandsford laid out the town, modelling it exactly on Alsinore, in Italy. He also introduced hay making

to the district and exploited the local anthracite mines.

Corrandhu Hill On the summit (836 feet/255 m) is a bivallate enclosure where prehistoric burials have been found. In 1600, 'Black' Thomas Butler, Lieutenant-General of Elizabeth I's army, was seized here by the Irish.

Dunmore Cave See Route 312.

Kilkenny See Route 311. Also links with Routes 312, 314, 342.

Route 344   43 miles   70 km
ATHLONE — MOUNTRATH

Bartholomew's ¼ inch:1 mile nos 2, 3
OS ½ inch:1 mile no. 15

Athlone See Route 333. Also links with Route 334.

a If you next intend to follow Route 333 to Kilconnell, you can turn to it here.

Clonfinlough and **Clonmacnoise** See Route 333.

Lemanaghan Pre-Romanesque oratory, and parts of a Romanesque church with six early gravestones.

Ferbane Early gravestones (NM) can be seen by the ruins of the 15th-century church.

Cloghan The 15th-century Clononey Castle has a well preserved tower, bawn and walled garden, and contains fine carpets and paintings (open).

Birr The gardens of the castle are famous for their box hedges, magnolias and maples (open). This was the site of the Rosse telescope, the largest in the world from 1845 to 1915 and now the important object of a museum.

Kilcormac The good 16th-century wooden pieta that can be seen in the church was buried in a bog for sixty years during Penal times.

Castle Bernard An ornate 19th-century mansion with the shaft of a high cross (NM) in the grounds.

Slieve Bloom Mountains Pleasant

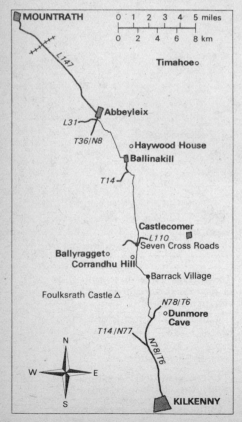

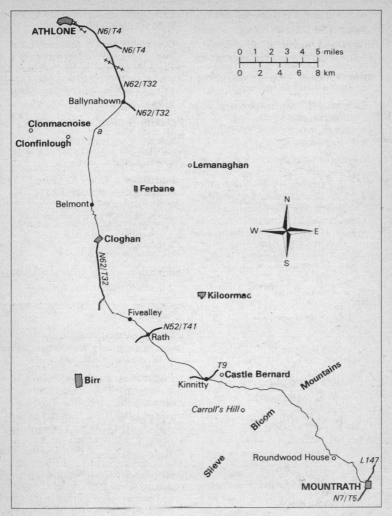

walks in these delightful hills.

Mountrath See Route 343.

Route 345   55 miles   88 km
SLIGO — BALLINA

Bartholomew's ¼ inch:1 mile no. 5
OS ½ inch:1 mile nos 6 (just), 7

Sligo Now a port and market town, Sligo has had a turbulent history. The name derives from the Irish for 'shelly river'. There are 13th-century Abbey ruins with good stone carving (NM); museum of local interest with W. B. Yeats exhibits. Links with Route 346.

a Boats for Lough Gill can be hired at Sligo.

Coney Island Pillars mark a low tide drive from the mainland to the island.

Strandhill Dolly's Cottage is a typical

early 19th-century rural cottage (open).

Knocknarea The great passage grave summit cairn is said to be the grave of the 1st century Queen Maeve or Mab. The Glen of Knocknarea on the south hill flank is a long, deep, wooded chasm.

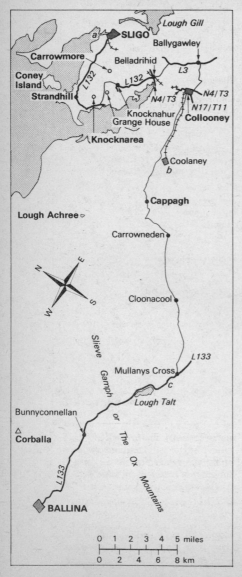

Carrowmore A great group of Bronze Age tombs, pillarstones and ring-forts (NMs).

Collooney Collooney Gap was strategically important in old times. The hand-cut Innisfree crystal works may sometimes be visited. To the north-east is a 'tidal' Holy Well.

b   A short cut to Route 357 can be made on lanes south.

Cappagh The area is rich in chamber tombs and gallery graves.

Lough Achree This is supposedly Ireland's newest lake, formed by a 15th-century earthquake.

c   If you next intend to follow Route 357 to Boyle, you can turn to it here.

Corballa Enniscrone YH.

Ballina See Route 329. Also links with Routes 328, 357.

Route 346   58 miles   94 km
DONEGAL — SLIGO

Bartholomew's ¼ inch:1 mile no. 1
OS ½ inch:1 mile nos 3, 7

Donegal A 15th-century castle and a Jacobean house stand on a Viking fortress site (NM). The ruined abbey is a claimant to being the place of writing of the *Annals of the Four Masters*, an old history of Ireland (NM). There are 18th-century houses, and the 20th-century church of the Four Masters. The factory for hand-woven tweed can sometimes be visited. Beaches. Links with Routes 347, 362, 363.

a   If you next intend to follow Route 363 to Enniskillen, you can turn to it here.

Brownhall In the estate is The Pullins, where the river flows through a gorge and cave system.

Rossnowlagh The friary houses the Donegal county museum. There is a surfing bay.

Lurgan Carn The summit of the low hill, with its ring and cairn, offers panoramic views.

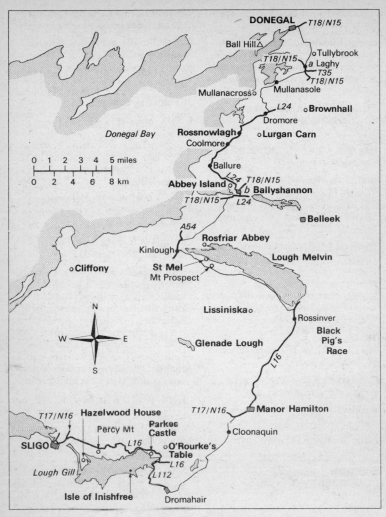

Abbey Island By a river island stand the remains of an abbey, with a cave used for mass in Penal times nearby.

Ballyshannon This is said to be Ireland's oldest inhabited town, sited at a strategic river crossing.

b To join Route 363 to Enniskillen, take the L24 south-east at Belleek.

Belleek The pottery producing lustre-finish china can sometimes be visited.

Rosfriar Abbey The lovely house near Lough Melvin also claims to be where four refugee scholars wrote the great 17th-century *Annals of the Four Masters*.

Cliffony Creevykeel Court Cairn, which has been well excavated, is considered the best in Ireland. Nearby is the massive, 19th-century Classiebawn Castle of the Mountbatten family.

St Mel Isolated abbey remains. The off-shore crannog has castle fragments and was the hiding place of a Spanish Armada captain.

Lough Melvin Both islands in the lough and its south-west side have several ruins, including Kilcoo Monastery which was founded or dedicated by St Patrick.

Black Pig's Race Some remains of the earthwork which was once the Ulster boundary.

Lissiniska The village lies in the scenic Glenaniff valley.

Manor Hamilton The town was founded in a strategic position in the 17th century by a Scotsman called Hamilton. There is a 17th-century stronghouse.

Glenade Lough To the north stands Dreffni Castle, where events gave Henry II a pretext for the Anglo-Norman invasion of Ireland, profoundly changing the country's history for centuries. Nearby are 16th-century Creevelea Friary (NM) and a thatched church.

Isle of Inishfree The island features in W. B. Yeat's poetry.

O'Rourke's Table A ritual rock commanding good views.

Parkes Castle A fine 17th-century castle (NM).

Sligo See Route 345.

Route 347   73 miles   118 km
DOOCHARRY — DONEGAL

Bartholomew's ¼ inch:1 mile no. 1
OS ½ inch:1 mile no. 3

Doocharry Links with Route 348.

a The main route between Doocharry and Ardara passes near several points of interest in valley and coastal lowlands, whereas the alternative route explores a higher, wilder valley.

Naran Large beach. At low tide the isle of Inishkeel with its ecclesiastical remains is accessible.

Dunmore Head The headland has two old forts, and offers good views.

Doon Lough In the lough is a great, ancient island fort.

Kilclooney Dolmen with a huge capstone.

Kilclooney Bridge Mass was celebrated by a large roadside rock in Penal times.

Ardara The Holy Family church has some 20th-century glass. Ardara is renowned for its needlework and homespun tweed.

Loughros Point A quiet peninsula with views of bays and headlands to either side.

Maghera A lonely hamlet near river falls, and caves exposed at low tide.

Glencolumbkille This was the retreat of St Colmcille, who is said to have vanquished demons over whom St Patrick had no power. The ruin of St Colmcille's dry-stone chapel is a station of a July pilgrimage circuit, as are many good prehistoric monuments (NMs). Celtic crosses; large souterrain in the churchyard. The area's poor soil has been improved by co-operative efforts.

Glen Head Precipitous cliffs with the impressive Sturrall promontory to the north.

Malin Beg Sheltered strand near natural rock bridges.

Slieve League The mountain gives superb views, and its cliffs are claimed to be the highest in Britain. There are many fine walks, such as 'One Man's Path', but some are dangerous so ask advice locally. The cliffs can be viewed from boats hired at Teelin.

Kilcar Hand-woven tweed factory.

Muckros Head Beach, and caves exposed at low tide.

Killybegs A fishing port. A carved slab can be seen in St Mary's Church. The factory making hand-tufted Donegal carpets is sometimes open to visitors.

Milltown Lace factory.

Killaghtee Ruined church with a floor of tomb slabs.

St John's Point An isolated peninsula with a beach and views of the mainland.

Inver Churchyard with the tomb of the inventor of the whaling gun-harpoon.

Mountcharles Famous for hand embroidery. Birthplace of the writer, S. Macmanus; also Lord Conyngham's Georgian house.

Donegal See Route 346. Also links with Routes 362, 363.

Route 348   53 miles   86 km
DUNFANAGHY — DOOCHARRY

Bartholomew's ¼ inch:1 mile no. 1
OS ½ inch:1 mile no. 1

Dunfanaghy Large strand. Links with Route 349.

Horn Head A lonely headland with fine cliffs and rich in sea-bird life. Cliff-top

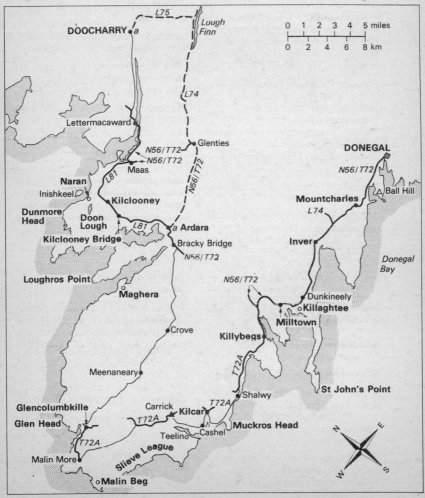

footpaths, including the one to Templebreaga or Marble Arch on the west side of the head.

Ray The great Celtic Cross is said to have been hewn from Muckish Mountain by St Colmcille.

Ballyconnell In the grounds of the house is a red-veined rock called Cloghaneely, said in legend to be a decapitated head.

a Ferries from the local quay to the Isles of

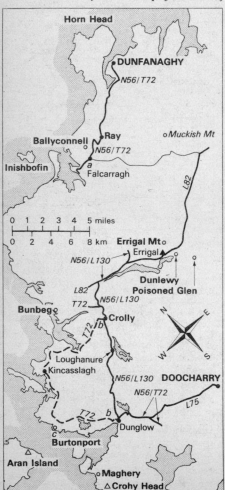

Inishbofin and Tory.

Inishbofin This island, and the larger Tory Island which lies further out to sea, are known as outposts of the old life-style, learning and religion.

Dunlewy Homespun tweed.

Poisoned Glen The impressive valley, which shelters the remains of some 5th- and 6th-century monastic beehive cells, gets its name from plants growing in it.

Errigal Mountain Made of quartzite, this is the highest mountain in County Donegal. The summit, which can be reached by a stiff climb on foot, affords a panoramic view.

Bunbeg Pretty harbour.

Crolly Crolly dolls are made here.

b The alternative route keeps closer to the coast, whereas the main option crosses the open Rosses area of rocks and tiny lakes to pass the lovely Lough Anure. Both choices contrast with the more mountainous scenery further north-east in the route.

Burtonport In the 18th century the Duke of Rutland founded a port on nearby Rutland Isle, and the Marquis of Conyngham founded Burtonport as a competitor. The former did not thrive, but Burtonport is still an important fishing port.

c Ferries to Aran Island.

Aran Island There is good cliff scenery on the island's western side.

Crohy Head Nearby are cliffs, caves and coves.

Maghery Beach. To the north is a ruined church, the object of pilgrimages every 7th July. There are graves of British soldiers who were washed ashore nearby.

Doocharry Links with Route 347.

Route 349   30 miles   49 km
DUNFANAGHY — RAPHOE

Bartholomew's ¼ inch:1 mile no. 1
OS ½ inch:1 mile nos 1, 4 (just)

An alternative to this fairly direct route is to link Dunfanaghy and Raphoe by a much longer ride through the peninsulas of Rosguill and Fanad to the east with their long beaches and occasional coastal rock formations.

Dunfanaghy Large strand. Links with Route 348.

Horn Head See Route 348.

Cashelmore Unusual 19th-century bell-tower.

Ards Peninsula Permission is sometimes granted to enter the lovely lowland estate now in the hands of an active monastery.

Doe Castle The ancient castle, although modernized around 1800, still has its bawn, keep and rock-cut ditch (NM). Nearby are old MacSweeney tombstones.

St Colmcille's Oratory The ruins are a place of pilgrimage. About 1 mile (1.5 km) to the south is a flagstone, said to mark St Colmcille's birthplace, and to cure anyone who sleeps on it of homesickness.

Doon Rock The rock was the inauguration place of the O'Donnell clan. The curative Doon Well is the goal of pilgrimages.

Conwal Ancient monastery site with old graves.

Raphoe See Route 362. Also links with Route 350.

Route 350   52 miles   84 km
DUNGIVEN — RAPHOE

Bartholomew's ¼ inch:1 mile no. 1
OS ½ inch:1 mile no. 4

Dungiven The 19th-century castle includes parts of a fortified Plantation bawn (NM). The ruined 12th-century priory church contains a good tomb (NM). Links with Route 351.

Banagher In the yard of the ruined church stands a tomb in the shape of a church, said to be that of St O'Heney,

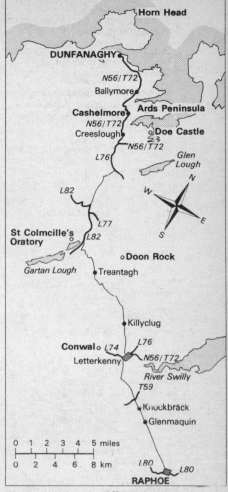

the church's founder (NM). The sand beneath the tomb is said to give success in contests to O'Heneys, and has been thrown at racehorses to help them win.

Stick Hill The hill overlooks the route as it passes through a large peat bog.

Draperstown The settlement was founded and named in 1818 by the London Company of Drapers.

Black Water Bridge Within a mile of the bridge are a group of stone circles, chambered tombs, a pillarstone and a double court cairn (NMs).

Castledamph Remains of a double stone circle. The area stretching between Glenroan Bridge and Meena-

gorp is unusually rich in prehistoric monuments of various kinds.

Evish Hill In Dergalt, to the west, is the ancestral home of USA President Woodrow Wilson (NM).

Sion Mills 20th-century church with interesting glass and carvings.

Strabane Gray's Printing Press contains a collection of 19th-century hand printing machines (NT, open). Both President Woodrow Wilson's grandfather and Captain Dunlap, the first printer of the American Declaration of Independence, worked here before emigrating.

Raphoe See Route 362. Also links with Route 349.

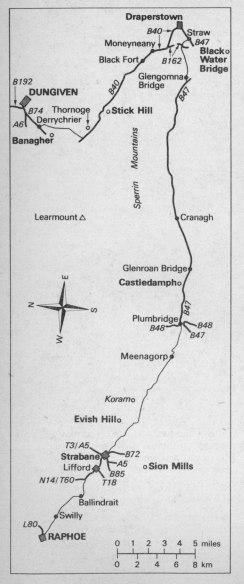

Route 351   42 miles   68 km
BALLYCASTLE — DUNGIVEN

Bartholomew's ¼ inch: 1 mile no. 1
OS ½ inch: 1 mile no. 2

Ballycastle Market town and seaside resort with sands. Marconi transmitted his first wireless message to Rathlin Island from here in 1905. Dunineny Castle ruins stand on a promontory. Links with Route 352.

Carrickerade Island In the summer months this basalt stack can be reached by means of a fragile rope bridge over a 90-foot (30-metre) drop. Excellent views include the Isle of Arran.

Dunseverick Castle Little remains of the stronghold once said to have been visited by St Patrick (NM), and later destroyed by the Cromwellians. There are good walks by cliff path to the Giant's Causeway.

Giant's Causeway This striking geological phenomenon has been caused by the extrusion of basalt; an outflow of volcanic rock which has cooled into thousands of polygonal columns. Legend has it that this is the giant's causeway over to Scotland.

Bushmills The pot-still whisky named Bushmills was called after this town.

Dunluce Castle Built in the 14th century, and romantically sited on a high rock cut off from the shore, the castle was besieged many times. It used guns salvaged from the wreck of a Spanish Armada ship. In 1639 a landslide jettisoned part of the castle and some of its servants in the sea. The gatehouse, towers and walls remain (NM).

Coleraine A port and manufacturing town. When the town was planned in the 16th century by Sir John Perrot, he had the oak frames for the houses prefabricated in London and shipped over to Ireland.

Mount Sandel Fort A motte (NM) standing high over the River Bann.

a The main route detours to the coast on small lanes and visits places of interest, while the alternative route follows more direct A and B roads.

Liffock The 17th-century thatched Hezlett House is of particular interest because of the unusual cruck—truss construction of the roof (NT, open).

Downhill Lions Gate of Downhill Castle was built in 1780 for the eccentric bishop of Derry, though little remains now. Just to the north is Mussenden Temple, a rotunda built on the cliff edge overlooking the mouth of Lough Foyle, with views along the Donegal and Antrim coasts (NT, open).

Sconce Hill At the top of the hill, at a height of 800 feet (245 m) is the Giant's Sconce (NM), a stone ring-fort.

Bovevagh There is an interesting church (NM), and to the south-west, Saint's Tomb (NM), built in the form of a stone-roofed church.

Dungiven See Route 350.

Route 352   67 miles   108 km
**BALLYCASTLE —
CARRICKFERGUS**

Bartholomew's ¼ inch:1 mile no. 1
OS ½ inch:1 mile nos 2, 5 (map 5 is currently unavailable)

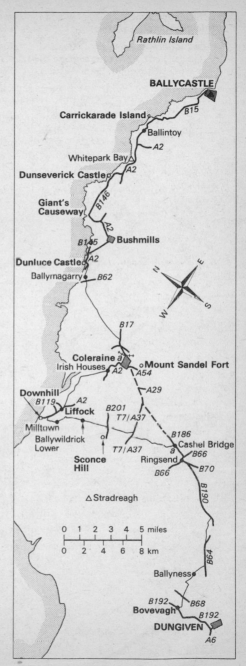

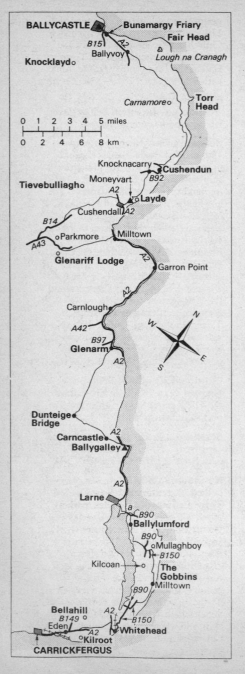

A ferry crossing between Larne and Ballylumford is used in this route.

The A2 is the renowned Antrim Coast road, popular with pleasure drivers, and may be busy depending on the season.

Ballycastle See Route 351.

Knocklayd The mountain, commanding views over inland ranges and the sea, has a great cairn.

Bunamargy Friary Ruins of a friary which was damaged by attack while being used as an English garrison (NM).

Fair Head Nearby are coal measures which were worked in the 18th and 19th centuries. A dry-stone revetted crannog, or man-made island, is in Lough na Cranagh, and nearby Doonmore is a motte-and-bailey carved in a basalt outcrop.

Torr Head Affording fine views, the promontory is Ireland's closest point to Scotland at 13 miles (21 km).

Cushendun Much of this estate village was built by Lord Cushendun and now belongs to the NT. By the River Dun were found worked flints, thought to be Ireland's earliest man-made objects.

Layde Ruins of a church which was the MacDonnell clan's burial place (NM).

Tievebulliagh Worked stones from the neolithic axe factory here have been found as distant as south-east England.

Glenariff Lodge The Glenariff valley is one of the finest of the beautiful Nine Glens of Antrim. The head of the valley, near the Lodge, is the Fairy Glen beauty-spot, with its river falls.

Glenarm Glenarm Castle, set in a lovely valley estate, has been the seat of the Mac Donnells of Antrim since 1636.

Dunteige Bridge To the east is Dunteige Giant's Cave, a wedge-shaped gallery grave (NM).

Carncastle To the west lies Sallagh Braes, a splendid amphitheatre of basalt.

Ballygalley Now used as a hotel, the 17th-century castle is Ireland's best-preserved Scottish baronial style house. Ruins of Carn Castle on a precipitous rock site.

Larne The Curran, whose name derives from the sickle shape of the land, has yielded so many worked flints that the Irish Mesolithic culture has been given the name of 'Larnian'. Ruins of the small, 16th-century Curran Castle (NM).

a Ferries run between Larne and Stranraer in Scotland.

Ballylumford Druid's Altar is a small, prehistoric tomb (NM).

The Gobbins The cliffs, rich in sea-bird life, can be reached on foot. In 1642 the island's Catholics were massacred and, it is said, their bodies thrown over the Gobbin Cliffs.

Whitehead Tower stump of 17th-century Castle Chichester (NM).

Bellahill Dalway's Bawn is the best-preserved of Ulster's Plantation 'bawn and flanker' towers (NM).

Kilroot Here Dean Swift, author of *Gulliver's Travels*, had his first living.

Carrickfergus See Route 353.

Route 353   74 miles   114 km
CARRICKFERGUS — DUNDRUM

Bartholomew's ¼ inch:1 mile no. 1
OS ½ inch:1 mile no. 4

A ferry between Portaferry and Strangford is necessary on this route.

Inevitably some busy roads have to be used near Belfast and the larger towns around it. Whilst this route has much to offer, it is interesting rather than peacefully scenic.

Carrickfergus The fine castle dates from the 12th century and has Tudor alterations (NM). Its possession was the key to a large area. In the 14th century it held out against attack for over a year. The public are admitted to *son et lumière*

performances. There are remains of the 17th-century town walls. St Nicholas' Church has Jacobean woodwork and Renaissance monuments; the Town Hall has an 18th-century facade. Links with Route 352.

Newtownabbey On Cave Hill, set around the 19th-century Belfast Castle, is a large park containing a zoo.

Belfast Having grown up around a 16th-century castle, Belfast expanded in the 19th century on the industries of shipbuilding and cotton, and it is noted for handwoven linen and damask. The city has been the capital of Northern Ireland since the 1920s, when the classical Parliament House at Stormont was built at a cost of £1¼ million. Buildings of interest include the City Hall, University, Belfast Charitable Institute in Clifton House, St Anne's Cathedral, St Malachy's Cathedral and the 19th-century custom house. Botanical gardens and museum; City Transport museum; Queen's Isle ship-yards are the largest of their kind in the world. Bedford Street has Victorian linen manufacturers' offices.

Dundonald Dundonald Fort is a Norman motte (NM). At Greengraves are The Kemple Stones, an impressive portal dolmen (NM).

Scrabo Hill Traces of ancient huts and earthworks (NMs). Around the Killy-neth River are lovely NT lands.

Newtownards The town was planned in the 17th century by a Scottish laird. There are ruins of a complex market cross, whose interior has served as a prison (NM). The church ruins (NM) are all that remain of a 13th-century friary, otherwise destroyed after the dissolution to prevent its use as a fortress. The Market House is 18th-century; the Town Hall has a lock-up. To the east is Movilla, the remains of an abbey which was renowned for scholarship, and where saints including Colmcille studied (NM).

Mount Stewart An 18th-century

house set in large grounds with formal vistas, terraces, and a rich variety of plants (NT, open). The Temple of the Winds, a copy of the one in Athens, overlooks Strangford Lough (NT, open).

Greyabbey Beautiful 12th-century ruins of a typical Cistercian abbey (NM).

Burial Isle This is the easternmost land of Ireland.

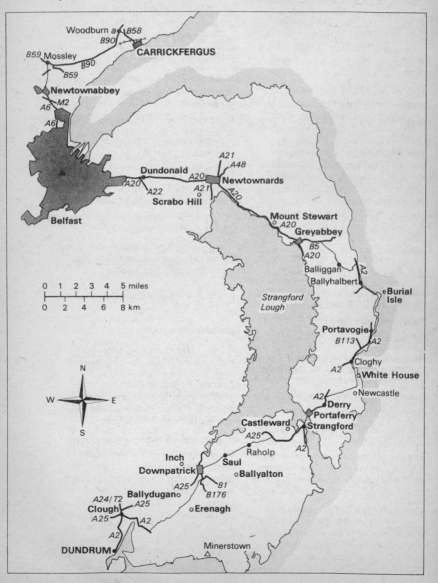

Portavogie Kirkistown Castle is a 17th-century tower house with a bawn.

White House The remains of a 17th-century plantation house.

Derry The ruins of two early churches with clay-bonded masonry.

Portaferry A small fishing port and resort. Presbyterian church in the Doric style; 15th-century castle ruins (NM).

Strangford The 16th-century Strangford Castle is considered to be Ulster's best example of a fortified town house.

Castleward An 18th-century house, part classical and part Gothic, with a Victorian laundry, and set in grounds with trees, shrubs and a wildfowl collection (NT, open). Nearby is 17th-century Castle Ward Plantation Castle, and the well-preserved Audley's Castle, the many castles in the area generally reflecting the insecurity of life hereabouts in medieval and later times. Prehistoric objects and thirty-four burials have been found in the complex cairn (NM) at Audleystown.

Saul By St Patrick's churchyard, on the site of an important monastery, are two stone-roofed mortuary houses. In legend, St Patrick had his first church in a barn here, after landing in Ireland.

Ballyalton Druidical ring (NM).

Downpatrick The 9th- or 10th-century high cross. It is said that St Patrick founded a church here.

Inch The beautifully sited ruins of St Mary's Abbey (NM).

Ballydugan The 18th-century flour mill, six storeys in height, used power from the nearby lake. Windmill stump.

Erenagh Here was Carrick Abbey, the earliest recorded abbey of a Continental order in Ireland. The monastery was used as a fortress and thus destroyed.

Clough Motte and bailey. The area has several good mottes.

Dundrum See Route 354.

Route 354   39 miles   63 km
DUNDRUM — NEWRY

Bartholomew's ¼ inch:1 mile no. 2
OS ½ inch:1 mile no. 9

Dundrum Fine ruins of one of Ireland's earliest castles (NM). Links with Route 353.

a The main route uses a pass over the Mourne Mountains, whereas the alternative keeps to the coastal lowlands.

Carnacavill Circular churchyard with the ruins of a church and a round tower, and early cross-slabs (NMs).

Newcastle Small port and resort. To the north-west, reached through Barbican Gate, is 1200-acre Tollymore Forest Park, with arboretum, river scenery, old estate follies and camp-sites.

Slieve Donard The summit affords fine views, including to Scotland.

Bloody Bridge Its name is taken from a massacre of Planters in 1641.

Silent Valley The mountain-girt valley contains the reservoir formed by the damming of the river Kilkeel.

Kilkeel Fishing resort. Medieval church ruins. The Crawtree Stone is a fine portal dolmen (NM).

Greencastle Remains of the Royal English Fortress of Green Castle (NM). Views of the Mourne Mountains and Carlingford Lough.

Mourne Mountains The beauty of these mountains has inspired poetry and song. The varied granite and shale rocks encourage a diverse flora.

Cloghmore An erratic 30-ton granite boulder. Kilfeaghan Cromlech has a 40-ton capstone (NM).

Rostrevor The church preserves the Bell of St Bronach, patron saint of seafarers.

Warrenpoint The catholic church has 20th-century glass.

b A ferry runs between Warrenpoint and Omeath, which is on Route 355.

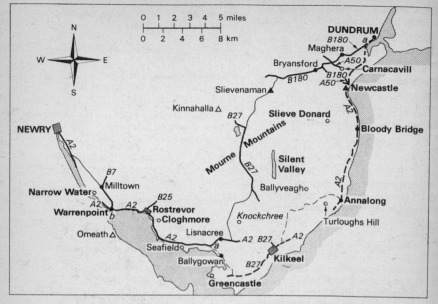

Narrow Water A lovely little castle, still well maintained (NM).

Newry See Route 355.

Route 355   41 miles   66 km
NEWRY — DUNDALK

Bartholomew's ¼ inch:1 mile no. 2
OS ½ inch:1 mile no. 9

Newry The name derives from a yew tree, said to have been planted by St Patrick. Due to its strategic position, Newry has suffered in many battles for control of the north; an attack in 1689 left only the church tower. The 18th-century canal linking Newry to Lough Neagh was the first major canal in the British Isles. The Town Hall is built over the river. Links with Route 354.

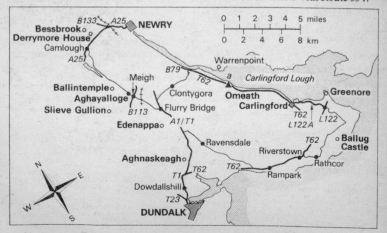

Bessbrook A 19th-century model linen village, founded without a public house or pawnshop by a Quaker.

Derrymore House Thatched, 18th-century manor house (NT).

Ballintemple Pre-Romanesque church ruins mark what was one of Ireland's most important nunneries (NM).

Slieve Gullion Dominating the Gap of the North, this mountain gives fine views. On one of its summits is Calliagh Birra's House, a passage grave in a great cairn. Slieve Gullion was the hideout of 17th-century outlaw Redmond O'Hanlon who terrorized the English after their seizure of his lands.

Aghayalloge Here is part of Dane's Cast, a defensive earthwork marking an ancient Ulster boundary (NM).

Edenappa The 8th-century Kilnasaggart Stone is the earliest positively dated Irish Christian field monument with fine inscriptions (NM).

Omeath This area was the last in Leinster where spoken Irish survived.

a A ferry runs between Omeath and Warrenpoint, which is on Route 354.

Carlingford Small port and resort. Ruin of King John's Castle, built on a rock (NM). The Mint and Taafe's Castle are fortified town houses. The Protestant church incorporates an old town wall tower. There are Dominican friary remains.

Greenore A decayed port.

Ballug Castle A 15th-century stronghold.

Aghnaskeagh An early ironworkers' furnace near two cairns (NMs).

Dundalk See Route 358. Also links with Route 365.

Route 356   61 miles   99 km
CAVAN — BOYLE

Bartholomew's ¼ inch:1 mile no. 2
OS ½ inch:1 mile nos 7, 8, 12

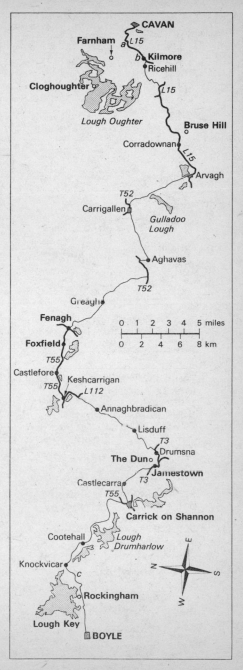

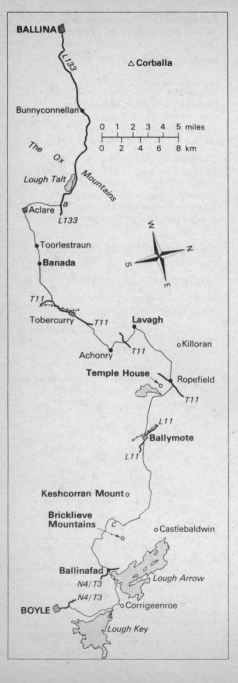

BALLINA

L133

△ **Corballa**

Bunnyconnellan

0 1 2 3 4 5 miles

0 2 4 6 8 km

The Ox Mountains

Lough Talt

Aclare
L133   a

Toorlestraun

Banada

T11

Tobercurry   *T11*   **Lavagh**

Achonry   *T11*   ○Killoran

Temple House   Ropefield

T11

L11

Ballymote

L11

Keshcorran Mount○

**Bricklieve
Mountains**   c   ○Castlebaldwin

Ballinafad
N4/T3   *Lough Arrow*

N4/T3

BOYLE   ○Corrigeenroe

Lough Key

Cavan See Route 361.

a If you next intend to follow Route 364 Enniskillen, you can turn to it here.

Farnham The house and demesne have, since the 17th-century, been the seat of the Maxwells from Scotland.

Cloghoughter On the lough island stand the remains of a fine example of the Irish 13th- and 14th-century circular tower-castle (NM).

Kilmore A modern Gothic cathedral with a good Romanesque doorway from an old monastery; Anglo-Norman motte and bailey.

Bruse Hill The summit gives views over lakes and highlands. At the north foot stands a pillar stone, called 'Finn Mac Cool's Finger Stone'.

Fenagh The site of an early monastery, burnt in 1360. The Royal Irish Academy now holds the Book of Fenagh, an ancient catalogue of the monastic assets and miracles. Remains of two old churches (NMs).

Foxfield At the priest's house is kept the medieval bell of St Caillin's.

The Dun An earthwork ditch and bank some half a mile long, cuts off a loop of the River Shannon.

Jamestown Named after James I, this town was founded to command a Shannon crossing; 17th-century fortified gate.

Carrick on Shannon This place is renowned for strong Protestantism. There is an 18th-century court house.

c Some of the lanes between Knockvicar and Rockingham are not shown on the Ordnance Survey map.

Rockingham The estate is a public park.

Lough Key There are 13th-century abbey remains on Trinity Isle; church ruins on Hog's Isle; and 17th-century castle remains on Castle Isle.

Boyle The fine remains of a 12th- to

13th-century abbey, previously of importance, including the gatehouse, cloister, kitchen, cellars and church (NM). Links with Route 357.

Route 357   65 miles   105 km
BALLINA — BOYLE

Bartholomew's ¼ inch:1 mile nos 2, 5
OS ½ inch:1 mile nos 6 (just), 7

Ballina See Route 329. Also links with Routes 328, 345.

Corballa Enniscrone YH.

a If you next intend to follow Route 345 to Sligo, you can turn to it at this point.

Banada Some 15th-century priory ruins on a lovely riverside site.

Lavagh Eerie remains of a 15th-century friary at Abbey Court. The name of nearby Knocknashee means 'Hill of the Fairies'.

b It is possible to short-cut here via lanes north to Coolaney on Route 345.

Temple House Nearby are the remains of a Knights Templars preceptory.

Ballymote The name derives from the Anglo-Norman motte to the west. Unusual 14th-century castle ruins (NM). The conical tumulus north of the town is the 'Fairy Mound of Laughter'.

c The roads between the mountains of Keshcorran and Bricklieve differ in shape more than usual between the two map series.

Keshcorran Mount The summit cairn stands on a hill rich in legends, including that of a King of Ireland suckled by a wolf. Traces of prehistoric occupation have been found in some of the limestone caves.

Bricklieve Mountains The great limestone ridges on the north side of the mountains have megalithic graves. There is an ancient village site with the foundations of forty-seven huts.

Ballinafad The 17th-century castle was built to control the important pass (NM).

Boyle See Route 356.

Route 358   33 miles   53 km
DUNDALK — DROGHEDA

Bartholomew's ¼ inch:1 mile no. 2
OS ½ inch:1 mile nos 8 (just), 13

Dundalk An important town of the English Pale in the Middle Ages. The portico of the 19th-century Court House is copied from the Temple of Theseus. Seatown 'Castle' is a 15th-century friary tower. Links with Routes 355, 365.

Stephenstown House A fine Georgian house by the river.

Clogfarmore Standing stone (NM).

Louth Ruins of an early monastery which suffered Norse raids (NM);

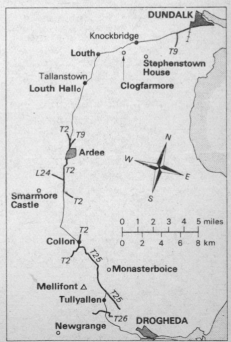

simple, stone-roofed St Mochta's House (NM); the 12th-century motte of an English royal fortress.

Lough Hall The 17th-century hall was for long a baronial seat.

Ardee The 13th-century keep of a border fortress of the English Pale is now a Court House.

Smarmore Castle A 14th-century castle; manorial church ruins. Manorial church.

Collon The new, 20th-century Mellifont Abbey.

Monasterboice An early monastic site famed for its carved high crosses (NMs). Other remains include a round tower and sundial (NMs).

Mellifont The fine ruins of 12th-century Mellifont Abbey, the first Cistercian abbey in Ireland.

Tullyallen William of Orange's army camped here before its victory at the Battle of the Boyne.

Newgrange An area famed for pre-historic remains (NMs) including an impressive passage grave, cairns, pillar-stones and earthworks.

Drogheda See Route 359.

Route 359   38 miles   61 km
DROGHEDA — DUBLIN

Bartholomew's ¼ inch:1 mile no. 2
OS ½ inch:1 mile nos 13, 16 (just)

Drogheda Medieval Parliaments were held here. The 13th-century St Lawrence's Gate; 18th-century Tholsel and grammar school buildings. The Boyne railway viaduct is a fine example of 19th-century engineering. Links with Route 358.

Donore The nearby hill was the Jacobite camp before the Battle of the Boyne.

Duleek Church with early gravestones (NMs) and high crosses (NMs). Ruins of St Mary's Abbey (NM); Duleek House estate.

Gormanstown The 14th-century castle is now a Franciscan school.

Balbriggan It was at the mouth of the River Delvin that St Patrick met and christened his successor, St Benignus.

Balrothery Church with 16th-century bell-tower. Long ago the Knights' Plots were given to those at council here, for grazing use during council. The plots still belong to their descendants.

Lusk Round tower (NM); monastery remains with a square tower added; well and double bullaun; church with good glass.

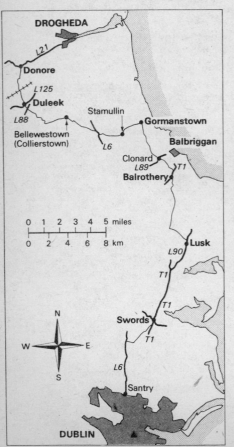

Swords Ruins of an archbishop's manorial palace (NM).

Dublin See Route 336. Also links with Routes 335, 340, 360.

Route 360   50 miles   80 km
KELLS (CEANANNUS) — DUBLIN

Bartholomew's ¼ inch:1 mile no. 2
OS ½ inch:1 mile nos 13, 16

Kells Also called Ceanannus, Kells was the site of an important 6th-century monastery, which produced great art works, now in museums. The remains include five fine high crosses, one of which was used as a gallows by the British: a round tower (NM) and Irish Romanesque St Columcille's House (NM). Links with Route 361.

Rathmore A 15th-century castle and church (NM).

Moymet The 16th-century Moymet Castle and the remains of a 15th-century manorial church.

Trim and **Hill of Tara** See Route 335.

Newtown Trim The riverside ruin of a 13th-century cathedral (NM); church ruin with an altar tomb.

Bective The ruins of 12th-century Bective Abbey which was partly converted into a fortified mansion after the Dissolution.

Dunsany A castle with good 18th-century features; the church ruin has interesting stone carving.

Killeen Castle A 19th-century castle. There are two manorial churches in the style of the Pale.

Dunshaughlin Pre-Romanesque church lintel (NM).

Dublin See Route 336. Also links with Routes 335, 340, 359.

Route 361   31 miles   51 km
CAVAN — KELLS (CEANANNUS)

Bartholomew's ¼ inch:1 mile no. 2
OS ½ inch:1 mile nos 8 (just), 12 (just), 13

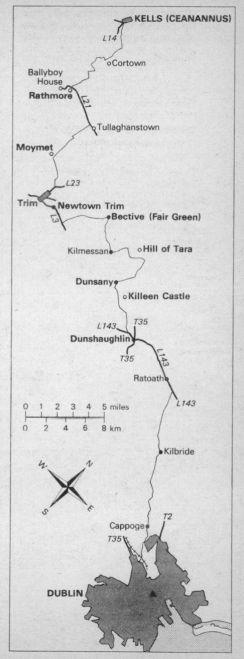

Cavan The town grew around a friary long since burnt by the English. Cathedral with sculptures by Power. There are many ring-forts in the area. Links with Routes 356, 364, 365.

Slieve Na Calliagh On the hill are large, complex remains of a passage grave cemetery, including thirty chambered cairns and tumuli, a ring-fort, a pillarstone and a cross (NMs).

Castlekeeran In the churchyard are three high crosses (NMs) which remain from an 8th-century monastery, and an Ogham stone. There are 14th-century church fragments (NM). St Ciaran's Well is still the goal of pilgrimages.

Kells See Route 360.

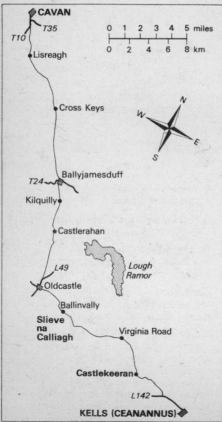

Route 362   32 miles   52 km
RAPHOE — DONEGAL

Bartholomew's ¼ inch:1 mile no. 1
OS ½ inch:1 mile nos 3, 4

Raphoe A monastery was founded here in the 7th century. Cathedral with ancient fragments; 17th-century castle, built with stones from a round tower. Links with Routes 349, 350.

Tops Hill On the summit is sixty-four stone Beltany Circle (NM).

Stranorlar The grave of Isaac Butt, a home rule founder.

Lough Mourne At the north end is Giant's Bed, a chamber tomb.

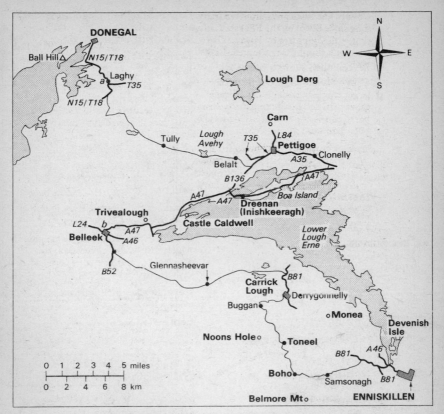

Croaghanierin Some hundred feet (30 metres) above the road and opposite the west end of the lough is a large ring-fort.

Barnesmore Gap The steep-sided valley was a haunt of robbers and highwaymen.

Lough Belshade From Edergole bridge it is possible to walk up the Corraber valley with its waterfalls to beautiful, cliff-ringed Lough Belshade.

Donegal See Route 346. Also links with Routes 347, 363.

Route 363   68 miles   110 km
DONEGAL — ENNISKILLEN

Bartholomew's ¼ inch:1 mile no. 1
OS ½ inch:1 mile nos 3, 7, 8

Donegal See Route 346. Also links with Routes 347, 362.

a If you next intend to follow Route 346 to Sligo, you can turn to it at this point.

Pettigoe The frontier between Northern Ireland and Eire divides the village.

Carn A bothog, or timber hut, which was used as a shelter for Mass in Penal times, is preserved in the graveyard.

Lough Derg Here is St Patrick's Purgatory, a cave where he fasted for forty days. Pilgrims used to follow his example until excesses led to a ban. Thousands still make the pilgrimage to Lough Derg. Station Isle has a good basilica, and Saint's Isle has a cave and ruins of a priory and church.

Dreenan In Caldragh ancient churchyard stand figured stones (NMs).

Castle Caldwell By the gate to the 17th-century castle ruins is a stone fiddle, commemorating a fiddler who fell from a pleasure boat and drowned.

Trivealough Lough-side ruins of an 'abbey' on an ancient monastery site (NM).

Belleek The pottery producing lustre-finish china can sometimes be visited. The fast river is harnessed for hydro-electric power.

b   If you next intend to follow Route 346 to Sligo, the L24 north-west is a short-cut to it at Ballyshannon.

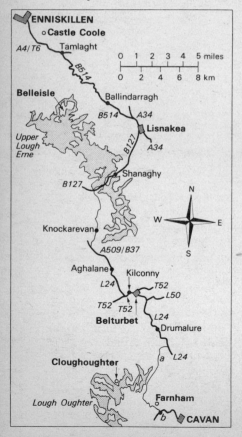

Carrick Lough By the shore are the ruins of a church built by a 15th-century husband and wife (NM).

Noons Hole Ireland's deepest swallow-hole.

Monea The remains of the 17th-century Plantation castle have some Scottish features (NM). Protestant church with a good 15th-century window.

Toneel Fragments of a high cross in the churchyard (NM). Nearby are the six Reyfad Stones with cup and ring markings (NMs).

Boho Series of complex limestone caves, swallow and pot holes.

Belmore Mountain On the mountain, which affords extensive views, are Moylehid Giant's Grave, a cairn and a cashel (NMs).

Devenish Isle Fine early and medieval ecclesiastical remains (NMs).

Enniskillen See Route 364.

Route 364   38 miles   61 km
ENNISKILLEN — CAVAN

Bartholomew's ¼ inch:1 mile nos 1 (just), 2
OS ½ inch:1 mile no. 8

Enniskillen The town stands in a strategic island position in Lough Erne. On Fort Hill are the remains of a 17th-century star fort, and a column to a Peninsula War here. Enniskillen Castle was long used as a barracks and has a fine water-gate (NM). Oscar Wilde was a pupil at the Portera Royal School, founded 1618. Links with Route 363.

Castle Coole Ireland's finest classical mansion, in grounds with the country's only breeding colony of grey-lag geese. Gortgonnell standing stone (NT, open).

Lisnakea The Corn Market cross incorporates parts of an early high cross. The ruins of Castle Balfour, a 17th-century plantation castle, are in the churchyard (NM).

Belleisle The 15th-century Annals of Ulster were compiled here.

Belturbet The motte on Turbet Isle was built by the Anglo-Normans in their attempt to penetrate the north.

a A short stretch of lane is not shown on the Bartholomew's map of 1977.

Cloughoughter and **Farnham** See Route 356.

b If you next intend to follow Route 356 to Boyle, you can turn to it here.

Cavan See Route 361. Also links with Routes 356, 365.

Route 365 51 miles 82 km
DUNDALK — CAVAN

Bartholomew's ¼ inch:1 mile no. 2
OS ½ inch:1 mile no. 8

Dundalk See Route 358. Also links with Route 355.

Castletown Dun Dealgain is a large motte and bailey (NM), with the ruins of 18th-century Castlefolly on the summit. The 15th-century crenellated Bellows Castle stands near the ruins of a manorial church.

Castle Roche The ruins include parts of the gatehouse, curtain wall and great hall. The rocky site affords good views.

Inishkeen Scant remains of an early monastery and round tower (NM). The poet P. Kavanagh, who describes the local life of his time, was born here.

Donaghmoyne Mannan Castle is a 12th-century hilltop motte-and-bailey.

Carrickmacross A convent now stands on the site of an Elizabethan castle built by the Earl of Essex. The renowned hand-made lace industry was established in 1820.

Shantemon Hill The inauguration place of the O'Reilly Lords was on this hill, possibly by the pillarstones called 'Finn Mac Cool's Fingers'.

Cavan See Route 361. Also links with Routes 356, 364.

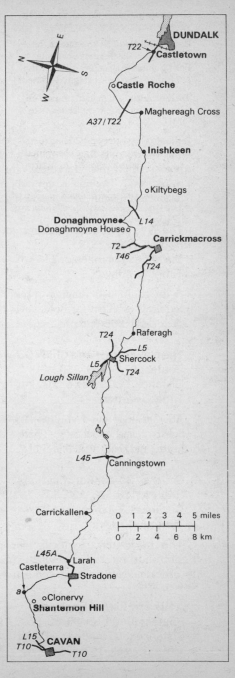

SELECTED TOURS

The twelve tours suggested below are intended to illustrate the scope of the book rather than represent any tours which we would specially recommend. The time scales indicated are arbitrary, but allow for a daily distance of roughly between twenty and fifty miles.

The Wye and Golden Valleys, and the Forest of Dean
Routes: 208, 223, 217
Distance: 134 miles or 216 km
Time: 3–7 days

A delightful tour ranging over many different landscapes. The varied terrain is excellent for newcomers to cycle-touring who want to discover their capabilities and preferences.

The New Forest and Chalk Downlands
Routes: 97, 96, 69, 100
Distance: 130 miles or 209 km
Time: 3–7 days

Another short tour over quite easy terrain which passes the ancient cities of Salisbury and Winchester. There are rolling chalk downlands and the open heaths and shady woodlands of the New Forest.

Scottish Border Fortifications
Routes: 125, 126, 127, 139, 137, 120, 121, 146, 144
Distance: 293 miles or 472 km
Time: 6–10 days

This moderately strenuous tour passes forests, moorlands, peaceful farmlands and sandy beaches. Strongholds of the Roman Wall, great castles and battlemented church towers tell of past border struggles.

A Historic Part of England
Routes: 9, 100, 68, 93, 85, 86, 87, 21, 18
Distance: 305 miles or 488 km
Time: 1 week–10 days

A fairly easy tour linking some of the country's best known historic sites. It includes the chalk downlands of Wessex and the Cotswolds. Stonehenge, Avebury, Winchester, Salisbury, Bath and Oxford are all on the route. The tour can be started at Godalming and finished at Windsor, both being close to London and Gatwick and Heathrow airports.

The Dales, Moors, and Wolds of Yorkshire
Routes: 132, 131, 130, 162, 165, 164, 160, 159, 166, 163
Distance: 333 miles or 536 km
Time: 1 week–10 days

As you wend through the richly varied landscape of Yorkshire on this moderately strenuous tour you will discover many fascinating and beautiful ruins of medieval monasteries and abbeys.

Devon
Routes: 109, 110, 111, 80, 81, 82, 107, 108
Distance: 356 miles or 569 km
Time: 1 week–10 days

A strenuous circular tour which passes through picturesque fishing villages on the spectacular coasts of Devon as well as visiting the bleak expanses of Dartmoor. Exeter is a good place to start and finish.

East Anglia
Routes: 37, 36, 33, 34, 39, 40, 41, 42, 43, 44
Distance: 365 miles or 585 km
Time: 1 week–10 days

A good beginners' tour on quiet roads and over easy terrain through the rural backwaters of England. The attractive old towns of Cambridge, Norwich and Bury St Edmunds are included and there are good rail links. The tour is also handy for cyclists using the Harwich ferry.

Wales and the Marches
Routes: 223, 214, 210, 216, 205, 230, 229, 227, 232, 233, 219, 218
Distance: 382 miles or 612 km
Time: 1–2 weeks

A strenuous tour visiting the rugged mountains of Snowdonia, the lonely hills of central Wales and the quieter farmlands of the Marches, an area with many castles and villages.

Cork and Kerry
Routes: 290, 291, 292, 293, 294, 295, (294), 296, 298, 299
Distance: 436 miles or 698 km
Time: 2–3 weeks

Using the port of Cork as a starting and finishing point, this tour explores the wild and rocky peninsulas of south-west Ireland. The cycling is fairly easy and the scenery includes fine cliffs, sandy beaches, mountains and inland hills.

Scottish Highlands and Islands
Routes: 278, 258, 257, 256, 255, 254, 251, 250, 249, 248, 260
Distance: 543 miles or 869 km
Time: 2–3 weeks

A strenuous tour for adventurous cyclists. It starts and finishes at different places and makes use of rail links. The route meanders through some of the best mountain and coastal scenery in the British Isles, offering opportunities to visit the Scottish islands.

Ireland's Pastures and Mountains
Routes: 335, 334, 333, 332, 323, 324, 325, 326, 327, 328, 357, 356, 361, 360.
Distance: 668 miles or 1076 km
Time: 2 weeks–3 weeks

Scenes of emerald pastures and of wilder, sombre lands: reminders of the ancient Celtic traditions and of the English influence of centuries past. Fairly easy cycling.

A Taste of Every Country
Routes: 225, 231, 229, 228, 360, 361, 364, 363, 347, 348, 349, 350, 351, 352, 184, 195, 190, 189, 120, 180, 176, 172, 171, 179, 117, 116, 115, 114, 155, 154
Distance: 1200 miles or 1930 km
Time: 3 weeks–2 months

The countries that make up the British Isles are remarkably varied in their customs and ways of life. This circuit provides the opportunity to visit each country, while leading through landscapes of great beauty.

APPENDIX 1

Highways and Byways

There are four classes of metalled public roads in Britain, of which only the motorways and motorway standard A roads (labelled (M) on commercial maps) are prohibited to cyclists. Although the types of road included within each classification vary considerably, a useful rule of thumb is that A roads link city to city, B roads link town to town and the unclassified roads, usually just called lanes, link village to village. (In Eire the A roads are classified 'N' or 'T', and the B roads 'L'.)

Since most motor traffic needs to travel quickly from one city to another, the larger A roads are generally busy and if you are wise you will use them only when there is no other option (such as when an A road crosses the only bridge over a river for miles) or when they have exceptional attractions (as with the outstanding scenic north Devon coast road). In mountain areas so few roads can be built because of the terrain that most of them are classified A, but the low population usually keeps them quiet.

B roads are moderately busy with cars, and although they do not give the most intimate view of the countryside they can be reasonably pleasant. They are useful if you want to make good time by following a clearly signposted road rather than picking a way through the maze of lanes.

Much of the dense network of lanes is ideal for peaceful cycling. They are often narrow and their many bends and corners make them unpopular with motorists and therefore quiet, although a few local people who know their way may tear unwisely fast around corners made blind by high hedges or walls, on the assumption that they have the road to themselves. You should always keep well to the left hand side of the road at corners.

The amount of traffic on the roads varies not only according to season and time of day, but also with the region. B roads in south-east England can be as busy as A roads elsewhere, whereas some north Scottish A roads could be taken as lanes in other parts of the country.

The very characteristics which make the lanes so pleasant for cycling also demand careful map-reading, and there are a couple of points to watch. Firstly, signposts are erected with the motorist in mind: sometimes they may direct you to the next town or large village not via the lanes but via a 'faster' but often longer route using A or B roads. The rule here is to use the signposts as clues but not orders, and to believe your map rather than the signposts. Secondly, although most lane junctions are furnished with signposts, not all of them are. There are many surfaced, private roads leading to isolated farms, and it is occasionally difficult to tell at a junction whether a road is private or not. In such cases, if you don't have a 1:50 000 map, ask locally or risk it taking you miles up a dead-end.

Paths, Tracks and Rights of Way

In the days before motor traffic, when most journeys were over much shorter distances and undertaken by foot, on horseback or with a cart, a fine network of unsurfaced paths and tracks grew up, many of which survive. In England and Wales many have been legally defined as rights of way, meaning that the public has absolute right to use them, but paths which have not been so defined can be used only with the permission of the landowner. Foot rights of way are open only to pedestrians, while bridle-ways are open to pedestrians, horse-riders and cyclists, though in practice the cyclist of today is not always able to follow particularly steep or muddy paths which horses can negotiate. The 'Byway open to all traffic' right of way, often following an ancient way of importance such as a drove road, is open to all forms of traffic. Although all rights of way should be signposted where they leave public roads, they have many confusing junctions with each other or other paths. A 1:50 000 map is vital for exploring them because the smaller scale maps do not show most of the tracks and paths or their legal status.

Riding over paths and tracks is fondly called 'rough-stuff' by cycle-tourists. The going varies enormously from very good over well-laid gravel to dreadful or useless where the path is just a legal line drawn over a ploughed field. Trying out a right of way tends to be a bit of a gamble. Their advantages are that they can get you truly 'away from it all', and that they can be used as vital links between lanes where busy roads would otherwise have to be resorted to. Pace on them is, of course, slow and some, while useable during one or other season, are overgrown in summer or muddy in winter. A few rights of way have been used in the routes in this book, but except in a very few cases, which have been made absolutely clear, there are road alternatives either suggested or immediately obvious from commercial maps.

Two special sorts of paths and tracks deserve mention. Firstly there are the towpaths alongside canals or navigable rivers. Many of them have become rights of way on foot, but you can buy low-cost permits enabling you to cycle some of those in the care of the British Waterways Board, although you must give way to other users of the towpaths such as anglers. Secondly there are the firm, gravelled forestry roads in Forestry Commission areas which, although they often go nowhere but to the depths of a plantation, can provide peaceful 'dead-end' exploration. The Forestry Commission officially allows walkers and horse-riders on many of them, but not cyclists who must seek permission in each individual case.

The rights of way laws are different in Scotland and Ireland. In Scotland the cycle is regarded as a 'mechanical aid to walking' and you are allowed to cycle on all paths open to walkers. However, the legal status of paths—whether they are rights of way or not—are not shown on even the OS 1:50 000 maps, and there is no infallible way of discovering whether a track is a right of way. You would be unlikely to be challenged on a path or track, except in the months of September and October when deer-stalking closes many paths to everyone. In Ireland it has not proved necessary for rights of way to be defined: try any track you fancy, getting permission or advice locally if possible. But always bear in mind that the landowner has the right to turn you off.

The 1:50 000 or 1 inch:1 mile maps are essential for exploring paths and tracks over the whole British Isles, and a compass is necessary in woods or in mountains. Also, if you are using strenuous or long tracks in mountainous or wild districts, follow all the codes of conduct that apply to hill walkers: take spare food and clothing, allow yourself lots of time, carry a whistle (six blasts per minute is the distress call), and know what to do if weather conditions change for the worse.

Cycling Regulations

The highway code applies to cyclists as well as motorists, and it is a good idea to look through it both to see what advice it has to give, and how it advises motorists to behave towards cyclists. You can buy it in ordinary bookshops.

It is common sense that you should always keep your cycle in good working order. You are obliged by law to have two independent braking systems. At night you must have a white lamp at the front, and a red lamp and reflector (which can be combined) at the back. The lights must meet certain size, position and brightness conditions which your dealer can clarify for you. You are not obliged to have a bell, as any audible warning of approach will do, but the bell has the advantage of being immediately understood by almost everyone.

APPENDIX 2

Climate

If a simple word had to be chosen to describe the British climate, it would be 'variable'. Sometimes the weather is lazy, not changing for a whole fortnight, but at others it is quite impish and about-turns from rain to sun overnight, only to change its mind by mid-morning and so on throughout the day. The moral of this for the cycle-tourist is never to be down-hearted by bad weather as it may well change very soon. Equally do not venture out without clothing for wind and rain, even if the weather is idyllic when you set off.

Contrary to the popular belief of foreigners, the sun does shine in Britain, and quite often, too! But the weather can be disrespectful of what it is supposed to do 'on average' in the various regions. You may have long downpours of driving rain on the South Downs in the 'sunny south-east', and ten days of unbroken heat and sunshine in 'Scotland's wet west'. A tour in the British Isles without any rain at all is rare, but once you venture into the outdoor life you will be pleasantly surprised. The proportion of wet weather is really not as great as those who stay indoors think.

The western side of Britain is always wetter, with the eastern lowlands of England and Scotland the driest area. Risk of rain increases both to the west and over high land so that the Lake District for example, is notorious with about four times as much rainfall as eastern England. Rain falls at any time of year, and in winter can turn to snow which sometimes blocks roads for days. The high, northern areas have most snow, with the Scottish highlands scoring some fifty days of snow lying annually, whereas most of southern England and Ireland scores less than ten on average. Now and then there is mist, particularly in the western mountains of Ireland. Scottish weather is quite unpredictable, and the Grampians and western Highlands in particular offer little shelter should you find yourself in a heavy shower. The Scottish midge is ferocious, so remember to take supplies of insect repellent.

The temperature varies a lot at all times of the year, depending on sunshine, the strength of the wind and whether you are sheltered from it, and the height of the land. However, in mid-winter the temperature averages about 4°C (38°F) and is lowest in the east, whereas in mid-summer it averages about 16°C (60°F) and is lowest in the north. This is not to say that it doesn't remain in the upper 70°F for considerable periods. If you are thinking of camping you should bear in mind that there are only eight months of the year completely free from frost in southern England, ranging right down to three months in Scotland's high Grampian plateau.

Wind is also variable regarding both strength and direction, although it does come slightly more often from the west and south-west. It is particularly noticeable in the more westerly parts of Ireland. A fortnight's cycle-tour would be likely to average a couple of days of headwind which you have to work against, irrespective of where the tour is or in what direction it is going, but only very occasionally does the wind become so strong or gusty as to make cycling difficult or unsafe. If you do meet a headwind, you will suffer most from it in a flat area such as the Fens, where you will never be in the lee of anything, and you would do well to change your plans and turn with the wind.

The seasons are marked not only by changes in weather, but also by changes in the colouring of the landscape. However, the most practical aspect is that of the changing hours of daylight. In southern England there are only about eight hours of daylight in mid-winter, whereas in mid-summer there are about sixteen, allowing time for exploration, pitching of tents and so on till about 9.30 pm. It is light until about 7.30 in March and September. The further north you go, the shorter the winter days, while the summer ones stretch out so that you can even just read a book at midnight in Scotland's far north.

APPENDIX 3

Maps

Except in the remote highland areas of the British Isles it is vital to use country lanes to enjoy cycle-touring, and as there are so many it is generally necessary to have maps which show all the lanes. There are three series of maps which are suitable, and which one you choose depends on the length and type of your tour, and how much money you can afford; also how much weight you are prepared to carry. Maps relevant to each route are indicated at its head.

OS 1:250 000: This scale approximates to four miles to the inch, which is just sufficient for all the lanes except dead-ends to be marked, but too small for all the villages and other clues to navigation to be included. Only nine sheets are required to cover all of Britain, so this series is suitable if you are short of cash, or are planning a long tour for which you must carry all the maps at once. This series has the extra advantage of showing height by shading clearly. Ireland is covered at a scale of four miles to the inch (1:253 440) by Bartholomew's.

Bartholomew's 1:100 000: This more detailed scale has room to show all villages, and a few extra details such as windmills, all of which are a help in navigation. It also shows a selection of unsurfaced tracks, but can be a bit confusing in this respect as some of the tracks are shown by the same symbol as some of the roads, and the legal status of the tracks is not given. Height is shown by shading. There are 62 sheets covering Britain, so this series is suited to cyclists who want more detail than the OS 1:250 000 can give, and who are touring a moderately wide region (Wales requires eight sheets, for example). Ireland is covered at a scale of two miles to the inch (1:126 720) by the Irish Ordnance Survey.

OS 1:50 000: These are luxurious maps to use, showing great detail which helps both in navigation and in finding features of interest, such as private roads, rights of way, churches, orchards, ancient ruins and so on. These are very accurate maps, and show height by means of contour lines. As they are expensive, and some two hundred of them are required to cover Britain, they are suited to the cyclist who wishes to explore a small area in detail, and they are very important for anyone wanting to use bridleways or tracks. The OS also produce a few tourist maps at the scale of 1 inch:1 mile (which is almost the same as 1:50 000) specially for popular holiday areas which straddle the join between two or more sheets of the 1:50 000 series, and these have been mentioned in the routes where relevant. There is no easily available equivalent series for Ireland although the Irish Ordnance Survey do produce maps at 1 inch:1 mile.

Construction of roads and buildings goes on continually, and it is important that you use maps which are as up to date as possible, especially in the faster developing regions.

If you are trying to save weight in your luggage, don't forget that you can always cut the covers off the maps.

If you have not yet decided where to go cycle-touring, or if you are planning a long tour, you might find that a map of the entire British Isles on one sheet gives a useful overview. Choose one that shows major roads and cities, and which gives an idea of height through shading. The Bartholomew's 1:1000 000 map of the British Isles is a good one.

Even in the big cities it can sometimes be difficult to buy detailed maps of areas which are far away as the demand for such maps is not great. Membership of the CTC could help you here, as it has a mail-order shop dealing in maps for cyclists.

APPENDIX 4

Food and Drink

In all but the mountainous parts of the British Isles you will find yourself well catered for regarding provisions. Towns offer the greatest choice, with shops, pubs and eating places of all kinds. Supermarkets generally offer the greatest variety of food, although fresh foods such as meat, fish, fruit and vegetables will often be cheaper when bought from smaller shops, and even more so from a market. In large towns and cities there is usually a market offering all kinds of food, while in ports fresh fish can be bought from the quayside. The larger villages have a village store which will stock anything from bootlaces to baked beans. The small and friendly village store is a disappearing feature of our landscape and nowadays not all villages have them. If you need to find one, ask locally and in any case stock up with food when a good chance presents itself.

For eating out, you will find that the larger places offer a wide range of 'take away' food (fish and chips, Indian and Chinese meals). Cafés where a light meal can be eaten at a table can be found in most towns and there is always a selection of more expensive restaurants and hotels where you can eat in style (it is best not to enter these establishments wearing a dripping cape or straight after a hot ride!). You will not find many transport cafés on the routes for these are usually situated on main roads, being primarily for the use of truck drivers. They offer large meals at cheap prices. Chain restaurants, which are usually built for the motorist, tend to be expensive. Cycling through small towns you well may spot a tea shop, a very English institution where you can buy pots of tea, sandwiches, cakes or light meals. They are a most welcome haven and many are listed in the CTC Handbook.

Whether you are riding through town, village or open country, the most frequently found, and often most enjoyable, source of sustenance is the pub (public house). Rural pubs tend to be pleasanter than those in towns which are more expensive and commercialized. All serve alcoholic and non-alcoholic drinks, although availability of food varies enormously. Some offer a 'ploughman's lunch' or similar light meal at midday, others will offer a hearty feast and some do no food at all. Most Scottish hotels have a public bar. In Eire, as well as pubs there are bars which often share premises with the village store and seem to operate similar opening hours.

Shopping here can be quite fun!

It is not a good idea to take water from streams and rivers for drinking unless you add sterilizing tablets first. Petrol stations usually oblige thirsty cyclists with fresh water and there are few private houses that would turn away a polite request to refill a water-bottle.

Opening Hours

Please note that the times given are only intended as a rough guide, and they do in fact vary from district to district. On Sunday mornings some general stores and newsagents/confectioners are open, while over public holidays everything is usually closed.

Banks: 10 am–3.30 pm Monday to Friday, closed on Saturdays and Sundays. Small banks open for shorter hours on odd days of the week.
Post Offices: 9 am–5.30 pm Monday to Friday, and Saturday morning. Small Post Offices close early one day a week, and close for lunch.
Supermarkets: 8.30 am–5.30 pm Monday to Saturday. Some also open for one evening during the week.
Shops: 8.30 am–5.30 pm Monday to Saturday. They sometimes have an early closing (midday) one day per week—usually Wednesday or Thursday—and small shops close for lunch between 1 pm and 2 pm.
Markets: 8.30 am–5.30 pm, one day per week in small towns and up to seven days per week in large towns and cities.
Restaurants, cafés, fish and chip shops: 11 am–3 pm, and 6 pm–11 pm Mondays to Saturdays.
Transport cafés: All day, seven days a week, and some all night also.
Tea shops: Vary in opening times, but generally the same as shops.
Pubs: 11 am–2.30 pm and 6 pm–10.30 pm seven days a week, with local variations.

Accommodation

According to your purse and taste you have a choice of several types of accommodation. If your tour is on a tight schedule and you wish to use youth hostels, bed-and-breakfast or hotels then you can make certain of a nightly roof over your head by booking well in advance. If you are less worried about having to adapt your itinerary on the spot because of, say, a full youth hostel, then you can plan accommodation stops by phoning them a day or so beforehand. These are the various options open to you, starting with the cheapest.

Wild camping: The most flexible and simple solution, which is to pitch your tent in open country or a farmer's field if you have permission. This is generally easiest in hill or mountain areas where there are few buildings and few alternative types of accommodation anyway. Scotland and Wales are examples. Choosing your own campsite each night means that you can stop cycling more or less when you wish, and often pick sites in exhilarating places. You should remember though that every bit of land does belong to somebody and if it is possible to request the permission of the landowner then you should do so. It goes without saying that you should clear up after you and be as discreet as possible.

Official camping: Official campsites tend to be concentrated in popular touring areas and here you will probably be sharing a field with cars and caravans. These sites have the advantage that they offer basic facilities such as toilets and a washing place although these are often fairly rudimentary. Several books are published each year providing up-to-date lists of campsites, their charges and facilities.

Youth Hostels (YH): These are often sited in areas of fine scenery or interesting towns and sometimes the buildings themselves are of merit. They are the cheapest alternative to camping and are clean but basic, informal, open to all ages and offer the chance to meet fellow travellers. Some provide meals and all have self-cooking facilities. The British Isles is covered by four separate organizations, the Youth Hostels Association (England and Wales), the Scottish Youth Hostels Association, An Oige (Eire) and the Youth Hostels Association of Northern Ireland. Each publishes a handbook listing addresses and details of hostels. If you already belong to a hostelling organization then you can use hostels throughout the British Isles without applying for further membership. You can get a copy of the International Youth Hostel Handbook, which lists all hostels.

Bed-and-Breakfast (B and B): These are usually found in private homes, often letting one or two rooms only, with breakfast and sometimes an evening meal. More often than not you will find your hosts to be a friendly family and for this reason staying in a B and B is a good way of meeting local people. B and B's bridge the gap in price and comfort between the dormitory accommodation of a Youth Hostel and the more reclusive luxury of a hotel. The CTC Handbook lists recommended addresses, and you can often find a B and B by asking locally.

Hotels and Inns: The most expensive type of accommodation, although prices and quality do vary a great deal. They are usually found in towns or popular tourist areas and on main roads. Village inns sometimes offer accommodation, though often they do not advertise the fact.

APPENDIX 5

Equipment

One of the features that makes cycle-touring a carefree pursuit open to virtually everyone is that little specialist equipment is needed above and beyond the bicycle itself. You will find that you can gather together much of what you need from the clothes and kit that you possess anyway. Many books have been written which look at the question of equipment in more detail (see Appendix 7). Here just the most fundamental points will be mentioned.

You can buy expensive bags for your equipment, but if you haven't got the cash to hand, you can make do with any bags which can be attached securely to the carrier. Keep the weight low down, leaving nothing in danger of getting mixed up with the spokes. In deciding clothing, remember that you may get alternatively hot and cold as you ride up and down hills or go with or against the wind, so layers of thin pullovers give better adjustability than one thick jacket. Thinner clothes are easier to dry should they get wet. Hands must stay warm for the job of working the brakes, so carry gloves: even in mild weather your hands can get cold on a long descent. If you are cycling in cold conditions a warm hat will do more to keep you warm than many times its weight in pullovers, and your feet will tend to get cold as they are relatively inactive, so take extra socks. Options in rainproof clothing are the old-fashioned cape which keeps you dry without making you sweaty inside it, but it does catch the wind; an anorak or cagoule may make you sticky but acts less like a sail. Try always to wear something light-coloured or bright, especially at night, so that you are clearly visible to other road-users.

The repair kit is dealt with below, but remember that you must keep not only your bicycle running but yourself too. Leave space in your bags for food, and always carry 'a little something' as ravenous hunger can strike suddenly. Thirst can turn an otherwise pleasant ride into a torture, so take a water bottle. Be prepared with a medical kit and 2p and 10p coins for phone boxes just in case of emergency.

Try to keep the weight of your luggage to a minimum. People vary widely in how much they take, but an average load for a fortnight's tour is about 20 pounds. Every extra pound has to be dragged up every hill!

Before you try out a cycle-tour lasting more than a few days, it is a good idea to do a trial weekend run, staying away from home overnight if you can. That way you will be able to discover the things you forgot before it is too late, and you will learn the pace that suits you best.

As for choice and equipping of the bicycle itself, detailed advice will be found in other books. Don't think that you must have an expensive and complicated machine to enjoy cycle-touring. Of course a cycle designed with touring in mind is bound to make things easier, especially as it will have gears which enable hills to be climbed even with a full load: those who already have such bikes will know that they can tackle even the West Country hills with ease. But if you just want to have a go on an ordinary bike, possibly with just a three-speed hub gear, choose one of the gentler areas of the British Isles and content yourself with the prospect of a leisurely pace.

Spares and Repairs

You can cycle for hundreds of miles without anything ever going wrong with your bicycle, assuming that you started out with it in good repair, but if anything does go wrong, your tour will probably have taken you far from any cycle shop or repairer. In any case, repairers are likely to be fully booked in summer. It is therefore wise to carry the tools and spares to deal with the likeliest problems. Again, other books deal with techniques and tools in detail, but this is a list which we have found adequate on virtually all our cycle-tours in Britain.

Tools:
> Assorted spanners to fit all nuts and cones
> Screwdriver
> Spoke nipple key
> Small file (for filing new spokes down to the right length)
> Chain rivet extractor
> Freewheel block remover
> Tyre levers
> Allen keys (if your bike needs them)
> Oil. You will be glad of this if you cycle in the wet or over tracks. Alternatively, you can often get some drops of oil from old cans left in garages.
> Rag

Spares:
> Puncture repair kit
> Inner tube (not essential, but it is much easier to swop tubes if you get a puncture than mend it on the road, especially if it is raining)

Spokes of the right length and gauge

Long brake cable (preferably adaptable to stand in as a spare gear cable if necessary)

Spare bulbs for both lamps

Length of thin galvanized steel wire (handy for those little jobs such as making a temporary substitute for a broken saddle-bag strap)

Spare tyre. If you start with tyres in good condition you need only carry a spare if going to areas where bike shops are very scarce such as northern Scotland or western Ireland. The best way to carry it is folded into three circles: once you get someone to show you how you will find it easy.

And don't forget:

Pump

Lock

Water bottle

Cycle Hire

It is possible to hire bicycles at a few centres in most counties. Although the hire charges can be expensive, you may like to hire to save the bother of transporting your cycle over a long distance. The standard of cycles on hire varies enormously, so check in advance that the dealer has a bike which is not only of the type and in a condition suited to cycle-touring but also the correct size for you. There is always the risk that the bicycle has been badly maintained, and if possible it is a good idea to go to a centre such as London or Oxford where there are several hirers in business so you have a choice, though the competition is in any case likely to keep standards high. At present there are not enough hire bicycles to go round the people who want them in certain areas, so book a machine in advance if you can, especially over weekends and during summer. Addresses of cycle hirers can be obtained from regional tourist boards, and the CTC compiles a list for the whole of the British Isles for its members.

APPENDIX 6

Passports

If you are resident in a country outside the British Isles there are normally no restrictions of entry beyond having a passport, unless you are travelling from a country where there has been a recent outbreak of infectious disease.

If you are resident in England, Wales or Scotland you will need a passport only if touring in Eire, and vice versa. Details and costs can be obtained from main post offices.

Insurance and Health

Depending upon your philosophy and finances it can be a wise precaution to insure yourself against personal accident, medical expenses, third party claims and loss or damage to cycle and luggage. Membership of the CTC offers you insurance policies to cover these unfortunate eventualities, but the policy must be taken out on British soil and a British address provided. Membership also offers you free third party insurance.

Currency

There is no restriction on the amount of money that can be brought into the country by foreign visitors. Scottish notes have a design different from those used in England and Wales, but they are accepted throughout the British Isles. Coins and notes of Eire are again different in design but have the same units and values; British money can be used in Eire but Irish money cannot be used in Britain. It is safest to carry the bulk of your money in the form of travellers' cheques (or normal cheques if you have a British bank account).

Language

English is spoken throughout the entire British Isles, although you will sometimes have to listen very hard to detect it under the disguise of thick but fascinating regional accents. Each of the three Celtic countries, Ireland, Wales and Scotland, have their own forms of Gaelic which are spoken in parts, but almost all the Gaelic speakers are fluent in English too. The distribution of areas which use predominantly Gaelic or English in the Celtic countries does not follow any easy rule, depending on many quirks of history. Dyfed (formerly Pembrokeshire) in the far south-west corner of Wales, for instance, is one of the most anglicized parts of that country, as it was easily accessible to the Anglo-Normans by sea.

APPENDIX 7

Useful Organizations and Sources of Information

Cyclists' Touring Club The CTC is the world's largest club for cycle-tourists and the knowledge and experience accumulated in over a hundred years of service to its members can help in the enjoyment of your cycling. Its aims are to encourage recreational cycling and to protect cyclists' interests. The routes in this book were initially developed as part of the CTC's services and they have been improved in the light of comments from hundreds of CTC members who have ridden them. Other services offered by the CTC include information and selected routes for cycling in many other countries of the world, expert technical advice regarding cycles and equipment, insurance covers, a bi-monthly magazine and the chance to ride with other cyclists in the many District Associations scattered throughout the country.

Further details of membership can be obtained from the National Headquarters, Cotterell House, 69 Meadrow, Godalming, Surrey, GU7 3HS (tel: 04868 7217).

Youth Hostels Association (England and Wales) National Office, Trevelyan House, 8 St Stephen's Hill, St Albans, Herts AL1 2DY (tel: 0727 55215)

Scottish Youth Hostels Association National Office, 7 Glebe Crescent, Stirling, FK8 2JA (tel: 0786 2821)

An Oige (Irish Youth Hostels Association) 39 Mountjoy Square South, Dublin 1 (tel: Dublin 745734)

Youth Hostels Association of Northern Ireland 93 Dublin Road, Belfast BT2 7HF (tel: Belfast 24733)

Rough Stuff Fellowship Secretary: F. E. Goatcher, 65 Stoneleigh Avenue, Worcester Park, Surrey KT4 8XY (tel: 01-337 9522)

A club devoted to the enjoyment of cycling on rough tracks, with its own bi-monthly magazine.

Tandem Club Membership Secretary: Peter Hallowell, 25 Hendred Way, Abingdon, Oxfordshire (tel: Abingdon 5161)

Aimed at the encouragement of tandem cycling, with spares, information service and bi-monthly magazine.

British Tourist Authority Tourist Information Centre, 64 St James's Street, London SW1 (tel: 01-730 0791)

General tourist information, coming events and address list of regional offices and information centres.

The five Tourist Boards listed below all supply tourist information including restaurant and hotel guides, free brochures etc.

English Tourist Board 4 Grosvenor Gardens, London SW1 (tel: 01-730 3400)

Wales Tourist Board 3 Castle Street, Cardiff (tel: 0222 27281)

Scottish Tourist Board 23 Ravelston Terrace, Edinburgh 4 (tel: 031 332 2433)

Bord Failte Eireann (Eire Tourist Board) Baggot Street Bridge, Dublin 2 (tel: Dublin 765871)

Northern Ireland Tourist Board River House, 48 High Street, Belfast BT1 2DS (tel: 0232 31221)

Countryside Commission John Dower House, Crescent Place, Cheltenham, Gloucester GL50 3RA

Information on designated long distance paths, National Parks, Country Parks, Areas of Outstanding Natural Beauty.

The National Trust 42 Queen Anne's Gate, London SW1H 9AS

Aimed at the preservation of places of historic interest and natural beauty in England, Wales and Northern Ireland. Members of the National Trust have free admission to properties, and a booklet listing all those open to the public is available from this address.

National Trust for Scotland 5 Charlotte Square, Edinburgh 2.

As above.

Forestry Commission Headquarters 231 Corstorphine Road, Edinburgh EH12 7AT (tel: 031 334 0303)

Addresses of the Conservancy (regional) Offices, for any enquiries concerning Forestry Commission land.

British Waterways Board PO Box 9, 1 Dock Street, Leeds LS1 1HH; *or* Willow Grange, Church Road, Watford, Herts, WD1 3QA; *or* Dock Office, Gloucester GL1 2EJ

Addresses of where permits allowing cycles on towpaths may be obtained.

Caledonian MacBrayne Ltd The Pier, Gourock (tel: 0475 33755)

The company which runs most of the Scottish ferries, and from where timetables may be obtained.

The Gatliff Trust c/o Frank Martin, 20 Cornwallis Avenue, Bristol BS8 4PP

Edward Stanford Ltd 12–14 Long Acre, London WC2E 9LP

Shop with mail order service stocking all types of maps for the British Isles.

HMSO Bookshops London address: 49 High Holborn, London WC1V 6HB (Shops also in Cardiff, Edinburgh, Manchester, Bristol, Birmingham, and Belfast)

Government bookshops selling publications relating to Britain, including the guide to ancient monuments and historic buildings.

Publications

Cycletouring: The bi-monthly magazine of the CTC, covering all aspects of cycle-touring.

Cycling: Weekly paper available from large newsagents, with an accent on racing, but with touring articles and features on equipment.

Cycling World: Monthly magazine dealing especially with utility cycling and touring.

International Cycling Guide: Annual paperback book covering touring, racing and domestic cycling.

Tim Hughes, *Adventure Cycling in Britain,* Blandford, 1978. A good cycle-touring text book, with technical information and hints on how to get the most out of your equipment and Britain.

Richard Ballantine, *Richard's Bicycle Book*, Pan, 1979. A well-illustrated paerback on bike maintenance.

E. Jorgensen and J. G. Bergman, *Fix Your Bicycle*, Clymer Publications (US), 1973. A well-illustrated and clear guide to cycle maintenance.

D. G. Moir, *Scottish Hill Tracks and Drove Roads,* Bartholomew, 1975. Two volumes, one for northern Scotland, one for the south, listing and describing rough tracks in Scotland.

Britain: Caravan and Camping Sites Published by the British Tourist Authority, intended for the motorist and listing more expensive types of campsites.

Historic Houses, Castles and Gardens Published annually, this is a comprehensive list of interesting properties open to the public, noting opening times and prices and covering the British Isles.

Museums and Galleries A full list with brief details of each place and published annually. Covers the British Isles.

If you are interested in finding out a little more about the countryside that you will be cycling through then you may like to read one or two of the following books. They are a few which we found fascinating and easy to read, but there are of course many more.

R. A. Buchanan, *Industrial Archaeology in Britain*, Penguin, 1972
L. Dudley Stamp, *Britain's Structure and Scenery*, Fontana, 1969
Jacquetta Hawkes, *Guide to the Prehistoric and Roman Monuments of England and Wales*, Chatto and Windus, 1973, and Cardinal, 1974
W. G. Hoskins, *The Making of the English Landscape*, Penguin, 1970
The Shell Guides to England, Scotland, Wales, Ireland and Britain (separate volumes)

GLOSSARY

Barrow prehistoric grave-mound

Basalt dark, hard rock, which cooled from a molten state

Bawn fortified enclosure

Blow-hole hole connecting a sea-cave with the land surface, through which water sometimes spouts

Broch ancient fortification with rooms in the thick walls

Bullaun man-made hollow in a boulder which was used in grinding corn

Cairn or **Carn** man-made pile of stones

Cashel rampart, ditch, or drystone wall of a ringfort

Corrie or **Cwm** semicircular valley in a mountain

Court grave prehistoric gallery grave with an entrance forecourt

Covenanter strict Scottish Presbyterians who were sometimes persecuted in the 17th century for holding to the terms of nullified Covenants which had given them rights.

Cromlech or **Dolmen** prehistoric chamber of great stones

Cruck curved timber roof support

Currach small, keel-less boat of canvas or hide

Cwm see Corrie

Dolmen see Cromlech

Fortnight two weeks

Gazebo a structure, e.g. a summer-house or pavilion, built for admiring views

Highland Clearances 18th- and 19th-century expulsion of Scottish peasants from their crofts by landowners, partly to make way for large-scale sheep-farming

Mass rock rock at which mass was celebrated when catholicism in Ireland was illegal

Misericords in churches, tip-up seats often with carved undersides

Monolith single large stone

Ogham 4th- and 5th-century alphabet used for inscriptions

Pale the boundary of English control in Ireland, which moved frequently

Penal times during the 17th and 18th centuries Penal Laws in Ireland limited the rights of catholics

Plantation the settling of immigrant Scots or English on land confiscated from the native Irish

Preceptory community or buildings of the Knights Templars or Hospitallers

Rath prehistoric hill-fort

Reredos the ornamental screen behind the altar in churches

Right of Way see Appendix 1.

'Rising' In Scotland, the Jacobite Rebellions of 1715 and 1745 which sought to put the Stuart family back on the British throne

Rocking Stone a natural and heavy, critically balanced stone which can be rocked

Rood screen in churches, the carved screen separating the choir from the nave

Rough-stuff see Appendix 1: *Paths, Tracks and Right of Way*

Round tower in Ireland, a tall, tapering tower, being a stronghold and belfry combined

Scree loose rocks on or below a slope

Scarp the steeper of the two sides of a hill range

Sedilia in churches, the seats, usually three, for the clergy

Tumulus prehistoric mound, some-times over a grave

Tympanum richly carved wall area especially as found over church doorways